INTERNATIONALISATION AND ECONOMIC INSTITUTIONS

Internationalisation and Economic Institutions

Comparing European Experiences

MARK THATCHER

OXFORD

UNIVERSITY PRESS

OXFORD
UNIVERSITY PRESS

Great Clarendon Street, Oxford ox2 6DP

Oxford University Press is a department of the University of Oxford.
It furthers the University's objective of excellence in research, scholarship,
and education by publishing worldwide in

Oxford New York

Auckland Cape Town Dar es Salaam Hong Kong Karachi
Kuala Lumpur Madrid Melbourne Mexico City Nairobi
New Delhi Shanghai Taipei Toronto

With offices in

Argentina Austria Brazil Chile Czech Republic France Greece
Guatemala Hungary Italy Japan Poland Portugal Singapore
South Korea Switzerland Thailand Turkey Ukraine Vietnam

Oxford is a registered trade mark of Oxford University Press
in the UK and in certain other countries

Published in the United States
by Oxford University Press Inc., New York

British Library Cataloguing in Publication Data

Data available

Library of Congress Cataloging in Publication Data

Thatcher, Mark.
Internationalisation and economic institutions: comparing European experiences / Mark Thatcher.
p. cm.
ISBN-13: 978-0-19-924568-0 (alk. paper)
1. France–Economic policy.   2. Great Britain–Economic policy.   3. Italy–Economic policy.
4. Comparative economics.   5. Globalization.   I. Title.
HC276.T48 2007
330.94–dc22
2006102400

Typeset by SPI Publisher Services, Pondicherry, India
Printed in Great Britain
on acid-free paper by
Biddles Ltd., King's Lynn, Norfolk

ISBN   978-0-19-924568-0

1 3 5 7 9 10 8 6 4 2

To Giuseppe, Malcolm, and the memory of Vincent Wright

Preface

The present study brings together three strands of my academic work: cross-national comparison, a historical approach involving the study of lengthy time periods, and the integration of international factors into the analysis of domestic politics. Each has its benefits: avoiding national insularity, an appreciation of what is novel and important, and what is not, and placing domestic decisions in a wider international context.

The ability to undertake such work owes much to research support from several sources. The Robert Schuman Centre, European University Institute, Florence provided a congenial and tranquil place for research leave. Funding for different parts of the project has come from an ESRC grant L216252007 within the Future Governance programme and the Centre for the Analysis of Risk and Regulation (CARR), LSE. The ideas presented here have greatly benefited from comments and criticisms by students and colleagues at LSE.

Many individuals have contributed to this work. Invaluable research assistance has been provided by Maria Kampp, Anneliese Dodds, Francesco Salerno, Alfredo della Monica, Khaled Madi, and Kevin Young. Interviewees have given their time and expertise generously. I wish to thanks those who read chapters and made extremely useful comments, including Julia Black, Peter Hall, Peter Cameron, Frank Vibert, Stephen Wilks, Noel Whiteside, Andrew Walter, Ken Shadlen, Virginie Guiraudon, Desmond King, Handley Stevens, Martin Staniland, Sandra Eckert, Guy Peters, and Raymund Werle. Mathias Koenig-Archibugi, Colin Scott, and Martin Lodge read the entire manuscript and made excellent suggestions, for which I am very grateful. Dominic Byatt at OUP was a patient editor who allowed me the time needed to finish.

I dedicate the book to three people who in very different ways made it possible. Vincent Wright inspired my academic life and his enthusiasm and *joie de vivre* are much missed. Malcolm Rushton has been a constantly encouraging and understanding presence. Giuseppe Rizzo has offered the wonderful combination of optimism, support, and a sense of perspective.

Contents

List of Tables

Introduction: A Policy Analysis of Market Internationalisation and National Economic Institutions

Internationalisation of markets occurs when external forces beyond the control of domestic policy makers create pressures for the opening of national markets. It raises two sets of issues. One is how and why it arises. The other concerns its effects on domestic politics. This book looks at the second, which relates to central debates in political economy and comparative politics over whether, how, and why nations respond differently to common international pressures.

The overall question posed by the study is: How and why does internationalisation of markets affect the reform of national economic institutions? In tackling this broad issue, the book pursues several specific questions. What does 'internationalisation of markets' mean? Who are its carriers within domestic institutional reform debates? Through which mechanisms does it operate in those debates? What are the institutional outcomes in the face of internationalisation, both historically and comparatively across nations?

To respond to these questions, the book draws on two literatures that are rarely combined, but which both speak directly to its theme. The first is the second image reversed (SIR) approach, which focuses on how internationalisation affects domestic politics.[1] The second are comparative institutionalist works, notably historical institutionalist and 'varieties of capitalism' studies, which look at how past and existing domestic settings affect institutional change and policy.[2] Despite their different *foci*, both sets of approaches treat internationalisation of markets as meaning increased trade, capital flows, or economic shocks. Both underline the difficulties that obstruct institutional reform. They often give pride of place to distributional conflicts among socio-economic groups and the efficiency of existing institutions for such groups. Both argue that in the face of common international pressures, nations maintain different institutional frameworks or alter them in diverse ways that reflect past institutional settings.

The present study develops a 'policy analysis' of market internationalisation and domestic institutional reform that builds on the SIR and comparative institutionalist literatures but also seeks to respond to their limitations. It goes beyond trade,

---

[1] Notably Gourevitch (1978, 1986), Katzenstein (1978, 1985), Keohane and Milner (1996).

[2] See, e.g. Hall and Soskice (2001*a*), Berger and Dore (1996), Kitschelt et al. (1999), Schmidt (2002), Zysman (1996), Hollingsworth and Boyer (1997), and Crouch and Streeck (1997).

capital flows or economic shocks to include policy forms of internationalisation, such as the decisions of overseas policy makers in powerful nations or regulation by international organisations. At the national level, it examines the effects of market internationalisation on institutions as part of domestic policy debates, processes and struggles. It therefore looks at governments and other public actors as well as socio-economic interests as possible carriers of internationalisation. It offers mechanisms that relate directly to the policy process as well as those based on economic efficiency. It allows scope for institutional reform and cross-national similarity, as well as maintenance of inherited cross-national differences. Overall it treats decisions to maintain or modify institutions as matters to be explained rather than merely responses by public policy makers to an altered environment.

The study applies its 'policy analysis' approach to five strategic sectors—securities trading, telecommunications, electricity, airlines, and postal services. It compares across four European nations that represent very different varieties of capitalism (Britain, France, Germany, and Italy) over a lengthy period (the mid-1960s–2005). Hence it uses cross-national, cross-sectoral, and temporal comparisons to draw out the role of internationalisation in domestic decision-making.

In answering its questions about internationalisation and institutional reform in these sectors, the book has three broad objectives. First, it seeks to analyse the links between two increasingly important phenomena: market internationalisation, which is transforming industries from communications to financial services; reforms of sectoral economic institutions that have occurred in countries across the world, notably privatisation, liberalisation and the creation of independent regulatory agencies.

A second aim is to offer claims about the effects of different forms of market internationalisation on sectoral economic institutions in industrialised nations. The book argues that whereas revolutionary transnational technological and economic developments are often met with institutional inertia, policy forms of internationalisation can undermine well-established sectoral economic institutions. They can contribute to the spread of similar formal economic institutions across nations with very different macro-level institutions and histories, albeit that countries can reach similar outcomes through diverse routes. Hence, whilst accepting specific national reform processes, the findings run counter to rather conservative views of institutional reform in much comparative writing which presents domestic institutional reform as slow, difficult, rare and/or different across nations even in the face of powerful international forces.

Third, the study seeks to integrate internationalisation of markets and policy making through its 'policy analysis' framework. It responds to an over-narrow focus by SIR and comparative institutionalist works on international capital and trade flows and concentration on socio-economic interests driven by economic efficiency. Instead, it seeks to give due weight to policy making at both the international and domestic levels. It underlines the role of governments and public officials in forming and leading reform coalitions. It shows how policy forms of internationalisation were influential because of their role in the policy process. By bringing in the policy process, it explains the surprising findings found in the cases, notably the lack of impact of transnational technological and economic developments, the importance of policy forms of internationalisation and the spread of similar sectoral economic institutions across four diverse countries.

PREVIEW OF APPROACH AND CENTRAL FINDINGS

The study defines internationalisation of markets as the appearance of new or strengthened factors that put pressures on national policy makers to open up domestic markets but are outside the control of those policy makers. The book argues that internationalisation of markets can take the form of trade, capital flows, or economic shocks, but is also broader, including policy forms—that is decisions by overseas policy makers and international organisations.

The study therefore looks at three forms of internationalisation. One is transnational technological and economic developments. The other two are policy forms: regulatory reforms in the largest world economy, the US; supranational regulation of markets by the European Union (EU). Each form can give rise to pressures to open domestic markets. Transnational technological and economic developments can alter costs to aid-cross-border flows and put pressure on national monopolies and public ownership. The US accounts for 40%–50% of the world market in sectors such as securities trading, telecommunications and airline services, and even electricity and postal services; American regulatory reforms can offer not only an example of liberalisation for other nations but also affect competition in the world market and stimulate overseas expansion by large US firms in ways that undermine national monopolies and public ownership abroad. EU regulation can establish legal frameworks that open domestic markets to competition and set rules to ensure that such competition is 'fair and effective'; it can also give rise to forces that alter competitive pressures on suppliers, weaken public ownership, and undermine governments holding regulatory powers.

Investigation of the effects of these three forms of internationalisation on key economic institutions reveals often surprising results. Five central findings from the cases can be underlined: transnational technological and economic developments were met with institutional inertia; policy forms of internationalisation had significant influence on institutional reform; the carriers of internationalisation were domestic actors, and its mechanisms were regulatory competition, opportunities offered by EU regulation for domestic actors and selective learning from overseas examples; radical reform of deeply rooted sectoral institutions had been introduced by 2005 that were similar across the four countries; but change took place through nationally specific routes.

A first finding is that even sweeping technological and economic forms of internationalisation were usually met with institutional inertia, or at most, modest reforms that differed across the four nations. Policy makers faced major pressures linked to technological and economic developments, such as failures to meet growing demand and difficulties in raising capital. In all four countries governments saw traditional institutions as inadequate and attempted to introduce reforms during the 1960s and 1970s. But they were unable to forge deep alliances with the managements of incumbent national suppliers, whereas opponents of change formed determined and broad coalitions. Instead of institutional alterations, other policies were found to respond to pressures arising from transnational technological and economic developments. When these failed, institutions that were widely regarded as inefficient, nevertheless endured. The finding is at its most striking in securities trading and telecommunications: revolutionary technological and economic developments that transformed the two sectors did not lead to major institutional reforms between the mid-1960s and early/mid-1980s.

A second finding, in sharp contrast to the first, is that the two policy forms of market internationalisation had much greater influence on the reform of economic institutions. In securities trading and telecommunications, overseas reforms (in the US and then Britain), and EU regulation were significant in rapid and comprehensive reforms being introduced from the 1980s onwards. Moreover, cross-sectoral comparisons show that the influence of policy forms of internationalisation did not depend on the presence of technological and economic changes: the two policy factors also played significant roles in the airline and electricity sectors in the period from 1990 until 2005 when transnational technological and economic developments were limited and indeed had weakened compared with previous decades. Policy forms of internationalisation were even influential in the reform of postal services, an unlikely candidate for change.

The study analyses the carriers and mechanisms for internationalisation, to aid an explanation of its findings. It shows that policy forms of internationalisation operated by influencing the strategies of powerful domestic actors, notably governments and domestic firms. Overseas actors were rarely central participants in domestic decision-making; rather, their influence was more indirect, through fears of international competition. Policy forms of internationalisation aided governments and incumbent suppliers to form strong reform coalitions. They did so through three main mechanisms. One was regulatory competition, or fear of it: national policy makers worried that firms in relevant rival nations were gaining institutional advantage (e.g. from being privately owned). EU liberalisation increased these fears. The second mechanism was the use of EU regulation to provide political impetus for reform, by providing good opportunities to reconsider existing institutional structures and to legitimate changes, notably by aiding claims that national policy makers had little choice and that promotion of existing national champions required institutional changes. Finally, reforms in 'relevant' overseas nations were selected as examples to illustrate the virtues of alternative institutional frameworks.

The fourth finding is that by 2005, all four nations had greatly altered deeply rooted institutions that often dated back decades and sometimes centuries. They had adopted comprehensive and similar institutional reforms in most sectors—that is 'international isomorphism' had taken place concerning formal institutions. Thus public ownership of national suppliers had been replaced with private ownership in telecommunications, stock exchanges, airlines and electricity, and sometimes even in postal services. Long-standing monopolies that dated back to the nineteenth century or earlier had been abolished. Instead, they had been replaced with rules designed to aid 'fair and effective competition'. Governments had created independent sectoral regulatory agencies and delegated powers to them. Thus contrary to SIR and comparative institutionalist claims, institutional similarity and often convergence occurred, even across four countries with diverse domestic settings and histories. The book shows how policy forms of internationalisation contributed significantly to the changes, although they were not the sole cause.

However, similar outcomes did not mean similar paths or explanations. Thus a fifth finding is that there were important differences in the role of internationalisation across nations. Britain followed a different route than its continental neighbours in all five sectors: reform was initiated and driven more by domestic factors than internationalisation; insofar as the latter played a significant role, it was through the use of examples from the US to legitimate choices. In contrast, policy forms of internationalisation were crucial for reforms in France, Germany, and Italy, including in decisions to initiate change. Policy makers looked to Britain rather than the US, as a source of regulatory competition as well as of ideas and experience. But the most important international factor in the three continental European countries was EU regulation. Whereas the EU played almost no role and indeed was regarded with suspicion in Britain, it was significant in institutional debates in France, Germany, and Italy, through a mixture of fear of the consequences of failing to adapt to EU liberalisation and by offering opportunities for policy makers to legitimate change.

Thus overall, the book suggests that a policy analysis approach is well suited to understand the effects of internationalisation of markets on national institutional reform. It includes policy forms of internationalisation as well as technological and economic ones. Indeed, the study argues that policy forms of internationalisation are more influential than the latter because they operate directly through the domestic policy process. They affect the strategies and coalitions of powerful domestic actors. They offer fear of loss of business for existing national incumbent suppliers and provide political impetus and legitimation for institutional reform. Hence they contribute to undermining well-entrenched and long standing economic institutions and to aiding the spread of similar new institutions, albeit through different routes due to contrasts in the domestic politics and structures of nations.

RESEARCH DESIGN AND CASE STUDIES

The book uses a historical case study approach in comparing five sectors across four countries (Britain, France, Germany, and Italy) between the mid-1960s and 2005 to generate wider arguments. The comparative historical research design using case studies enables several methods to be combined to maximise analytical penetration.[3] Historical process tracing identifies the central actors in domestic decision-making concerning economic institutions and establishes

---

[3] cf. Mahoney and Reuschemeyer (2003), Gerring (2004), and George and Bennett (2004).

the causal mechanisms that link internationalisation and the strategies and choices of those actors. It also permits contrasts between periods before and after the presence of different forms of internationalisation (allowing 'within unit' comparisons, where the sector is a unit). Cross-sectoral comparison permits different combinations of forms of the independent variable, internationalisation, to be studied. Cross-national comparison is used to examine whether and how the effects of internationalisation vary according to diverse national-level institutional and political settings.

Five network industries have been selected for analysis. Two—stock exchanges for trading company securities and telecommunications—are subjected to very detailed analysis and used to generate initial findings. Thereafter, those findings are refined and tested in three other network industries—electricity, airlines, and postal services. Why are these sectors and nations interesting for examining internationalisation of markets and domestic institutional reform? First, the sectors are economically and politically strategic. They have 'horizontal' cross-sectoral effects—on the ownership and capital of firms, the technological infrastructure and the supply of communications, transport, and power. They lie at the core of modern capitalist states.

Second, the sectors allow analysis of different forms of market internationalisation and various combinations of such forms. In securities trading and telecommunications, extremely powerful transnational technological and economic developments, strong US regulatory reforms, and detailed EU regulation all developed between the mid-1960s and 2005. All three forms of internationalisation challenged traditional institutions that closed markets in Western Europe, such as public ownership of suppliers, monopolies for those suppliers, and the allocation of regulatory powers to governments or associations of suppliers. Moreover, the three forms emerged at different times, aiding analysis of their individual effects through 'periodisation' (cf. Lieberman 2001), distinguishing the times before and after new international factors became powerful.

In securities trading and telecommunications, all three forms of internationalisation developed and cumulated. One possibility is that the effects of policy forms of internationalisation are dependent on the prior presence of technological and economic internationalisation. To check this, the study takes three other sectors—electricity, airline transportation, and postal services—in which one or both of the two policy forms of internationalisation grew but transnational technological and economic developments were relatively weak by the late 1980s (although sometimes they had been significant in earlier periods). Hence the three additional cases expose the effects of more policy forms of internationalisation in the absence of major technological and economic changes.

The three sectors also present important variations that allow deeper investigation of the causal mechanisms whereby policy forms of internationalisation affect national decision making. Thus in electricity, the US introduced regulatory reforms that offered an example for European nations but had relatively little effect on world competition; hence the case tests the ideational power of reforms in the US. In airlines, strong US reform affected international competition; the

Table 0.1. Forms of market internationalisation and their strengths in network sectors

	Transnational technological and economic forces	US regulatory reforms	EU regulation
Securities trading	Very strong	Very strong	Very strong after early/mid-1990s
Telecommunications	Very strong	Very strong	Very strong after early/mid-1990s
Electricity	Weak by late 1980s	Weak for competition, strong as example	Strong after late 1990s
Airlines	Weak by late 1980s	Very strong	Strong after mid-1990s
Postal services	Weak	None	Strong after 2000

case therefore exposes a sector in which direct international competition can be strong. Postal services saw no US reforms, but only the development of EU regulation. They allow study of the effects of EU regulation in a 'low tech' sector without reforms in the US to offer either an example or competitive pressure for reform.

Table 0.1 summarises variations in the strength and timing of different forms of market internationalisation across the five sectors. 'Strength' refers to degree of pressure placed for opening national markets and against traditional national institutions in the four European countries.

A third reason for choosing the cases is that they are 'hard' ones for cross-national institutional change and convergence. Internationalisation met well-entrenched sectoral institutions, many of which dated back decades. Indeed, sectors such as telecommunications and financial capital are frequently cited as cases showing cross-national institutional stability and contrasts despite international pressures for change during the 1970s and 1980s.[4]

Finally, the four nations represent 'hard cases' for the spread of similar institutional forms. They have different numbers of veto players and veto points with Britain having few but Italy many, and France and Germany lying in-between.[5] Moreover, comparative institutionalist literatures have presented the four as different 'varieties' or 'models' of capitalism—notably that Britain is a liberal market economy, Germany a 'coordinated market one' and France a state-enhanced or 'mixed market' one—which follow diverse institutional reform paths.[6] The four countries thus offer much variation within Europe in macro- or national-level

---

[4] cf. Vogel (1996), Thatcher (1999), Cawson et al. (1990), Zahariadis (1992), Grande (1989), Deeg and Lütz (2000), and Lütz (2002).

[5] See Tsebelis (2000, notably p. 104).

[6] For greater detail, see Chapter 1; recent works include Hall and Soskice (2001a), Schmidt (2002a, b), Berger and Dore (1996), Kitschelt et al. (1999), Zysman (1996), Hollingsworth and Boyer (1997), Albert (1993), Crouch and Streeck (1997), and Hayward (1995); among older works, see for instance Shonfield (1969) and Hayward (1976).

political and economic institutions (as distinct from the sectoral ones studied in the book). Given differences in veto points/players and types of capitalism, diverse institutional responses to internationalisation are expected.

It is worth underlining that the book looks at formal sectoral institutions concerning the organisation of the main national incumbent supplier(s) (notably ownership, and if state-owned, legal position within the public sector and fragmentation), competition (i.e. rules governing entry) and the allocation of formal sectoral powers, particularly between governments (central and subnational), regulatory agencies and business associations. It does not look at behaviour within formal institutional frameworks nor at economic outcomes, which would have been beyond the scope and length of the present work.[7] However, it is based on an assumption that formal market institutions matter, both as an object of study in themselves and for the behaviour of policy makers and economic actors.

Thus overall, the five sectors represent strategic economic and political domains with well-entrenched domestic institutions. If internationalisation of markets can undermine these institutions, then it could be expected to do so in other domains with less long-standing structures. Equally, given the differences in national-level institutions and past historical trajectories among the four countries, SIR and comparative institutionalist analyses would predict continuing differences in institutional development. Using hard cases both because of the deep roots of national sectoral institutions and differences across the four nations helps in offering stronger claims from the specific examples studied that can be expected to apply across different industrialised countries and sectors.[8]

Plan of the Book

Using a critique of two major relevant literatures, SIR and comparative institutionalism, Chapter 1 sets out a framework for analysing market internationalisation and domestic institutional reform that pays attention to policymaking at both international and domestic levels. It argues that market internationalisation can take both policy and economic forms. It defines and discusses three forms that are analysed in the study: transnational technological and economic developments, and two policy forms, namely reforms in a significant overseas nation (in this case, the US) and supranational regulation (by the EU). It then discusses possible mechanisms whereby these different forms of internationalisation can influence domestic decisions about national institutions.

The empirical chapters are divided by first looking at stock exchanges for securities trading (Chapters 2–5) and then the telecommunications sector (Chapters 6–9) before turning to electricity, airlines, and postal services

---

[7] In particular, similar formal institutions may not necessarily lead to similar relationships among actors, strategies or economic outcomes—for a discussion in network industries, see Thatcher (2007), and for regulatory behaviour after delegation, Coen and Thatcher (2005).

[8] The conclusion discusses extending the study's claims to less-industrialised nations and sectors.

(Chapters 10–12). For each sector, the chapters examine the three forms of internationalisation from the mid-1960s until 2005 and then study their effects on institutional reform in Britain, France, Germany, and Italy.

Chapter 2 analyses how three sets of international factors revolutionised markets for securities trading. From the mid-1960s onwards, transnational technological and economic developments, such as the increasing use of computerisation, expansion of the securities market, higher cross-border flows, and strong trends towards large corporate investors and suppliers, transformed company securities trading. Then reforms took place in the US between the late 1960s and early 1980s that both influenced the world securities market and offered an example of reform. Finally, European Union (EU) sectoral regulation grew from the late 1980s and established a legal framework that outlawed monopolies and aided competition. The three forms of internationalisation put severe pressures on traditional European institutions for securities trading.

Chapter 3 argues that the transnational technological and economic developments and reforms in the US were met with institutional inertia in France, Germany, and Italy in the period between the mid-1960s and 1985 (i.e. just before major reforms in Britain and then EU regulation). Sectoral institutions in the mid-1960s were very long-standing and protective of suppliers. In the three countries, they included public ownership of stock exchanges, legal monopolies, and the allocation of regulatory powers to governments and associations of brokers and exchanges. Many policy makers acknowledged that traditional institutions faced increasingly strong pressures from transnational technological and economic developments and between the mid-1960s and mid-1980s, there were debates on modest proposals designed to expand securities trading and allow greater entry to stock exchanges in the three countries. Yet even limited alterations were largely blocked, due to the failure of governments to form a strong alliance with the leaders of stock exchanges that could overcome opposition to change. The result was inertia or very limited reforms that increased existing cross-national differences.

Securities trading in Britain is treated separately from the other three countries (Chapter 4). One reason is that Britain had a different starting point, in that the London Stock Exchange was a privately-owned club, run according to informal norms and self-regulation and having its own particular internal organisation of trading. Another is that Britain reformed earlier than the other three countries and then influenced them.[9] Third, the role of internationalisation differed from that in the other three nations, and followed a specific 'British reform path' (which is also seen in other sectors). Finally, the swing from institutional conservatism to revolution offers a good intra–national example of when and why different forms of internationalisation affect institutional reform.

---

[9] The chapter structure is a response to 'Galton's problem', where the cases studied are interdependent; in this study, the US acted before the other European nations and was not influenced by them; similarly, Britain reformed before the other three nations and was not influenced by their decisions.

Between the mid-1960s and the early 1980s, pressures on domestic institutions arose from transnational technological and economic developments. But traditionalists in the LSE successfully fought to retain their inheritance, while the US example was rejected as inferior. However, the position changed greatly after the early 1980s. The LSE was transformed from a private British club into a profit-making listed company open to takeover, including by overseas bidders. Reversing decades of self-regulation, regulatory powers were delegated to new independent financial regulatory authorities. The 'British reform route' involved changes being triggered for domestic reasons and led by British state actors. But international factors became important thereafter, as British policy makers became concerned about regulatory competition from the US and selectively used new institutions in the US to justify changes. EU regulation was not significant in domestic decisions and indeed was regarded with suspicion.

Chapter 5 shows how policy forms of internationalisation were important in radical reforms that transformed institutions for securities trading in France, Germany, and Italy between 1986 and 2005 and stood in sharp contrast to the earlier period of inertia. After initial modest changes in the late 1980s, rapid and sweeping changes were introduced from the mid-1990s onwards that broke with long-standing sectoral institutions. Thus stock exchanges were privatised and made into profit-making companies; legal monopolies were ended and regulatory powers were transferred to independent sectoral regulatory authorities. Moreover, long-standing national specificities were ended.

New policy forms of internationalisation were crucial in these changes. Policymakers feared regulatory competition due to new institutional arrangements in overseas countries, notably Britain, while also looking to Britain as a successful example of reform. But a second, more important factor was that unlike earlier periods, detailed sectoral EU regulation insisted on liberalisation of national markets. The two factors increased fears of securities trading moving elsewhere. They aided the formation of strong reform coalitions between governments and the managements of incumbent suppliers and provided arguments to legitimate changes. The chapter shows that similar institutional outcomes were reached to those in Britain, but through a different route: whereas in Britain, change began because of domestic factors, policy forms of internationalisation were more significant in both initiation and implementation of reforms in France, Germany, and Italy. Moreover, policy makers looked to Britain rather than the US. In sharp contrast to Britain, EU regulation was a central factor. Nevertheless, the outcome by 2005 was the adoption in all four countries of similar formal sectoral institutions. Tables 0.2 and 0.3 summarise institutional features in securities trading in 1965 and then in 2005 (more detailed tables are provided in individual chapters).

Chapters 6–9 examine telecommunications. Their arguments are similar to those for securities trading: even sweeping transnational technological and economic forces failed to result in institutional change, whereas policy forms were significant in comprehensive restructuring of well-entrenched institutional arrangements. They also follow a similar structure to the analysis of securities. Thus Chapter 6 shows how internationalisation transformed the telecommunications

Table 0.2. Sectoral institutional features for securities trading in 1965

	Britain	France	Germany	Italy
Organisational position of stock exchanges	London Stock Exchange— private club of individual male British members	Paris Bourse— publicly owned	Several exchanges owned by regional chambers of commerce	Publicly-owned city exchanges under control of city Chambers of Commerce
Rules governing competition	Monopoly for members of LSE and trading as individuals; trading split between wholesale and retail; fixed commissions	Legal monopoly for publicly appointed brokers (*Agents de change*) trading as individuals; two markets for same securities	Legal monopoly on exchanges for publicly appointed brokers— (*Kursmakler*), trading as individuals; domination of trading by banks	Legal monopoly for publicly-appointed brokers (*Agenti di Cambio*), trading as individuals; banks could trade on own account and as intermediaries and accounted for larger trades
Allocation of regulatory powers	Self-regulation led by LSE Council and Bank of England, mostly through informal norms	Most powers in hands of Ministry of Finance and Banque de France	Regions (Länder) responsible for legal supervision of their exchanges	Dispersion between local chambers of commerce, local assembly, Treasury, and Bank of Italy

Table 0.3. Sectoral institutions for securities trading in 2005

Institutional feature	Britain	France	West Germany	Italy
Organisational position of stock exchanges	London Stock Exchange a listed company	Paris Bourse listed company, part of international company (Euronext)	One dominant exchange, Deutsche Börse, listed company	One national exchange, Borse Italia; privately-owned company, listing planned
Rules governing competition	Competition through market makers setting commissions and free to engage in retail and wholesale trading; several exchanges for trading	Brokers open to take over and entry allowed for companies, including banks	Brokers open to take over and entry allowed for companies, including banks	Brokers open to take over and entry allowed for companies, including banks
Allocation of regulatory powers	Sectoral regulator with detailed powers of rule-making and enforcement	Strengthened sectoral regulator	Strengthened federal sectoral regulator; significant powers remain with regional governments (Länder)	Strengthened sectoral regulator

market. Transnational technological and economic developments, especially dig-italisation, began to revolutionise the sector from the mid-1960s. The US greatly altered its regulatory institutions, especially in the 1970s and early 1980s, provid-ing an example for other nations and also affecting the overall world telecommu-nications market. Detailed EU regulation grew from the late 1980s to provide a comprehensive framework based on competition. The three sets of international forces put pressures on closed national markets and traditional institutions.

Chapter 7 shows how and why transnational technological and economic developments and regulatory reforms in the US failed to result in major institutional changes in France, West Germany, and Italy between 1965 and 1987 (just before detailed EU regulation began). Institutional arrangements for telecommunications were highly protective of national suppliers in the mid-1960s. In all three countries, publicly-owned suppliers, usually Posts and Telecommuni-cations ministries, had a monopoly over services and most equipment; limited cross-national differences existed, notably in Italy, which had several suppliers, some of which were minority privately owned companies. During the 1960s and 1970s, suppliers faced major problems, including lack of investment and inabil-ity to meet demand, even for fixed telephone lines. Existing institutions were widely regarded as inefficient and unable to meet transnational technological and economic pressures. Governments attempted to introduce modest reforms. Yet these were blocked by a determined coalition led by trade unions, employees, and political parties. Instead, policies that did not require major institutional changes were used and/or inefficiencies were tolerated. Insofar as limited reforms were made, they widened cross-national contrasts.

As in securities trading, the book argues that Britain followed its own distinct route to reform in telecommunications (Chapter 8). Despite large-scale failures of supply, arising in part because of transnational technological and economic developments, only limited changes were introduced in 1969 and thereafter inertia reigned. This position altered dramatically in the 1980s. A determined govern-ment pushed through privatisation of the incumbent operator, British Telecom, ended its monopoly and transferred important regulatory powers to a newly created independent sectoral regulatory agency. The policies were initiated for domestic reasons, but thereafter examples of institutions in the US were used selectively to legitimate new arrangements.

In 1987, France, Germany, and Italy had well-entrenched institutional arrange-ments that had survived attempts to introduce even modest alterations. Chapter 9 shows how and why policy forms of internationalisation helped to undermine existing institutions. Policy makers feared regulatory competition from Britain. In addition, EU regulation offered occasions for change, arguments to legitimate reform and opportunities for national champions to become international ones. Aided by these two international factors, governments and national suppliers formed broader alliances, whereas their opponents lost some of their 'nation-alistic' members and arguments for defending traditional institutional arrange-ments. The reform coalitions were therefore able to overcome strong resistance and introduce sweeping institutional changes, notably privatisation of incumbent

Table 0.4. Sectoral institutions in telecommunications in 1965

	Britain	France	West Germany	Italy
Organisational position of incumbent	Part of civil service linked with postal services	Part of civil service linked with postal services	Part of civil service linked with postal services	Several incumbents, one part of civil service linked with postal services, others majority publicly owned
Rules governing competition	Monopoly over almost all services and terminal equipment	Monopoly over almost all services and terminal equipment	Monopoly over almost all services and terminal equipment	Monopoly over almost all services and terminal equipment
Allocation of regulatory powers	Central government	Central government	Central government	Central government

suppliers, termination of monopolies, and delegation of powers to independent sectoral agencies.

Thus by 2005, Britain, France, Germany, and Italy had broken with deeply-rooted domestic institutions that protected national suppliers from competition. Instead, they had adopted an institutional model of a liberalised market with private suppliers regulated by independent agencies and governments (compare Tables 0.4 and 0.5 below that set out institutions in 1965 and 2005). Policy forms of market internationalisation had played a significant role in that movement, although their role had differed, notably between Britain and the three continental nations.

Table 0.5. Sectoral institutions in telecommunications in 2005

	Britain	France	Germany	Italy
Organisational position of incumbent	100% privately-owned company	Majority privately-owned company	Majority privately-owned company	100% privately-owned company
Rules governing competition	Entire sector open to competition—no legal monopolies	Entire sector open to competition—no legal monopolies	Entire sector open to competition—no legal monopolies	Entire sector open to competition—no legal monopolies
Allocation of regulatory powers	Shared between government and sectoral independent regulatory authority	Shared between government and sectoral independent regulatory authority	Shared between government and sectoral independent regulatory authority	Shared between government and sectoral independent regulatory authority

The study then examines institutions in electricity, airlines, and postal services across the four nations (Chapters 10–12). It argues that although these sectors have been subject to much less technological and economic internationalisation than telecommunications and securities trading in the period between the mid-1980s and 2005, policy forms of internationalisation still affected domestic institutional decisions. Thus reforms in the US and Britain, and EU regulation aided the formation of alliances between governments and incumbent suppliers that sought change to prepare national firms for international competition. The reform coalition overcame entrenched opposition, notably by trade unions and employees. The mechanisms were similar to those uncovered in securities and telecommunications, namely increasing fears of regulatory competition and providing political impetus for change by offering occasions for reform and arguments to legitimate it. The importance of EU regulation is shown by its significant effects even in an unpropitious low tech sector such as postal services. The cases of airlines and electricity also shed light on the effects of overseas reforms: cross-national learning is superficial and selective being highly dependent on its usefulness for domestic policy reformers in legitimating changes desired for unrelated reasons, whereas its effects through regulatory competition are more direct.

The three cases confirm differences in national reform routes between Britain and the three Continental countries. Britain acted earlier and initiated change for domestic reasons; insofar as internationalisation was important, it was the US as a source of legitimation and menu of alternative institutional features. In France, Germany, and Italy international factors were more significant, notably regulatory competition from British suppliers and especially EU regulation. Nevertheless, the outcome of the reforms was a similar movement towards commercial (usually privately-owned) national suppliers, liberalisation of markets, and often delegation of powers to independent sectoral regulatory agencies. Tables 0.6 and 0.7 summarise key economic institutions in the three sectors in 1965 and 2005.

The final chapter summarises the findings of the book and relates them to broader debates about internationalisation of markets and domestic institutional reform. It presents a policy analysis approach of market internationalisation and economic institutions that builds on, but develops, SIR and comparative institutionalist approaches. The framework put forward differs from these last two by adopting a broader definition of internationalisation, one that includes international policy decisions. It suggests that carriers of internationalisation are not just socio-economic interests but also political and state actors, especially governments. It argues that internationalisation affects national decisions through a broader range of mechanisms than economic efficiency or distributional conflicts, and highlights those mechanisms that feed in directly to the domestic policy process and involve governments. It suggests that nations that represent very different varieties of capitalism can adopt similar sectoral institutions, but that they do so through diverse routes that reflect their domestic politics.

Table 0.6. Sectoral economic institutions in electricity, airline transportation, and postal services in 1965

	Britain	France	Germany	Italy
Electricity	Supplier: several state-owned public corporations Rules governing supply: monopoly Regulatory powers: government	Supplier: state-owned public corporation Rules governing supply: monopoly Regulatory powers: government	Supplier: several private, regional, and municipal-owned companies Rules governing supply: monopoly Regulatory powers: municipalities and regional governments	Supplier: state-owned public corporation Rules governing supply: monopoly Regulatory powers: government
Airlines	Main incumbent: state owned Rules governing supply: duopoly Regulatory powers: government	Main incumbents: majority state owned Supply: mostly monopoly Regulatory powers: government	Main incumbent: majority state owned Supply: mostly monopoly Regulatory powers: government	Main incumbent: majority state owned Supply: mostly monopoly Regulatory powers: government
Postal services	Supplier: part of civil service Rules governing supply: monopoly Regulatory powers: government	Supplier: part of civil service Rules governing supply: monopoly Regulatory powers: government	Supplier: part of civil service Rules governing supply: monopoly Regulatory powers: government	Supplier: part of civil service Rules governing supply: monopoly

Finally, the book relates its findings to three broader themes. First, it discusses how to test the conclusions from the case studies more widely in order to expand their scope, both within Europe and elsewhere in industrialising or developing countries. Second, it links its findings to recent debates on cross-national policy diffusion or transfer. In particular, it discusses the nature of cross-national policy learning, which it argues is often superficial, selective, and dependent on domestic politics. It also underlines that countries can arrive at similar institutional outcomes through different international diffusion processes. A third broader theme concerns Europeanisation. The chapter uses the book's material to argue that Europeanisation goes well beyond 'goodness of fit' between EU legal requirements and existing domestic institutions. Instead, it suggests that the EU has wider repercussions due to the ways in which European regulation is used within the domestic policy making process. It links these uses to questions of winners and losers from Europeanisation, since EU regulation can aid governments and firms to alter national institutions well beyond EU requirements and for motives other than meeting EU law.

Table 0.7. Sectoral institutional features in 2005 in electricity, airline transportation, and postal services

	Britain	France	Germany	Italy
Electricity	Incumbents: privately-owned companies Rules governing supply: competition in entire sector Regulatory powers: independent sectoral regulator and government	Incumbent: majority state-owned company Rules governing supply: competition in most of sector and in entire sector by 2007 Regulatory powers: independent sectoral regulator and government	Incumbents: dominance of a few privately owned companies, plus regional and municipal owned Rules governing supply: competition in entire sector Regulatory powers: independent sectoral regulator and government	Incumbent: majority privately owned company Rules governing supply: competition in most of sector and in entire sector by 2007 Regulatory powers: independent sectoral regulator and government
Airlines	Incumbent: BA privately-owned company Rules governing supply: competition allowed, limits on slots and US flights Regulatory powers: independent sectoral regulator	Incumbent: Air France majority privately owned Rules governing supply: competition allowed, limits on slots Regulatory powers: government	Incumbent: Lufthansa privately owned Rules governing supply: competition allowed, limits on slots Regulatory powers: government	Incumbent: Alitalia- majority privately owned Rules governing supply: competition allowed, limits on slots Regulatory powers: government
Postal services	Incumbent: Royal Mail state-owned limited company Rules governing supply: competition allowed except in reserved area Regulatory powers: independent sectoral regulator and government	Incumbent: La Poste state-owned public corporation Rules governing supply: competition allowed except in reserved area Regulatory powers: independent sectoral regulator and government	Incumbent: Deutsche Bundespost majority privately-owned company Rules governing supply: competition allowed except in reserved area Regulatory powers: independent sectoral regulator and government	Incumbent: state-owned public corporation Rules governing supply: competition allowed except in reserved area Regulatory powers: government

Overall, the book presents internationalisation as part of the policy process. Policy forms of internationalisation are crucial for decisions about national economic institutions. Their importance lies in their role within domestic policy processes. The result can be much greater institutional change and cross-national similarity than expected from current theories of internationalisation and comparative institutionalism.

1

Analysing Market Internationalisation and National Institutions

The present study examines how different forms of market internationalisation affect sectoral economic institutions in industrialised countries. This chapter engages with two major literatures in comparative political economy that deal directly with both internationalisation and domestic institutions: second image reversed (SIR) studies and comparative institutionalist works. They are chosen because they offer good examples of relevant literatures, are well-established and provide several complementary strengths and weaknesses. A critique of the two is used to develop a third approach, a policy analysis of market internationalisation and domestic institutional reform that is then applied in the book.

The chapter is divided into two parts. First, it briefly sets out the key elements of SIR and comparative institutionalist analyses that relate most directly to the effects of market internationalisation on domestic institutional reform. It then offers a brief critique of each, highlighting valuable elements and *lacunae*, notably concerning the definition of internationalisation, carriers and mechanisms, and the treatment of institutional change.

Thereafter, building on the previous discussion, it puts forward the policy analysis framework used in the present study. It argues that a broader concept of internationalisation of markets is needed than trade or capital flows, which are the focus of many studies. It therefore includes two policy forms of internationalisation—changes in overseas policies and supranational regulation—and more specifically in this study, regulatory reforms in the US and EU regulation. It suggests that both socio-economic and state actors can be carriers of internationalisation. It offers a range of mechanisms for the different forms of internationalisation that include both economic efficiency and other more political mechanisms such as legal coercion, the cross-national spread of norms and international mimetism. It develops a framework that can be applied to institutions at the sectoral level. Finally, it differentiates market internationalisation from a potential rival, 'globalisation', and justifies the utility of the separate concept of internationalisation.

More detailed discussion of the findings from the case studies and the implications for analyses of internationalisation and domestic institutional reform are developed in Chapter 13.

ANALYSES OF MARKET INTERNATIONALISATION AND COMPARATIVE DOMESTIC INSTITUTIONAL CHANGE

A host of studies have looked at how market internationalisation affects domestic institutions. The two that deal most explicitly with the field and are well-developed are: SIR analyses and comparative institutionalist works. The following section does not attempt to offer a complete literature review. Rather, drawing on major works, its purpose is to set out the salient features that recur concerning three issues: the definition of internationalisation of markets; carriers and mechanisms whereby internationalisation affects domestic institutional reform; and predicted institutional outcomes.

Second Image Reversed Analyses

Studies in the SIR tradition examine how events at the international level influence domestic politics.[1] They therefore reverse the 'second image' which looks at how internal state structures and domestic politics influence international conflicts.[2] Gourevitch (1978) divides international events into political and economic, and pithily summarises each as 'war' and 'trade'. Many writers in the SIR tradition have largely followed him on the latter, looking at trade, capital flows, or international economic 'shocks'.[3] Thus Frieden and Rogowski define internationalisation as 'an exogenous decrease in the costs, or an increase in the rewards, of international economic transactions', which then give rise to increased cross-border trade and investment.[4] The cost decrease can be due to lower transport costs, improved infrastructure, or altered government policies that reduce technical, economic, or political barriers to cross-border flows. Higher rewards can arise from economies of scale and greater disparities between nations in total factor productivity. Some writers add the requirement that easing of cross-national exchanges produce 'observable flows of goods, services, and capital'.[5] 'Exogeneity' means 'changes that are not only exogenous to any one nation's policy but that resist manipulation by any one government'.[6]

An exogenous easing of international exchange will lead to pressure for change because it affects the relative value or 'prices' of policies and institutions as

---

[1] The most explicit and developed recent work is the collection edited by Keohane and Milner (1996); for other major works that mostly concern industrialised countries see Gourevitch (1978); see also Katzenstein (1978, 1985), Gourevitch (1986), and Smith (1993). For a review of literature on the effects of internationalisation on domestic politics until the late 1980s, see Almond (1989); for other works, see notably the Cornell Studies in Political Economy series edited by Peter Katzenstein, Cornell University Press.

[2] The 'first image' involves studying international conflict through examining individual and human nature and the 'third image' by looking at the international community—Waltz (1954).

[3] e.g. Milner (1988), Milner and Keohane (1996*a*), Frieden and Rogowski (1996), and Garrett and Lange (1996).

[4] Frieden and Rogowski (1996: 26).   [5] Keohane and Milner (1996: 4).

[6] Frieden and Rogowski (1996: 27).

well as goods and services (Frieden and Rogowski 1996). In particular, it will increase calls to liberalise international trade and inflict increasing welfare costs on countries that fail to do so. However, more precise mechanisms are put forward. It is argued that internationalisation affects domestic politics through conflicts among socio-economic actors arising from its distributional consequences. One analysis is based on conflict between three factors of production—notably labour, landowners, and capitalists.[7] Rogowski (1989) argues that an exogenous easing of international exchanges offers incentives for owners of abundant factors of production. They form alliances to press for free trade in opposition to owners of scarce factors, who seek protection. Depending on which factors are abundant in a country, different coalitions and cleavages will occur.[8] A second approach presents conflicts as lying between sectors.[9] Owners of assets that are sector-specific and hence cannot be switched among sectors according to returns available, will have incentives to lobby for favourable policies (owners of mobile assets will simply switch those assets according to the highest returns and hence lack such incentives). If the sector is uncompetitive on world markets, owners of assets will seek protection; if it is competitive, they will press for liberalisation. A third approach differentiates between types of firms. Thus for instance, large firms, which can enjoy internal economies of scale, will seek liberalisation to have access to larger markets, whereas smaller ones that cannot reap such economies will seek protection. Similarly, firms that are already adapted to world markets will seek liberalisation, whereas those that would need to make large adjustments oppose it.

Altered preferences of socio-economic actors and conflicts among them do not automatically translate into domestic policy changes, for they are mediated by 'macro-level' national institutions. Garrett and Lange (1996) suggest that the responsiveness of governments to internationalisation depends on at least four institutional factors. Regime type is important, as democratic regimes are more responsive than non-democratic ones. Methods of aggregating preferences (e.g. electoral systems) influence the extent to which governments are dependent on specific groups, which can then demand protection; hence electoral systems that make politicians accountable to wider electorates increase the likelihood of liberalisation, since those politicians can represent gainers and compensate losers. The number of veto points also matters: the higher they are the lower the likely responsiveness of a nation to internationalisation.[10] Finally, the

---

[7] Itself deriving from the Stopler–Samuelson theorem of the effects of changes in the costs of international transactions—cf. Hiscox (2002).

[8] Thus in advanced industrialised countries, if land is scarce but labour is abundant, capital and labour form a free trade alliance against land, leading to an urban–rural cleavage, whereas if land is abundant and labour is scarce, a land–capital alliance opposes labour which seeks protection, resulting in class cleavages; if both land and labour are scarce, then they will ally against free-trade capital; these coalitions also hold if there is an exogenous impediment to trade.

[9] This derives from the Ricardo–Viner approach that underlines how changes in relative prices affect sectors.

[10] Hallerberg and Basinger (1998).

more power is delegated to independent bureaucratic agencies that are partially insulated from elected politicians, the lower the responsiveness of policy makers to internationalisation (although the likelihood of liberalisation may rise).[11] Since national institutions vary across countries, most SIR studies underline differences in responses to market internationalisation, be it an increase in international trade or an economic shock.[12]

The implications of internationalisation for institutional change are usually given little consideration in general SIR models, which instead concentrate on policy making and economic decisions. The national-level institutions that they examine are seen as deeply rooted in history, being the product of events such as the timing of industrialisation, wars, or traditions.[13] Powerful coalitions grow up within nations to defend existing institutions. Hence Garrett and Lange (1996: 54) assert that although internationalisation of markets can create incentives for governments to reform formal institutions (by causing conflicts between policies that perform well in the changed international conditions and policies required to meet institutionally-shaped political pressures), reform will nevertheless be very difficult because governments will have to act contrary to the wishes of their (institutionally-shaped) constituencies.

Insofar as institutional reform is considered, it is presented as being diverse across nations. Garrett and Lange (1996: 69–74) suggest three factors that condition whether governments seek institutional responses to policy pressures arising from internationalisation. They are: the risk aversion of governments, the length of time until governments are held accountable to its citizens (e.g. the time period between elections), and whether conjunctural conditions such as the health of the international economy are favourable (by offsetting the costs of institutional change). Since the first two of these factors differ across nations, so will institutional change. However, their analysis is suggestive rather than well-developed. Only when sectoral studies are undertaken, is greater attention given to institutional reform. Thus for instance, Deeg and Lütz (2000) argue that economic integration of financial markets and international regulation have led to the centralisation of national regulatory structures at the expense of subnational ones in stock exchanges and banking in the US and Germany. Again however, they underline how existing national institutions mediated international pressures in financial markets. In particular, they argue that differences in subnational competition and legislative fragmentation led the two countries to take diverse paths of sectoral institutional adaptation to international pressures and hence convergence was limited.

---

[11] cf. Frieden and Rogowski (1996: 44).

[12] Thus e.g. in the face of increases in world trade, oil shocks or industrial crisis nations pursue dissimilar industrial and economic policies concerning protectionism, support for companies, labour market policies or fiscal policies (e.g. Katzenstein 1978; Katzenstein 1985; Gourevitch 1986; Louriaux 1991; Keohane and Milner 1996).

[13] Gourevitch (1978) and Rogowski (1989).

Comments on the SIR Treatment of Market Internationalisation and National Institutions

Second image reversed studies offer many valuable elements for studying market internationalisation and domestic politics. They allow for several sources of internationalisation. They not only recognise that market internationalisation can directly impinge on domestic decisions but also follow that insight through, by looking at its effects on preferences, strategies, and coalitions. They build sophisticated stylised models of those effects.

However, major criticisms can also be made. First, there is a paradox in the treatment of market internationalisation. Several sources (political, economic, and technological) are accepted but are bundled together, without discussion of how they may have diverse impacts on domestic debates and decisions. Indeed, such bundling may result in the omission of important differences in their dynamics and effects. Yet thereafter, the apparently broad conception of internationalisation can rapidly become focused only on the effects of alterations in trade and capital flows, especially in general models concerning industrialised nations.[14] (In contrast SIR works on developing nations provide a much broader treatment of market internationalisation.)[15]

A second criticism is that internationalisation is defined as exogenous, in the sense of being entirely beyond the control of any national governments. It is unclear how this is compatible with the claim that government policy offers one source of easing of international exchanges. Moreover, the definition excludes policies by governments of very powerful nations and neglects the potential for governments acting collectively. Some, but not all, public policy makers may be able to influence the internationalisation of markets.

A third criticism is that the state is reduced to playing a passive role. It is presented as responding to altered preferences of socio-economic groups, but not leading reform or having its own preferences. Indeed, the policy processes whereby the demands of socio-economic coalitions are translated into government decisions are not explained. Implicitly, policy is driven by economic developments, ignoring other sources arising from the political process and government bureaucracy.

Fourth, analysis of institutional change is limited. State structures affect responses to changes in the international environment but are themselves largely fixed. In part, this is due to macro-level national institutions being selected that are difficult to alter. In part, it is due to focusing on the preferences of socio-economic actors and their effects on trade liberalisation rather than institutional frameworks. However, when sectoral institutions are analysed (e.g. Deeg and Lütz 2000), the potential for market internationalisation affecting institutional reform is revealed, suggesting a promising line of analysis.

---

[14] See Rogowski (1989) and Milner (1988); indeed, Keohane and Milner (1996) appear to require cross-border flows.
[15] See for instance, Maxfield (1997) and Haggard (1990).

A fifth question concerns the mechanisms whereby market internationalisation affects national policy change. Discussion has been focused on one mechanism—namely efficiency-driven demands by socio-economic groups who seek liberalisation or protection. However, other mechanisms for institutional reform are often ignored, such as cross-national learning or coercion.[16] Moreover, there is an implicit assumption of the existence of a single institutional equilibrium that is known beforehand to deliver the policies desired by the dominant coalition in response to market internationalisation. If multiple institutional equilibria, incomplete knowledge, and inefficiencies are permitted, the model would become more realistic. It would permit a richer study that could include learning, power relations, choice between competing institutional alternatives, and uncertainty.

Finally, the attention given to cross-national differences can be queried. It seems a paradox that studies of a common set of pressures and opportunities should devote so much attention to cross-national differences. Equally, the relative absence of convergent responses invites a research strategy to examine these rare birds, since they might throw light on why, when, and how mediation of market internationalisation by national institutions does not lead to divergent responses.

Overall, SIR models have great strengths in considering how increased trade affects preferences and coalitions. However, they downplay more political aspects, notably the role of governments, and pay too little attention to how cross-national institutional reform can take place.

Comparative Institutionalist Analyses

Comparative institutionalist studies—notably historical institutionalism and work on 'varieties' or 'models of capitalism'—claim that nations are characterised by long-established institutional differences.[17] Market structures, rules, and norms vary greatly across countries—for example, concerning public ownership and privatisation, the extent of 'deregulation', the role of the state, and the power of firms and organised labour. Even in a confined and highly interdependent area such as Europe, several varieties or models of capitalism persist.[18] In turn, diverse national institutions lead to cross-national differences in policy-making, the strategies of firms, and economic performance.

Empirically, most analyses suggest that Germany offers a good example of a 'coordinated market economy' with strong coordinating institutions that aid cooperation between firms, whereas Britain has a liberal market economy in which the state's role in markets is primarily to ensure competition; traditionally France has had a *dirigiste* and statist structure but may be a 'mixed market economy'

---

[16] This applies to studies of industrialised countries but much less to those of developing ones.

[17] For overviews, see Peters (1999), Thelen (1999), and Hall (2007).

[18] Hall and Soskice (2001a), Berger and Dore (1996), Kitschelt et al. (1999), Schmidt (2002), Zysman (1996), Hollingsworth and Boyer (1997), Albert (1993), Crouch and Streeck (1997), and Rhodes and Apeldoorn (1998).

between liberal and coordinated market economies.[19] Italy is often seen as an economy with widespread state intervention matched by great fragmentation and politicisation.[20]

Pressures on national institutions from market 'internationalisation' or globalisation are usually conceived in terms of increased trade and factor mobility, especially that of capital. Thus for instance, Hall and Soskice (2001b: 55) define globalisation as 'developments that have made it easier for companies to locate operations abroad', including trade liberalisation, deregulation, and expansion of international financial markets, access to and expansion of former communist countries and declining transport and communication costs.[21] Factor mobility may put pressures on policy makers to alter 'inefficient' domestic institutions by threatening the profitability of firms, attracting capital to other countries, and undermining employment and the financing of the state.

Earlier historical institutionalist works argued that because domestic institutions are supported by coalitions of actors who have strong interests in their continuation, national reform is extremely rare (following a pattern of 'punctuated equilibrium') and/or slow.[22] More recent studies have accepted that in the face of economic and financial internationalisation, institutional change does occur. Nevertheless, they maintain that it is highly bounded. Thus Hall and Soskice (2001b) argue that liberal market economies such as Britain or the US tend to choose deregulation (policies that remove obstacles to competition, expand the role of markets, and increase market incentives), which advantages their firms, whereas coordinated market economies tend to introduce less deregulation and maintain mechanisms that allow business and labour to cooperate. Hence change is highly path-dependent, as initial institutional directions are reinforced. Streeck and Thelen (2005b) suggest that although 'transformation' of the functioning of institutional regimes has occurred, it has done so without 'disruption': existing formal institutional regimes have been maintained, but instead their functioning has been gradually modified.

Several explanations are advanced as to why institutional change is so limited. One relies on the heavy hand of existing domestic institutions. Thus Hall and Soskice develop a firm-centred analysis of market institutional change in which existing 'institutional complementarities' condition the relative advantages of reform strategies for firms and policy makers. In the face of globalisation, nations will reinforce existing advantages: 'much of the adjustment process will be oriented towards the institutional recreation of comparative advantage' and hence 'nations often prosper, not by becoming more similar, but by building on their

---

[19] Hall and Soskice (2001b), Hancké (2001), Wood (2001), Schmidt (1996, 2002), and Hayward (1995).

[20] cf. Locke (1995: ch 2) and Cassese (2000: ch. 2.)

[21] See also Schmidt (2002), Berger and Dore (1996), Hollingsworth and Boyer (1997), Swank (2002); Streeck and Thelen (2005b: 3) do not define internationalisation and globalisation, but point to rising competition in world markets. They also cite international pressures such as the development of micro-electronics and demographic changes.

[22] cf. Krasner (1984), Hall (1986), and Cortell and Peterson (1999).

institutional differences' (Hall and Soskice 2001*b*: 60, 63). In similar vein, Vivien Schmidt argues that the effects of globalisation and Europeanisation are mediated by national circumstances—economic vulnerability, national legacies, and the preferences and reform capacities of policy makers (Scharpf and Schmidt 2000; also Schmidt 2002). Ideational explanations also claim that countries use long-standing national models when learning from abroad. The cross-national spread of ideas is greatly conditioned by existing national institutions and institutionally-established interests, policy legacies, and distributions of power.[23] Hence, differing domestic institutions produce nationally distinct and often bounded patterns of learning. Another approach suggests that easier adaptation strategies than altering existing institutions are available. Streeck and Thelen (2005*b*) put forward five mechanisms that build on existing formal institutions without requiring these to be drastically altered: displacement (the slow rise of previously subordinate institutions within an overall regime); layering (attaching new institutional elements to old regimes that alter the functioning of the latter); 'drift' (deliberate neglect of institutions that therefore lose power); conversion (new uses of existing institutions); exhaustion (the gradual withering away of institutions).

The result of highly bounded change is that national institutional differences persist in the face of market internationalisation/globalisation. Even if policies and economic performance may converge, institutions do not (Boltho 1996; Boyer 1996). Instead, the national level remains vital for market institutions: 'so many of the institutional factors conditioning the behaviour of firms remain nation-specific and depend strongly on statutes or regulations promulgated by nation states' (Hall and Soskice 2001b:16). Different varieties of capitalism endure. At most, Streek and Thelen (2005*b*) accept that there is a secular trend towards 'liberalisation', including 'privatisation, deregulation, self-reliance, and a general opening up of social and economic arrangements to the logic of "free" competitive markets' (2005*b*: 4). However, it has been gradual and its timing, pace, direction, and extent vary across countries, depending in large measure on how common exogenous forces have combined with country-specific endogenous ones (Deeg 2005; Streeck and Thelen 2005*b*).

Comments on Comparative Institutionalism's Treatment of Market Internationalisation and National Institutions

The comparative institutionalist literature offers a rich analysis of institutional change. It investigates domestic politics, which is essential since national institutional reform involves debates and decisions by actors within countries. It also incorporates the effects of previous institutional frameworks, as change does not take place on a 'blank page'. It provides good arguments about why radical modification of national institutions is difficult and bounded.

---

[23] Dobbin (1994), Immergut (1992), Rueschmeyer and Skocpol (1996), Hall (1989), King (1992, 1999), Hansen and King (2001), and Weir (1992).

Nevertheless, five limitations in the treatment of internationalisation and institutions can be pointed out. First, the conception of market internationalisation is confined to that adopted by early 'strong globalisationalists', namely increased cross-border capital and trade flows.[24] However, other forms of globalisation, such as that of firms, regulation, and markets are ignored.[25] In particular, more political forms of globalisation through policy decisions are omitted.

A second problem is that although international factors such as globalisation are accepted as significant pressures on national institutions, analysis of their effects on domestic debates about institutional reform is not pursued. Instead, they are treated as a form of external shock, and thereafter, attention is focused on how existing institutions mediate them rather than examining directly their effects. However, this may downplay or sometimes obscure how international factors can influence decision-making within domestic arenas (cf. Thatcher 2004).

A third and surprising question concerns the role of state actors. Change in domestic market institutions is largely analysed in terms of the needs of firms.[26] Governments are presented as highly responsive to these needs. Thus implicitly, they merely seek to maintain the efficiency of firms in the face of international pressures.[27] However, this is an apolitical view of governments and other state actors, who may have own interests and strategies autonomously from firms. The analysis is all the more surprising given the recognition in much comparative institutionalist works that institutional change involves decisions by public policy makers.

More generally, institutional change appears highly driven by economic efficiency, albeit efficiency set within national institutions and hence liable to be met with different institutional solutions. The role of ideas, uncertainty or imposition by powerful actors are all downplayed, in a not dissimilar way to SIR models.[28] This is again surprising since many comparative institutionalist writers have underlined the importance of learning in the international transmission of ideas.[29] The restricted focus on market efficiency stands in stark contrast to sophisticated treatment of the role of pre-existing national institutions in moulding change or the rich empirical material offered by comparative institutionalist case studies.

Finally, the overwhelming emphasis in much comparative institutionalist work is on cross-national differences in response to international market pressures. This may be because many studies have covered entire countries and/or have examined a mixture of institutional reform, policymaking, and the strategies of firms

---

[24] cf. Strange (1986, 1996), Andrews (1994), and Goodman and Pauly (1993).
[25] For a discussion of these, see Braithwaite and Drahos (2000) and Held et al. (1999).
[26] For instance in Hall and Soskice (2001a).
[27] Streeck and Thelen (2005b: 3) suggest that governments have in part accelerated and called upon globalization and internationalization to deal with ever-rising demands from their constituents but do not develop this point further.
[28] For a similar critique of historical institutionalist models, see Peters, Pierre, and King (2005).
[29] See, for instance, Hall (1989), King and Hansen (2001), and King (1992).

(Hall and Soskice 2001*a*). Yet even those studies that identify some degree of similarity in national responses limit their pursuit of why common trends arise; thus for instance, Streeck and Thelen (2005*a*) accept a cross-national movement towards liberalisation, but focus their attention on why change in formal institutional regimes can be gradual. While studying cross-national differences can offer a valuable antidote to simplistic 'strong globalisation' approaches (cf O'Brien 1992; cf. Andrews 1994), it risks Susan Strange's sharp criticism that 'comparative social scientists are misnamed: they do not compare nearly as much as they contrast' (Strange 1997: 183).

A POLICY ANALYSIS OF MARKET INTERNATIONALISATION AND DOMESTIC INSTITUTIONAL REFORM

The SIR and comparative institutionalist literatures both look at how existing institutions condition national responses to international changes. They offer complementary strengths and weaknesses. The former identifies several sources of internationalisation and provides a well-developed analysis of its effects on preferences, strategies, and coalitions, but is weaker on consideration of institutional change. The latter presents a relatively 'thin' analysis of internationalisation but a rich menu for studying the influence of existing national contexts on institutional change. Interestingly, both sets of literatures often adopt a narrow economic view of market internationalisation (treated as trade, capital flows, or economic shocks) and analyse change in efficiency-driven terms. They downplay the role of governments and say little about how the pressures arising from internationalisation play out in the policy process. Both also assume or claim institutional stability and devote more attention to cross-national differences in the face of market internationalisation rather than looking at common trends.[30]

This book draws on the strengths of the two sets of approaches and seeks to respond to some of their weaknesses. It offers a policy analysis by treating internationalisation and its effects on decisions concerning national institutions as part of public policy making.[31] It assumes that at both international and domestic levels, public policies are not merely a reflection of socio-economic forces and interests but have at least some autonomy from them (without negating the importance of such forces, a weakness in 'old institutionalist' analysis that focused on laws and regimes but downplayed the wider socio-economic context). At the international levels, this means that policies can shape markets as well as being shaped by them. At the domestic level, it integrates internationalisation with domestic policy

---

[30] With a few partial exceptions—notably Streeck and Thelen (2005*a*) or Milner (1988); even here, common directions of change are acknowledged but receive limited attention.

[31] The term policy analysis is used in different senses, from examination of the making of public policy to more restricted usages relating to particular theories or explanations of policy; here it is used in the former broader sense; among major overviews of policy analysis, see for instance, Jenkins 1978, Parsons 1995, Hill 1997, Wildavsky 1987, John 1998.

making. It treats the responses of policy makers to market internationalisation as matters to be explained rather than automatic responses to altered market conditions. It looks at the interests, ideas and role of governments and officials, as well as socio-economic interests. It includes non-price mechanisms for internationalisation to affect domestic institutions, as well as economic efficiency ones. It takes a 'meso' or sectoral approach, for frequently policy analyses underline the separation of different parts of a polity due to policy networks and the segmentation of governments and seek to produce 'middle-range' theories that link organisations and macro-level political systems, rather than offering claims covering entire economic or countries.[32]

This section sets out the key elements of the analytical framework. It then ends with a brief discussion of how internationalisation relates to 'globalisation'. The final chapter (13) relates the empirical findings to the analytical framework.

(i) *Forms of market internationalisation*: Building on the SIR literature, the study defines 'market internationalisation' as new or strengthened factors that put pressures on national policy makers to open up domestic markets but are outside the control of those policy makers. Market internationalisation can arise from several sources, not just technological or economic cost changes, but also policy decisions—for instance by overseas policy makers or international organisations. This study selects three major forms that create pressures to open domestic markets: transnational technological and economic developments; regulatory policy in a dominant nation (the US); 'supranational regulation' (by the EU). It thus compares the effects of economic forms of market internationalisation with two policy forms.

The importance of technological and economic factors, notably those that aid cross-border flows of information and capital, is recognised in both the SIR and comparative institutionalist literatures, as well as work on globalisation.[33] Two of the sectors examined, securities trading and telecommunications, have been transformed by such developments. In particular, micro-electronics have enormously eased cross-border flows of capital and information. Demand for cross-border transactions has also risen. Moreover, micro-electronics has weakened national monopolies, which have become increasingly difficult to sustain. Hence the book looks at how these transnational developments created pressures and opportunities for policy makers in domestic institutional debates.

Regulatory change in the US is the second form of internationalisation studied. A growing literature on cross-national policy transfer shows how decisions in one country can influence those in other nations through cross-national learning,

[32] Benson 1982; cf. Hill 1997.

[33] cf. Keohane and Milner (1996*b*), Frieden and Rogowsk (1996), Hall and Soskice (2001*b*), and Streeck and Thelen (2005*b*) for globalisation, see Held, McGrew, Goldblatt, and Perraton (1999), O'Brien (1992), and Andrews (1993), Goodman and Pauly (1994).

imposition or 'regulatory competition'.[34] The most important nation is the US, which accounts for 40%–50% of total world markets in domains such as telecommunications, securities trading, electricity or airline services. In these sectors, the US introduced major regulatory reforms, which had repercussions for other nations. They altered competitive opportunities and pressures in the world market, due to the size of the US. They affected regulatory competition among nations, by giving American companies institutionally-derived advantages.[35] They influenced the overseas strategies of US firms and policy makers, for instance by allowing the establishment of very large firms with the capacity to expand in Europe and/or by creating incentives for them to do so. They provided an example of reform as well as apparent opportunities for European firms to enter the large and enticing US market, with consequent repercussions on the strategies of European policy makers. Hence regulatory reform in the US resulted in incentives and pressures for European policy makers to open their home markets.

As Fligstein (2001) points out, markets are social constructs, created in part by rules, norms, and understandings. International organisations can affect domestic markets by altering rules and norms on matters as diverse as ownership, entry, 'unfair competition' or regulatory structures. The EU offers a highly developed example of supranational governance and studies suggest that 'Europeanisation', particularly the development of EU legal frameworks, creates adaptation pressures on national institutions.[36] In the sectors studied, the EU has created an increasingly comprehensive set of rules and norms that open up national markets—notably to end monopolies and establish a regulatory framework for 'fair and effective competition'. The book therefore considers how EU regulation affected national institutional reform.

European governments and policy makers lacked the market power to affect transitional technological and economic developments and had no substantial influence on US regulatory decisions. Hence the first two factors were clearly exogenous to the nations studied here. EU regulation is more complex, since it arises out of processes involving supranational organisations such as the European Commission and European Court of Justice (ECJ), national governments acting collectively through the Council of Ministers and the directly elected European Parliament. However, EU regulation can be said to be exogenous to any one government, because no single country controls decision-making and because supranational organisations, even if established by national governments, are beyond the control of individual countries, and in any case, have a degree of autonomy from their principals.[37] Lack of control by any one country is especially

---

[34] For general discussions about policy transfer see Dolowitz and Marsh (2000), Rose (1993), and Bennett (1991); for an excellent discussion of Americanisation and industrial production systems immediately after the Second World War, see Djelic (1998).

[35] See below for definition and discussion of regulatory competition.

[36] Green Cowles, Caporaso, and Risse (2001), Schmidt (2002*b*), Featherstone and Radaelli (2003), Knill and Lemkuhl (2002), and Knill and Lenschow (2005).

[37] For discussions of agent autonomy by international organisations using the principal–agent framework, see Pollack (2003) and Tallberg (2002).

true for the sectors examined, as most EU legislation was passed by qualified majority voting in the Council of Ministers, so no one member state could block it, and some was even passed by the Commission on its own.[38] Hence the study treats EU regulation as a third international factor.[39]

(ii) *Carriers and mechanisms of internationalisation in domestic institutional reform*: SIR and comparative institutionalist analyses have highlighted socio-economic actors such as firms or labour as carriers of internationalisation. However, governments and other state actors also need to be considered as possible carriers because they are likely to be significant actors in domestic institutional debates.[40] Hence the study examines how market internationalisation affects the objectives, resources and constraints of firms, governments, independent regulatory agencies, and trade unions. It pays particular attention to coalitions and alliances, since in a multi-actor 'regulatory space', reform is likely to require cooperation between several actors.[41]

In looking at the mechanisms whereby market internationalisation can affect domestic decisions, the book includes political mechanisms as well as ones based on economic 'efficiency'. DiMaggio and Powell (1991) distinguish two forms of isomorphism (i.e. homogenisation): competitive and institutional.[42] The former, they suggest, involves market competition, niche change, and fitness measures. It is driven by efficiency. However, the latter can take the forms of coercion (resulting from formal and informal pressures exerted by other organisations, be this through force, persuasion, or collusion); mimetic modelling or imitation; normative pressures, due to professionalisation.[43]

DiMaggio and Powell are studying organisations rather than national institutions, but their insights can be applied to internationalisation and sectoral economic institutions. To take their first category, 'competitive isomorphism', internationalisation can alter material payoffs from domestic institutions, changing the institutional framework that is most efficient for domestic actors.[44] Policy makers

---

[38] Notably in telecommunications, acting under Article 86 [ex-Article 90] (3) of the Treaty of Rome—see Chapter 6.

[39] Chapters on internationalisation look very briefly at how governments of the four nations participated in EU regulatory decision-making, in order to aid understanding of their strategies within the 'two-level' European game played at both domestic and EU levels, and the extent to which whether EU regulation was imposed on them; for discussions of two-level games, see Putnam (1988) and Evans et al. (1993); for general debates on European integration and the role of the Commission, European Court of Justice and national governments, see Moravscik (1998), Sandholtz and Stone Sweet (1998), and Stone Sweet (2004).

[40] cf. Djelic (1998: 65–127), who argues that actors in institutions that border the state and economy were the central agents of Americanisation in France and Germany after the Second World War.

[41] On regulatory space, see Hancher and Moran (1989) and Scott (2001).

[42] The discussion illustrates how terms are used differently: DiMaggio and Powell use the term 'institution', but look at organisations rather than nations or the sectoral formal institutions studied in the present work.

[43] Djelic (1998: 129–221) develops and applies a similar typology, but the present one differs in extending coercion by including indirect coercion via regulatory competition; see also Braithwaite and Drahos (2000: 15–26) who list no fewer than seven mechanisms for globalisation.

[44] See Simmons and Elkins (2004).

may thus compare possible institutions and alter existing ones to maximise payoffs in the light of the altered international environment. However, internationalisation can also operate through regulatory competition among countries: if a nation modifies its regulatory institutions, this can also change its advantages relative to other nations, whose suppliers and users are therefore affected if competing for markets.[45] In more concrete terms, if one country adopts advantageous institutions (such as standards or forms of ownership), this may help its firms and hence put pressure on other nations to respond to maintain their competitiveness. Regulatory 'races to the top' or 'to the bottom' may take place, as countries compete by establishing high or low domestic standards.[46] More generally, regulatory competition offers an example of 'institutional advantage', as countries seek to aid their suppliers by ensuring better institutional frameworks than their competitors.[47]

With respect to the second category of institutional isomorphism, three mechanisms suggested by DiMaggio and Powell can also be applied in the present study. Coercive mechanisms involve national policy makers being pressurised against their preferences to reform domestic institutions. Coercion can be economic and financial, but can also take political and legal forms, through binding rules and decisions by international organisations, in this case the EU, on unwilling domestic policy makers; examples could include requiring liberalisation, alteration of ownership of suppliers or modification of regulatory systems.[48] Equally, powerful overseas nations or companies may oblige weaker countries to alter market institutions through lobbying or threats.[49]

Normative changes involve the diffusion of professional norms.[50] Transnational epistemic communities or policy networks can be important vehicles for transmitting norms across nations, while being beyond the control of policy makers in individual countries.[51] The EU offers not just a source of imposition but also of norms. It can stimulate or create formal and informal trans-European networks.[52] Moreover, if European regulatory norms develop, these may influence domestic policy makers as to what 'appropriate' market institutions should be.[53]

Mimetic isomorphism involves policy makers copying each other, through cross-national 'policy learning' or 'policy bandwagoning'.[54] It can take the form

---

[45] For a good discussion, see Radaelli (2004).   [46] cf. Vogel (1995).

[47] For a good discussion of comparative institutional advantage, see Hall and Soskice (2001*b*).

[48] For a discussion based on the role of adjudication using the example of the EU, see Stone Sweet (2004).

[49] Simmons (2001), Simons and Elkins (2004), and Ohmae (1990).

[50] Chapter 13 offers a discussion of diffusion.

[51] For epistemic communities see Haas (1992); for transnational networks, see for instance Slaughter (2004) and Stone (2004).

[52] cf. Eberlein and Kerwer (2004), Eberlein and Grande (2005), and Schneider and Werle (1991).

[53] Radaelli (2003), Knill and Lehmkuhl (2002), Eising and Jabko (2001), and Eising (2002).

[54] Different authors use slightly different concepts—for instance, Bennett (1991) refers to 'emulation', while Rose (1993) discusses cross-national learning and Braithwaite and Drahos (2000) refer to 'modelling' for cross-national policy learning and the spread of ideas, see Hall (1989, 1993), King (1992), Hansen and King (2001), Blyth (2002), and Majone (1991); for 'policy transfer' generally see Dolowitz and Marsh (2000), and for a critique James and Lodge (2003).

of attempts at rational analyses of overseas experiences and their applicability domestically. However, it can also be part of political struggles, for as Blyth (2002) argues, ideas are 'weapons' in institutional reform, and work on framing and 'discourse' shows that 'learning' is often used to shape debates and legitimate decisions. Nor does 'mimetism' require straightforward copying, as examples can be translated and interpreted.[55] Thus, reform in one country may offer examples (positive or negative) for overseas policy makers. Equally, EU decisions may provide a model for national institutions but also be used as part of discourse to justify change.[56]

The purpose of the foregoing discussion is not to set out an exhaustive list of mechanisms. Rather it is to underline that the present study does not confine its search for the mechanisms of market internationalisation to changes in the prices of institutions following altered demand by socio-economic groups. Instead, it has drawn on the policy transfer and diffusion, and Europeanisation literatures to present other possibilities. The empirical chapters focus on the process of institutional reform, including the effects of international developments on actors' strategies, coalitions, and conflicts, in order to identify which mechanisms operated. Chapter 13 will not only discuss the mechanisms found but relate the findings to diffusion/policy transfer and Europeanisation literatures.

(iii) *Institutional change: sectoral regulatory reform*: Both SIR and many comparative institutionalist studies have focused their attention on macro-level domestic institutions such as electoral systems, or coordinating institutions between business and employees. However, this introduces a conservative bias into the analysis, since these institutions are often difficult to alter. Moreover, they are relatively remote from market internationalisation, thereby risking underestimating the influence of the latter.

The book examines how market internationalisation affects three sectoral economic institutions: the ownership and organisation of suppliers; the formal rules governing competition; and the allocation of market rule-making powers (e.g. between governments and sectoral regulators). For firms and users, these sectoral institutions are often the most direct ones that structure markets. Alterations in these institutions in the form of privatisation, liberalisation, and delegation of powers to independent regulatory agencies have been identified as major changes in the reform of markets.[57] Indeed, these sectoral institutions are at the core of debates about how markets are organised.

(iv) *Internationalisation and globalisation*: The concept of internationalisation of markets faces a sibling that may be seen as a rival: globalisation. Sometimes the

---

[55] Indeed, Bennett (1991) refers to 'emulation' while Braithwaite and Drahos (2000: 25) talk of 'modelling' in which globalisation of regulation occurs through 'observational learning with symbolic content'; on 'translation', see Campbell (2004, ch. 3).

[56] Schmidt and Radaelli (2004), Schmidt (2002*a*, *b*), and McNamera (1998).

[57] Feigenbaum et al. (1999), Majone (1996), Cassese (2000), Coen and Héritier (2005), Schmidt (2002*b*), Levy and Spiller (1996), Vickers and Wright (1989), Clifton, Corrin, and Fuentes (2006), Wright (1994), and Thatcher (2002). The term 'de-regulation' is generally avoided or placed in inverted commas for as Vogel (1996) points out, freer markets (i.e. liberalisation) often leads to more rules.

two terms are used interchangeably or are not even defined (see e.g. Garrett and Lange 1996; Morgan, Whitley, and Moen 2005).

Globalisation has become a very popular term. Initially, strong globalisation-alists treated it as increased cross-border capital and trade flows but its scope has now been widened to include other forms, and to cover effects on national autonomy.[58] Yet the extent to which globalisation has occurred in recent years has been the subject of bitter debate.[59] Critics have claimed that changes in cross-border flows and trade have been limited and remain below levels seen in the nineteenth century. Some writers have simply treated globalisation as a phenom-enon that goes back to the Ancient World (Braithwaite and Drahos 2000). Even in fields such as banking and securities, the globalisation thesis has been chal-lenged by evidence that the international developments do not amount to glob-alisation.[60] Critics also argue that far from leading to homogenous 'neo-liberal' policies and institutions, nations have responded to globalisation in highly diverse ways.[61]

How does internationalisation of markets relate to globalisation? On the one hand, it is a narrower concept, since it is restricted to international developments that affect economic exchanges. On the other hand, it is broader in that it includes developments that may be regional rather than global, and which may continue to involve strong nation states (e.g. which cooperate internationally). Hirst and Thompson (1999: 8–13) provide a useful distinction between globalisation and internationalisation of economies. They argue that in a 'globalised' economy 'distinct national economies are subsumed and rearticulated into the system by international processes and transactions'. Nation-states lose autonomy. They con-trast it with an international economy in which, although cross-border trade and multinational companies can grow, 'the principal entities are national economies' (1999: 8). They argue that empirically, the main changes in recent years have been internationalisation not globalisation.

Thus internationalisation of markets refers to significant events that create pressures to open national markets even when they do not constitute economic globalisation. They include decisions that are under the collective control of national policy makers such as regional treaties or agreements. Internationalisa-tion avoids arguments about whether nation states as a group have lost power or whether national frontiers have become irrelevant for trade, capital, and compa-nies. Equally, it separates international changes and their effects on nations (in this case, institutions). It allows analysis of the effects of those changes within domestic politics to proceed without necessarily reaching agreement on whether they constitute 'globalisation'.

---

[58] cf. Strange (1986, 1996), Andrews (1994), Goodman and Pauly (1993), and Giddens (2000).

[59] For attacks, see Fligstein (2001) and Hirst and Thompson (1999).

[60] See Sobel (1999) and Helleiner (1994).

[61] See for instance Garrett (1998, 1995), Hall and Soskice (2001b), Berger and Dore (1996), Schmidt (2002), Zysman (1996), and Hollingsworth and Boyer (1997).

Concluding Comments

Second image reversed and comparative institutionalist literatures offer valuable attempts to integrate internationalisation and domestic politics. A critique of the two has uncovered their strengths as well as their limitations. Following that critique, a policy analysis framework has been set out that encompasses both economic and policy forms of market internationalisation. It allows for both socio-economic and state actors to be the carriers of internationalisation. It seeks both efficiency mechanisms and more political mechanisms for the three forms of internationalisation examined.

The analytical framework is now used in the empirical chapters to show that policy forms of internationalisation had more influence on reform of sectoral institutions than transnational technological and economic changes. They did so because their carriers were powerful domestic actors who could interpret and use them for their own purposes. They were both a pressure and an opportunity for these domestic actors. While technological and economic forms of internationalisation were often met with institutional inertia or sometimes cross-national divergence, regulatory reforms in neighbouring nations and supranational regulation contributed to remarkably comprehensive and similar reforms. The implications for SIR and comparative institutionalist frameworks as well as broader questions of why market internationalisation operates in these ways are explored in the final chapter.

2

The Internationalisation of Securities Markets

'Today equity and capital markets are global. Today competition for capital is global'. John Thain, NYSE Chief Executive, April 2005[1]

In the mid-1960s, markets for company securities were relatively small and highly nationally segmented. Most company securities were traded on domestic stock exchanges using people and paper. Individual investors were predominant. But in the period until 2005, increasingly powerful international forces transformed markets, putting strong pressures on national policy makers to alter traditional national economic institutions and open domestic markets.

This chapter examines three central international forces in securities markets. The first are transnational technological and economic developments, such as the computerisation of trading, increased cross-border dealing and capital flows, the global expansion of stock markets, trends towards the growth of large institutional investors, and the international expansion of financial firms. These developments altered the nature of securities trading—its costs, demand, and types of products. They began in the mid-1960s and continued thereafter. The second set of international forces arose from reforms in the US, the world's largest market for securities trading, that modified the operation, openness, and attractiveness of American markets and offered an example of institutional change. Finally, EU legislation was passed; it set rules that member states had to follow in regulating securities trading.

The three forces were international in that they applied across borders and were largely outside the control of policy makers in Britain, France, Germany, and Italy; even EU legislation was decided collectively by member states, together with the European Commission. They emerged progressively, aiding tracing of the effects of each in later chapters; in particular, transnational technological and economic forces and US reforms developed before EU sectoral regulation. The chapter does not explain why the three forms of internationalisation occurred, but rather sets out the pressures they created on institutions that closed markets in European countries, notably the organisation of stock exchanges as clubs of domestic individuals, rules preventing competition and the mixture of regulation by governments and self-regulation by stock exchanges and traders. Subsequent

---

[1] The *Financial Times* 21.4.05.

chapters examine the effects of these pressures on institutional reform in Britain, France, Germany, and Italy.

The chapter begins by offering a brief overview of common features of stock exchanges in major industrialised countries, in order to appreciate the importance of internationalisation. It then sets out the three sets of international forces and considers the potential pressures and challenges that each offered to traditional institutional arrangements. It looks at markets for trading company securities (i.e. equity shares), but it excludes other financial instruments such as company or government bonds. The choice is made because stock markets for company securities have been at the core of debates about financial institutions and because they relate directly to a central issue for firms, namely their ownership.

SECURITIES MARKETS IN THE MID-1960s IN WESTERN EUROPE AND THE US

In the mid-1960s, the operation of securities trading was well established and divided along national boundaries in most industrialised countries, in terms of markets, technology, and regulation. Markets were dominated by long-standing stock exchanges, such as the London Stock Exchange (LSE) in Britain, the Paris Bourse in France, or the New York Stock Exchange (NYSE) in the US.[2] Some were publicly owned (in Continental Europe), others privately owned (Britain and the US). Most exchanges were organised as forms of 'club': only members could trade on the exchange; those members had to be individuals or partnerships of individuals rather than limited companies; admission processes limited numbers and excluded 'undesirables'. The purposes of an exchange were to protect its members and ensure a central market for trading securities, not to make profits for itself.

Stock exchanges can perform many functions, from listing companies whose shares can be traded to post-trade functions of clearance and settlement. However, as trading systems—that is ways of bringing buyers and sellers together—they have three central functions: providing public information about the prices at which securities are bought and sold; routing orders from investors and financial intermediaries to traders/dealers; order execution and settlement, whereby buying and selling prices and quantities are agreed and implemented.[3] In the mid-1960s, these three functions were highly 'material'. The technology of securities trading was human: traders gathered on the public 'floors' of stock exchanges to agree prices and quantities, communicating their offers by 'open cry'—shouting and gesticulating. Prices were often written on blackboards. Trades were then

---

[2] There were also regional exchanges; some were small (e.g. in the UK, France, and Italy) but others were large (notably in West Germany, which lacked a dominant national exchange and the US); in some countries, trading took place off exchanges, but even here trading was influenced by such exchanges—for instance, in terms of reference prices being set by the exchange.

[3] cf. Lee (1998: 1–3) for a discussion.

confirmed, cleared, and settled through a paper process, which included physical share certificates.

Competition within countries for securities trading was limited. Thanks to legislation or powerful norms, stock exchanges held monopolies over several elements of public trading of securities: listing of companies whose shares could be traded on the exchange, the provision of information about prices, routing orders and public trading of securities,[4] and clearance and settlement of public trades. There was little or no competition among exchanges. Within the exchanges, fees ('commissions') were usually fixed, further limiting price competition.

The rationale for many rules and norms was the protection of individual investors. Countries frequently invented a mythical vulnerable female investor whose interests had to be safeguarded—Aunt Mathilda in the US, Aunt Agatha in Britain, and the 'veuve [widow] de Carpentras' in France. Rules were justified by the need to ensure that such individual investors had equality of access to market information and trading with large institutions. In practice, this meant cross-subsidisation of small trades by large ones and rules designed for personal investors with little knowledge or capital. It also meant placing barriers to entry by institutions into stock market trading to ensure that traders were individuals rather than powerful financial corporations (in particular, banks were usually excluded from exchanges).

Markets for securities were highly nationally segmented. Most companies were only listed on their domestic stock exchange. Traders were national, with foreigners usually being excluded by law. Buyers and sellers of securities were also largely domestic.[5] Thus cross-border trading was limited.[6] A high proportion of trading was undertaken for individual investors, who were domestic citizens. Even in markets with significant institutional investors, such as the NYSE and LSE, individual investors were very important—for instance, representing 54% of ownership of UK equities in 1963.[7]

Regulatory arrangements were decided at the national level. They comprised a combination of oversight by governments and central banks with a high degree of self-regulation by the financial community. In practice, a small national 'policy community' predominated. International bodies such as the Féderation Internationale des Bourses de Valeurs (FIBV), had almost no powers over member stock exchanges, while the European Community did not regulate securities trading.

Securities markets remained small relative to domestic economies, whether measured by volume or by market capitalisation of firms listed, even in those

---

[4] In contrast to private arrangements, whereby banks or other intermediaries could match buy or sell requests.

[5] One indication is that foreigners owned few shares in companies—in Germany, they owned only 6% of shares in 1960 and 8% in 1970—Story (1997: 252), quoting the Bundesbank.

[6] In 1965, total sales and purchases of US and foreign stocks by foreigners on the NYSE were $9,376 million (c0.26% of GDP)—adapted from NYSE Factbook Historical Statistics; in 1970, cross-border transactions in bonds and equities combined was only 2.8% of GDP in the US and 3.3% in Germany—Lütz (1996: 16), citing figures from the Bank of International Settlements.

[7] Michie (1999: 631).

nations that had larger stock exchanges (e.g. Britain and the US). Thus for instance, in 1965, turnover on the LSE represented 0.77% of Britain's gross domestic product (GDP), and on the NYSE, 2.06% of the US GDP (see Table 2.1 below).

TRANSNATIONAL TECHNOLOGICAL AND ECONOMIC TRANSFORMATIONS

From the 1960s onwards, transnational technological and economic/financial developments began to transform the market for company securities. Key changes were: computerisation and the use of telecommunications, growth in securities markets, trends towards institutional investors, new products, cross-border capital flows, and international expansion by key financial actors.

Computerisation and the Use of Telecommunications

Computing and telecommunications revolutionised securities markets. They became increasingly used in different stages of share trading—providing information about share prices, routing orders, and, clearance and settlement through paperless electronic transactions.[8] One effect was to create strong pressure on incumbent national exchanges by weakening their monopolies over trading.[9] Computerisation made it easier for competitors to offer alternatives to all the traditional stock market functions. Information on stock market prices could be provided electronically, at low cost and with high reliability; indeed, by 1974 Reuters had a system that enabled LSE prices to be displayed in countries as far away as Japan in a few seconds.[10] From the early 1970s, new electronic stock markets or 'alternative trading systems' appeared that allowed brokers to work away from the physical floor of exchanges and offered lower costs, especially for large trades, the most profitable part of dealing.[11] One prominent example in the US was the National Association of Securities Dealers Automated Quotations (NASDAQ), which began in 1970.[12] Then in the 1980s and 1990s, 'fully automatic' dealing systems appeared which matched the orders of buyers and sellers and fixed prices electronically, without brokers or physical exchanges.[13] It also became easier for buyers and sellers to bypass central exchanges altogether and deal directly with each other, through telephone systems in the 1960s and then electronic systems in the 1970s.[14]

---

[8] Clark and Sherrington (1980), Hamilton (1986: 40–9), Degryse and Achter (2002), and Muniesa (2003: 72–91).
[9] cf. Allen, Hawkins, and Sato (2002).
[10] Michie (1999: 507), Muniesa (2003: 74–6), and *The Banker* (December 1994).
[11] Michie (1999: 502–13) and Blanden (1974).
[12] Michie (1999: 504); for the US, see Haney (1984).
[13] cf. Michie (1999: 615) and Aguilar (2000).   [14] Michie (1999: 457) and Blanden (1974).

A second effect of new electronic technology was to aid cross-border dealing. It made purchasing and selling shares by overseas actors easier, as they could monitor prices on screens in their own countries. It allowed investors and companies to obtain several quotes for a deal and hence greater choice over which national exchange to trade on.[15] Moreover, it permitted traders situated in one country to trade on the exchange in another country ('remote trading'). Thus the potential for international competition was increased as investors and traders could switch between national exchanges.

Finally, new technology created strong reasons for large-scale investment by exchanges. Computerisation offered lower costs, fewer errors, increased capacity, greater transparency and faster trading, clearing, and settlement.[16] At the same time, there were competitive pressures for its application, as rival domestic and international exchanges could use it to attract trading. However, the new technologies required heavy capital expenditure. New electronic dealing systems cost large sums—for instance, LSE's electronic SEAQ system was reputed to cost £5 million, while its SEQUENCE system in 1996 cost £81 million.[17] Similarly, computerised settlement systems involved significant spending.[18] In addition, computerisation required spending by exchange dealers.[19]

Higher capital spending created great difficulties for traditional exchanges organised as non–profit-making clubs composed of individual members with limited personal capital. It created incentives for exchanges to allow corporate members to enter. It also resulted in pressures for exchanges themselves to become companies in order to raise their own capital rather than relying on their members. Indeed, by April 2005, the venerable NYSE, despite being the world's largest stock market and after 212 years as a club, decided to become a limited company.[20]

Expansion of Securities Trading

Internationally, equities markets grew dramatically over the period from the mid-1960s. Their capitalisation value and turnover rose rapidly both absolutely and

---

[15] cf. Greene (1981).

[16] For an analysis of electronic trading and falling transaction costs, see Degryse and van Achter (2002), Haney (1984), Harington (1993), and Domowitz and Steil (2002: 325) suggest 28%–33% savings on total trading costs from using automated systems; Michie (1999: 451) states that an IBM 360 in 1964 saved £42,600 per annum, while a new computer in 1966 reduced the number of man-hours required for processing to c. 8%; LSE's automated dealing system SEAQ in the mid-1980s could handle 70,000 transactions per hour—more than double the then existing volume of sales—Haney (1985: 82).

[17] Haney (1985) and Michie (1999: 614).

[18] In 1990 the cost of a settlement service was put at £30–£35 million per annum—McDougall (1990: 14); for instance, LSE's TALISMAN system was estimated to cost £15.7 million in 1975, while its TAURUS system had cost £75 million in 1993 when it was abandoned and even the more modest CREST system cost £30 million in 1996—Michie (1999: 511, 608).

[19] Even in the 1960s, computerisation made trading by jobbers and brokers in London more capital intensive (Michie 1999: 434); the sums then rose vertiginously so that by the 1990s, LSE members had spent an estimated £320 million preparing for the TAURUS settlement system (Michie 1999: 608).

[20] The *Financial Times* 21.4.05.

relative to national GDPs. Table 2.1 presents figures for turnover; it looks at major exchanges separately since they collected figures differently. Table 2.2 sets out the rise of market capitalisation of listed domestic companies.

Table 2.1. Turnover of equities (millions of US dollars) and as percentage of national GDP

Year	NYSE	% of US GDP	London	% of UK GDP	Tokyo	% of Japan's GDP	France	% of France's GDP
1960	37,690	1.35	—	—	53	0.01	n/a	n/a
1965	73,200	2.06	6,043	0.77	37	<0.01	n/a	n/a
1970	103,063	2.46	15,310	1.73	84	<0.01	4,229	0.50
1975	133,819	2.80	30,484	3.10	386	0.02	5,872	0.59
1980	397,670	6.90	53,511	3.71	200,000	9.08	10,990	0.95
1985	1,023,202	15.22	175,935	14.84	n/a	n/a	31.613	2.54
1990	1,300,000	16.46	1,070,748	35.80	200,000	6.14	132,262	9.09
1995	3,100,000	34.73	2,527,799	79.10	900,000	25.59	194,434	12.54
2000	11,100,000	96.73	9,546,473	259.27	2,300,000	61.40	1,424,559	79.58
2003	9,700,000	78.27	6,386,219	190.12	2,000,000	52.76	1,179,963	63.30

Sources: London: until 1980, from a table of 'UK Equity turnover'; after 1980, from table: Global comparison of annualized value of trading, in NYSE Facts and Figures. *NYSE*: 1960–80: table of 'Market value of shares sold on registered exchanges (mils.) (1935–85)'; after 1980, from table: Global comparison of annualized value of trading in NYSE Facts and Figures. *Tokyo*: 'Total Stock Trading Value (Domestic Stocks)' and 'TSE listed foreign stocks', from the Tokyo Stock Exchange Factbook; figures for foreign stocks only included from 1975, up to 1980; after 1980, from table: Global comparison of annualized value of trading in NYSE Facts and Figures. *France*: Historical series, domestic and foreign shares, from Bourse website. Figures for GDP from 'Groningen Growth and Development Centre and the Conference Board, Total Economy Database, May 2006, http://www.ggdc.net', Table 'Total GDP, in millions of 2005 US dollar (converted to 2005 price level with updated 2002 EKS PPPs)'. All figures have been converted from domestic currency to US dollars using the xe.com currency converter.

Table 2.2. Market capitalisation of domestic listed companies in billions of US dollars

	All World Federation of Exchange members	NYSE	NASDAQ	NYSE and NASDAQ as % of US GDP	London	London as % of UK GDP	Tokyo	Tokyo as % of Japan's GDP	Deutsche Börse	Deutsche Börse as % of Germany's GDP
1980	2,900	1,200	n/a	20.84	200	18.57	400	18.16	70	4.99
1990	9,600	2,700	300	37.98	900	64.44	2,800	85.90	400	20.25
1995	17,500	5,700	1,200	77.30	1,300	85.69	3,500	99.52	600	27.93
2000	30,900	11,500	3,600	138.34	2,600	146.54	3,200	85.43	1,300	54.78
2005	40,900	13,300	3,600	136.37	3,100	156.09	4,600	115.43	1,200	48.68

Sources: As Table 2.1; figures for Germany are for West Germany only until 1990.

Behind the expansion of securities markets lay several structural forces that operated cross-nationally. Firms sought disintermediated borrowing—that is funding through issuing securities rather than borrowing from banks.[21] On the demand side, securities were increasingly bought by financial institutions such

[21] Walter (1996: 91–7), cf. Houthakker and Williamson (1996: 48–77), and Sobel (1999: 53–67).

as pension and investment funds, driven by long-term factors such as increasing savings for pensions and investment by the middle classes.

These developments increased the economic importance of securities markets which became evermore central to providing capital and for holding wealth, not just for a few firms and rich individuals but for many companies and millions of people (albeit indirectly through collective savings institutions such as pension and mutual funds). The disadvantages of poorly functioning securities markets rose for nations.

Institutional Investors and Suppliers

The nature of securities investors and suppliers of financial services also altered. The importance of individual investors declined whereas that of institutional investors such as pension and mutual investment funds or insurance companies rose from the 1960s onwards. Verdier (2002: 176–7) calculates that over the period 1980–late 1990s, the share of financial assets held by institutional investors rose in all the industrialised nations he examined. Thus for instance in the US, households owned 73% of stock (by value) in 1955 but 54% by 1976, and then approximately 40% in the late 1990s, while institutional investors accounted for approximately 25% of public share trading in the 1950s but over 60% after 1969.[22] In Britain, individual ownership of UK equities dropped from 54% of the total in 1963 to 17.7% in 1993.[23] The size and internationalisation of financial conglomerates also increased.[24] The most striking developments were by banks and American securities houses. Thus for instance, increasing numbers of banks began to establish overseas offices from the mid-1960s and US securities houses and other financial conglomerates expanded their overseas operations.[25]

The move towards institutional investors and international financial conglomerates increased competitive pressures on stock exchanges. Large investors were much better placed than individuals to switch exchange or bypass dealers and exchanges by using electronic systems, in order to lower their costs. Their financial clout and knowledge aided them in negotiating on matters such as dealing fees and commissions. The increasing predominance of institutional investors ran counter to the traditional priority given by stock exchanges to individual investors, both in regulation and in the frequent cross-subsidisation of small trades by larger ones. Equally, the rise of large internationalised conglomerates provided powerful competition to domestic securities firms and also aided investors to use overseas exchanges for trading.[26]

---

[22] Fraser and Rose (1980: 326).   [23] Michie (1999: 631) and Plender (1980).
[24] cf. Hamilton (1986).
[25] Fry (1969: 619), Blomquist (1970), Donnell (1970), *The Banker* (November 1970, November 1972, November 1974, November 1977), and Leper (1979).
[26] Even the listing of firms on overseas exchanges, a difficult procedure, increased somewhat (Sobel 1994: 56–9); in the 1980s, international syndication of equity issues began—Hamilton (1986: 75).

New Financial Instruments

The spread of new financial instruments, aided by the application of electronics and innovation in the US, also altered the nature of securities markets.[27] Examples included 'warrants' and 'options' (the right to buy or sell shares at a specified time and price), financial 'futures' (contracts based on future events), and especially 'derivatives' (instruments based on the value of other financial assets—such as tracking share indices).

New instruments represented an alternative to ordinary listed securities, and could be traded in markets other than traditional stock exchanges. They could offer indirect competition to the latter. But perhaps more importantly, new markets for instruments such as derivatives could be organised differently from traditional stock exchanges since they lacked the same institutional 'baggage'. In particular, they could be organised as automated electronic markets, without rules insisting on trading on physical floors or even using dealers.[28] They thereby provided alternative examples of how to organise financial markets in contrast to traditional stock exchanges.

Cross-Border Financial Flows

Increased cross-border flows, both in absolute terms and as a share of total transactions, represented another major economic development for securities markets. The measurement of cross-border capital flows is subject to major methodological difficulties and ignores potential capital flows, which cannot be measured but can strongly affect behaviour.[29] Nevertheless, most studies suggest that cross-border flows have greatly increased.[30] Thus for instance, in 1988, $10 trillion of securitised funds moved across national borders.[31] In 1990, an estimated 11.8% of all equity trading was cross-border—that is firms' stocks were purchased on its national exchange by foreigners.[32] Cross-exchange trading (i.e. when a firm's shares are purchased on foreign exchanges) grew by an estimated factor of 8 between 1986 and the early 1990s.[33] To give just one example, aggregate foreign purchases and sales of securities in US markets rose from $26 billion in 1977 to $75 billion in 1980 to $416 billion by 1989 and also rose as a proportion of total transactions.[34] Equally, purchases and sales by US investors of securities abroad rose from $5 billion in 1977 to $18 billion in 1980 to $232 billion in 1989.[35] Table 2.3 offers figures for purchases and sales of US securities and overseas by foreigners on the NYSE.

---

[27] Vittas (1985).   [28] cf. Muniesa (2003: 84).

[29] A key issue is the classification of overseas buying and selling of shares (cf. Grundfest 1990).

[30] Although the extent of 'globalisation' has been contested (Grundfest 1990; Hamilton 1986; Walter 1988; for differing views, see Sobel 1994).

[31] Grundfest (1990: 349, quoting evidence by Merill Lynch).

[32] Coleman and Underhill (1995: 495, quoting evidence by Salomon Bros).

[33] Coleman and Underhill (1995: 495) and cf. Michie (1999: 623).

[34] Grundfest (1990: 353) and Sobel (1994: 52).

[35] Grundfest (1990: 357) and Sobel (1994: 52).

Table 2.3. Transactions by foreigners on the NYSE in US and foreign securities

Year	Transactions in US stocks: foreigners' purchases from Americans ($)	Transactions in US stocks: foreigners' sales to Americans ($)	Transactions in foreign stocks: foreigners' purchase from Americans ($)	Transactions in foreign stocks: foreigners sales to Americans ($)	Transactions in foreign stocks: net capital flow ($)
1960	1,977	1,775	509	592	−83
1965	3,720	4,133	906	617	289
1970	8,927	8,301	1,033	998	35
1975	15,355	10,678	1,542	1,730	−188
1980	40,298	34,870	7,897	10,044	−2,148
1985	81,995	77,054	20,861	24,803	−3,941
1990	173,293	188,419	122,641	131,863	−9,222
1995	462,950	451,710	345,540	395,831	−50,291
2000	3,605,196	3,430,306	1,802,185	1,815,273	−13,088
2003	3,115,244	3,077,713	1,382,774	1,445,048	−62,274

Source: Adapted from NYSE Factbook Historical Statistics.

Cross-border flows formed part of a broader international economic context, notably increased financial imbalances across Europe, the US, and Japan, the end of the Bretton Woods fixed exchange rate regime and reduced capital controls (cf. Helleiner 1994). They meant both that capital was more mobile and that the potential overseas markets for securities trading had risen. They undermined highly segmented national securities markets.

Conclusion: Transnational Technological and Economic Pressures

Overall, transnational technological and economic developments transformed securities trading. The market became increasing computerised, subject to competition, and open to new products. It also expanded rapidly, saw higher cross-border flows, and became increasingly dominated by institutional investors.

These changes put pressures on traditional national regulatory institutions that protected domestic markets for securities trading. The organisation of stock exchanges as clubs of individual nationals, excluding foreigners and financial firms, faced problems of higher capital spending to introduce new technology, much greater volumes of trading, a world dominated by corporate investors and suppliers, and rival exchanges both for securities and new financial products. Restrictions on competition were threatened by the bypass of existing exchanges because of the rise of alternative exchanges and cross-exchange trading, especially by the increasingly dominant corporate investors and financial suppliers. A regulatory system that combined powers held by national governments with strong self-regulation by stock exchanges and traders was challenged by greater diversity of actors and interests, international actors that lay outside national 'communities' and increasing complexity as trading volumes and cross-border flows rose. The enhanced economic importance of securities provided strong incentives for the development of institutions that allowed national stock markets to invest in new technology and be prepared to deal with large capital flows, overseas business, and powerful corporations.

REFORMS IN THE US

In the early 1960s, there were several organisational features that were common to the US and European nations, especially Britain. The largest stock exchange was the NYSE, although several regional exchanges existed.[36] Similarly to the London Stock Exchange, the NYSE was run as a private club by its individual members, who bought 'seats'. Trading took place on the floor of the exchanges. The securities market was also highly domestic, a parallel with continental European nations: NYSE members had to be American; the vast majority of trading was by US investors in US shares;[37] American financial actors such as securities houses and banks had very little overseas business. As in many European nations, securities were separated from other financial services. In particular, the 1933 Glass-Steagall Act obliged banks to choose between commercial banking and investment banking (engaging in securities-related business such as underwriting and brokerage), thereby hindering the rise of 'universal banks' (i.e. banks dealing with financial services across the board). The major difference with Europe was that a federal sectoral regulatory agency, the Securities and Exchange Commission (SEC) existed from 1934. The SEC enjoyed considerable independence from elected politicians, although the latter retained important powers such as nominations to its board and setting its budget.

Changes in US Securities Markets

Major changes took place in US securities markets, especially in the 1970s and early 1980s. Three are highlighted here: competition to existing exchanges, the ending of fixed commissions, and the emergence of financial conglomerates.

Competition to the NYSE and other traditional regional stock exchanges developed from alternative markets. In 1971, the NASDAQ (National Association of Securities Dealers Automated Quotations) system began. It allowed dealing without a physical central market by using an electronic network of leased lines linking a central computer with terminals in dealers' offices that displayed prices

[36] Regional exchanges accounted for only 8%–12% of all trades, while the NYSE accounted for more than 50% of all listings from the mid-1960s onwards and 76% of all trades by 2002—Arnold et al. (1999), Van Ness, Van Ness, and Warr (2003); in addition, the American exchange ('AMEX') in New York also exists.

[37] Only in 1957 were overseas stocks allowed to be listed on the NYSE.

and quotes; buyers and sellers then had to contact brokers directly to trade. In the early 1970s, NASDAQ often offered better quotations than the NYSE and decided to include securities listed on the existing exchanges.[38] In 1983, NASDAQ began electronic trading, so that shares could be traded through its computer system.

NASDAQ grew rapidly: the number of terminals rose from a few thousand in 1972 to 120,000 by 1985, when more than 16 billion shares were traded, with a value of $200 billion, so that NASDAQ was the third largest stock exchange in the world.[39] During the 1990s, NASDAQ grew further, being a favoured market for trading high technology shares in companies that were not willing to go through the process of being listed on an older exchange such as the NYSE.[40] Further competition to established exchanges came from other electronic markets that not only displayed information but also allowed electronic trading, such as Institutional Networks Corporation (Instinet) formed in 1969, which offered an electronic trading system for institutions; it too expanded rapidly, with 320 million shares being traded in 1984. Another was Intex that permitted dealing from abroad.[41] Thus by the 1980s, the NYSE faced rival markets that were electronic and indeed fully automated—dealing could take place from terminals outside a physical market.

The regulation of securities dealing on the NYSE was altered from the late 1960s onwards. Fixed commissions on trades provided a measure of certainty for dealers and also meant that small investors were cross-subsidised by larger ones.[42] However, they came under increasing attack, notably by the SEC, the Justice Department, and by institutional investors who generated a rising share of trading.[43] In 1971, the NYSE ended fixed commissions for large trades and in 1975 the SEC abolished fixed commissions for all trades. The results were largely beneficial for both investors and many dealers.[44] Brokerage rates for large trades fell sharply, reducing costs for institutional investors; yet they also declined for individuals. Moreover, turnover on the NYSE rose. Although several brokerage firms went out of business or were forced to merge, by the 1980s there was a greater concentration of business and higher profits for the remaining firms.

More generally, the internationalisation, size, and diversity of financial markets and firms rose in the US. The NYSE allowed foreign membership in 1977. Listing and trading of overseas companies on the NYSE rose (see Table 2.3). American banks and brokerage houses began to expand overseas in the late 1960s, while overseas banks increasingly entered the US market.[45] New instruments and markets also developed from the early 1970s onwards, such as warrants trading (1970), financial futures and options (1972–3), and then stock index futures

---

[38] Walmsley (1985: 38).   [39] Hamilton (1986: 43).
[40] Trading rose from $15.3 billion in 1984 to $2.4 trillion in 1995—Sardesai (1997).
[41] Hamilton (1986: 44–5) and Muniesa (2003: 86).   [42] cf. Gart (1994: 74).
[43] cf. Phillips and Zecher (1981: 53–89) and Walmsley (1985: 35).
[44] Gart (1994: 77–8) and Walmsley (1985).
[45] Pringle (1966), Fry (1969), Walmsley (1980: 99), and Canal (1974).

and derivatives in the early 1980s.[46] These markets grew very swiftly—by 1983 the value of trading in futures on the stock market index exceeded that of the NYSE, which responded by opening its own markets for futures instruments.[47] However, the most important change was the development of large, powerful, international market firms from the 1970s onwards, often covering several aspects of securities (e.g. underwriting, advising, and takeovers).[48] The most significant included Merill Lynch, Shearson Lehman, Salomon, or Drexel Burnham Lambert. During the early mid-1980s, most securities brokerage houses were bought up by large financial corporations.[49] In 1999, the Glass-Steagall Act was repealed, reducing regulatory protection of securities business and aiding the growth of large, multi-service financial conglomerates able to operate internationally. As a result, by the mid-1980s, the US had a set of large, diversified financial conglomerates that dwarfed most securities firms and investment banks in European countries.

Effects of US Changes on Europe

The changes in the US greatly increased the gap between the US model of regulation and that in Europe, and put pressure on traditional European institutions. They affected the global market as the US represented the largest world market for shares, accounting for approximately half of the global market (e.g. in 1980, the NYSE alone accounted for 44% of trading on stock exchanges of World Federation of Exchange markets).[50]

Four effects relevant for European policy makers can be underlined. First, US reforms increased competition with other exchanges, especially the most lucrative parts of the securities market, namely large trades for institutional investors in major companies ('blue chips'). In particular, the NYSE offered an alternative market for listing and trading of shares in European firms. Its size made it an attractive market for large firms to issue shares. Moreover, NYSE reforms reduced costs for large investors, notably through the end of fixed commissions.

Second, reforms in the US aided the emergence of markets for new financial instruments such as derivatives and futures that were often separate from incumbent exchanges and used electronic trading. They offered an attractive alternative model of securities trading to the traditional stock exchanges, especially when they grew rapidly and engendered highly profitable new activities. They also added a host of new products that did not fit into traditional institutional arrangements developed for trading ordinary company securities.

Third, the emergence of large internationalised American financial conglomerates placed greater competitive pressures on European firms. US conglomerates were well equipped to lobby, expand, and compete abroad. In addition, US policy

---

[46] Sobel (1994: 28) and Hamilton (1986: 72–4).
[47] The New York Futures Exchange in 1980 and then index options in 1983.
[48] Hamilton (1986: 78–110).
[49] See Hamilton (1986: 85–8).   [50] *Source*: calculated from WFE statistics.

makers pressed European nations to open their markets to American conglomerates.[51] Small- or medium-sized European financial companies were vulnerable in their domestic markets and disadvantaged overseas. Changes in the US moved the international securities market further from the previous world of relatively small specialised firms offering personalised services to individual clients towards a financial services industry dominated by a few large multi-service international companies. They created competitive pressures on European nations to concentrate their financial companies and to strengthen the role of banks, often the only financial companies that were large relative to American firms.

Finally, US reforms offered an example for other countries. They showed that new stock markets using electronics could be created and compete with incumbents with physical trading floors. Reforms of NYSE illustrated the benefits of abolishing fixed commissions. Moreover, the creation of conglomerates offered a powerful example of how the securities industry could be reshaped. Changes in the US were noted in Europe from the mid-1960s onwards[52] and could be used in cross-national policy learning, providing reformers in Europe with empirical evidence and ammunition to justify change. They also underlined the vulnerability of incumbent exchanges to competition.

EUROPEAN UNION REGULATION[53]

Until the 1990s, there was little EU law specifically concerning securities trading. Instead most legislation dealt with other financial services; insofar as it concerned stock exchanges, it covered raising capital (notably listing and bringing securities to markets), and market abuse (e.g. insider trading).[54]

Passing EU legislation for securities trading proved slow and difficult. A study for the European Commission (Wymeersch 1977) argued that differences across national stock exchanges concerning rules for access and operations constituted a significant barrier to integration and the efficient use of capital in Europe. But the response was merely a Code of Conduct in 1977 that offered non-binding recommendations.[55] Moreover, one of its key principles was 'concentration'—i.e.

---

[51] This even began in the mid-1960s, when the US Secretary of State for the Treasury, Douglas Dillen, claimed that European capital markets were riddled with monopoly, causing the capital flows to the US and hence balance of payments imbalances—Kindleberger (1993: 438).

[52] For instance, in 1966, the EEC produced the 'Serge report' underlining that national markets in Europe were too closed—Kindleberger (1993: 439).

[53] EU is used here, although legally legislation comes under the European Community 'pillar' of the EU and the term EEC was used before the 1990s; the international securities organisation the International Organisation of Securities Commissions (IOSCO) drew up important rules for securities firms, notably concerning capital adequacy and accounting rules but not for market structure directly and such rules only emerged in the late 1990s after years of negotiations; they were much less significant for European exchanges than EU regulation and are not examined here.

[54] cf. Moran (1994: 159).

[55] Commission Recommendation 77/534/EEC concerning a European code of conduct relating to transactions in transferable securities [1977] OJ L212/37.

that financial intermediaries should execute their orders on an organised market (such as a stock exchange) unless the principal (i.e. the buyer or seller) had given explicit orders to do otherwise. Concentration therefore militated against the development of competition to established exchanges.

When the European Commission finally proposed an Investment Services Directive (ISD) in 1988 that offered detailed rules for securities trading, it aroused fierce battles between two groups of member states, 'Northern' states led by Britain and Germany, and the 'Southern' group led by France, Italy, Spain, and Belgium.[56] They fought over the extent to which EU rules should protect existing stock markets or aid competition to them. Behind their disagreements lay powerful domestic interests, notably stock exchanges. The Northern group wished to permit increased competition which they believed would advantage their national exchanges. They also supported the creation of new exchanges and forms of trading (such as 'over-the-counter' trading). The Southern group feared the entry of new exchanges and sought to protect their traditional stock markets, notably through regulation that would limit use of overseas exchanges or the creation of rival exchanges.[57]

After more than four years of negotiations, the ISD finally became law in 1993; many of its requirements came into force from 1996.[58] It represented a compromise: it liberalised access to securities exchanges, but its rules for competition through aiding the development of new markets were more limited. It said little about the allocation of regulatory powers within member states. Moreover, its provisions allowed member states considerable discretion.

Access to Securities Markets

The ISD distinguished between 'regulated' and 'unregulated' securities markets; traditional stock exchanges clearly fell within the former. It insisted that member states abolish any national rules limiting numbers of persons having access to a regulated market.[59] To aid cross-border entry, the ISD created a European-wide 'passport': firms authorised in one member state were to have access (including membership) to regulated securities markets in other member states. Moreover, the principle of 'home country control' applied so that a national stock exchange could not prevent trading by firms authorised in another EU member state.

The ISD sought to aid cross-national 'remote access' to electronic markets— that is trading without a physical presence in the market (e.g. by using electronic screens). It stated that if a market in one member state allowed remote access, other member states were obliged to provide facilities to firms based in their

---

[56] Coleman and Underhill (1995) and Brown (1996).

[57] See Steil (1996: 115–26) and Moloney (2002: 653).

[58] Council (1993a); it went beyond equities, but here the focus is just on tradable company securities; for a legal analysis, see Moloney (2002: 654–74); for a critical view, see Steil (1996).

[59] If access were limited due to the legal structure or technical structure of a market, the member state was to ensure that both were to be regularly adjusted.

territory for trading on that overseas market. Thus for example, if the LSE allowed remote access, the French authorities were obliged to permit firms in France to trade on the LSE. This was important since it provided an alternative to trading on domestic exchanges. Finally, credit institutions (e.g. banks) were included in firms given access to exchange markets.[60]

However, member states kept powerful tools to keep out undesired overseas firms. Remote access to exchanges was allowed but not imposed by the ISD. Moreover, the 'access passport' only applied to investment firms authorised under the ISD, those firms had to comply with requirements such as those laid down in the Capital Adequacy Directive. Firms were also obliged to meet certain rules of the host regulated market, on matters such as the constitution and administration of the firm, professional standards for staff, rules for clearing and settlement, and record keeping. These requirements could be used to make access difficult.

Competition Through New Exchanges

Liberalisation of access to exchanges was counter-balanced by ISD provisions that allowed governments to restrict competition to incumbent stock exchanges from new 'alternative exchanges'. Member states could choose to apply the 'concentration principle', namely to require transactions in investment services covered by the ISD to be carried out on a 'regulated market' (Article 14). Although subject to certain conditions and waivers,[61] the concentration principle still represented a potentially powerful tool for national governments to limit domestic competition among exchanges. In addition, member states and not the European Commission classified exchanges as 'regulated markets', which gave them considerable discretion as the ISD had several qualifying conditions that many newer markets did not always meet.[62] Hence the 'concentration principle' gave member states much scope to exclude new exchanges.[63]

Allocation of Regulatory Powers

The 1993 ISD also gave member states much discretion over the allocation of regulatory powers. It required member states to designate the competent national authorities for the application of the directive but defined those authorities very broadly, allowing member states to recognise organisations (including private

---

[60] A temporary derogation until 31 December 1996 was given to several countries including France and Italy.

[61] Such as only applying to 'domestic transactions' and obliging member states to offer a waiver so that investors could choose to have transactions carried outside regulated markets.

[62] For instance, newer quote-driven markets had problems over rules for publication of prices and volumes of trades at the start and end of the trading day and within short periods of the execution of trades (Coleman and Underhill 1995: 500; Maloney 2002: 669–71); the ISD left considerable discretion to the national level over applying its requirements—e.g. over publication of trading prices.

[63] Article 15(5).

ones, such as stock exchanges) as competent authorities.[64] It is important to note that the ISD did not require member states to establish independent regulatory authorities nor did it offer any rules over whether such authorities should cover just securities or other financial services.

Overall View of the ISD

While the ISD liberalised access to regulated markets, it contained many potential loopholes for governments to restrict such access. It relied on indirect competition among national exchanges by aiding remote access and regulatory competition among exchanges rather than the creation of new exchanges within member states. It allowed considerable discretion for member states over competition and the allocation of regulatory powers. It contained no provisions concerning ownership of exchanges.

EU Regulation after the 1993 ISD

The period between 1999 and 2005 saw further developments of EU sectoral legislation for regulatory institutions in securities markets. In 1999, the Commission passed a Financial Action Services Plan that envisaged EU legislation to break down barriers to creating a single financial market.[65] In 2000 it reviewed the 1993 ISD (Commission 2000) and put forward new rules to aid alternative trading markets (which would be subject to much less stringent rules than regulated markets by being treated as investment firms), the end of the concentration principle and stronger requirements on the immediate publication of trades.

The Action Plan and Review were followed by the 2004 Markets in financial instruments directive (MIFID), which replaced the 1993 ISD.[66] MIFID covered many fields, and its detailed requirements will be implemented between 2005 and 2007, and hence after the period studied in this book. Nevertheless, three aspects can be highlighted that are most directly relevant to securities trading. First, it helps cross-border trading. Thus it extends 'passporting'—that is firms being authorised in one member state to provide financial services in other member states[67]—and it broadens home country control of cross-border transactions and

---

[64] Wymeersch (1998); Article 22(2) of the ISD says competent national authorities shall be 'either public authorities, bodies recognised by national law or bodies recognised by public authorities expressly empowered for that purpose by national law'.

[65] European Commission (1999) and Moloney (2002: 25–32); it had broad scope, but with respect to securities trading it envisaged the development of alternative trading markets, allowing a single company prospectus for cross-border capital raising, adopting a market abuse regime, and extending investor protection for cross-border provision of services.

[66] European Parliament and Council (2004).

[67] In particular, it clarified that passporting covered alternative securities markets (called 'Multilateral Trading Facilities' in the Directive).

business.[68] These provisions reduce paperwork (since firms only have to meet one set of national requirements) and the ability of national authorities to restrict entry by other EU firms. Second, it increases EU detailed regulation, reducing the scope for member states to make their own rules.[69] Finally, it aids cross-border raising of finance.[70] Overall, it represents a further step towards weakening national barriers to entry to domestic stock exchanges.

CONCLUSION

In the mid-1960s, securities markets in industrialised nations were relatively small compared to 2005. Most stock exchanges were organised as clubs, open to only a limited number of members and closed to foreigners. Traders and many investors were individuals. Cross-border trading or listing was limited.

The period until 2005 saw powerful internationalisation of securities markets. Transnational technological and economic forces transformed the costs, demand, products, and size of the industry; reforms in the US, the largest national market for securities, both affected the world market and offered a powerful example of reform; supranational regulation by the EU insisted on a degree of liberalisation, especially for cross-border access to exchanges. These three forms of internationalisation developed over time and they cumulated with each other. Thus transnational technological and economic forces began from the mid-1960s onwards; US reforms followed; EU legislation only began in earnest from the 1990s onwards.

The three forms of internationalisation put pressures on traditional regulatory institutions for securities trading in similar ways. They increased the scope for competition both among exchanges and within them. It became easier to create new electronic exchanges and hence challenge monopolies. The US offered concrete examples of the success of such exchanges from the early 1970s. At the same time, higher cross-border flows, the acceptance of listing of overseas companies and the rise of institutional investors all augmented competition among exchanges.

Internationalisation also undermined the traditional internal structure and ownership of exchanges based on a limited number of individual members and fixed commissions. New technology required investment by exchanges and brokers/dealers, which individuals found difficult to fund. Equally, increased competition for securities trading raised pressures for increased efficiency. Corporate investors were better placed than individual ones to demand change, while the US offered a powerful example of the benefits of reforms such as abolishing fixed

---

[68] For instance, covering reporting of transaction and supervising conduct of business and organisational requirements on passported (i.e. cross-border) firms.

[69] For instance, it laid down pre- and post-trade transparency requirements for different types of market (regulated markets, MTFs and over-the-counter trading), including by investment firms that are 'systematic internalisers'—i.e. which deal on their own account by executing orders outside an organised market, and hence can compete with established stock exchanges.

[70] For instance, by its provisions for a single company prospectus.

commissions. Finally, the rise of large financial conglomerates underlined the vulnerability of individual traders operating with little capital. Thus stock exchanges and their members faced an increasingly competitive market dominated by large companies.

Traditional informal self-regulation, cross-subsidisation, and protection of individual investors were also challenged by internationalisation. As the size of securities markets grew and their importance for the provision of capital to companies and the holding of wealth went up, so the economic and political stakes of institutional choices rose. Equally, institutional investors were well placed and had incentives to attack structures and rules that were not efficient for them—for instance, those that protected exchanges, traders, or individual investors. Moreover, as new financial instruments developed, markets grew and internationalisation of firms and financial flows rose, so it became more difficult to rely on informal rules or self-governance by domestic policy communities.

Whether the international forces that affected securities markets throughout the world led to 'global' competition for securities and capital as claimed by NYSE's chairman in 2005 is a matter for debate.[71] However, it is clear that international forces were beyond the control of policy makers in individual nations such as Britain, France, Germany, or Italy. Equally, they transformed the nature of the industry, putting great external pressures to alter traditional domestic sectoral institutions that protected domestic markets for securities trading. Following chapters examine how national policy makers responded to those pressures.

---

[71] For contrasting views, see Strange (1988), Helleiner (1994), Sobel (1994), and Verdier (2002).

3

Common Pressures, Diverse Paths: Securities Trading in France, West Germany, and Italy 1965–85

In the mid-1960s, France, West Germany, and Italy had well-established institutions governing the trading of securities that dated back decades and often centuries. Those institutions greatly protected existing national suppliers. Thus the public trading of company securities was the monopoly of state-owned stock exchanges. Within those exchanges, brokers appointed as state officials but doing business as individuals had a monopoly over trading. Governments (national or subnational) held most regulatory powers over stock exchanges: there were no independent regulatory agencies.

Institutions in the three countries differed considerably from those in Anglo-Saxon nations.[1] Stock exchange were publicly owned, in contrast to privately ownership in Britain and the US. Governments held many regulatory powers, unlike the US, which had an independent regulator (the SEC), and Britain where self-regulation was strong. In addition, stock exchanges were much smaller than in Britain and the US. At the same time, however, important differences also existed among the three continental European nations themselves over the degree of centralisation of trading, the allocation of regulatory powers, and the role of banks. Differences often matched those predicted by comparative institutionalist literatures, which suggest that France has a highly centralised and interventionist state, whereas power is more dispersed among associations and subnational levels in Germany, while Italy has a highly fragmented set of institutions.

International factors placed strong pressures on the long-standing institutions in France, West Germany, and Italy. Policy makers became concerned that existing institutions were inappropriate to meet increasing powerful technological and economic internationalisation. They looked at overseas examples, especially in the US and Britain, that offered an alternative institutional model. Serious debates on reform of institutions for securities trading took place in the late 1960s and early 1970s. Modest proposals to open and expand securities trading to respond to the changed technological and economic nature of the industry and match overseas nations, such as the US, were made. However, even these limited changes were generally blocked: institutional inertia was the predominant response to

[1] See Chapter 2 for the US and Chapter 4 for Britain.

international pressures. Reformers were unable to form strong determined coalitions to overcome opposition from supporters of existing institutions. Insofar as institutional changes were introduced, they often widened existing cross-national differences. Moreover, debates and reforms peaked in the late 1960s or early 1970s, with a decline thereafter, although internationalisation grew steadily stronger.

With respect to the general argument of the book, securities trading in France, West Germany, and Italy between the mid-1960s and 1985 thus provides strong evidence about the limited impacts on domestic institutional reform of transnational technological and economic developments and of reforms in the US. National policy makers, especially governments, saw that these two forms of internationalisation posed challenges to traditional institutions that were acknowledged to be inadequate. Yet they were unable to form strong domestic reform coalitions or to impose change on actors enjoying protection from existing institutional arrangements. As a result, the three countries largely maintained those institutions, or altered them in limited and diverse ways, so that the countries followed their own specific institutional paths. The chapter therefore shows the importance of the domestic policy process in institutional responses (or lack of them) to transnational technological and economic developments and reforms in the US.

The chapter looks at each country in turn, beginning with a brief overview of economic institutions for securities trading in the mid-1960s and then looking at reform debates and changes. The conclusion seeks to explain why the transnational technological and economic developments and reforms of securities regulation in the US between the mid-1960s and 1985 failed to lead to cross-national convergence or even widespread reform.

FRANCE

Institutions and Markets for Securities in the Mid-1960s

Institutions for share markets in France were deeply rooted in history.[2] *Agents de change* (brokers) held a legal monopoly over the sales and purchases of shares, originally from an *ordonnance* of Phillipe le Bel in 1304 and confirmed by an edict of 1705 and the Napoleonic Code of 1807.[3] Brokerage rates were set by law. *Agents* had to be members of a professional association (*syndicat*), which decided whether to admit members, often transferring a vacant seat to sons and heirs. Only individuals could be *Agents* and members of a brokerage house (*a charge*). They had unlimited personal liability and were jointly liable for each others' losses, including if an *Agent* went bankrupt, an interdependence that created strong shared interests.

---

[2] For a history of the French stock exchange, see Lehmann (1997).
[3] Tomasi (2002: paragraph 86).

Trading on the Bourse de Paris took place in the magnificent early-nineteenth century Palais Brongniart in a raised circle surrounded by a balustrade known as the *corbeille*.[4] It began at 12.30 (a time chosen to allow the mail carriage to arrive from Lyons) and ended at 14.30. Prices were set by open cry among the *Agents* and written in chalk on a large blackboard. The state was intimately involved in regulation. Thus although the *Agents de change* were private profit-making individuals, they were also 'ministerial officers', appointed by ministers and acting within regulations set by the latter. Sectoral regulatory organisations were controlled by the Ministry of Finance, the Banque de France and the *Agents de change*. In particular, the main regulatory body for exchanges, the Comité des bourses de valeurs, created in 1942, was chaired by a deputy governor of the Banque de France, with a *directeur* of the Trésor and members of the financial community. It was responsible for rules governing share trading.

The French stock market faced considerable difficulties by the mid-1960s.[5] Share prices and ownership were in decline, and the *Agents* were in poor financial condition. The market depended heavily on state support, notably via purchases of shares. The Comité des bourses de valeurs was weak, and the exchanges had few formal rules to protect investors, suffered from complexity and were easily subject to manipulation.[6]

Discussions of Reform and Internationalisation 1965–85

Serious debates on reform of institutions for securities trading took place in the late 1960s and early 1970s. They were led by the political executive, especially the Finance Ministry. In particular, Valéry Giscard d'Estaing strongly encouraged stock market reform as Finance Minister (1969–74).[7] The political executive created a sectoral regulator, the Commission de la Bourse (COB) in 1967 (see below), which then pressed hard for further reforms.[8] Its views were influential not only because of its institutional position but also due to leadership by distinguished figures from the French state.[9] Its efforts were supported by government-appointed ad hoc Commissions on stock market reforms chaired by very senior figures from the financial, administrative, and political worlds; they included the 1971 Caplain

---

[4] Seven regional stock exchanges existed, but the Paris exchange accounted for over 95% of capitalisations and transactions by value, *Le Monde* 28.3.66; in addition, a market for non-quoted stocks (*hors-cote*) existed in Paris.

[5] See Lehmann (1997: 82–6); Conac (2002: 25–6); *Les Echos* 20.6.66, the *Financial Times* 24.6.66, *Le Nouvel Observateur* 12.10.66, and *Le Nouveau Journal* 22.2.68.

[6] cf. Lehmann (1997: 58–87), Conac (2002: 24–5), and *Le Monde* 31.8.67; for a British critique, see *The Times* 6.7.70.

[7] cf. *Les Echos* 25.11.71 and *La Nation* 17.5.72.

[8] For the COB's proposals and details of reforms, see Decoopman (1979: 149–82).

[9] For instance, Pierre Chatenet (president 1968–72) was a former interior minister—*Le Monde* 4.10.67; Jean Donnedieu de Vabres (president 1974–80) was a former *directeur de cabinet* of Pompidou when prime minister and then secretary-general of the government—*Le Monde* 9.8.74.

report, the 1972 Baumgartner report, and then later the 1980 Pérouse and 1985 Tricot reports.[10]

Although domestic actors dominated discussions of institutional reform, international pressures were clearly present. Policy makers drew on overseas examples and comparisons, especially with the US and Britain.[11] They pointed out that the Paris Bourse had lower trading volumes and capitalisation and fewer listed stocks than the LSE and NYSE and that shareholding was more limited in France than in the US and UK.[12] Almost no foreign shares were traded on French exchanges, and there were fewer international investors than in Britain and the US. The Paris Bourse lacked liquidity, with many stocks being quoted but very rarely traded. Overseas exchanges were already using new technology, especially computerisation, giving them advantages in terms of speed, costs, and reliability.[13] Competition to the Paris Bourse from the LSE after Britain joined the European Community in 1972 was even mentioned, including the danger that trading in French shares could migrate to London.[14]

The COB and the ad hoc Commissions claimed that the Paris Bourse suffered from institutional and fiscal disadvantages compared to its overseas rivals. They argued that the Paris Bourse had to expand internationally, and sought changes that would make it attractive to overseas investors.[15] Their rhetoric referred to the Paris Bourse as having 'an appointment with Europe'[16] and to matching LSE and Frankfurt.[17] The COB's first secretary-general set out a strong position: 'Vis-à-vis the outside world, which represents an important potential clientele for French shares, it is essential to protect the French market from all risk of being provincial. For this, it is helpful to consider domestic institutions from the point of view of the foreigner: every difference seems a handicap'.[18]

---

[10] Caplain (1971), Pérouse (1980), and Ministère de l'Economie et Finances (1972) [Baumgartner report]; Ministère de l'Economie (1985) [Tricot report]; Michel Caplain was president of the financial company Suez and of the banking committee of CNPF (the employers' association), and Wilfred Baumgartner was a former finance minister, governor of the Banque de France, and head of Rhone-Poulenc.

[11] Caplain (1971: 4,7), *La Nation* 20.3.70, *La Vie Française* 29.1.71, *Le Monde* 18.1.71, *Le Nouvel Journal* 18.7.71, *Le Monde* 18.7.71, *L'Agence Nouvelle* 28.7.71, *Le Monde* 26.11.71, *La Nation* 17.5.72, *La Croix* 18.5.72, *Les Echos* 27.5.72, Ministère de l'Economie et Finances (1972) [Baumgartner report], *La Vie Française* 3.2.72, *Les Echos* 29.5.72, *La Croix* 17.5.72, *Le Monde* 22.5.72, Pérouse (1980), *La Vie Française* 28.1.85, *Le Monde* 24–5.3.85, *Libération* 26.3.85, and *Le Point* 3.6.85.

[12] Thus for instance, in 1971, the capitalisation of French exchanges was 117 billion francs as compared with 390 for Britain and 5,500 for the US, the value of transactions was 28 billion francs compared with 194 for LSE, only 830 firms were quoted in France as against 3,307 on LSE and 10,000 for the NYSE alone and only 1 in 33 French people owned shares, as against 1 in 22 Britons and 1 in 7 Americans. Sources: Turot (1973), 1971 Baumgartner Commission—*Le Monde* 18.7.71 and Pérouse (1980: 43–6).

[13] Pérouse (1980: 56–80).   [14] *Le Monde* 8.8.72; cf. Turot (1973: 26–8).

[15] *La Vie Française* 8.9.80, *Les Echos* 22.3.85, *Le Monde* 24–5.3.85, *La Vie Française* 28.1.85, and Tricot report; De Witt (1985).

[16] Pierre Chatanet, COB president, *Le Monde* 7.4.72.

[17] *Le Point* 3.6.85, Dupont (head of the *Agents'* company) (1986: 95), cf. *Le Monde* 16.10.80 (Pérouse Commission 1980).

[18] Burgard (1970: 864).

However, reform faced a key obstacle, namely the *Agents de change*. Their professional association (*syndicat*) was at the centre of discussions but was reticent about change. In particular, it successfully defended several market practices that allowed the *Agents* to enjoy high turnover and continue as individual traders. Furthermore, alterations that threatened jobs were politically dangerous, as employees of the Paris Bourse were willing and able to go on strike. In practice, reformers could muster support only for modest modifications that did not threaten the profits of the *Agents* and the jobs of Bourse employees or at times when the *Agents* were in real difficulties. Hence the most significant changes were made in the mid- or late 1960s; thereafter reforms were very modest.

Reforms Introduced and Those Blocked

The Allocation of Regulatory Powers: The COB, a Sectoral Authority

The most important institutional reform was the creation of the COB (La Commission des Opérations de Bourse) in 1967. In the mid-1960s, the government (notably the Finance Minister Michel Debré) looked at overseas regulators—the SEC in the US, and to a lesser extent, the Belgian securities regulator and the LSE.[19] It noted that these bodies were separate from the government and were able to combat market abuse, thereby offering protection to investors. Drawing directly from overseas examples, it therefore decided to alter the supervision of the markets by creating a sectoral regulator.

The COB was established as a public regulatory body.[20] It was organisationally separated from the *Agents de change* and the government. It enjoyed a degree of independence from the latter in that its members were designated for fixed terms, its personnel were under the authority of its head and it took its own decisions.[21] It was made responsible for the proper functioning of the market for shares as well as the publication of information by firms and listing or delisting of shares, and its major powers related to the supply of information.[22]

The COB represented a major institutional innovation, not just for French stock exchanges, but also for the entire administrative system in France, since sectoral regulators separated from central ministries were a rarity at that time.[23]

---

[19] Decoopman (1979: 1), *Le Monde* 31.8.67, *Le Nouveau Journal* 22.2.68, and interview senior financial regulator 1.

[20] In the 1980s, it was classified as an 'autorité administrative indépendente' (the French version of an independent regulatory body); for discussions of the legal status of the COB, see Donnenieu de Vabres (1980), Decoopman (1979: 5–17), Guillaume-Hofnung (1982), and Robert and Labboz (1991: 47–58).

[21] Originally members were nominated for five years, reduced to four; the President was nominated by decree in the Council of Ministers, the other four members by the Minister of Economics.

[22] Its powers included receiving complaints, undertaking enquiries, and approving the publication of information; these were strengthened by the law on insider trading in 1970 which increased the COB's investigative and sanctioning powers—Lehmann (1997: 89) and Lascoumes (1985); for detailed discussions, see Decoopman (1979: 17–37, 162–5).

[23] Decoopman (1979: 1).

It arose from overseas lesson-drawing and its central purposes included attracting international investors, avoiding differences with other competing foreign markets and preventing the outflow of capital abroad; indeed, the 1967 legislation stated that the COB was to aid the development of the stock market and to 'allow the financial market and the Paris stock exchange to play a wider international role that should be theirs'.[24] At the same time, and despite the lesson-drawing from the US, the COB remained a much weaker organisation than the SEC.[25] The government enjoyed considerable formal controls over the COB, notably through the nomination of members, setting its financial and personnel resources and the presence of a government commissioner in deliberations of the COB's members. The COB's powers were often limited. In particular, it could not take cases to court itself, set legal rules governing information, issue general 'cease and desist' orders or exercise general disciplinary powers over the *Agents*.[26] Thus the COB offered a major institutional change for France but remained very different from the SEC.

The Organisation of the Market and the Position of the Agents de change

In the mid-1960s, France had both weak share traders and a major peculiarity in the organisation of securities markets, namely the coexistence of two markets for the same shares on the Paris Bourse. With respect to the first, the *Agents de change* were suffering from falling profits and numbers, but faced many legal restrictions on their activities. They matched buy and sell orders but were not permitted to trade on their own account (*contre-partie*) or outside the market, thereby reducing market liquidity and limiting trading to the Bourse's opening hours (12.30–14.30 weekdays). Nor were they permitted to engage in other work such as providing investment advice.[27] They were highly fragmented between different brokerages (*charges*). As individuals, they lacked capital for large trades.

The second involved different prices for securities depending on the form of settlement (i.e. payment and delivery of shares) used. On the *marché au comptant*, settlement occurred swiftly after a transaction; but on the *marché à terme*, the *Agents* only had to settle at the end of the month.[28] The *marché à terme* offered investors and *Agents* free credit as they only had to settle the net amount they owed at the end of the credit period. It aided individual investors/speculators, who lacked capital and encouraged trading, thereby increasing volumes for the *Agents*. But it meant that for some shares, two prices were offered according to whether the trade was *au comptant* or *à terme*, a system that was difficult to understand, especially for overseas investors.

Significant reforms were debated in the early 1970s. The Caplain, Baumgartner, and Pérouse reports compared the position in France with that of overseas

---

[24] l'ordonnance du 28 Septembre 1967; Burgard (1972: 861–4), cf. Lascoumes (1985: 6–7).
[25] See Conac (2002).   [26] Conac (2002: 56–7, 113, 116–17).
[27] Only in the mid-1960s were they allowed to manage investment portfolios and advertise for clients.
[28] cf. Rizzo (1975: 567–77).

exchanges, including the NYSE and the LSE, where dealers/jobbers were authorised to trade on their own account and continuous trading took place.[29] They
pointed out the frequent lack of liquidity for certain shares, and the fact that most
prices were set at the beginning of the trading session with little activity thereafter.
They also argued that overseas investors wanted to understand prices easily, rather
than relying on figures written on a blackboard in the Paris *corbeille* for two hours
a day, a particular problem for investors outside Paris (notably foreigners in other
time zones).[30] In order to increase liquidity, simplify the market and ensure constant trading, the Baumgartner Commission (1971), with the support by the COB
and head of the compagnie (association) des Agents,[31] suggested unifying the
two markets (*au comptant* and *à terme*). It, the Caplain Commission and the
Pérouse Commission also called for continuous, computerised trading, and
the development of Paris as an international market.

However, the *Agents* feared that these proposals would further reduce their
numbers, by decreasing the volume of trading (because of the end of free credit
offered by the *marché à terme*) and by increasing their capital requirements.[32]
Trade unions were strong among the *Agents'* employees, and the prospect of
redundancies and complaints of low pay because of the reduced numbers of *Agents*
and computerisation led to prolonged strikes in 1968, 1974, and 1979 that closed
the Paris Bourse.[33] In this position, attempts to merge the *marchés au comptant*
and *à terme* were blocked by the *Agents* in 1977–8.[34] Discussion of ending the
Agents' monopoly over dealing, that would have allowed new entrants such as
banks to trade shares, also aroused opposition and no modifications were implemented.[35] Although the opportunities for replacing the *corbeille* with electronic
systems were recognised,[36] the introduction of computing remained limited; in
particular, it was not used for dealing.

Policy makers shied away from confronting the *Agents* and feared strike action
by their employees.[37] Only limited institutional reforms were introduced. In
1972, Giscard d'Estaing as finance minister announced that in order to help the
Bourse to compete with foreign exchanges (notably London and New York),
the government would legislate to allow the *Agents* to engage in a restricted
form of *contre-partie* outside Bourse hours.[38] Previous requirements for special

---

[29] *Le Monde* 18.1.71 and *Les Echos* 10.2.72.
[30] See interview, Yves Flornoy (head of Compagnie des Agents de change), *La Vie Française* 8.9.80,
Pérouse (1980), *Le Monde* 16.10.80, and *Le Point* 3.6.85.
[31] *La Vie Française* 8.3.76, *Le Monde* 26.11.76, *Le Nouveau Journal* 28.5.78, 4.5.79, interview, Yves
Flornoy, head of the companie des Agents, and *Les Echos* 9.4.79.
[32] *L'Express* 14-20.3.77, *La Vie Française* 6.12.76, and *Le Nouveau Journal* 28.5.77.
[33] cf. *La Vie Française* 27.12.76, *Le Figaro* 15.9.76, 16.3.79; numbers of brokerages of Agents (*charges*)
fell from 83 in 1962 to 45 in 1979, and *Les Echos* 9.4.79.
[34] *La Vie Française* 27.12.76, 24.1.77, 14.2.77, 30.4.79.   [35] *Le Figaro* 31.3.79.
[36] Interview, Yves Flornoy, *La Vie Française* 5.1.76, *Les Echos* 4.4.79, *Les Echos* 24.1.78, *Le Monde*
10.2.79, and *La Vie Française* 27.12.76, 17.12.79.
[37] *Le Figaro* 15.9.76, *L'Express* 14.3.77, cf. *Le Monde* 17.4.79, and *Les Echos* 9.4.79.
[38] Trading outside market hours but at prices set during the 12.30-14.30 sessions of the Paris
Bourse—Ministère de l'Economie et Finances (1972), *La Nation* 17.5.72, *La Croix* 15.5.72, *La Vie
Française* 18.5.72, *Les Echos* 29.5.72, Lehmann (1997: 93), and *Le Nouveau Journal* 8.8.73.

government authorisation for the quotation of foreign shares on the Paris Bourse were lifted.[39] Yet more significant alterations were not attempted. Instead, fiscal measures were used to increase the attractiveness of shares, such as an extension in 1973 of tax breaks (the '*avoir fiscal*') from French investors to overseas ones, liberalisation of exchange controls over the outflow revenues from selling shares and the creation of new forms of savings under the 1978 *loi Monory*.[40]

Thus in 1985, France still had brokers who had a monopoly over share trading but operated during very limited hours as individuals with little capital. It retained a system of dual prices for the same stock, an institutional feature that was difficult to understand but aided individual investors through free credit and supported the *Agents* by encouraging trading.

WEST GERMANY

The 1960s: Federalism and Bank Domination

Before 1914, German capitalism and stock markets had developed strongly. But, under the Nazis, severe restrictions were placed on share trading and investors were seen as speculators.[41] By the 1960s, stock exchanges played only a minor role in the German economy.[42] Few companies were publicly quoted ('AGs') and most firms tended to raise their capital by borrowing from banks.[43] The share of household wealth held in the form of equities was extremely low—2% for the 1950–9 period. Instead, Germany had a bank-dominated financial system. The banks enjoyed a close long-term relationships with firms: they owned most shares in the publicly-quoted AGs, provided the majority of capital to firms (both for AGs and for private limited liability companies) and derived most of their business from the stable and profitable activity of providing loans.[44]

Stock exchanges in West Germany were not only small but also fragmented. Eight regional exchanges shared equities trading, although the Frankfurt exchange was the largest.[45] The exchanges were public law institutions, owned by the regional Chambers of Commerce. The official brokers (*amtliche Kursmakler*) were public officials appointed by the regional stock exchange supervision authorities (*Börsenaufsichtsbehörde*), but traded as individuals with personal liability and mutual liability for each other. They had a monopoly over trading on the official exchanges and setting prices.[46] Share trading was very limited, and the exchanges were open two hours per day between 11.30 and 13.30.[47]

---

[39] *Le Nouveau Journal* 9.6.73.   [40] *La Vie Française* 3.2.72 and *Le Monde* 18.7.71.

[41] Interview senior banker 1; see e.g. Franke (2001) and James (1998).

[42] See, e.g. Storey (1997) and Czada (2000).

[43] For general discussions of how the structure of the German economy affected stock exchanges, see Storey (1997) and Lütz (1997, 2000).

[44] Interview senior banker 1.   [45] Lütz (1998: 156).

[46] A second category of brokers, the *Freimakler*, who were not regulated by public law, acted as intermediaries for banks on exchanges, and also traded in unlisted shares and on the small unofficial markets. Hadding and Schneider (1987) and Schwark (1994: 225–54).

[47] Story (1997: 251–3, 261).

A well-established legal framework governed stock markets, mostly dating from before 1945. The regional governments (the Länder) had been responsible for legal supervision of their respective exchanges since 1896, appointing 'state commissioners' to oversee them. The 1946 German Constitution (Basic Law) confirmed this position. Thus regulatory powers were shared between national and regional governments so that institutional changes required agreement by both. Moreover, significant legal restrictions existed on markets, notably a prohibition on futures and options trading under the 1934 banking law. Legal requirements to protect investors were limited: price transparency on exchanges was weak; there were few reporting requirements for companies; insider trading was not illegal.

The relative absence of detailed legal rules meant that stock exchanges were marked by strong self-regulatory and cartel arrangements.[48] The Länder confined themselves to legal supervision of the exchanges, largely leaving regulation of behaviour to private actors.[49] In practice, this meant that banks dominated decision-making.[50] The majority of share trading was done via banks who passed orders to the brokers (*Makler*). Moreover, the banks held many seats on the boards of exchanges whose presidents were, by tradition, private bankers.[51] The banks and the brokers used their position to limit competition, both among themselves for services and across exchanges. The result was that share listing and trading costs were high, and informal rules protected the smaller regional exchanges.[52]

Thus in the mid-1960s a powerful domestic coalition existed that benefited from the status quo: the banks, who dominated the supply of capital to firms and share trading; the Länder who had their regional exchanges and a powerful position vis-à-vis the federal government; the exchanges themselves who did not compete with each other.

Discussions of Reform, Internationalisation, and Inertia

Institutional reforms were debated on several occasions in the period from the early 1960s until 1985. Attempts at legislative reform were led by the Federal Economics Ministry, which repeatedly called for change throughout the late 1960s and set up several expert committees to put forward proposals.[53] The stock exchanges, some banks and the employers' association, the Bundesverband der Deutschen Industrie (BDI), supported non-legislative measures to 'modernise'

---

[48] Lütz (1998: 155–7).   [49] Interview senior exchange official 2.
[50] Interviews senior banker 1 and 2, senior exchange official 1 and 2.
[51] Interviews senior banker 1, senior exchange official 3.
[52] For instance, the informal obligation for larger firms to have their shares listed and traded on all exchanges, which raised their costs.
[53] A standing committee, the Stock Exchange Expert Commission (Börsensachverständigenkommission) composed of representatives from all interested parties, including banks and exchanges also offered reform advice, interview senior exchange official 3, see Beyer-Fehling and Bock (1975); *Die Welt* 2.7.66, article by a senior government official in the Ministry, *Frankfurter Allgemeine Zeitung* 5.7.66, *National-Zeitung, Basel* 16.1.68, and *Süddeutsche Zeitung* 13.1.69.

German exchanges.[54] For both sets of actors, international factors were important reasons for reform. They feared that small stock markets failed to meet the capital needs of German firms who would therefore lose out in the face of increasing international competition.[55] They noted that exchanges in Britain and the US were larger and more internationalised (in terms of overseas investors) than German ones.[56] With greater internationalisation of capital markets, German exchanges needed reforms to compete with overseas rivals and attract foreign shares, as well as boosting domestic trading.[57]

Reformers argued that German exchanges needed to modernise and reach 'international standards' by adopting institutional features of exchanges overseas, notably those in Britain and the US.[58] These features included: greater independence for exchanges from banks, creating one dominant national exchange similar to the LSE instead of several small regional exchanges,[59] and allowing futures and options markets.[60] Reformers also sought greater protection and information for investors;[61] there was even mention of stock exchanges creating their own supervisory body modelled on the SEC.[62]

Serious attempts at change were made in the late 1960s. A 'study commission' was created in 1964 that examined the conditions for re-establishing futures and options trading.[63] In 1968, the government drafted legislation designed to make the exchanges more transparent, larger and more internationally competitive, drawing strongly on the US and Britain as models.[64] In particular, it sought

[54] *Frankfurter Allgemeine Zeitung* 12.6.61, *Industriekurier* 29.1.63, 20.3.69, *VWD-Wirtschaftspiegel* 19.5.67, *Handesblatt* 11.11.67, *Zeitschrift, Kreditwesen* 1.4.69, and *Finanznachrichten* 16.5.69.

[55] *Handeslblatt* 11.7.66; interview senior banker 2.

[56] *Zeitschrift für das gesamte Kreditwesen* 15.11.61, *Frankfurter Allgemeine Zeitung* 12.12.67, *Die Welt* 13.9.72; Karl Otto Pöhl, President of the Bundesbank, *Handelsblatt* 7.5.85; *Handelsblatt* 16.4.85, *Frankfurter Rundschau*, 10.4.1985; interview senior banker 1.

[57] *Die Welt* 2.7.66, *Zeitschrift für das gesamte Kreditwesen* Heft 13, 1967, *Zeitschrift für das gesamte Kreditwesen*, vol. 14, no. 22, 15.11.1961, *Frankfurter Allgemeiner Zeitung*, 12.6.61, 5.7.1966, *Handelsblatt*, 11.7.1966, *Finanznachrichten*, 11.11.1966, Nr. 44, *Die Zeit*, 22.9.1967, *Süddeutsche Zeitung* 17.1.68, *Handelsblatt* 8.3.71, *Handelsblatt* 2.4.75, Frankfurt Stock Exchange organisation—*Handelsblatt* 16.4.85; Karl Otto Pöhl, President of the Bundesbank, *Handelsblatt* 7.5.85, 22.8.85; Wolfgang Röller, President of German banking association—*Handelsblatt* 31.10.85, 31.12.85.

[58] *Süddeutsche Zeitung* 6.11.63, 17.1.68, *Finanznachrichten* 11.11.66, *Handelsblatt* 11.6.66, 11.11.67, *Die Welt* 2.7.66, Regierungsdirektor in Federal Economics Ministry *Frankfurter Allgemeine Zeitung* 12.12.67, *Frankfurter Allgemeine Zeitung* 5.7.66; interviews senior banker 1, senior exchange official 2.

[59] *Die Welt* 2.7.66, *Zeitschrift für das gesamte Kreditwesen* Heft 13, 1967, *Süddeutsche Zeitung* 17.1.68, 13.1.69, and *Handelsblatt* 23.12.68.

[60] *Frankfurter Allgemeine Zeitung* 13.11.54, 12.6.61, *Zeitschrift für das gesamte Kreditwesen* 15.11.61, and *Industriekurier* 29.1.63.

[61] Interview senior exchange official 3.

[62] Suggestions by private banker A von Metzler, *National-Zeitung, Basel* 16.1.68 and by Ernst Bracker, manager of German Corporation for Securities (Deutsche Gesellschaft für Wertpapier), *National-Zeitung, Basel* 8.6.70.

[63] *VWD-Wirtschaftsspiegel* 2.1.67.

[64] *National-Zeitung, Basel* 16.1.68, *Blick durch die Wirthschaft* 16.1.68, *Süddeutsche Zeitung* 17.1.68; draft legislation has been documented in Beyer-Fehling and Bock (1975: 17–79).

to limit the influence of the banks by insisting that share trades be executed by brokers on the public exchanges. It also put forward increased publication requirements, for instance for share trades and company reports. In 1969, an expert committee established by the Federal Economics Ministry recommended concentrating trading on stock exchanges, increased transparency for trades, more frequent publication of company reports, the reintroduction of futures and options trading, improvements in the organisation of the exchanges, measures against insider trading and changes in taxes.[65] In 1969, a working committee of the Länder began work on revising the law on stock exchanges, notably to strengthen the role of the brokers and the independence of the exchanges.[66]

However, reformers faced strong and determined opponents. The Länder, who held most regulatory responsibilities and owned the exchanges, resisted increased federal powers and feared the loss of the smaller regional exchanges.[67] They and the banks were hostile to formalisation of regulation.[68] In any case, many banks saw little need for change and the central bank, the Bundesbank, gave no support to reform.[69] The exchanges were divided, notably between larger exchanges such as Frankfurt and Dusseldorf, which saw opportunities from reforms, and smaller exchanges which were fearful that they would lose out to competitors.[70] Opponents argued that legislation was not needed for change, and indeed that voluntary measures could achieve the government's aims.[71] They rejected copying the US or UK, claiming that they differed from Continental Europe and hence their institutional models were inappropriate for Germany.[72] Finally, they suggested that change in Germany should await European Community and international regulatory reform.[73]

Opponents of institutional change were successful. Thus the government's 1968 draft proposals faced a wave of criticism from the stock exchange committees, banks, and credit institutions.[74] Legislation needed to be passed by the Bundesrat, the upper house of parliament composed of representatives of the Länder. Faced with strong opposition from the latter and the banks, the government did not attempt to pass significant reform.[75] Instead it accepted the voluntary route to

[65] *Industriekurier* 20.3.69 and *Finanznachrichten* 16.5.69; see Bremer (1976).

[66] *VBW-Wirtschaftsdienst* 14.3.69.

[67] Interviews senior exchange official 2 and 3, Korwitz; *VBW-Wirtschaftsdienst*, 14.3.1969 and *Handelsblatt* 20.10.1971.

[68] *Handelsblatt* 23.1.1968, 2.2.71, 6.4.72, *Frankfurter Allgemeiner Zeitung* 21.2.1969, *Zeitschrift Kreditwesen* 1.4.1969, and *Die Welt* 19.11.70.

[69] Interviews senior banker 1 and 2, senior Bundesbank official.

[70] Interview Breuer; *Frankfurter Allgemeine Zeitung* 31.7.85 and *Handelsblatt* 15.2.80, 5.3.85, 16.4.85, 20.12.85, 23.12.85, 31.12.85.

[71] *VWD-Wirtschaftsspiegel* 2.1.67, 15.8.67, *VWD-Firmen* 16.11.67, 22.1.68, *Handelsblatt* 23.1.68, *Zeitschrift für das gesamte Kreditwesen Heft* 13, 1967, 1.4.69 and *Deutsche Zeitung* 18.3.63.

[72] *VWD-Wirtschaftsspiegel* 15.8.67, *Der Volkswirt* 31.10.69, *Wirtschaftswoche* 12.11.71, and *Frankfurter Allgemeine Zeitung* 1.8.72.

[73] *Süddeutsche Zeitung* 6.11.63 and *VWD-Wirtschaftsspiegel* 19.5.67.

[74] *VWD-Firmen* 22.1.68 and *Handelsblatt* 23.1.68. [75] Interview senior exchange official 3.

change and hence only minor institutional modifications were made.[76] Proposed alterations such as obliging share trades to pass through exchanges rather than between banks, the prohibition of insider trading, or alteration of the 1934 banking law prohibiting futures, and options trading did not obtain consensus and hence were not introduced.[77] The failure of the government to obtain agreement to reform legislation in 1968 was followed by almost two decades of inertia until after 1986 (see Chapter 5).

ITALY

The Position in the Mid-1960s

In the mid-1960s, there were several regional stock exchanges in Italy, although the Milan exchange was by far the largest. But Italian capitalism was dominated by the state, para-public organisations and banks. Trading of shares was small and stock exchanges had been in decline since 1945.

The exchanges had been created by royal decree and were publicly owned and under the control of the Chamber of Commerce (*Camera di Commercio*) of the city in which they were located. Stock exchanges were classified in legal doctrines as a public service, akin to telecommunications, electricity, or railways. Most institutions dated back to legislation passed in 1913 and 1925.[78] By law, public trading of quoted shares was the monopoly of the *Agenti di Cambio*. The *Agenti* were state officials but were not paid by from the public purse, and lived on the profits of buying and selling shares. The *Agenti* traded as individuals, with personal liability, being forbidden from forming companies or having any links with banks. Trading was by open cry, with prices written on blackboards, taking place for only a few hours a day. Banks were specifically excluded from undertaking public share trading but could trade on their own account or act as intermediaries between buyers and sellers.

Formal regulatory powers were dispersed among three main regulatory organisations: the local chambers of commerce, a local assembly, and the Ministry of the Treasury.[79] Although the *Agenti*, as public officials, were subject to complex rules (e.g. for recruitment), they enjoyed considerable self-regulation since they were represented in the city assembly and had influence over the city Chambers of Commerce. At the same time, despite the existence of local exchanges, many decisions needed the approval of the Treasury Ministry.

---

[76] A minor revision of stock exchange legislation was passed in 1975—the Börsengesetz (stock exchange law)—which strengthened the position of the brokers, while the banks altered their general business conditions so that explicit agreement was needed for share trading to take place off the exchanges (Schwarke 1994: 38ff.); Bremer (1976); interviews senior exchange official 2, senior regulator; *Börsen-Zeitung* 4.7.68, *Handelsblatt* 23.12.68, and *Frankfurter Allgemeine Zeitung* 30.4.68.

[77] *Frankfurter Allgemeine Zeitung* 21.2.69, *Süddeutsche Zeitung* 13.1.69, *Handelsblatt* 2.2.71, 28.2.73, and *Wirtschaftswoche* 12.11.71.

[78] Terzo (2000: 2198–9) and Torchia (1992: 44–59).

[79] Giurisprudenza Commerciale (1975) and Cassese (1976: 645).

Pressures for Change and the Process of Reform

Until the late 1960s, the small size and stagnation of the stock exchanges limited the perceived need to introduce reform and little attention was given to securities trading.[80] Although ideas for modifications were put forward in the late 1940s, no changes were made. However, from the mid-1960s serious discussions took place. The government, notably the Treasury Ministry, set up a commission in 1966, put forward detailed proposals in 1968 and then led the process of passing legislation.[81] In the background, the central bank, the Banca d'Italia, also pressed for change.[82]

Discussions of reform were driven by the weaknesses of Italian stock exchanges. Italy's financial markets appeared evermore unsuitable for a large industrial economy. The personal sector had high savings.[83] Companies increasingly needed funds to expand, as self-financing of investment fell (from 81% in 1968 to 28% in 1971 or 45% in 1972). Yet stock exchanges were very small relative to the total economy. Thus by 1975, the capitalisation of the Italian stock exchanges was $15 billion, the same level as Holland, lower than Switzerland ($18 billion), and far behind Germany ($58 billion) or Britain ($74 billion). Most individual savings were in the form of deposit accounts with banks and the post office.[84] Thus the stock exchanges were failing in their function of bringing together savers and investors.

Exchanges in Italy suffered from several major problems that contributed to their small size.[85] Since the *Agenti* were small, many larger trades passed through the banks rather than the stock exchanges, which were bypassed.[86] The strongest actors in the sector were the banks, but they were specifically excluded from exchanges. In contrast, the *Agenti* were weak: they lacked capital and hence could not trade on their own account (as in France, they could not offer *contre-partie*), limiting the liquidity of the market. They faced problems of liability, since they were individuals but were also collectively responsible for each other's debts. Their role was unclear, since they were both seen as 'mediators' between buyers and sellers of shares and as profit-making agents; there were several scandals concerning insider trading and conflicts of interest which arose in part from this ambiguity. Finally, trading was dispersed among several exchanges which lacked their own legal personality and were subject to an array of diverse controls by the Banca d'Italia and local and central authorities.

Reform was far from easy. The Banca d'Italia held major powers over the banks, which it wished to protect; hence two systems of regulation grew up, with

---

[80] Torchia (1992: 59–65), Sotgia (1966: 736–7), and Cassese (1976: 112–13).

[81] Sotgia (1966) and Campi (1968).

[82] Giurisprudenza Commerciale (1975) and Cesarini (1998: 634).

[83] e.g. an average of 15% of GDP in the period 1961–72; figures from Giurisprudenza Commerciale (1975: 632–3), Cesarini (1998) and 660 (Tagi), and Cassese (1976: 116–19).

[84] 60.6% for the period 1964–72.   [85] Sotgia (1966) and Giurisprudenza Commerciale (1975).

[86] Giurisprudenza Commerciale (1975: 649), Cassese (1976: 654) (Gaetano) and 663 (Tagi).

difficulties of overlaps and duplication.[87] Moreover, the *Agenti* were hostile to greater public control or an 'US-style' SEC.[88] Legislation had to receive approval from two houses of parliament in a complex multiparty system. Parliament was worried about excessive 'discretion' being given to a sectoral regulatory body.[89]

Allocation of Regulatory Powers: Creating a Sectoral Authority, Consob

The most significant reform in the period 1965–85 came with the law of 1974, which created a sectoral regulator, La Commissione per le società e la borsa (Consob), headed by a president and four members with a term of five years.[90] Consob arose from a search for new institutions due to the domestic economic crisis of the early 1970s and scandals.[91] The SEC was cited in debates, as was the creation of the COB in France in 1967.[92] Consob obtained two broad types of powers.[93] The first concerned the operation of exchanges, notably over the listing of shares, quotations, and trading. Exchanges were now placed under the supervision of Consob. The second were powers over transparency concerning companies whose shares were quoted on exchanges.

At first glance, the creation of Consob appears a radical institutional reform, being an independent regulatory authority in a country where such bodies were virtually unknown in the 1970s. Yet the changes of 1974 were in fact limited. Consob enjoyed only limited autonomy.[94] It was under the authority of the Treasury, whose directives it had to follow, and indeed, was treated as a unit within the Treasury.[95] It lacked its own legal personality and hence many of its decisions required ministerial decrees issued by the Treasury and it had limited autonomy over its own finances and internal organisation.[96] The Treasury retained important powers, notably over the establishment of exchanges, selection, and nomination of the *Agenti* and overseas shares. It also maintained ultimate responsibility under the 1974 law for overall policy towards stock markets.[97] Finally, the Banca d'Italia and the Treasury had broad powers over much of the financial sector, especially over the banking and investment sectors, that affected securities trading and hence could bypass Consob.[98]

The early and mid-1980s saw some enhancement of the Consob's legal role and independence. International factors played a significant role in the charges. One factor was the example of the COB in France, which was also strengthened in the 1980s and helped reformers to justify giving further powers to Consob.[99] Another

---

[87] Marchetti (1987).　　　[88] Giurisprudenza Commerciale (1975) and Minervini: 683.

[89] Landi (1975: 2).

[90] Law 216/1974; also degree laws 95/1974 and 138/1975; for a detailed analysis, see Landi (1975); the members were put forward by the Prime Minister (Presidente del Consiglio) and nominated by decree by the President of the Republic; their terms were renewable once.

[91] Belcredi (1994: 85).　　　[92] Mignoli (1991) and Belcredi (1994: 29, 85–6).

[93] Cassese (1976: 113–16).

[94] Torchia (1992: 67–88), Giurisprudenza Commerciale (1975), Minervini 683, Cassese (1976: 648–9).

[95] Landi (1975).　　　[96] Torchia (1992: 82).　　　[97] Torchia (1992: 72, 84–5).

[98] cf. Marchetti (1987).　　　[99] Mignoli (1991).

was European Community regulation of financial services, which did not require that powers be given to a sectoral regulator, but did provide a justification and occasion for strengthening Consob. Thus for instance, in 1983, Consob's powers were broadened to cover mutual investment funds and financial products sold through public offerings as part of implementing the first European Community directives on investment services and banking(1977) and listing of shares (1979).[100] Importantly, in 1985, Consob was given its own legal personality and its powers were extended to non-quoted firms.[101] This allowed it to issue its own decisions and provided, at least legally, for greater freedom over its own internal organisation and finances. Nevertheless, in 1985, Consob's main activities still concerned provision of information by quoted companies and savings rather than the operation of the stock exchanges.[102] It also remained highly subject to the powerful Banca d'Italia.

The Organisation of the Market and the Position of the Agenti di cambio

Despite the many problems of Italian stock exchanges, reforms between 1974 and 1985 did not greatly alter the structure of the stock exchanges or the rights of the Agenti.[103] Privatisation of the exchanges was ruled out and even more limited ideas of giving them legal personality were not introduced despite being discussed from the mid-1960s onwards.[104] Proposals to allow the Agenti to trade as companies or establishing schemes to deal with liability when an individual Agente went bankrupt were not implemented.[105] The banks continued to be excluded from the exchanges, while at the same time, unofficial markets were not regulated. Thus the major problems of Italian stock exchanges concerning the weakness of the Agenti, inadequate mechanisms to ensure transparency and fair practices, integration of the banks, or the lack of autonomy of the exchanges from local controls were not tackled. The result was that by 1985, the stock exchanges were still small and underdeveloped and lacked a good reputation for trading securities.

CONCLUSION

In the mid-1960s, the institutional framework for securities trading in France, West Germany, and Italy was largely inherited from past centuries or decades and differed considerably from that in the US and Britain. Stock exchanges were publicly owned and their traders were state-appointed officials who had legal monopolies over trading on the exchanges but did business as individuals. Trading

[100] Law 77/1983; EC Council 1977 and 1979; Cassese (1986), Jaeger (1985: 952), and Piga (1986: 285, 288).

[101] Law 285/1985, Torchia (1992: 81–2), and Marchetti (1987: 15).

[102] Nardozzi and Vaciago (1994: 19–20), Belcredi (1994: 88–91), and Cassese (1986).

[103] Giurisprudenza Commerciale (1975) and Cassese 647.   [104] cf. Stogia (1966: 739, 744).

[105] For discussion in 1975 see Giurisprudenza Commerciale (1975), Cassese (1976: 646–7), Campi (1968: 672–7).

took place on physical exchanges open for a few hours per day. Finally, many formal regulatory powers were held by governments (national or international).

At the same time, significant differences existed across France, West Germany, and Italy. France had one powerful exchange, the Paris Bourse, and the national government held most regulatory powers, while banks were excluded from securities trading. In contrast, there was much greater decentralisation in West Germany, as trading was spread among several powerful regional stock exchanges and most regulatory powers lay at the regional level. Moreover, West Germany had a bank-dominated system, as the banks had powers over exchanges, control of most securities trading, and provision of the majority of finance. Finally, in Italy, exchanges were based at the level of cities, while regulatory powers were dispersed and banks were important for off-exchange trading. These features are summarised below in Table 3.1.

The institutional features of securities trading in France, West Germany, and Italy appeared ill-suited for a modern economy and serious reform debates took place in all three countries. Policy makers worried that their stock exchanges were very small, which limited the ability of firms to raise funds through issuing equity and also created problems in matching individual savings with the capital requirements of firms. Traders were individuals and lacked capital, restricting their capacity to execute large share trades or trade on their own account to provide liquidity to the market. In West Germany and Italy this meant that most significant

Table 3.1. Major institutional features of securities trading in 1965

Institutional feature	France	West Germany	Italy
Organisational position of stock exchanges	Publicly-owned exchanges, dominated by Paris Bourse.	Several exchanges owned by regional chambers of commerce (Länder)	Publicly owned under control of city chambers of commerce.
Competition	Legal monopoly for *Agents de change*— publicly-appointed individuals with personal liability	Legal monopoly over trading on exchanges and price setting for official brokers (*Kursmakler*), appointed by regional exchange supervision authorities and trading as individuals with personal liability; coexistence of unofficial traders and domination of trading by banks	Legal monopoly for *Agenti di Cambio,* publicly-appointed individuals with personal liability; but banks could trade on own account and as intermediaries and accounted for larger trades
Allocation of regulatory powers	Most powers in hands of Ministry of Finance and Banque de France	Regional governments (Länder) responsible for legal supervision of their exchanges; shared powers with federal government	Dispersion between local chambers of commerce, local assembly, Treasury, and Banca d'Italia

trades were undertaken by the banks off the exchanges. Lack of trading and small markets resulted in stagnation for stock exchanges and traders, who were often in decline by the 1960s. Policy makers drew unfavourable comparisons between their small exchanges and those in the US and Britain. Indeed, the stock exchanges in the three countries were largely incapable of attracting international business, either by investors or overseas firms, as their rules were arcane, their business hours limited and the protection offered to investors very limited.

Yet despite discussions of reform, concerns about pressures from changing technological and economic conditions and overseas examples in the US and Britain, very few major organisational modifications were introduced in France, West Germany, and Italy between 1965 and 1985. Central institutional features such as individual traders, limited opening hours, or legal monopolies for traders remained. Insofar as institutional alterations were made, they differed across the three countries, with France and Italy creating weak independent sectoral regulators and Germany not doing so. Paradoxically, the most significant reform debates and changes took place in the late 1960s and early 1970s, whereas transnational technological and economic developments strengthened from the 1960s onwards and the US introduced major institutional reforms in the 1970s. Thus by 1985, the only major change in Table 3.2 involved the final line on the allocation of regulatory powers.

Why was institutional reform so limited? One reason is that powerfully entrenched domestic interests who drew benefits from the existing institutional framework were able to block reforms. In France and Italy, they included the *Agents/Agenti*, and in Germany, the banks and regional governments. A second factor is that non-institutional responses to problems were sometimes used. Thus for instance, in France, fiscal measures to boost investment in equities were preferred to altering the structure of the Bourse. A final factor is that the example of the US was examined but often found to be only partially applicable or attractive and not copied. Hence for example, France looked at the SEC to inspire the creation of a sectoral regulator (the COB) but failed to copy it, while opponents of change in West Germany argued that the large and powerful American stock markets were not necessary or even efficient compared to the domestic bank-dominated financial system.

Table 3.2. Allocation of regulatory powers in 1985

	France	West Germany	Italy
Allocation of regulatory powers	Government, Banque de France, and independent sectoral regulatory authority, COB, with own legal personality and sanctioning powers	Regions (Länder) responsible for legal supervision of their exchanges; shared powers with federal government	Dispersion between local chambers of commerce, local assembly, Treasury, Bank of Italy, and weak independent sectoral regulatory authority, Consob

Overall, the case of stock markets in France, West Germany and Italy between 1965 and 1985 shows how powerful transnational technological and economic developments and reforms in the world's largest securities market, the US, can be met with institutional inertia or divergent reforms in medium-sized industrialised countries. Even institutions regarded as inadequate to meet these developments and criticised as inferior to those overseas nations were maintained, as governments failed to form strong reform coalitions and overcome resistance by actors with vested interests in existing arrangements. The two forms of internationalisation—transnational technological and economic developments and reforms in the US—were insufficient to overcome blockages in the domestic policy process. In 1985, France, West Germany, and Italy still had an institutional framework designed for domestic individual investors and traders, not for an internationalised market composed of large financial corporations.

4

From Conservatism to Revolution: British Stock Exchanges 1965–2005

In the mid-1960s, the London Stock Exchange (LSE) offered a classic example of British institutional and political conservatism. It was run as a long-standing gentleman's club composed of individual members. It was largely self-governing, relying on informal social norms and rules that had developed over the previous three centuries and protected its members. It lay at the heart of the British financial and political 'establishment'. Many of its features were anchored in the past, symbolised by LSE brokers wearing a recognisable uniform—dark suits and bowler hats.

Internationalisation placed considerable pressures on these institutions (see Chapter 2). Transnational technological and economic developments from the 1960s onwards such as the use of electronics in trading, the rise of large institutional investors, and the growth of cross-border business all ran counter to LSE's position as a small British club. Reforms in the US from the 1970s and 1980s increased overseas competition to LSE and offered an example of reform.

Most second image reversed (SIR) studies suggest that national institutions remain resistant to change despite economic internationalisation. Between 1965 and the early 1980s, British economic institutions for stock exchanges strongly supported this hypothesis. Despite facing pressures for change, LSE mounted a stout and successful defence of traditional institutions. Reformers who sought to modernise LSE were brushed aside, with only minor alterations being made. Bowler-hatted brokers working in their club according to British traditions seemed impervious to internationalisation.

Yet from the mid-1980s onwards this situation altered dramatically. Key domestic actors, notably the government and Bank of England, reversed their previous support for inherited arrangements. Although this was initially for domestic reasons, international factors soon became crucial to their strategies. Public policy makers led a reforming coalition that introduced a regulatory revolution—in terms of the speed and scale of changes—best known as the 1986 'Big Bang'. That revolution was then continued in the 1990s. Rules protecting LSE and its members from competition were abolished. LSE itself was transformed from a gentleman's club into a profit-making limited company, and large financial institutions, many from abroad, took the place of partnerships of individual traders. Informal governance was replaced with statutory regulators and formal regulation. By 2005, economic institutions governing securities trading were unrecognisable compared with those existing only a few years earlier. Previously hallowed institutional features had disappeared, including the bowler-hatted gentleman traders.

The move from conservatism to revolution in the UK offers a fascinating case for examining the effects of internationalisation on national economic institutions for four reasons. First, it allows analysis of why long-standing sectoral institutions are maintained despite technological and economic internationalisation. The chapter argues that alternative strategies to institutional reform can meet transnational technological and economic pressures. Moreover, when public policy makers are unable or unwilling to lead change, protected suppliers are able to defend their protected position, even if it is in decline and institutions appear increasingly unsuitable for the altered conditions of the sector. Thus it confirms the findings of Chapter 3 about transnational technological and economic developments being met with institutional inertia.

Second, the British case shows how and why such institutions can be altered quickly and comprehensively. Hence it allows consideration of the conditions under which institutions persist despite internationalisation, and then those under which they are reformed. In particular, it shows the importance of public policy makers driving change, creating domestic reform coalitions, and overcoming resistance.

Third, the chapter traces a British reform route. Change had begun for domestic reasons, but thereafter international factors, especially the US, were important in the strategies of British policy makers: they feared regulatory competition from the US, and they used the US example to legitimate new institutional arrangements. But they engaged in only superficial learning and did not copy wholesale US institutions. Instead, the US example provided a useful source of fear and inspiration that was used selectively in the domestic policy process to justify change.

Fourth, reforms in Britain were important for those in continental European nations—both as a source of competition and as an example. Hence once introduced, they formed an endogenous part of the process of internationalisation (these effects are explored in Chapter 5 on France, Germany, and Italy 1986–2005).

This chapter begins by briefly summarising the key institutional features of securities markets in the mid-1960s. It then looks at three phases: conservatism from the mid-1960s until 1980, when the traditional City coalition defended existing arrangements, the Big Bang revolution from 1980 to 1986, and the extension of that revolution until 2005. The chapter considers when, how, and why internationalisation was significant in reform.

ECONOMIC INSTITUTIONS FOR SECURITIES TRADING IN THE MID-1960s

In the mid-1960s, almost all trading of company securities (mostly referred to as shares or 'equities') took place on the LSE.[1] LSE was a large well-established

---

[1] For our purposes, we will focus only on LSE, the dominant exchange, although there were 22 regional exchanges, these steadily merged with LSE, which became the sole exchange for Britain and Ireland in 1973.

exchange whose origins went back to a law of 1697 that required brokers and jobbers to be licensed.[2] During the nineteenth century, it had been the pre-eminent exchange in the world and although by the mid-1960s, it had lost its dominant position (especially due to the rise of the NYSE) it remained of significant size internationally and its turnover was higher than stock exchanges in other European countries, both in absolute terms and relative to GDP.[3] In part, this reflected the nature of British capitalism, particularly the development of limited companies reliant on equity capital. In part, it was also because LSE was more internationalised than its continental European counterparts, in that foreign investors and shares accounted for a significant share of trading.

Unlike other exchanges in Europe, formal rules split trading between 'retail' and 'wholesale' functions—a division of roles known as 'single capacity'. Brokers undertook retail functions by dealing with investors, who gave them buy or sell orders. Brokers were not allowed to deal with each other but only with 'jobbers', who would quote buy and sell prices. Jobbers were responsible for wholesale functions. They bought and sold shares themselves, thereby providing liquidity to the market. Since 1911, commissions charged by brokers were fixed by the LSE. Trading was done on the floor of LSE, where brokers and jobbers met and agreed buy and sell orders, which were then written into their notebooks and had to be honoured (giving rise to the expression 'my word is my bond').[4]

LSE operated in a manner similar to a British gentleman's club. Brokers and jobbers were members of LSE, but had to be 'nominated' and take the place (for a fee) of a previous member. Foreigners and women were not allowed to be members and frequently brokers and jobbers were chosen due to family connections and social standing. Securities trading was an individualised business: brokers had personal links to clients and fund managers; long City lunches were renowned. Brokers and jobbers were organised into partnerships or unlimited liability companies so that ordinary partners had unlimited personal liability.[5] Public advertising was not permitted—brokers could only send information if requested and jobbers did not have contact with investors.

LSE formed part of 'the City of London', with the Bank of England, banks, trading houses, and insurance brokers.[6] The City operated through 'self-regulation' or 'club government'—a group of men linked by professional and social networks who knew each other and worked through a mixture of self-created and self-enforced formal rules and informal social norms.[7] Thus regulation of trading was undertaken by the Stock Exchange Council, elected by LSE members. But the most powerful actor was in the background—the Bank of England. It and

[2] For comprehensive histories, see Michie (1999) and Kynaston (2001); see also Clarke (1979), Morgan and Thomas (1962), McRae and Cairncross (1984), and Chapman (2002).

[3] For international comparisons, see Chapter 2, but one example is that in 1970, LSE's turnover represented 1.73% of UK GDP whereas the figure for France was 0.5%; another example is that in 1973, the total market capitalisation of UK and Irish company equities exceeded the total of all the other EEC stock markets—LSE (1978: s89); for LSE's own analysis of its decline, see LSE (1978: s79–s81).

[4] McRae and Cairncross (1984: 137–8) and Clarke (1979: 75–6).   [5] Revell (1973: 63).

[6] cf. Clarke (1979).   [7] Moran (2003).

the Stock Exchange Council operated through informal 'persuasion' and social norms more than formal enforcement. In contrast, the legal framework governing share trading was extremely limited—for instance, no legal monopoly over the trading of shares existed.

The City of London enjoyed great economic and political power in Britain. It accounted for a high proportion of Britain's wealth and invisible exports. Many Members of Parliament came from City backgrounds (including LSE stock-broking) and the City had a close formal and informal relationship with the Treasury. Moreover, the Bank of England protected the City and acted as a bridge between it and the government. Thus in the mid-1960s, LSE formed a central element in the City of London and more generally the British ruling establishment.

CONSERVATISM: RESISTANCE TO CHANGE 1965–80

Transnational technological and economic developments put considerable pressures on traditional British institutions in the 1960s and 1970s, in addition to domestic forces for change. Three features came under particular attack: LSE's internal rules for fixed commissions on trades and single capacity; LSE's status as a club of British individuals; and self-regulation.

LSE's fixed commissions for buying and selling shares avoided 'ungentlemanly' bargaining over fees, while the single capacity system separating wholesale and retail trading was argued to ensure that all investors, including small ones, obtained the best possible prices.[8] But fixed commissions prevented institutional investors from negotiating lower rates for large trades, which in practice meant that they cross-subsidised smaller trades, especially by individuals.[9] The 'single capacity system' of brokers and jobbers led to two sets of charges.[10] Both rules appeared inappropriate for changing market conditions.[11] In particular, large institutional investors such as pension and life insurance funds accounted for a rising share of LSE trading.[12] They manifested increasing unhappiness about fixed commissions and strongly opposed rises in LSE nominal commission rates in the 1970s, which were needed to meet inflation.[13] Institutional investors also

---

[8] LSE (1978: s14–s27).   [9] *The Times* (3.8.67, 13.12.71).

[10] Brokers charged vendors and buyers a commission fixed by LSE; the jobber's revenue came from his 'turn'—i.e. the difference between buying and selling prices. The latter could be large—one estimate for a large trade of £50,000 was 5%–11%—*The Times* 3.8.67.

[11] See Michie (1999: 491–513) and Clarke (1979: 76–82); moreover, large investors found ways round fixed fees and single capacity, such as demanding 'soft commissions' (e.g. 'free research' or computer equipment) in return for large orders or their brokers 'crossing' trades (i.e. offsetting buy and sell orders) which were then 'put through' a jobber at a much reduced jobber's turn.

[12] Thus the proportion of UK quoted ordinary shares held by savings institutions rose from 26% in 1963 to 52% by 1977, and they accounted for 60% of LSE turnover by the late 1970s—LSE (1978: s99) and *The Times* 25.8.78.

[13] *The Times* 8.1.69, 13.12.71, 8.12.75.

sought to bypass LSE altogether. They used the 'third market', whereby merchant banks dealt directly with each other and with large institutional investors.[14] Most threateningly of all, in 1973 a group of merchant banks, unhappy with LSE's commissions, created Automated Real Time Investment Exchange Limited (ARIEL), an electronic system to rival LSE and directly inspired by the successful US Instinet system.[15] ARIEL allowed investors to make offers anonymously for shares in companies listed on LSE using terminals, matched potential buyers and sellers and then enabled the two parties to negotiate a price. Its computerised system provided opportunities for alternative markets and hence allowed large investors to avoid LSE brokerage commissions and to negotiate their own terms.[16] It was particularly suited to large investors and its commissions were lower than LSE's.[17]

Fixed commissions and single capacity were argued to impede LSE's hopes of capturing a greater share of overseas securities markets. Overseas brokers working in London (especially American ones) were not allowed to be LSE members and could simply avoid LSE for trading while LSE members were not allowed to engage in 'dual capacity' (combining retail and wholesale trading of securities), even overseas.[18] Worse still, active trading of UK shares took place on overseas exchanges, especially in the US, which thus represented a growing risk to LSE's monopoly even over domestic shares; its importance grew as overseas ownership of UK shares, especially in the US, rose.[19] LSE acknowledged that it had increasingly lost its position as an international centre for securities trading.[20]

International and domestic factors also made LSE's existence as a club for British individual members less comfortable from the late 1960s onwards. Introducing new technology into LSE required large capital expenditure,[21] while brokers and jobbers faced higher costs for their own operations (e.g. for offices and computer equipment). These demands increased financial pressures on LSE's members, especially smaller brokers and jobbers who lacked capital.[22] At the same time, there were difficult market conditions in the late 1960s and then after the 1973 oil crisis.[23] Competition from ARIEL saw commissions reduced or held down despite rising costs; thus for instance, in 1975, commissions were increased by 4% despite an estimated 46% rise in unit costs for stockbrokers over the previous two years.[24]

These problems were serious because brokers and jobbers, as partnerships of individuals with unlimited liability, found it difficult to raise capital.[25] LSE rules

---

[14] *The Times* 3.8.67.
[15] Blanden (1974), Kynaston (2001: 468–9), and *The Times* 16.8.72, 30.1.73, 12.2.74; indeed, Instinet's founder sat on ARIEL's board, while ARIEL's managing director sat on Instinet's board— *The Times* 30.1.73.
[16] cf. *The Times* 3.8.67, 8.1.69, 17.11.78.   [17] *The Times* 18.4.73, 4.11.74 and Blanden (1974).
[18] *The Times* 3.10.77, 13.12.71, 15.1.79 and Michie (1999: 465–8).   [19] Michie (1999: 474).
[20] LSE (1978: s79–s88).
[21] For instance, the estimated cost of the TALISMAN settlement system in 1974–5 was £15.7 million (Michie 1999: 511).
[22] *The Times* 20.2.67, 2.10.68, 27.10.75, 17.11.78 and the *Financial Times* 27.1.79, 10.2.79, 12.2.79, 26.4.79.
[23] Michie (1999: 429–32, 513–18).   [24] *The Times* 18.12.75.
[25] Interview, senior LSE official.

that all partners had to be LSE members and could have no occupation apart from broking or jobbing made matters more difficult. Worse still, there were major cost overruns on computerisation of LSE's clearance and settlement system (called TALISMAN), leading to strong complaints, especially by smaller partnerships.[26] Jobbing and broking became less financially attractive occupations, and the number of jobbers fell sharply, as did overall LSE membership in the late 1960s.[27] Yet the LSE's ban on overseas members impeded LSE brokers from establishing overseas operations, since it prevented LSE from offering reciprocity; at the same time, within Britain, American brokerage houses were expanding their operations, but were excluded from LSE.[28]

Finally, in addition to international pressures, self-regulation and fixed commissions also faced increasing domestic political and legal threats by the end of the 1970s. In 1976, the government set up a committee, headed by the former Prime Minister Harold Wilson, to look at the City after criticisms of the financial sector by the Labour Party.[29] More seriously, services were included under general competition law in 1976, but no exemption was given to LSE. In 1977, the Office of Fair Trading (OFT) decided to open an investigation into fixed commissions and single capacity.[30] LSE sought intervention by the government to halt the OFT's case, with support from the Bank of England. But the government did not intervene and in 1979 the OFT referred LSE's rule book to the Restrictive Practices Court arguing that it was potentially in breach of competition law.[31]

In the face of these pressures, LSE's leadership and the Bank of England paid close attention to threats to London's position, such as foreign investors bypassing LSE by going through foreign brokers who operated in London and LSE members being restricted from overseas expansion by LSE rules.[32] They wished to ensure that the LSE became the main securities market in Europe and internationally through lower costs, increased flexibility, and abolition of restrictions such as controls on capital flows.[33] But this was to be achieved through investing to make LSE more efficient and attractive for investors and traders rather than major institutional alterations.

Thus one prong of LSE's strategy was to introduce new technology, especially computers, which offered lower costs and quicker, more reliable information, clearing, and settlement. From 1974, LSE began to implement the TALISMAN system for clearing and settlement, which was to produce savings of £8.3 million

---

[26]   *The Times* 27.10.75 and the *Financial Times* 27.1.79, 10.2.79.

[27]   The number of jobbers had fallen from more than 400 in the 1920s to 100 in 1960 to 14 firms by the mid-1970s—*The Times* 3.8.67, 1.3.78; the overall number of LSE members declined by 275 between 1963 and 1967—Michie (1999: 439–41, 456).

[28]   Michie (1999: 468–71).

[29]   Earlier, the Department of Trade had opened an inquiry into the supervision of capital markets, following criticisms that the stock exchange lacked the determination to deal with scandals; in response, the Law Society argued for a statutory regulator—*The Times* 15.1.75.

[30]   Kynaston (2001: 573–4).   [31]   *The Times* 30.9.77 and the *Financial Times* 10.2.79, 12.2.79.

[32]   *The Times* 3.10.77, 1.3.78, 15.1.79.   [33]   cf. *The Times* 13.12.71, 27.3.72, 21.6.76, 3.8.78.

per annum for its members. The system also aided LSE to compete with rivals such as ARIEL who had electronic systems. Another prong was to alter its prices and attack ARIEL. In particular, LSE sharply reduced its commissions for large trades in 1972 and then in the mid-1970s, implemented only small nominal increases, especially for large trades.[34]

Confronted with difficulties in attracting members with sufficient capital, LSE introduced minor alterations to its organisational position. Thus in 1967 it removed limits on the number of members a partnership could have and in 1969 it ended the system of nominations whereby a new member had to take the place of a departing member. Also in 1969 it permitted broking and jobbing partnerships to become limited liability companies, but subject to stringent rules that left LSE members with both control and liability.[35] After a battle lasting several years, LSE members finally voted to accept foreigners and women as LSE members in 1971 and 1972.[36]

Finally, LSE continued to defend self-regulation which it claimed was flexible and effective because it was undertaken by expert practitioners.[37] It and the Bank of England rejected overseas examples. In particular, US institutional arrangements such as a statutory sectoral regulator, the SEC, were criticised for creating a high and costly level of legal formalism.[38] As the chairman of the City Capital Markets Committee, which examined policy issues under the auspices of the Bank of England, put it, there was 'no case at all for slavish imitations of systems imported from elsewhere'. Overall the British securities system was seen as superior to overseas alternatives.[39]

Non-institutional strategies to defend LSE appeared successful. The LSE's rival, ARIEL, was in sharp decline at the end of the 1970s while the fortunes of LSE's traders were aided by a stock market revival.[40] An investigation by the Department of Trade's into securities trading concluded that self-regulation could be improved but should continue.[41] The Wilson Committee did not recommend a statutory regulator for securities. Indeed, the Department of Trade told the Committee that the existing system gave no cause for 'much sustainable criticism', whereas a US-style SEC would be a 'fundamental departure in our constitutional terms' because it would enjoy too much freedom from parliamentary

---

[34] *The Times* 16.8.72, 18.12.75.

[35] LSE members had to hold at least 51% of the voting rights and had to assume personal liability for company debts, while outside investors were limited to a maximum 10% of share capital—*The Times* 2.5.69 and Michie (1999: 435–8).

[36] Michie (1999: 469) and *The Times* 23.3.71, 22.5.71, 3.5.72.

[37] LSE (1978: s69–s78) and *The Times* 3.4.75, 30.3.75; indeed, faced with criticism of institutional arrangements, LSE, in cooperation with the Department of Trade and Bank of England, created a new self-regulatory body in 1978, the Council for the Securities Industry.

[38] LSE (1978: s69–s73), *The Times* 13.12.71, 22.10.76, 27.6.7, 30.9.77, 1.1.77, and the *Financial Times* 30.3.79, 30.5.79; interview, senior LSE official.

[39] *The Times* 18.12.74.

[40] *The Times* 18.12.75, 21.4.79, 29.5.79, 31.5.79 and Kynaston (2001: 498–9).

[41] *The Times* 22.10.76.

control and that the government was opposed to such a body.[42] The only cloud on the horizon appeared to be the OFT's decision to refer its case against fixed commissions to the Restrictive Practices Court, but a Conservative government, which could be expected to be more favourable to the City than the Labour one of 1974–9, was elected in May 1979. Overall, LSE's traditional alliance with the Bank of England and the government appeared to block any major institutional reforms, non-institutional responses were used to counter technological and economic pressures and the US was rejected as an example of alternative sectoral arrangements.

REVOLUTION 1980–86

The Process of Change—Key Actors and Their Strategies

Yet, after the inertia of the 1960s and 1970s, the institutions of securities trading were revolutionised in the mid-1980s.[43] The break with the past was symbolised by the term 'the Big Bang' for the changes of 27 October 1986, when fixed commissions and single capacity were replaced with 'market makers' free to set their commissions and trade with each other, and electronic trading was established that soon replaced the physical trading floor. Other major modifications were the reorganisation of LSE away from a closed British club of individuals to an international organisation, and moves from self-regulation to statutory regulation through the creation of a statutory regulator, the Securities and Investment Board (SIB) under the 1986 Financial Services Act. Thus the rules governing securities trading, LSE's own organisation, and the allocation of regulatory powers were all comprehensively reformed.

Institutional change was triggered by two British 'outsiders' from the traditional City of London policy community. One was the head of the Office of Fair Trading, Sir Gordon Borrie. The OFT's legal case against the 'restrictive practice' of fixed broking commissions (begun in 1979) led directly to the 1986 Big Bang. The second was Jim Gower, a retired commercial law professor whose major report for the government on investor protection in 1984 inspired the 1986 Financial Services Act.[44] Nevertheless, behind the two outsiders lay traditional British 'insiders', namely the Bank of England, the government, and eventually the leadership of LSE.[45] After 1981, the Bank crafted a new strategy designed to prepare the City of London for changing markets and international competition.[46] The government,

---

[42] Quotes from Mr PAR Brown, the *Financial Times* 30.3.79.

[43] For a good narrative, see Reid (1988) and Michie (1999: ch.12); for the views of key participants, see Institute of Contemporary British History (1999) ('Witness seminar') and Gower (1988); for a corporatist analysis, see Moran (1991: ch. 3); for an analysis of the framework, see Black (1997: ch. 2).

[44] Gower (1984); he also issued an interim report in 1982.

[45] cf. The *Financial Times* 12.10.83, 30.4.84, 21.8.86; see also Reid (1988: ch. 2) and Plender (1987).

[46] Interview, senior financial regulator 3.

notably the Department of Trade and Industry (DTI), commissioned the Gower report, negotiated the settlement of the OFT's case with the LSE, and passed the 1986 Financial Services Act. After initial opposition, LSE's senior management led by its Chairman Sir Nicholas Goodison accepted structural reforms, and became centrally involved in their detailed implementation.[47]

Although domestic factors triggered the process of change, international ones were crucial for British policy makers deciding to press for radical reform and in justifying a comprehensive overhaul of institutions.[48] Reformers argued that UK regulation had to adapt to two sets of transnational forces. The first was economic internationalisation, notably the growth in international trading (i.e. trading of firms' shares outside their home nation's stock market), the emergence of cross-border firms, and the creation of new electronic markets.[49] On the one hand, these changes offered opportunities for the City of London to capture a share of growing markets. In particular, overseas financial firms were crucial market actors whose business had to be attracted to London but created difficulties for the previous informal club regulation.[50] Their importance increased after the 1986 Big Bang, as they entered the LSE, especially as purchasers of UK brokers/jobbers. On the other hand, they increased its vulnerability, as large investors and dealers accounted for an increasingly large proportion of LSE's business, had the capacity to trade securities outside LSE and attacked LSE costs.[51] British policy makers became concerned about LSE's share of both the home market and the expanding market in international securities. The *Financial Times* claimed that 'the Bank [of England] some time ago lost patience with the clubby, inward-looking Stock Exchange which was opting out of international markets'.[52] The Bank's view was soon adopted by the government. Eventually, faced with the danger of losing its dominant position in share trading, LSE's senior management underlined the need for sweeping reforms in order to prevent 'fragmentation' of securities markets.[53]

The second international factor was the decisions and strategies of US policy makers and firms, which became an important element in British reform debates.[54] The Bank of England and LSE's senior managers were worried about competition from the NYSE—both for international equities trading and for

---

[47] The *Financial Times* 9.12.83, Reid (1988: ch. 2), cf. senior LSE official (1988); indeed, Goodison had already thought of ending dual capacity in the late 1970s, but had lacked support—Kynaston (2001: 528); interview, senior LSE official.

[48] Interview, senior LSE official.

[49] For general overviews, see Reid (1988: ch. 2), Moran (1991: ch. 3), Plender (1987), and Gower (1988: 2); the *Financial Times* 28.1.81, 15.8.83, 15.11.83; interview, Alex Fletcher, the *Financial Times* 13.12.83; Institute of Contemporary British History (1999: 103–4); for electronics the *Financial Times* 7.10.85; 15.9.83, 7.10.85, and more generally the *Financial Times* 21.2.86, 24.3.86.

[50] Black (1997: 52) and Kynaston (2001: 611–13).

[51] Reid (1988, ch. 2); The *Financial Times* 30.1.80, 17.3.82, 6.10.83, 15.8.83, 30.4.84, 1.5.84.

[52] The *Financial Times* 30.4.84 and cf. Moran (1991: 76).

[53] The *Financial Times* 15.8.83, 17.10.85, cf. Goodison (1988); comments by Sir Nicholas Goodison, the *Financial Times* 18.10.85, 17.1.86, 3.12.86.

[54] cf. Moran (1991: 57–8, 74) and Reid (1988: ch. 2).

domestic UK securities.[55] They sought changes that would enable LSE to compete with the NYSE. Reformers quoted overseas examples to support their case. This was clearest in the DGFT's case against LSE 'restrictive practices', which drew inspiration from NYSE's abandonment of fixed commissions in 1975. Learning from the US's SEC was more ambiguous. In public, reformers rejected the US model as being 'excessively legalised and bureaucratic'.[56] But as policy makers sought to reinforce London's position internationally, previous attitudes of superiority of the British system of self-regulation compared with the SEC weakened. Nevertheless, policy makers did not engage in deep learning from the US. Thus members of the OFT, the Bank of England, and LSE made a few visits to the US, usually after they had already decided to undertake reforms;[57] as one senior policy maker put it, 'we looked at the US but not comprehensively', and undertook little research since 'I knew enough about the US'.[58] Overall, the US provided a source of fear of losing business and of inspiration for institutional features, but it was not a model that was copied.

To prepare the City of London for international competition, the Bank of England, government, and LSE leadership pursued a strategy that had four related elements.[59] First, they wished to attract trading of overseas securities to LSE by lowering costs (e.g. of commissions) and ensuring an efficient centralised exchange. Second, they welcomed the entry of overseas companies into the City, including LSE. Third, they actively encouraged the development of well-capitalised securities firms that were owned or at least based in London and could compete with overseas rivals.[60] Finally, they pursued a modernised efficient regulatory system, as judged against overseas rivals, particularly the US.[61] The new strategy involved radical alterations of traditional institutions based on entry barriers, partnerships of individuals, and self-regulation through informal norms policed by LSE.

Reform met strong opposition from within LSE and in parliament. A significant number of LSE members, especially those in smaller firms, feared that

---

[55] See for instance, the *Financial Times* 7.10.85; Goodison—'a grave risk' that securities might be 'regulated away' from Britain altogether—the *Financial Times* 18.10.85; 21.8.86; Sir Kenneth Berrill, then chairman of a large stockbroker Vickers da Costa, the *Financial Times* 12.11.83, arguing that LSE needed to respond to US reforms to compete; cf. the *Financial Times* 21.10.83; interview, senior LSE official.

[56] For instance, Alex Fletcher (then Minister for Corporate and Consumer Affairs) stated that 'I am not an SEC man'—the *Financial Times* 13.12.83; Gower report—nothing 'as elaborate' as the SEC, the *Financial Times* 19.1.84; comments by Michael Howard, then Minister for Corporate and Consumer Affairs—the *Financial Times* 28.11.85.

[57] Interviews, senior financial regulators 2 and 3.   [58] Interview, senior financial regulator 3.

[59] Plender (1987), Moran (1991), and Institute of Contemporary British History (1999).

[60] The *Financial Times* 15.12.83, Normal Tebbit (Secretary of State, DTI), parliamentary debate the *Financial Times* 23.11.83, 21.12.83, 21.12.83, interview, Alex Fletcher (minister with special responsibility for City Affairs, DTI)—'there is a need for financial conglomerate', the *Financial Times* 13.12.83; policy statement by Robin Leigh Pemberton (governor of Bank of England), the *Financial Times* 12.3.84, 27.10.86, 27.10.86.

[61] Alex Fletcher, Minister for Corporate and Consumer Affairs, FT 20.1.84; Gower report 19.1.84; comments, Norman Tebbit 25.9.84, 21.8.86.

competition arising from the Big Bang reforms would endanger their livelihoods and the structure of LSE, especially when they looked at the experience of the US after reforms of the NYSE.[62] In parliament, Conservative backbenchers with City links questioned whether the reforms were necessary and/or beneficial to investors, while the Labour–Liberal Democrat opposition called for more sweeping moves towards statutory regulation.[63] But, a determined coalition of the government, Bank of England, and eventually LSE's management, overcome opposition, armed with the new internationalisation strategy and arguments.

Competition: Single Capacity and Fixed Commissions

In 1980, competition in securities trading was still limited by LSE rules setting fixed brokerage commissions for most trades and by single capacity that obliged brokers to pass through the wholesale jobbers on LSE's trading floor. In 1979, the head of the Office of Fair Trading, Sir Gordon Borrie, had begun a legal case against LSE, arguing that fixed commissions were an illegal restrictive practice. LSE vigorously defended its position, claiming that single capacity offered investors, especially individuals, greater protection against exploitation than dual capacity systems.[64]

However, LSE's repeated appeals to the government to stop the case were rejected, despite the Conservative Party being in government after 1979.[65] Indeed, LSE's traditional ally, the Bank of England, encouraged the OFT's legal action as a central element in its modernisation strategy. In 1983, as the case finally came before the Restrictive Practices Court, the LSE's senior officials, led by (Sir) Nicolas Goodison, preferred to reach an agreement with the government on reforms of market structure rather than allow the Court to make a ruling.[66] In particular, LSE agreed to end fixed commissions as part of the Big Bang of October 1986. Instead, it introduced a new system of market makers who would determine their own commissions, combine retail and wholesale trading and could trade directly with each other.

International factors were central to ending fixed commissions and single capacity. Changes in the US offered an example for British reformers.[67] In particular, the OFT filed evidence about the end of fixed commissions in the US in 1975, and resulting fall in commissions, and the absence of prohibitions on dual capacity to support its case against LSE before the Restrictive Practices Court.[68] Indeed, Sir Gordon Borrie stated that the NYSE's abandonment of fixed commissions was

[62] The *Financial Times* 15.9.83, 5.10.83, 12.10.83, 27.10.86 and Lawrence (1996: 325–6); interview, senior LSE official.

[63] The *Financial Times* 23.11.83, 1.12.83, 14.1.87.

[64] The *Financial Times* 24.9.80, 28.1.81, 2.2.81, 10.10.83.   [65] Moran (1991: 69–70).

[66] The government passed a short act to exempt LSE from the Restrictive Practices Act—Borrie (1986); for a history, see Kynaston (2001: 616–30).

[67] Interview, senior competition official; Institute of Contemporary British History (1999: 102).

[68] The *Financial Times* 1.2.83, 5.4.83.

'one of the keys' to the case.[69] After a visit to the US, the government minister for corporate affairs declared that he was 'unafraid of dual capacity', expected it to occur and hoped that it would follow the examples he had seen in North America.[70]

For their part, the Bank of England and LSE's own senior leadership were worried that the City of London was becoming internationally uncompetitive, especially after reforms in the US in the 1970s.[71] LSE was failing to attract international securities trading.[72] Single capacity was seen as a hindrance to international expansion because it contributed to LSE being composed of brokers and jobbers who had narrow expertise and were under-capitalised relative to overseas financial firms, especially in the US.[73] Even within the domestic market, an increasing share of UK shares was being traded abroad because large investors were less prepared to cross-subsidise small investors by paying high commissions and could bypass LSE through foreign firms that were not subject to LSE's rules and could hence execute their orders either on the NYSE or 'off exchange' in their own offices. This danger grew after the abolition of exchange controls in 1979 which made trading by UK investors on overseas exchanges much easier.[74] US exchanges offered particular competition: commission rates on large trades were put at 0.4% in London and 0.15% in the US, and by 1983, 7% of UK equities trading took place in the US.[75]

The Bank of England's strategy, which was shared by the government, was to push through reforms that allowed LSE to compete for business worldwide and aided the development of large securities firms with the size and capital to compete internationally.[76] It thus sought to end single capacity and fixed commissions and to encourage the development of large broadly based financial groups, notably through the entry of merchant banks into securities trading. To some extent, events seemed to bear this out—after the Big Bang, LSE gave greater importance to international equities trading, commissions fell for large trades (but rose for small ones), and foreign business rose.[77]

The Organisation of LSE

In the 1980s LSE faced the dangers of rising costs, small members, and losing business to international competitors.[78] Foreign bankers and financial actors

[69] The *Financial Times* 5.4.83, 1.2.83.

[70] Alex Fletcher, interview, the *Financial Times* 13.12.83.

[71] The *Financial Times* 21.8.86, 27.10.86 and Reid (1988: 33–4, 43–4).

[72] The *Financial Times* 17.10.85.

[73] The *Financial Times* 5.2.80, 6.2.80, 15.2.80, 15.9.83, 19.9.83, 21.12.83 and Reid (1988: 33–4); interview, senior LSE official.

[74] Poser (1988), the *Financial Times* 28.1.81, 21.10.83, 7.10.85, Reid (1988: 11), Moran (1991: 76), Michie (1999: 544), and Kynaston (2001: 600); interview, senior LSE official.

[75] Laurence (1996: 326).

[76] The *Financial Times* 15.11.83, 22.11.83, 12.3.84, 21.8.86, 27.10.86.

[77] The *Financial Times* 3.12.86, 27.10.87; for a discussion, see Reid (1988: 89–102).

[78] The *Financial Times* 2.1.81, 2.2.81, 15.8.83, 7.10.85, 17.10.85.

in London created their own organisation, the international securities regulatory organisation (ISRO) in 1985 to regulate international securities dealers and consider establishing its own exchange.[79] Moreover, the creation of a new exchange, the London International Futures Exchange (LIFFE) in 1982 offered a striking example of the rewards from innovation and dropping LSE rules such as single capacity.[80] At the same time, LSE's costs were rising (including to pay for new technology), but the number of jobbers and brokers were falling and their revenues and profits were under pressure; however, attempts to increase commissions in 1982 provoked a fierce revolt by large investors.[81] Finally, LSE members lacked capital, especially relative to overseas financial conglomerates.

In response, the government, Bank of England, and LSE's leadership altered LSE's internal organisation as part of a wider strategy to create an internationally competitive City of London composed of larger financial firms. They accepted and indeed welcomed the entry of overseas firms into LSE.[82] As part of its settlement with the government of the OFT's legal case against it, LSE was obliged to change its internal workings.[83] Thus in 1986, sweeping reforms allowed 100% outside ownership of LSE members and foreign companies to become members. LSE created a specialised international electronic market the Stock Exchange Automated Quotation International (SEAQI) and opened it to overseas companies in 1985.[84] Moreover, membership of LSE became attached to firms instead of individuals and unlimited liability of LSE members was ended. Allowing external investors to buy LSE members and terminating unlimited liability were essential elements in the Bank of England's strategy of creating strong UK financial groups that could match overseas ones.[85] The LSE's internal governance structure was altered, so that by 1986, one-third of LSE's Council were non-practitioners, to make it more responsive to forces for change.

The reforms aroused unease and sometimes opposition—for instance, reforms to LSE's membership rules in 1985 failed to obtain the 75% needed to pass, and were delayed until 1986, while Conservative backbench MPs with links to the City were worried about overseas firms taking over British ones.[86] Nevertheless, faced with a reform strategy pursued by the government, Bank of England, LSE leadership and the Office of Fair Trading, opponents were unable to resist the changes.

The 1986 Big Bang changed the face of LSE. Large firms, from Britain and abroad, bought up stockbrokers and jobbers, so that almost all independent firms

---

[79] The *Financial Times* 17.10.85, 31.10.85.   [80] Michie (1999: 557–9).

[81] The *Financial Times* 17.3.82, 18.3.82, 25.3.82.

[82] The *Financial Times* 23.11.83 (comments by Norman Tebbit on the advantages of foreign institutions entering LSE), comments by Alex Fletcher, the *Financial Times* 17.2.84.

[83] The *Financial Times* 9.9.83, 13.9.83, 16.9.83.

[84] Kynaston (2001: 688); cf. the *Financial Times* 21.3.85, 9.10.85, 3.3.86, 20.3.86, 27.10.87.

[85] The *Financial Times* 17.3.82, 15.8.83, 19.9.83, 15.11.83, 12.3.84.

[86] Notable examples included Anthony Beaumont-Dark, Peter Tapsell, and Nick Budgen—the *Financial Times* 23.11.83.

disappeared.[87] However, the result was an inflow of capital into LSE members. Moreover, large users did not establish a rival exchange to LSE; indeed, in 1986, ISRO decided to merge with LSE to form international LSE, claiming that its aims had been achieved thanks to LSE's new rules that gave greater attention to international securities, and because many LSE stockbrokers had been bought up by ISRO members.[88] The international securities market, SEAQI, grew rapidly and by 1990 handled more business than LSE's domestic stock market.[89] LSE had been transformed from a club for selected British individuals into an association open to companies from all over the world and a force in the international securities market.[90] The revolution was symbolised by the increasing use of electronic systems by LSE members who were now mostly owned by large well-capitalised financial groups; by January 1987 LSE's trading floor was deserted.[91]

Regulatory Organisations and Framework

Financial services regulation in Britain was profoundly altered by the 1984 Gower report and 1986 Financial Services Act. Both were primarily driven by domestic scandals and the desire to protect small investors in financial services outside share trading.[92] Nevertheless, they also affected LSE, greatly reducing its traditional self-regulation. Two international factors were important for securities regulation. One was the example of the US. The 1984 Gower report argued that change was needed to avoid scandals and maintain international confidence, although it claimed that a British equivalent of the SEC should be avoided.[93] The government and the Bank of England agreed that stronger investor protection was needed to enhance financial services at home and overseas.[94] Once the decision to create a financial regulator was made, policy makers visited the SEC. But they did not take the US regulatory system as a model, seeing it as 'inappropriate' to Britain because it was 'too fragmented'.[95] The government praised certain aspects of the US regulatory system, but it too rejected a British SEC, arguing that the SEC was too legalistic and bureaucratic.[96] A second international factor was the changing nature of the City as it moved away from a small club of British insiders. Instead, the internationalisation of markets, the formation of more integrated financial

---

[87] By 1991, 358 of 410 LSE members were companies, many being foreign-owned subsidiaries of North American, Japanese, and Continental European financial institutions—Michie (1999: 603).

[88] The *Financial Times* 3.12.86; interview, senior financial regulator 1.

[89] The *Financial Times* 17.5.90.

[90] Kynaston (2001: 696–8); for figures and examples, see Michie (1999: 580–92).

[91] Only the traded options market was left.

[92] Gower (1988: 6–10); interviews, senior LSE official, senior financial regulators 2 and 3.

[93] The *Financial Times* 19.1.84 and Gower (1984).

[94] The *Financial Times* 12.10.83, comments, Fletcher, the *Financial Times* 20.1.84; interview, senior financial regulator 2.

[95] Interviews senior financial regulators 2 and 3.

[96] Comments by Fletcher, the *Financial Times* 23.10,84; however, the opposition Labour Party called for the creation of a SEC—the *Financial Times* 1.10.82, 17.7.84, 17.12.85, 14.1.87, 14.1.87.

firms, and the increasing number and diversity of players (including overseas ones) were seen as weakening self-regulation, which operated best in a small 'village' community.[97] Although LSE defended self-regulation,[98] it was unable to prevent changes under the 1986 Financial Services Act that greatly diminished its autonomy over rule-making. The Act introduced a complex framework in which law and publicly created or licensed regulators played much more prominent roles than previously, together with supposed 'self-regulatory organisations' (SROs).[99] A sectoral regulatory agency, the Securities and Investment Board (SIB), was established, whose chairman and board were appointed by the Bank of England and Chancellor of the Exchequer.[100] The Secretary of State for Trade and Industry delegated powers to the SIB. In particular, the SIB had powers to license SROs, approve their rules and establish rules itself. The major SRO for trading securities became The Securities Association (TSA), which took most of LSE's regulatory powers;[101] in turn, the TSA was merged with the Association of Futures Brokers and Dealers in 1991 to form the Securities and Futures Authority (SFA) in 1991.

Although the new arrangements were supposed to offer 'self-regulation within a new statutory framework',[102] the SIB rapidly created a highly detailed framework and was well described as 'a statutory wolf in self-regulatory sheep's clothing'.[103] Powers over share trading were held by a self-regulatory body, that body was licenced and under the authority of the SIB.[104] While policy makers had officially rejected a SEC, the first head of the SIB, Sir Kenneth Berrill, stated that the SIB would 'to all intents and purposes, be exercising the powers of an SEC'.[105]

1987–2005 EXTENDING THE REVOLUTION

Processes of Reform: Actors and Strategies

Regulatory reform continued after 1987, notably to increase statutory regulation and to encourage competition. It was led by domestic actors, particularly the government and statutory regulators, the SIB and its successor the Financial Services Authority (FSA). Two traditional regulators—LSE and the Bank of England—were largely excluded from regulation after 1997. This marked a

---

[97] The *Financial Times* 1.10.82, 15.11.83, 21.12.83, 30.4.84, 15.11.85; interview, senior LSE official.
[98] The *Financial Times* 24.7.82, 16.1.84.   [99] See Black (1997: ch. 2).
[100] Although, technically, the SIB was legally a private limited company, which enabled it to avoid civil service pay and conditions.
[101] London Stock Exchange retained power over listing, but this too was transferred first to the UK Listing Authority as part of the Financial Services Authority in 2000.
[102] Quote, Alex Fletcher, DTI Minister, the *Financial Times* 18.10.84.
[103] The *Financial Times* 13.2.88.
[104] Black (1997: 77–80) characterises this as 'mandated self-regulation'.
[105] Moran (1991: 58).

remarkable change, as these two bodies had been central participants in policy-making for two centuries.

Internationalisation was central to the strategies of reformers. The government, SIB/FSA, and Bank of England sought to protect London's competitive position internationally, especially relative to the US. This was visible in decisions to encourage competition to LSE provided it aided as part of enhancing London's attractiveness as a financial centre. Moreover, attitudes towards American style regulation continued to evolve, with much less hostility towards a 'British SEC'. In contrast, although the European market was seen as offering potential rewards for the City of London, British policy makers were suspicious of EU regulation, fearing that it would be a threat (notably in terms of higher costs and loss of UK competitive advantage), and hence they focused on how to influence EU regulation rather than using it in debates on domestic institutional reform.[106]

Competition Among Exchanges

The 1990s saw the creation of electronic exchanges based in London.[107] Although several aimed at capturing cross-border trading, they also competed with LSE for domestic share trading. Some were based on existing systems used in the US (e.g. Instinet). They had fewer restrictions and lower costs than LSE—notably by operating fully automated markets that did not require market makers but simply matched buy and sell orders.

LSE feared the expansion of new electronic exchanges: cross-border trading was its most rapidly growing market; it looked at the experience in the US, where the NYSE had lost substantial ground to new rivals (an estimated one-third of trading volumes on stocks listed on NYSE).[108] It sought to use its rules to discourage its own members from using alternative exchanges.[109] It argued that a central, unified marketplace for equities was in the public interest by ensuring best information and prices for participants.[110]

However, the government and independent regulators did not seek to protect LSE. On the contrary, they welcomed new exchanges as part of their strategy

---

[106] See for Goodison (1988); the *Financial Times* 17.11.88; or British reactions to the 'Lamfalussy group'—the *Financial Times* 12.7.2000, 15.7.2000, 22.7.2000, 15.9.2000 (article by Andrew Large, former head of SIB), the *Financial Times* 20.9.2000; interviews, senior financial regulators 1 and 4.

[107] For instance, Tradepoint (the oldest, dating from 1995), Instinet, E-Crossnet, and Posit—the *Financial Times* 4.10.99 and Michie (1999: 615).

[108] The *Financial Times* 11.3.93, 18.10.93.

[109] Examples included rules prohibiting LSE market makers from offering better prices than those advertised on LSE's own price system or allowing a delay on publishing very large trades so that a bloc of shares could be sold without other market makers knowing of the large change as it was going on—the *Financial Times* 11.2.93, 6.4.94, 25.11.94, 25.11.94, 18.3.95, 12.8.95, 18.8.95, 7.9.95, 27.11.95, 13.12.95.

[110] The *Financial Times* 18.10.93, 23.6.95.

of promoting London's overall international competitive position.[111] The SIB argued that electronic technology made it easy to trade shares and that the needs of investors had become very diverse, especially with the growth of overseas share dealing. Hence it accepted entry by any organisation, provided it could meet requisite standards rather than relying on a single centralised market (i.e. LSE).[112] On several occasions the OFT and the SIB investigated LSE's rules, forcing LSE to alter those that it believed unfairly damaged competition by new exchanges.[113] Moreover, when LSE's project for a computerised settlement system, TAURUS, collapsed the Bank of England stepped in to take over settlement, and established a new company, CRESTCo that was separated from LSE.[114] Hence LSE lost control of settlement, previously one of its core functions and a potential source of competitive advantage (through vertical integration).

The Ownership and Organisational Position of LSE

In 1991 individual membership of LSE was formally ended, marking the end of several hundred years of history. In March 2000, LSE demutualised and became a listed company, whose shares were traded.[115] The main purposes of demutualisation were to allow LSE to raise capital more cheaply and aid it to compete with new electronic exchanges.[116] Indeed, LSE's strategy was to focus on becoming a company competing for markets internationally.[117] LSE had thus made a complete transition from a gentleman's club of the 1960s to a commercial company.

Rapidly LSE became involved in attempts at international mergers and takeovers. It received overtures to join Euronext, a three-way merger between the Paris, Brussels, and Amsterdam exchanges, but rejected these; the main factor was its belief that British regulation was much more favourable to investors than that of other European nations.[118] Instead, LSE sought a partnership with Deutsche Börse in 1998 and then a full merger in 2000 in order to capture a large share of European equities trading and to counter alternative alliances (notably the Euronext group).[119] However, the attempt failed: in addition to commercial and technological blockages (e.g. issues of valuation or trading platforms), regulatory differences between Britain and Germany were crucial, notably rules over disclosure of trading, market transparency, and investor protection.[120] Fully-blown

---

[111] Treasury Committee (1996: paragraphs 73–87) and the *Financial Times* 18.10.93, 29.8.2000; interview, senior financial regulator 4.

[112] Interview Sir Andrew Large, chairman SIB; SIB 1995, the *Financial Times* 23.6.95.

[113] Michie (1999: 599) and the *Financial Times* 11.2.93, 25.11.95, 18.3.95, 18.8.95, 23.9.95, 13.12.95, 24.7.97.

[114] CRESTCo merged with Euroclear in 2002.

[115] Shares were distributed to members (numbering c300) which they could buy and sell—the *Financial Times* 22.5.2000, 21.8.2000.

[116] The *Financial Times* 4.10.99.   [117] The *Financial Times* 17.5.90, 23.7.94, 4.10.99.

[118] The *Financial Times* 26.4.2000.

[119] The *Financial Times* 26.4.2000, 4.5.2000, 22.5.2000, 9.9.2000, 9.9.2000, 13.9.2000, 30.10.2001.

[120] The *Financial Times* 26.10.98, 6.5.2000, 22.5.2000, 21.8.2000, 29.8.2000.

hostile takeover attempts by foreign companies then ensued in 2004–5, notably by Deutsche Börse, the Swedish exchange OM, and the Australian company McQuarry.

The Treasury and Bank of England remained in the background of these merger activities. They welcomed LSE's attempt to merge with Deutsche Börse on the grounds of consolidation of the world's stock exchanges, ignoring a call by the Conservatives for a delay to consider issues of ownership and regulation,[121] but did not play a direct role in seeking to resolve obstacles to the merger.[122] They were even more distant with respect to OM's hostile bid, described as 'a commercial decision for the LSE'.[123] Their main concern was the City of London's overall international position rather than treating LSE as a British entity to be protected against foreigners.[124] For its part, the FSA 'couldn't care less' about ownership of LSE provided it did not cause regulatory confusion.[125] As of 2006, takeover bids for LSE had failed, but this occurred because of withdrawals by bidders on financial grounds rather than decisions of the government or regulators.

Regulatory Organisations

Major reforms after 1990 greatly extended the move away from traditional British self-regulation that had begun in the 1980s. In 1997 the incoming Labour government ended the previous 'half-way house' between statutory regulation by the SIB and SROs run by practitioners, including the SFA. Instead, powers were concentrated in one statutory regulator, the Financial Services Authority (FSA).[126] The Bank of England's supervisory role for financial services was ended: under the 1998 Bank of England Act, its powers were transferred to the FSA. The LSE's remaining regulatory powers were also ended, notably over listing (transferred to the FSA).[127] The 2000 Financial Services and Markets Act formalised the change from the traditional regulation of stock exchanges via informal norms led by the LSE and the Bank of England to regulation by a statutory sectoral regulator.[128]

The FSA, like the SIB, was formally a private limited company. Nevertheless, the Treasury enjoyed important powers over the FSA. It appointed the FSA's board and chairman, and had the power to dismiss them. It could conduct reviews and enquiries into the FSA. The 2000 Act also set the FSA's objectives, notably: maintaining market confidence; promoting public understanding of the financial system; securing the appropriate degree of protection for consumers; and reducing financial crime.

---

[121] The *Financial Times* 29.8.2000.   [122] The *Financial Times* 29.8.2000.
[123] The *Financial Times* 29.8.2000.
[124] The *Financial Times* 29.8.2000, 29.7.2005 and *The Guardian* 31.3.2005.
[125] Quote, senior financial regulator 4.
[126] The legal form was complex in that the FSA legally acted under contract on behalf of the agencies it replaced until 2000.
[127] The *Financial Times* 4.10.99.   [128] For overviews, see Blair et al. (2000) and James (2001).

The creation of the FSA concerned most of the financial services industry, and hence explaining its establishment would require going far beyond stock exchanges. Domestic factors were crucial, especially scandals.[129] However, international factors played an important role with respect to regulation of stock exchanges. In part due to transnational technological and economic changes, reformers argued that boundaries between different financial activities were weakening, making a system of separate regulatory organisations based on those boundaries obsolete and inefficient.[130] The SEC was used increasingly as a positive example by those advocating greater powers for regulators, notably the head of the SIB and large institutional investors.[131] However, fears of its legalism continued and it was an argument for change rather than a model that was copied by British policy makers.[132] Indeed, policy makers also looked at other overseas debates, notably the Wallace Commission of Inquiry in Australia that recommended one regulatory system that covered different financial institutions and products.[133] London's international competitive position was argued to be weakened because of a proliferation of regulatory bodies.[134] The institutional choice was to create the FSA as a single statutory regulator with powers to make formal rules and enforce them. The outcome was a long way from informal self-regulation of the mid-1960s.

CONCLUSION

In the mid-1960s LSE was a well-established club of individuals with unlimited personal liability. As in other countries, competition was limited through fixed commissions and entry barriers to membership. However, LSE differed from its continental European counterparts in being privately owned, having internal rules that separated retail and wholesale trading (single capacity), and enjoying remarkably wide informal self-regulation.

The period between 1965 and 1980 provides considerable insights about why well-established existing national institutions remain stable despite pressures from transnational technological and economic developments. LSE was vulnerable due to its rules restricting competition (fixed commissions and charges from both jobbers and brokers) and reliance on large investors cross-subsidising small ones. It faced losing its de facto monopoly over trading in British securities: it could be

---

[129] cf. Laurence (2001: 88–98) and Blair et al. (2000: 13–15); examples included the Maxwell and Barlow Clowes frauds or pensions mis-selling; for the political process, see Keegan (2004: 176–91).

[130] Spalek (2001: 76–7) and Blair et al. (2000: 10–12).

[131] Interview, Andrew Large, the *Financial Times* 3.11.92, Laurence (2001: 97); interview, senior financial regulator 1.

[132] Interview, senior financial regulator 4.   [133] Interview, senior financial regulator 4.

[134] Report by Professor Richard Brealey, commissioned by the then Securities Association—the *Financial Times* 8.7.92; comments by Labour's spokesperson on City Affairs Mo Mowlam on profusion of regulatory bodies confusing Britons and foreigners alike—the *Financial Times* 26.4.91; SIB comments that self-regulation not understood on the Continent—the *Financial Times* 25.1.90.

bypassed either through trading on overseas exchanges or by a new rival (ARIEL) with lower costs, modern technology, and a specific aim of large institutional investors. Worse still, LSE members faced a combination of low profits and higher capital costs, all borne by individuals rather than limited companies.

Yet only minor institutional modifications were made for twenty years. Why was this? One reason was that LSE adopted a non-institutional strategy to respond to technological and economic challenges. Thus for example, it computerised its own clearing and settlement systems to enhance its efficiency and lower costs, and reduced commissions for large trades to compete with ARIEL. Another factor was that despite international decline and financial difficulties, LSE members were highly conservative, and appeared content to live off their monopoly of UK share trading. Finally, a decisive factor was the lack of action by the government and the Bank of England: they remained spectators, content to let LSE decide its own responses to transnational technological and economic developments, and unwilling to intervene to drive through reforms.

In contrast, the period between the early 1980s and 2005 shows how and why long-standing institutions can be rapidly and radically reformed. Change was led by British actors. In particular, the government, together with the Bank of England, Office of Fair Trading, and eventually LSE's leadership, all altered their strategies and became active participants in reform. Reform was triggered by domestic factors such as the OFT's legal case against LSE. However, international factors were crucial in the altered strategies of policy makers. Two can be underlined. One was the danger of regulatory competition, as the US offered more attractive markets and hence drained LSE of international and UK securities trading. The other was the US example, which was important in legitimating change.

Table 4.1. Institutional changes between 1965 and 2005

	1965	1986 (post-Big Bang)	2005
Organisational position of the incumbent—LSE	Privately-owned club composed of individual male British members	Privately-owned club open to British and overseas companies	Quoted company
Competition in trading	Limits on competition due to fixed commissions and LSE rules on advertising and single capacity; LSE main stock exchange with minor regional exchanges	Competition through market makers setting commissions and free to engage in retail and wholesale trading	Competition through market makers setting commissions and free to engage in retail and wholesale trading; several exchanges for trading
Regulatory organisations and powers	Self-regulation by club government (led by LSE Council and Bank of England)—strong informal norms	Statutory regulator, the SIB, and overseeing self-regulatory organisations	Statutory regulator, the FSA, with detailed powers of rule-making and enforcement

Hence British policy makers used the end of fixed commissions in the NYSE and to a lesser extent the role of the SEC to justify new institutional arrangements such as the 1986 Big Bang or the creation of a statutory regulator. But this involved superficial rather than deep learning and policy makers only looked seriously to the US after decisions to alter institutions had already been taken. Although the US provided a source of fear of loss of business and of inspiration for institutional features to be used or avoided, it was not a model that was copied wholesale.

As part of legitimating change, reformers adopted objectives of making London an international financial centre by attracting overseas investors and firms and creating large, internationally-competitive financial suppliers. To achieve these aims, reformers put forward a new model of regulatory institutions, namely one that was open to competition, to overseas companies, and was policed by a strong independent statutory body. The outcomes were a new set of sectoral arrangements that overturned institutions encrusted for decades and sometimes centuries. Table 4.1 summarises the institutional changes between 1965 and 2005 in the three aspects examined in the book.

Overall, the case of securities trading in Britain shows that traditional sectoral institutions can survive in the face of powerful unfavourable transnational technological and economic pressures. In contrast, when governments and other public bodies participate actively in reform, and are able to use policy forms of internationalisation—in this case reforms in the US—changes can be revolutionary in their speed and extent. Thus public policy makers are shown to be initiators and central actors in change, creating coalitions and overcoming opposition, even from powerful vested interests. Moreover, reforms overseas are significant in change through their role in the domestic policy process: for reformers, they are valuable in offering the fear of regulatory competition and as an example to legitimate change, without requiring deep learning or wholesale emulation. The British case underlines the importance of a policy form of internationalisation (overseas reforms) and its interaction with the domestic policy process.

The British route to reform involved international factors entering decision-making after domestic ones had set off the reform process. It also saw attention paid to the US rather than European nations or EU regulation. Chapter 5 contrasts this with the reform route followed in France, Germany, and Italy.

5

Transformation and Convergence: Stock Exchanges in France, Germany, and Italy 1986–2005

Between 1986 and 2005 France, Germany, and Italy adopted similar sweeping reforms that transformed deeply entrenched sectoral institutions. Monopolies over securities trading were abolished. The organisation of stock exchanges was radically altered from publicly owned meeting places for traders into privately owned profit-seeking companies running electronic markets. Independent sectoral regulators were created or strengthened. The changes were remarkable: they stood in sharp contrast to the inertia or divergence that had taken place between the mid-1960s and 1985 (see Chapter 3); they ended institutional features that had stood for decades and even centuries; they removed institutional protection of domestic suppliers; and they involved convergence with institutions in Britain.

Internationalisation of markets played an important role in these transformations. Transnational technological and economic developments continued to give rise to pressures for change. Equally, the US offered both an example of an alternative framework and a possible source of regulatory competition. However, these two factors had not led to reform before 1986. The novelty after 1986 was that two new forms of internationalisation emerged. First, in 1986, Britain's Big Bang radically altered the organisation of the LSE (see Chapter 4). Second, EU regulation increased from the late 1980s onwards. Given the timing of these two new forms of internationalisation, the chapter takes 1986 as its starting point.

The chapter argues that these two additional policy forms of internationalisation influenced the strategies, coalitions, and resources of actors in domestic debates on institutional reform. They aided the formation of determined coalitions for change and weakened the membership and capacities of their opponents. Reforms in Britain increased fears of regulatory competition and provided an example of new institutional forms. Transposing EU law provided occasions for reconsideration of institutional structures. More broadly, EU regulation increased fears of loss of business to other European exchanges and legitimated reforms that went beyond those required by EU law.

In terms of the book's broader argument, securities trading in France, Germany, and Italy between 1986 and 2005 shows the impact of policy forms of internationalisation. EU regulation and reforms in Britain made significant contributions to changes that were remarkable in their extent and stand in contrast to earlier inertia. They aided the spread of analogous institutions across three nations with different national-level political institutions, as well as convergence with Britain. This is particularly noteworthy because the four countries are usually presented in comparative institutionalist studies as contrasting varieties of capitalism. The chapter shows that the two policy forms of internationalisation were significant in domestic political struggles because they aided governments and other reformers in creating coalitions and gave them arguments to justify modifying traditional institutions. Hence it underlines that policy forms internationalisation can powerfully influence reform because of their impacts within the domestic policy process. Finally, the case sets out a 'continental European reform route' (in contrast to the British one) in which EU regulation and reforms in Britain were crucial in the initiation and implementation of change.

For each country, the chapter begins by looking at the effects of different forms of internationalisation on the strategies and coalitions of key policy makers. It then examines specific decisions concerning competition in trading, the organisational position of the stock exchange, and the allocation of regulatory powers between governments and sectoral regulators. The concluding section compares the position in 2005 and 1986, and considers why the impacts of internationalisation of markets differed from the inertia seen between 1965 and 1985.

FRANCE

The Process of Reform

In 1986, France still maintained traditional institutions, such as public ownership of the Paris Bourse, publicly-appointed brokers (the *Agents de change*) who held a monopoly over share trading, and a weak sectoral regulator, the Commission des Opération de Bourse (COB). In the period until 2005, these institutions were radically recast.

Reform was led by domestic actors, particularly the government.[1] It established high-level commissions that produced reports preparing the ground for changes, led discussions with other actors, provided key personnel (even to nominally private sector organisations), and passed new legislation, notably in 1988, 1989, 1996, and 2003.[2] The other key actors were the COB and financial institutions, notably

---

[1] Interviews senior legislator 1, senior financial regulator 1, senior financial practitioners 1 and 2; within the government, the Trésor and the Finance Ministry were usually central; key individuals included: Pierre Bérégovoy as Finance Minister 1988–92, Daniel Lebèque (*directeur du Trésor* 1984–7), Christian Noyer (*directeur du Trésor* 1993–5), and Philippe Jaffré (who held posts dealing with financial markets throughout the 1980s and early 1990s); within Bérégovoy's *cabinet*, Jean-Charles Naouri, and Claude Rubinowicz were key participants—*Le Matin* 7.10.85, *Journal des Finances* 9–15.7.88, the *Financial Times* 8.4.87, and *Le Monde* 11.3.87.

[2] Key commissions included the Pérouse Commission (1980), the Tricot Commission (1985), the La Portz report (1988), and the de la Serre report (1991); examples of public sector personnel taking major posts include the head of the Conseil des Bourses de Valeurs (1990–4), Bruno de Maulde, who was a senior civil servant on secondment ('détachement'), while the new head of the company, Paris

large banks which became central participants in securities trading. The traditionally powerful brokers, the *Agents de change*, were important in the late 1980s, but thereafter increasingly lost influence and were mostly bought by banks.[3] In contrast, although foreign institutions became significant as market players and investors, they did not form a separate group from French institutions.[4]

Nevertheless, international factors were 'omnipresent' through their influence on the strategies and coalitions of French actors, particularly the government's determination to press ahead with reform and its ability to obtain a high degree of acceptance for its plans among domestic actors.[5] Technological and economic pressures on institutional choices continued to be felt in the mid-1980s. The *Agents de change*, who traded as individuals, lacked capital for expansion, liquidity, or funding new computer systems for the Paris Bourse.[6] More indirectly, the rapid growth of markets in related financial products, such as the marché à terme international de la France (MATIF) for derivatives (created in 1986), which were not subject to the same restrictions as the Bourse de Paris, offered an example of the benefits of alternative institutional frameworks and encouraged the banks to expand their trading operations.[7] Finally, the diversity, sophistication, and international exposure of new financial products and markets provided arguments for altering the regulatory framework.[8]

However, these technological and economic developments offered background pressures for change. The most visible factors in reform discussions were international regulatory competition and EU regulation. All major French actors—the government, COB, *Agents*, and banks—compared French institutional arrangements, such as trading rules, settlement systems, and alternative regulatory organisations, with overseas exchanges.[9] They saw the US as an example of regulatory structures, but not as a rival for markets.[10] In contrast, they viewed LSE as a dangerous competitor, and also Frankfurt from the 1990s onwards.[11] They argued that the Paris Bourse had to modernise and expand internationally to match these exchanges in services, costs, and investor protection.[12] They became particularly

Bourse (La Société de bourse de Paris) and then Euronext, Jean-François Théodore, was seconded from the Trésor, *Le Figaro* 11.12.90; in addition, the head of the COB (1995–2002) and then of the AMF (2002–today), Michel Prada, was a former senior Trésor official.

[3] By 1995, only 4 of 52 brokers were independent—Lehmann (1997: 112), cf. *La Tribune de l'Expansion* 24.10.90, 5.7.91, and *Le Figaro* 11.12.90; interviews senior legislator 1 and 2.

[4] Interviews senior legislator 1, senior legislator 2, and senior financial practitioner 2.

[5] Quote senior financial regulator 2.

[6] Lehmann (1997: 111); *La Tribune de l'Expansion* 23.10.90; interview senior legislator 2.

[7] cf. Lehmann (1997: 107–14); interviews senior financial regulator 2, senior financial practitioner 1.

[8] Interview senior financial regulator 2; cf. Bézard (1989), Viandier (1989: 46–7).

[9] *La Tribune de l'Expansion* 2.1.90, 5.7.91, *Le Figaro* 27.6.90, *De La Serre* (1991), Marini (1994), and Gourlard (2003); proposals by Senator Philippe Marini, *Le Figaro Economique* 2.2.95, and *Le Monde* 29.3.95; *La Tribune Desfossés* 4.1.96, *Libération* 23.10.2000, and *Les Echos* 12.9.2002.

[10] Interview senior financial practitioner 1.

[11] Interviews senior financial practitioner 1, senior financial regulator 4, senior financial regulator 1.

[12] Dupont (head of the Compagnie des Agents de change) (1986: 95); *Le Point* 3.6.85, the *Financial Times* 7.4.87, 8.4.87, *Tribune de l'Economie* 15.6.87, and *Le Monde* 24–25.3.85, 2.12.87, interview, Régis

concerned about LSE after its Big Bang reforms in 1986, seen as 'an English strategy of domination'.[13] They were worried that the Paris Bourse was much smaller than its rivals and that dealing in French shares was migrating to other exchanges, notably to London: by the late 1980s/early 1990s, an estimated 15%–30% of French shares were traded on LSE's SEAQ-International system.[14] The dangers to Paris were put graphically: a member of the National Assembly justified the law of 1988 by underlining the risks of Paris being 'deserted' by investors unless it could offer the same services and degree of investor protection as other exchanges.[15]

Arguments for reform were strengthened by EU regulation and the move towards the Euro.[16] First, EU regulation increased competition among exchanges. In the late 1980s, policy makers pointed to the need to prepare French markets and firms for the opening of European capital markets as part of the Single Market ('1992').[17] The EU's 1993 Investment Services Directive (ISD) was seen as aggravating international competition by allowing firms authorised in one country to trade across the EC.[18] Second, they feared that lack of detailed EU re-regulation would allow member states to engage in regulatory competition by adopting 'deregulation'.[19] French policy makers worried that the Paris Bourse would be squeezed between LSE and Frankfurt, and argued that it had to become as good as other European exchanges through institutional modifications.[20] Third, transposition of the 1993 ISD provided a 'powerful lever' for reconsideration of the institutional structure.[21] It led to modifications going well beyond those laid down in EU law but which were justified, in part, by the effects of EU liberalisation.[22]

Rousselle (head of the Société des Bourse Françaises), *La Tribune de l'Expansion* 20.6.88; *La Tribune de l'Expansion* 15.1.90, *Les Echos* 22.2.95; cf. Choinel (1990); interview senior financial regulator 3; see reports by COB, Le Portz (1988); *La Vie Française* 28.1.85, *Le, Libération* 26.3.85, and *Le Point* 3.6.85.

[13] Quote—Dupont (1986: 92); *Le Monde* 16.1.86, *Le Figaro Economie* 20.10.86; cf. Courbis and Dupuy (1989); interviews senior legislator 1 and 2, senior financial practitioner 1.

[14] In 1989, the Paris Bourse had a capitalisation of 1.95 billion francs compared with 4.8 billion for LSE, while the value of transactions was 1/6 that of the German exchanges; for trading, see *La Croix* 6.2.86, the *Financial Times* 11.3.87, 7.4.87, 8.4.87, *Le Figaro* 25.6.87, *La Tribune de l'Economie* 15.6.87, *The Economist* 1.10.88, and *La Tribune de l'Expansion* 25.10.90 ; see also *La Tribune de l'Expansion* 23.10.90, 5.7.91, *La Tribune de l'Expansion* 10.7.91, and De La Serre (1991); interview senior financial practitioner 2.

[15] Philippe Auberger (RPR), *Le Monde* 2.12.87; see also comments by the head of the Compagnie des Agents de Change—Dupont (1986: 89).

[16] *La Tribune de l'Expansion* 5.7.91 and *Les Echos* 29.3.99.

[17] Comments by Eduard Balladur, finance ministers, National Assembly debates, *Le Monde* 2.12.87, *La Croix* 12.3.87, the *Financial Times* 7.4.87, *La Tribune de l'Economie* 15.6.87, Bézard (1989: 934), Viandier (1989: 46–7), and Choinel (1990: 48); interview senior legislator 2.

[18] Interview, Alain Ferri, president of the Association Française des sociétés de Bourse, *La Tribune Desfossés* 29.7.94.

[19] Comments, Jean-François Théodore (president of the SBF), *La Tribune Desfossés* 10.1.94.

[20] *La Tribune de l'Expansion* 10.7.91 and De La Serre (1991); interview senior legislator 1.

[21] Interview senior legislator 1; interview senior financial regulator 2.

[22] Notably restructuring regulatory authorities in the law of 2 July 1996—cf. *La Tribune Desfossés* 10.1.94, *Le Figaro Economique* 2.2.95, interview, Jean Arthuis (Finance Minister), *Les Echos* 11.7.96. Interview senior legislator 1, senior financial practitioner 2.

Although government policy makers were in favour of change, they met resistance. The *Agents de change* were the most reluctant about reform. Many were wedded to traditional conceptions of a central marketplace offering a 'public service' (*service public*). They also sought to maintain their privileges and remained suspicious of the power of the COB.[23] Arguments arising from the dangers of competition with other stock exchanges and EU regulation were essential for the government and the leaders of the *Agents* to gain acceptance of change. Usually, they enabled the government to achieve agreement among domestic actors.[24] However, they also helped to legitimate decisions that the government imposed on the *Agents de change*, notably sweeping reforms in 1988 and 1989 introduced by the Finance Minister Pierre Bérégovoy that allowed entry by banks and changes in 1996 that weakened the role of the central market in setting prices.[25]

Substantive Reforms

Competition in Trading Securities

In 1986, the trading of securities remained the monopoly of the *Agents de change*, who were appointed as public officials but then plied their trade as individuals with unlimited liability. The position of the *Agents* dated from the eighteenth century and before. Yet legislation in 1988 abolished the *Agents'* monopoly over brokerage, opening the door to the *Agents'* traditional enemies, the banks.[26] It permitted the *Agents* to become limited companies (known as *sociétés de Bourse*), ending their position as ministerial officers. It gave limited companies (including overseas ones) the right to take over part or all of the capital in the *Agents*, with 100% ownership possible by 1992. Brokerage charges were no longer set by law and became open to negotiation between banks and *Agents* for large orders, making share dealing more attractive for banks.[27]

These changes were implemented despite resistance by the *Agents*.[28] They were undertaken to make Paris competitive with other stock exchanges, notably LSE, a matter that became more urgent because of moves to a European Single Market in financial services.[29] Thus reforms sought to shift securities trading away from

[23] Interview senior financial regulator 2.

[24] Interviews senior financial practitioner 1 and 2, senior financial regulator 4, senior financial regulator 1, senior financial regulator 2.

[25] *La Tribune de l'Expansion* 1.6.89, 10.7.91, *Libération* 10.7.91, and *Les Echos* 3.1.96; interview senior financial practitioner 1.

[26] *La loi du 22 janvier* (1988); for a summary of change in December 1987 and 1988, see Couret (1988) and Cerny (1989).

[27] Robert and Laboz (1991: 91–4) and De Witt (1985).

[28] *Le Figaro-Economie* 20.10.86, and the *Financial Times* 8.4.87, interview, Régis Rousselle, head of the Société des Bourses Françaises, *Le Monde* 5.10.88.

[29] Bacot, Dubroeucq and Juvin (1989: 45–7, 56–8); *Le Monde* 2.12.87 (parliamentary debate); *La Croix* 12.3.87, the *Financial Times* 11.3.87, the *Herald Tribune* 11.3.87; see also the Tricot report (1985) (Ministère de l'Economie 1985)—*La Vie Française* 28.1.85 and De Witt (1985); cf. interview, Jean Arthuis, finance minister, *Les Echos* 11.7.96; interview senior financial regulator 2.

the small, poorly capitalised *Agents* towards larger financial institutions, especially banks, that could compete with traders in overseas exchanges, particularly London after its 1986 Big Bang.[30] They also sought to allow French financial institutions to expand in markets with international capital movements and an increasing range of financial products.[31] Perhaps surprisingly for a country known for its nationalistic economic policy, foreign entry was not resisted—for example, using the 1988 law, foreign firms took over existing share brokers and began to offer dealing and other services.[32]

In 1996, remaining restrictions on entry on the Paris Bourse were reduced through legislation that transposed the EU's 1993 ISD.[33] The long-standing monopolies of the *sociétés de Bourse* and Paris and regional Bourses over share trading were terminated.[34] In accordance with the ISD, legislation severely weakened the concentration principle (i.e. that all share trading must pass through a Bourse).[35] Perhaps surprisingly, France acted earlier than most other European countries. However, one reason was that transposing the ISD allowed French brokerage firms an 'authorisation passport' to trade on overseas exchanges, an attractive prospect for those in the industry.[36] Another was that reformers argued that competition and the authorisation passport made the Paris Bourse internationally competitive.[37] The changes were part of the strategy of aiding expansion overseas by French firms and attracting foreign capital to France, an approach that enjoyed considerable success.[38]

Organisation of the Bourse

In 1986, trading still took place by open cry in the ancient *corbeille* (pit) in the Paris Bourse between 12.30 and 14.30. The Bourse itself remained a non-profit making publicly owned body run by the *Agents*. However, its organisation was transformed in the late 1980s and early 1990s in order to compete with overseas exchanges. Policymakers argued that foreign investors wanted to be able to know prices and transmit orders easily, rather than being obliged to trade at prices written on a blackboard in Paris for two hours per day.[39] Thus in 1986, opening hours were extended to aid traders operating from overseas and increase liquidity.[40] Moreover, open cry trading in the *corbeille* (pit) was replaced with the

---

[30] Interview senior financial regulator 2.   [31] De Witt (1985).

[32] 13 of 58 brokers were majority foreign owned by 1991—the *Financial Times* 26.9.91.

[33] Loi de modernisation des activités financiers du 2 July 1996.

[34] *Les Echos* 3.1.96, *La Tribune Desfossés* 4.1.96, and *Libération* 4.1.96.

[35] In particular, derogations were allowed for large trades—Tomasi (2002: paragraphs 88–90).

[36] Interview senior legislator 1.

[37] Interview senior legislator 1; *La Tribune de l'Expansion* 24.10.90.

[38] In 2004, c30%–35% of orders on the Paris Bourse came directly from overseas and c50% of investment was by non-residents—interview senior financial practitioner 2.

[39] The *Financial Times* 7.4.87, interview, Régis Rousselle, président de la Société des Bourses Françaises, *La Tribune de l'Expansion* 20.6.88; *Option Finance* 27.2.88.

[40] *Le Monde* 16.1.86, 4.3.86, the *Financial Times* 16.1.86, *La Croix* 6.2.86, and *Le Figaro-Economie* 20.10.86.

CAC (*cotation assistée en continue*), an electronic system derived from that used on the Toronto Stock Exchange. The CAC began in 1986 and was progressively extended to more and more stocks, allowing continuous all-day trading. A new settlement system was introduced to match the rapidity and 'back-office' costs of other exchanges, and hence attract international investors.[41]

Modernisation required large-scale investment: for instance, computerisation was estimated to require 400 million francs in 1989.[42] The under-capitalised *Agents* could ill-afford to meet these costs.[43] To raise funds, the exchanges were transformed into a limited company, the Société des Bourses Françaises (SBF) by the 1988 law, with its own capital. To finance investment and cover losses, the banks offered substantial capital funds to the SBF; however, in return, they obtained 25% of the SBF's capital and 4 seats on the SBF's Board.[44] Thus the banks obtained much greater power over the Paris Bourse, which itself moved away from its traditional status as a *service public* or collective body for brokers towards a private profit-making company.

Thereafter, the SBF sought to become a pan-European exchange. Initially, it approached Deutsche Börse, underpinned by strong support by elected politicians.[45] In 1997 the two exchanges discussed creating a European Bourse. However, in the late 1990s the alliance with Deutsche Börse broke down, notably over the issue of whether to use the systems and technology of one exchange or the other. This was a 'hard knock' for France, which feared that the Paris Bourse would be squeezed between Frankfurt and LSE.[46] The SBF turned to other smaller exchanges and in 2000, the Paris, Brussels, and Amsterdam Bourses merged to form Euronext. Thereafter, Euronext became a listed company in 2002, whose shares are traded. It continued to expand abroad, for instance by buying the London International Futures and Options Exchange (LIFFE) in 2002, merging with the Portuguese Bourse in 2002 and creating a pan-European clearing system LCHClearnet in 2003. Thus by 2005, the Paris Bourse had been transformed from a non-profit market into an international quoted company.[47]

Two major 'specificities' of the internal organisation of the Paris Bourse for securities trading were also ended, in large measure to meet the perceived requirements of overseas investors. The first were rules on *contre-partie*—the *Agents*

---

[41] The *Financial Times* 8.10.85 and *La Tribune de l'Expansion* 2.5.89, 7.6.89; settlement times were reduced from over 3 weeks to a maximum 5 days.

[42] *La Tribune de l'Economie* 7.6.89.

[43] The position of the *Agents* was made worse by a major scandal in 1988 when the Bourse's reserve fund was badly invested resulting in a loss of 500 million francs—the *Financial Times* 15.6.88 and *La Tribune de l'Expansion* 2.5.89.

[44] The *Financial Times* 21.7.88 and *La Croix* 21.9.88.

[45] Interview senior financial practitioner 2; interview, Jean-François Lepetit, president of the CMF, *Les Echos* 4.12.98.

[46] Interviews senior legislator 2, senior financial practitioner 1, and senior financial regulator 3 and 4.

[47] In 2006, Euronext agreed to a merger with NYSE, marking a further step toward internationalisation.

trading on their own account and quoting their own prices rather than just matching buy and sell orders of third parties. Although *contre-partie* appears arcane, it represented a battle between two different conceptions of an exchange: the traditional French model of a *service public* with state rules to maintain a strong central market offering publicly known prices for all investors, regardless of size, in which brokers are intermediaries linking buyers and sellers; an Anglo-American, market makers model with brokers who trade on their own account and set the prices that they offer to clients.[48]

Until 1986, the *Agents* were only permitted to buy and sell on their own account outside trading hours and in response to client orders; moreover, they had to unwind the transaction by trading on the Bourse (and hence its official prices) within a set time period. Reformers severely criticised restrictions on the ability of *Agents* to engage in *contre-partie* in comparison with LSE and NYSE.[49] They argued that the rules limited liquidity, especially in conditions of rapid changes in prices and exchange rates. In contrast, market makers in London were permitted to buy and sell for themselves and had the capital to do so, especially after the 1986 Big Bang when they became limited companies. To compete with LSE, *contre-partie* was widened in 1986—traders were allowed to buy and sell on their own account, although they had to unwind the transaction at official Bourse prices within sixty days.[50] Moreover, the 1988 law allowed the *Agents* to become limited companies whose capital was open to other institutions; one of the major reasons behind the legislation was to create stronger financial institutions that had the capital to offer effective *contre-partie* and hence aid Paris in competing with London over liquidity and services.[51] Nevertheless, Paris kept the principle that all trades were conducted at prices set by the central market.

In the 1990s, worries increased that the Paris Bourse was losing large trades to LSE/SEAQ-International because of more stringent French rules over declaring large trades.[52] To counter Paris' apparent disadvantage, especially in preparation for European liberalisation under the ISD, the Paris Bourse's rules were altered.[53] In particular, brokers were allowed to deviate from central market prices and to delay declaring trades for large transactions for shares in selected major companies.[54] In 1998 investors were permitted to

[48] Courbis and Dupuy (1989).

[49] See for instance Tricot report (1985), *La Vie Française* 19.5.80, 28.1.85, *Le Monde* 24.3.85, the *Financial Times* 8.10.85, *Le Monde* 4.3.86, and *Le Figaro-Economie* 20.10.86; for a discussion of the problems of the Paris Bourse, see Humphreys (1986); interview senior legislator 2.

[50] *Le Monde* 4.3.86 and Courbis and Dupuy (1989).

[51] *Le Figaro-Economie* 20.10.86, Humphreys (1986), Courbis and Dupuy (1989); interviews senior financial regulator 1 and 2.

[52] An estimated one-third of trading of the CAC stocks was taking place in London by 1991—*La Tribune de l'Expansion* 23.10.90, 25.10.90, 5.7.91; 10.7.91 (report by Barbier de la Serre for Conseil des Bourse de Valeurs (CBV)); interviews senior legislator 2, senior financial practitioner 2, senior financial regulator 4, and senior financial regulator 1.

[53] cf. *La Tribune de l'Expansion* 6.7.91, 10.7.91 (report by Barbier de la Serre for CBV), 7.2.92 (report by Bacot to CBV), and *La Tribune Desfossés* 29.7.94.

[54] Lehmann (1997: 111) and *La Tribune Desfossés* 29.7.94.

ask their brokers to undertake a trade outside the market without having to obtain regulatory approval.[55] Thus by 1998, international regulatory competition had driven the Paris Bourse away from traditional public service notions of a central market setting the same public prices for all trades regardless of size.

The second French 'specificity' was the coexistence of twin methods of trading securities—the *marché au comptant* with immediate settlement and the *marché à terme* with settlement later, offering free credit. The arrangements dated back to the nineteenth century; they were particularly advantageous for individuals lacking capital, since they could buy or sell securities without having to borrow the money, and for the *Agents*, since they encouraged trading.[56] However, they were complex in that two prices for the same security existed, depending on which method of trading was used.

In 1989, the Paris Bourse tried to create one single market, but with free credit through the so-called *règlement mensuel* (monthly settlement).[57] However, the *règlement mensuel* was criticised as a French 'anomaly' that led to longer settlement times than in overseas exchanges and was not understood by foreign investors.[58] Initially, powerful opposition, notably by the *Agents*, blocked change: it was argued that the *règlement mensuel* aided individual investors, and increased the number of transactions, thereby aiding market liquidity (and also brokerage revenue).[59] But as criticism continued, notably on the grounds that the *règlement mensuel* was 'surprising' to foreign investors, notably Anglo-American ones,[60] the argument for an internationally comprehensible system won out over the protection of individual investors and traders, and in 2000, the *règlement mensuel* was ended.[61]

Regulatory Organisations

Although a sectoral regulator had been established in 1967, the COB, its powers and independence from the government and regulatees were limited. Its remit was restricted and it faced strong self-regulatory bodies staffed by practitioners.[62] During the mid-1980s and the 1990s, it was criticised for failing to deter and sanction malpractices. In part, attacks arose from domestic scandals and the desire to protect the increased number of small shareholders who had bought shares in the privatisations of state firms.[63] However, they also involved unfavourable comparisons between the institutional position of the COB and its foreign counterparts,

---

[55] *Les Echos* 18.2.98.   [56] Interview senior financial practitioner 2.

[57] *La Tribune de l'Expansion* and *Le Figaro* 1.7.89.

[58] *La Tribune de l'Expansion* 2.1.90, 7.2.92; and *La Vie Française* 7.4.90.

[59] *La Tribune Desfossés* 30.7.93.   [60] Interview senior financial practitioner 1.

[61] The only major concession was the use of new financial instruments, notably 'warrants' or stock options that provided a form of leverage to allow investors to trade above the capital that they had available—*Le Monde* 17.5.2000 and *Les Echos* 25.9.2000.

[62] Until 1996, the Conseil des marchés Financiers (CMF) and Conseil des Bourses des Valeurs (CBV), representing the intermediaries; thereafter, the two were merged into the CMF.

[63] Scandals included the Triangle-Pechiney and Société Générale affairs; interviews senior legislator 2 and senior financial regulator 4.

notably the SEC.[64] It was argued that the COB had to meet international standards in services and investor protection, since as the head of a major French bank put it, 'so long as Paris is an exchange that is under suspicion, or at least different, with an uncertain morality...we cannot behave as adults and Europeans'.[65] Finally, although EU law did not require reform of the COB, it did increase pressures for change: the transposition of the 1993 ISD offered an opportunity to debate regulatory structures, while greater competition for trading due to the ISD, the Single Market and the introduction of the Euro, were cited as intensifying the need for Paris to make changes.[66]

Major legislation was introduced in 1989 by the Finance Minister Pierre Bérégovoy, and in 1996, by a coalition of the Trésor, COB, and the Banque de France.[67] Their objectives were to respond to domestic financial scandals, to reassure international investors, and to import good overseas practices, especially from the US and Britain (particularly after the latter's Big Bang reforms of 1986).[68] The legislation significantly increased the COB's independence and powers, drawing to some degree on the example of the SEC.[69] The tenure and membership of the COB were altered to give it greater autonomy from the government.[70] The costs of the COB were placed on market players through a levy based on that used by the SEC.[71] In 1989, Bérégovoy insisted on giving the COB the power to take cases to court, again modelled on the SEC, despite fierce opposition from lawyers, the Senate, and the Justice Minister, who argued that the change was contrary to French traditions; although the modification was then ruled unconstitutional by the constitutional court in 1989, the COB was given new powers to take court action itself in 1996.[72] Finally, the 1996 law formally recognised the COB as an independent regulatory authority.[73]

[64] *Le Monde des Affaires* 6.2.88; see also *La Vie Française* 6.2.88, 3.2.89, *Le Figaro* 14.1.89, *Le Monde* 29.3.95, and *La Tribune Desfossés* 29.3.95; for a detailed comparison, see Grabar (1988) and Conac (2002).

[65] Marc Vienot, PDG of La Société Générale, *Le Monde* 10.3.89; interview senior legislator 2.

[66] *Le Monde* 29.3.95, *La Tribune Desfossés* 29.3.95, and *Les Echos* 7.12.95, 3.1.96.

[67] Loi du 2 août 1989 relative à la sécurité et à la transparence du marché financier du 2 août 1989 and Loi de modernisation des activités financiers du 2 July 1996; *Les Echos* 7.12.95, 3.1.96, and *Le Figaro-Economique* 31.5.96; for discussions of the changes in 1989, see Autin (1989), Viandier (1989: 46), and Benoit (1989).

[68] For international factors, see *Quotidien de Paris* 30.3.89, *La Tribune de l'Expansion* 16.1.89, 6.3.89, see the Pfeiffer Commission (Pfeiffer 1990), *Les Echos* 6.10.95, 17.11.95, 29.11.9525.4.96, interview, Michel Prada (president of the COB), *Les Echos* 4.12.95, *La Tribune Desfossés* 17.1.95, 4.1.96; for overviews and analyses of the reforms, see Bézard (1989), Viandier (1989), and Couret, Martin, and Faugérolas (1989); interview senior financial practitioner 2.

[69] Couret et al. (1989: 1, 6) and Benoit (1989: 156).

[70] The tenure of the president of the COB rose from 4 to 6 years, (non-renewable); although he or she remained nominated by the government, other members were designated by a series of other bodies such as the Conseil, d'Etat, the Banque de France, and Cour de Cassation; the Government's Commissaire who had sat on COB deliberations was abolished; the number of COB members was increased so that financial professionals were in a minority.

[71] cf. *Le Monde* 18.11.84, 8.8.85 and *Libération* 2.10.87.

[72] *La Tribune de l'Expansion* 12.10.88, 20.2.89, 9.6.89 and *Le Monde* 24.6.89, 30.7.89.

[73] Une autorité administrative indépendante, although recognised as such by courts before 1996.

The COB was further strengthened by legislation 2003.[74] It was renamed the Autorité des Marchés Financiers (AMF) and merged with two major self-regulatory bodies to widen its remit.[75] Moreover, it was given increased powers, notably to impose sanctions for breaches of law and regulation, and of professional codes that it had approved. It was recognised as a 'public independent authority' with its own legal personality, a significant advance since it allows the AMF to employ staff and use its revenues as it wishes. A major reason for the 2003 merger of the COB and self-regulatory bodies was that reforms in other countries had produced a single regulator for securities trading and that the French system of dual regulators was regarded as 'too complicated for foreigners'.[76] In particular, it was the French response to reforms in Britain (the creation of the FSA) and Germany (BaFin).[77] The changes were also born of a view that France had to meet international standards—otherwise its markets would lose out to competitors in Europe.[78] But perhaps the most important factor was EU regulation.[79] The 2003 directive on insider trading and market manipulation sought a 'single administrative body'.[80] More generally, simplification of regulators aided European integration and international cooperation.[81]

Thus between 1986 and 2005, the French sectoral regulator for securities had been transformed from a weak administrative body with limited independence into a much stronger organisation with its own legal personality, wider powers and a broader remit. Internationalisation played a major role in this development, which marked a sharp break from traditional French notions regarding administrative bodies and the regulation of markets.

(WEST) GERMANY

The Process of Reform

In the mid-1980s, West Germany had eight small regional stock exchanges that were owned by the regional governments (the *Länder*) and treated as public utilities. The exchanges were relatively unimportant in providing capital as few

---

[74] La loi Sécurité financière du 1er août (2003); for details, see Coquelet (2004), Frison-Roche (2004), and Thomasset-Pierre (2004).

[75] The Conseil des Marchés Financiers for investment service providers and the Conseil de discipline de la gestion financière which dealt with regulation of collective investment funds.

[76] Interview senior financial regulator 2; Decoopman (2003: 1817).

[77] Interview senior financial regulator 3 and senior financial practitioner 2; however, the AMF's remit remained more limited than the FSA's, especially concerning banking and insurance.

[78] Interview senior financial regulator 3.

[79] Frison-Roche (2004: paragraph 19) and Coquelet (2004: paragraph 1).

[80] European Council (2003: Article 11).

[81] Frison-Roche (2004: paragraph 19), Goulard (2003: 17), and Decoopman (2003).

companies were quoted or even established as joint stock companies.[82] Moreover, in practice, the banks dominated the financial system, including exchanges. There was no national sectoral regulator and most rules were either determined by the *Länder* or the exchanges and traders themselves.

By 2005, this situation had been transformed.[83] Policymakers had made the creation of a large, internationally competitive stock exchange their central aim. Indeed, Germany had one large predominant exchange (Deutsche Börse) that was a privately owned listed company. A federal regulator had been created together with formal rules to govern securities trading.

The changes were driven by the so-called 'Frankfurt coalition' that emerged in the late 1980s and 1990s. It was led by the traditionally dominant force in stock exchanges, namely German banks, mostly based in Frankfurt; the most important was Deutsche Bank (notably its head, Rolf Breuer).[84] The banks worked closely with the Frankfurt exchange, together with its home region (Land), Hessen.[85] In addition, the Federal Ministry of Finance gave sustained attention and leadership to stock exchange reform, with support from the central bank, the Bundesbank.[86]

The central strategy of reformers was to make the German stock market and financial institutions (*Finanzplatz Deutschland*) attractive to international capital to aid the financing of German companies and investment.[87] A key issue was increased competition for securities trading.[88] The use of information technology in share dealing, the expansion of cross-border trading, and increasing capital

---

[82] See Story (1997); in 1982, there were only 2,100 joint-stock companies of which 450 were listed on the exchange—Story (1997: 251–2); between 1956 and 1983, the number of listed companies fell from 686 to 442 (Pohl 1992: 323).

[83] For overviews, see Moran (1989, 1992) and Lütz (1998, 2002).

[84] For banks generally, see *Wirtschaftswoche* 3.1.86, *Handelsblatt* 16.10.87, *Frankfurter Allgemeiner Zeitung* 4.11.87, *Süddeutsche Zeitung* 27.9.88, and *Die Zeit* 17.10.91; for individual banks, see *Handelsblatt* 31.12.85, 26.6.86, 3.12.98, *Rheinischer Merkur* 14.6.91, *Wirtschaftswoche* 8.7.88, and *Süddeutsche Zeitung* 20.8.88; for Deutsche Bank, see *Handelsblatt* 3.7.85, 31.10.85, 9.6.86, 15.10.87, 22.4.88, 24.10.88, *Süddeutsche Zeitung* 27.4.89, *Die Welt* 27.4.90, and *Rheinischer Merkur* 14.6.91; interviews, senior banker 1 and 2 and senior exchange official 1.

[85] *Handelsblatt* 29.10.87, 23.11.95 and *Frankfurter Allgemeiner Zeitung* 12.5.87, 7.7.93; interview senior banker 1.

[86] *Handelsblatt* 11.11.90, 27.8.92, 22.7.96, 18.6.98, 28.3.2001, 10.9.2001, 17.1.2002, *Wirtschaftswoche* 30.8.91, *Süddeutsche Zeitung* 20.7.96, *Frankfurter Allgemeiner Zeitung* 4.4.97, and General-Anzeiger 24.1.90; speeches by Pöhl, Bundesbank president, *Tagesspiegel* 7.5.85, *Handelsblatt* 22.8.85, *Frankfurter Allgemeiner Zeitung* 24.6.89, *Wirtschaftswoche* 21.7.89, and *Süddeutsche Zeitung* 19.3.92; Bundesbank annual report—*Handelsblatt* 28.4.87, 15.4.88; interviews senior banker 1, senior Bundesbank official, senior exchange official 2 and 3, and senior regulator.

[87] Interviews senior banker 2, senior exchange official 3, and senior regulator.

[88] For its citation by different actors: Frankfurt stock exchange organisation—*Handelsblatt* 16.4.85; Karl Otto Pöhl, president of the Bundesbank, *Handelsblatt* 7.5.85, 22.8.85; reforms planned by the eight regional exchanges, *Handelsblatt* 22.4.86; presidents of the Düsseldorf and Frankfurt exchanges—*Handelsblatt* 31.12.86; Deutsche Bank, *Handelsblatt* 9.6.86, 15.10.87, 24.10.88; Wolfgang Röller, president of German banking association—*Handelsblatt* 31.10.85, 16.10.87, and *Süddeutsche Zeitung* 27.9.88; Federal Association of German Banks—*Frankfurter Allgemeiner Zeitung* 4.11.87; Bundesbank annual report—*Frankfurter Allgemeiner Zeitung* 15.4.88; see also *Handelsblatt* 7.8.87, 3.9.87.

mobility all created international competitive pressures on stock exchanges.[89] But urgency for change came from reforms in neighbouring nations, together with EU regulation. German exchanges were losing trading in domestic shares to London, New York, and Paris. London's 1986 Big Bang was of particular importance. On the one hand, it offered an example ('proof for the theory that a more liberalised industry environment would be beneficial');[90] indeed, it was more influential than the US, since the NYSE and SEC were seen as 'far away' and also open to criticism on grounds of being conservative and inefficient.[91] On the other hand, in the 1980s, London was seen as a major competitive threat. One senior member of the Frankfurt exchange coined the term 'Londonfurter'—shares issued in Frankfurt but traded in London.[92] Reformers underlined the extent to which German exchanges were backward and disadvantaged relative to others abroad.[93] Compared to Britain, Germany lacked a large, powerful central exchange, trading of overseas stocks, and a sector-specific regulator.

The effects of the EU also featured prominently in reform debates in three ways. First, the European Single Market and the introduction of the Euro increased competitive pressures, especially on Germany's regionalised system of exchanges.[94] The Frankfurt coalition argued that to function effectively in this market, Germany needed to modify its institutions—in particular, to create a strong national stock exchange and supervisory authority instead of regional markets and fragmented supervision.[95] Second, EU regulation had to be transposed into national law. In particular, EU provisions on investor protection and insider trading ran counter to Germany's traditional lack of legal penalties, and necessitated considerable legislative modification.[96] Third, implementing EU directives provided the

---

[89] Board member, Hamburg Vereins und Westbank—*Handelsblatt* 31.12.85; Ulricht Steiger, Economics Minister, Hessen—*Handelsblatt* 1.9.86; Alfred von Oppenheim, President of Düsseldorf exchange, Michael Hauck, Pres of Frankfurt Exchange and Steiger—*Handelsblatt* 31.12.86; Hermann Solms, FDP Financial affairs spokesman in Bundestag 30.11.88; *Wirstschaftswoche* 8.7.88.

[90] Quote interview senior banker 2; interviews senior exchange official 3 and 4.

[91] Interviews, senior exchange official 1 and 2 and senior Bundesbank official; the NYSE was criticised because of its system of specialists and its failure to introduce information technology, and the SEC for being too legalistic—interview senior banker 2.

[92] Hans Messer, president of the Frankfurt Chamber of Industry and Commerce IHK—Frankfurt Industrie und Handelskammer), *Handelsblatt* 3.9.87; Story (1997: 257–8, 261, 264) and Moran (1992: 146–8).

[93] See plans for reforms by the eight regional exchanges and prepared by the large banks—*Wirtschaftswoche* 3.1.86; first annual report of German Stock Exchanges' Association (Arbeitsgemeinschaft der Deutscher Wertpapierbörsen)—*VWD Europa* 5.6.87; article by W Hirche, Economics Minister Lower Saxony, *Handelsblatt* 21.7.89; cf. *Die Welt* 31.5.85, *Wirtschaftswoche* 8.7.88, *Handelsblatt* 29.11.89.

[94] *Handelsblatt* 15.2.80, *Süddeutsche Zeitung* 20.8.88, and *Frankfurter Allgemeiner Zeitung* 7.11.89; cf. Story (1997: 258); interview senior banker 2.

[95] Rolf Breuer, Deutsche Bank, *Die Welt* 27.4.90, Rüdiger von Rosen, 'Working group of German stock exchanges', *VWD Europa* 29.10.90; Banking Association call for major reform—*Handelsblatt* 12.11.96; Hessen Economics Minister and Deutsche Börse head, *Handelsblatt* 23.11.95, 11.9.96; CDU/CSU parliamentary financial experts, 7.7.96, the *Financial Times* 10.7.96; Gerhard Eberstadt, Dresder Bank Board, and *Handelsblatt* 3.12.98.

[96] *Handelsblatt* 8.12.88, *The Economist* 11.3.89, *Süddeutsche Zeitung* 14.6.89, and *Die Welt* 20.6.89.

occasion for self-criticism, cross-national comparison, and major reform legislation.[97] Indeed, it was used to justify wider changes not required by EU law, notably
the creation of a specialised independent federal agency and the introduction of
electronic trading.[98] Reforms met considerable resistance. The *Länder* and some of the smaller
regional exchanges opposed increases in federal powers, which they saw as weakening regional markets and their regulatory role.[99] This was important because
legislation needed to be passed by both houses of parliament, including the Bundesrat, which was composed of representatives of the *Länder*. The exchanges and
banks in the late 1980s and early 1990s attacked 'juridification' and obstructed
the creation of a 'German SEC', which they claimed was unnecessary; instead they
urged the continuation of self-regulation.[100] Indeed, there was general hostility
to an open market in equities and the 'Anglo-American' practice of contested
takeovers.[101]

Discussions were thus lengthy and difficult. However, gradually, broad agreement on certain changes developed, notably between the banks, regional
exchanges, and *Länder*. International factors were central in the alteration of
strategies of the key supporters of previous institutional arrangements (especially
the banks and exchanges), in the formation of the Frankfurt coalition and in
its ability to justify change. The outcome was that between 1986 and 2003, no
fewer than five pieces of legislation were passed: the *Börsenzulassungsgesetz* (stock
exchange admission regulations) of 1986, the 1989 *Börsengesetz* (Stock Market
Act) and then the first, second, third, and fourth Financial Market Promotion
Acts in 1990, 1994, 1998, and 2002. The later legislation involved fundamental changes that ran contrary to traditional German institutional structures for
financial markets.

Substantive Reforms

The Organisation and Ownership of the Stock Exchanges

During the late 1980s large commercial banks and some stock exchanges, notably
Frankfurt, became concerned that trading would go abroad, especially to LSE,
which enjoyed advantages of existing international clients, electronic trading, and

---

[97] *Handlesblatt* 14.8.91, 10.3.93, 28.12.94, 21.6.96, 22.7.96, 10.9.2001, *Frankfurter Allgemeiner Zeitung* 4.7.91, 21.6.96, *Süddeutsche Zeitung* 20.7.96, and *Wirtschaftswoche* 28.6.91, 30.8.91; interview senior exchange official 2.

[98] See comments by Rüdiger von Rosen, head of German stock exchanges working party, *Welt am Sonntag* 3.2.91, *Handelsblatt* 14.8.91, 31.10.91, Germany's oldest and largest association for private investors, the Deutsche Schutzvereinigung für Wertpapierbesitz (DSW), *Handelsblatt* 29.4.92.

[99] Story (1997: 256); DBT 26.4.91, *Rheinischer Merkur* 14.6.91, *Wirtschaftswoche* 30.8.91, 28.2.92, *Die Zeit* 17.10.91, *Süddeutsche Zeitung* 15.2.92, and *Handelsblatt* 17.1.2002.

[100] Alfred Schmidt, head of Stock Exchange Supervisory authority (*Börsenaufsichtsamt*), *Handels-blatt* 26.1.90, Rolf Breuer, Deutsche Bank, *Die Welt* 27.4.90, *Frankfurter Allgemeiner Zeitung* 11.10.90, *The Economist* 31.8.91, *The Times* 28.10.91, and *Handelsblatt* 23.8.93, 3.9.93.

[101] Story (1997: 255–6, 264–5), and Lütz (1998: 160).

the 1986 Big Bang.[102] (Interestingly, they saw the NYSE as backward in keeping floor trading and hence not a positive example.)[103] They argued that Germany had to alter its fragmented and state-dominated institutional framework.[104] Federal and *Länder* policy makers gradually accepted this view.[105]

An initial step came with the 1989 Stock Market Act. Until then, trading in futures and options was forbidden by law.[106] To take advantage of this situation, London and Paris created futures markets in German shares in 1988 specifically designed to attract trading in German-listed companies.[107] Fear of loss of business to these overseas exchanges was the driving force for reformers, led by large banks, to seek changes in the law.[108] Other policy makers, such as federal government politicians, the Frankfurt Stock Exchange, and the association of stock exchanges also called for a new exchange to stem loss of business abroad.[109] As a result, the 1989 Stock Exchange law allowed the creation of a financial futures exchange, the Deutsche Terminbörse (DTB), which was financed by the large banks and began operating in 1989.[110] The DTB marked a major innovation for the organisation of German exchanges and a political breakthrough for the Frankfurt coalition.[111] It was a German-wide exchange, breaking with the principle of regional exchanges and was based in Frankfurt, further enhancing the city's financial pre-eminence. It only had institutional members, mostly large commercial banks, and was fully electronic, eliminating a physical trading floor. It was created despite strong hostility to 'speculation', lack of any tradition since 1934 and opposition by the brokers (*Makler*) who feared the loss of the physical trading floor.[112]

The next step was to concentrate securities trading within Germany in a privately owned organisation. The process was led by the large banks (especially Deutsche Bank and Dresdner Bank), who claimed it was needed to increase efficiency and attract international capital; their key example was London's Big Bang.[113] Initially, they sought to subsume all the regional exchanges into a national German stock exchange that would compete with overseas rivals, notably London. But this failed due to considerable resistance by regional exchanges and

---

[102] *Handelsblatt* 31.12.86, 6.3.87, *Wirtschaftswoche* 7.8.87, *Handelsblatt* 3.9.87, 29.10.87, 24.3.88, 16.2.89, *Frankfurter Rundschau* 24.3.88, *Süddeutsche Zeitung* 24.3.88, and *Frankfurter Allgemeiner Zeitung* 9.6.89; interviews senior banker 2 and senior exchange official 1.

[103] Interviews senior banker 2 and senior exchange official 3.

[104] Rolf Breuer, Deutsche Bank, *Handelsblatt* 9.6.86; Michael Hauck, president of Frankfurt Stock Exchange Handelsblatt 31.12.86; Friedrich von Metzler, president, Frankfurt Stock Exchange, *Handelsblatt*, 24.1.90, Rüdiger von Rosen, Working Group of German stock exchanges, *VWD Europe* 29.10.90, Rolf Breuer, Deustche Bank, *Rheinischer Merkur* 14.6.91, *The Economist* 31.8.91, *Handelsblatt* 8.1.98, and Gerhardt Eberstadt, Dresdner Bank, *Handelsblatt*, 3.12.98.

[105] *Frankfurter Allgemeiner Zeitung* 12.5.87, 4.11.87, 15.4.88, 13.12.88, 24.6.89, *Handelsblatt* 1.9.86, 12.12.86, 29.10.87, 24.3.88, 29.11.88, Dr Hermann Solms FDP spokesman for financial matters in the Bundestag, *Frankfurter Allgemeiner Zeitung* 30.11.88, and *Wirtschaftswoche* 19.2.88, 8.7.88, 17.2.89.

[106] Under the 1934 Banking Law.   [107] Story (1997: 263–4).

[108] Interviews senior banker 2, senior exchange official 1 and 3.

[109] *Handelsblatt* 3.9.87, 18.9.87 and *VWD Europa* 5.6.87.   [110] Story (1997: 263–4).

[111] Moran (1992: 147–8); interviews senior banker 2 and senior exchange official 2.

[112] Interviews senior banker 2, senior exchange official 1 and 3.

[113] Interviews, senior Bundesbank official, senior banker 1, senior exchange official 1, 3, and 3.

the *Länder* governments.[114] A more indirect approach was then applied. The Frankfurt Stock Exchange was taken out of the hands of the Frankfurt Chamber of Commerce and transformed into a private law company, Deutsche Börse AG. This then became a holding company which owned several subsidiaries: some provided common services to all regional exchanges, notably for clearing and settlement, information technology, and electronic information; one owned the Frankfurt exchange; another owned the DTB. The main shareholders in Deutsche Börse were the banks, but the regional exchanges were also given shares, thereby allaying concerns about a takeover by Frankfurt. The result was that a single powerful organisation emerged. Although the regional exchanges continued to exist, most business (perhaps 90%) went through Deutsche Börse.

Deutsche Börse soon moved away from a physical trading floor towards an electronic system. A national information system, Inter–Banken–Informations system (IBIS) was established in 1989 and then transformed into an electronic trading and settlements system (named Xetra by 1997) designed to match overseas exchanges.[115] An important reason was that traders looked at similar systems in operation in London and Paris and feared loss of business to them, especially to LSE's SEAQ-I.[116] They drew parallels with the move of German futures trading to the other two exchanges in the 1980s.[117]

Deutsche Börse also sought overseas expansion. It believed that 'consolidation was overdue' among European exchanges to attract international investors, reap economies of scale and create a pan-European market in equities.[118] It was also attracted by the prospect of remote membership of exchanges that was legally permitted under the EC's 1993 ISD, but which in practice met obstacles from national regulatory authorities (NRAs) concerned to defend their exchanges.[119] Although the German federal government was not directly involved, it agreed that consolidation was needed in Europe to compete with the NYSE and Asian exchanges.[120] In the 1990s, Deutsche Börse tried to create links with the Paris Bourse, beginning with a joint trading system for their respective futures exchanges, the MATIF and the DTB. The plan failed at the final hurdle due to opposition by the Paris brokers who feared German 'domination'.[121] Thereafter, Deutsche Börse turned its attentions to LSE. In 2000 it attempted to merge with LSE and create an international exchange. It acted despite warnings of negative effects on Germany's domestic financial services industry.[122] Although the merger was unsuccessful, as were later attempts (see Chapter 4 on Britain), Deutsche Börse implemented

---

[114] *Frankfurter Rundschau* 28.4.90, *Frankfurter Allgemeiner Zeitung* 16.6.90, *Die Zeit* 24.1.92, the *Wall Street Journal* 8.10.92, DBT 26.4.91, *Rheinischer Merkur* 14.6.91, *The Economist* 31.8.91, *Capital* 1.9.91, and *Handelsblatt* 31.3.95; interviews senior banker 1 and 2, and senior exchange official 1 and 4, senior Bundesbank official.

[115] *Handelsblatt* 29.11.89; Lütz (2002: 236); Breuer and *Die Welt* 27.4.90, *Wirstachaftswoche* 28.6.91, *Frankfurter Allgemeiner Zeitung* 4.7.91, and *Handelsblatt* 23.11.95, 12.10.98.

[116] Interviews senior exchange official 1 and 4.   [117] Interview senior exchange official 4.

[118] Interview senior banker 2.   [119] Interview senior exchange official 1.

[120] Interview senior government official 1.   [121] Interviews senior exchange official 1 and 4.

[122] *Handelsblatt* 16.6.2000.

a key element of the plan, namely becoming a publicly-listed company in order to obtain financial flexibility for overseas expansion (in Europe but also the US).[123]

Thus by 2005, in sharp contrast to its earlier position as home of several small exchanges, Germany had one large national stock exchange operating with electronic trading of shares. That exchange was a privately owned quoted company seeking to become an internationally competitive exchange.

Competition in Trading of Securities

In 1986, official market brokers (*Kursmakler*) were appointed by the regional governments and traded as individuals. They had a monopoly over trading on exchanges. Although much trading took place off-exchanges, especially by the banks, the *Kursmakler* set the public prices at which trades were to be conducted.

The position of the *Kursmakler* was soon weakened in the 1980s. Their monopoly was not extended to new markets such as the futures exchange, the DTB (created in 1989). Moreover, banks and financial institutions were able to trade directly in the new electronic systems established in the 1990s (IBIS and then Xetra). The 2002 Financial Markets Promotion Act ended public price fixing for share trading. Thus the *Kursmakler* were largely rendered obsolete and many brokers filed for bankruptcy or merged or formed joint-stock companies. Securities trading and price setting were now open to competition, undertaken electronically and mostly in the hands of large financial institutions, rather than being the preserve of publicly appointed individuals.[124]

Regulatory Organisations

After 1986, considerable debate took place in Germany over whether a federal sectoral regulator with legal powers should be established to replace the traditional combination of oversight by the *Länder* and self-regulation by the exchanges. Reformers argued that significant powers should be given to a new agency, especially to outlaw insider trading and increase legal supervision of exchanges. However, change initially faced strong opposition. The *Länder* fiercely attacked any reduction of their role and proposed an inter-state supervisory agency.[125] They and the banks were hostile to increased federal legal regulation and the loss of self-regulation.[126] Moreover, the major overseas example of a sectoral regulator, the SEC, was treated by bankers and policy makers with suspicion due to its legalism

---

[123] Interviews senior exchange official 4 and senior Bundesbank official.

[124] *Handelsblatt*, 9.11.1999, 20.8.2002; interviews senior exchange official 1 and senior exchange official 2.

[125] *Wirtschaftswoche* 28.2.92 and *Handelsblatt* 27.8.92, 18.6.98, 17.1.2002; Lütz (1998: 164).

[126] *Wirtschaftswoche* 30.8.91, *Handelsblatt* 29.4.92, 23.8.93, 3.9.93, 12.6.97, and *Frankfurter Allgemeiner Zeitung* 8.10.96, 25.4.2002, 26.4.2002; interview senior exchange official 3.

and inflexibility—it was a 'horror picture' and policy makers wanted 'everything except the SEC'.[127]

International factors played a significant role in change. Reformers put forward the model of a powerful independent regulator that would punish offences, as part of the strategy of making German markets internationally accepted and attractive.[128] More specifically, the federal government, with support from the exchanges' association, claimed that Germany needed a national regulator to cooperate with overseas regulators (especially the SEC) over cross-border issues.[129] Thus, for example, cross-border memorandums of understanding (MOUs) between regulators became more important in the late 1980s because of US pressure on other nations to assist in regulation. But when the SEC sought to sign cross-border MOU with Germany and cooperate on insider trading in the late 1980s, it found no counterpart, and sought (or even demanded) an equivalent German authority to work with.[130] Pressure was increased by SEC decisions to prohibit the sale of German options in the US on the grounds that Germany lacked sufficiently high-regulatory standards.[131] Moreover, in international fora (e.g. the international organisation of securities regulators, IOSCO), Germany was disadvantaged by the absence of a specialised agency and the inadequate skills and resources of the *Länder*.[132] In addition, German exchanges such as the DTB were competing with overseas rivals for foreign members, and sought a clear regulatory framework.[133] As a result of these factors, by the late 1990s, even large banks believed that regional regulators were inadequate and supported a federal agency in order to attract international trading.[134]

Transposition of EU regulation aided the process of reform, in the face of continuing resistance to a federal sectoral regulator. The degree of legal imposition by the EU was low. Instead, EU regulation was used to trigger and justify wider reforms, which proceeded through limited steps and compromises. Thus the EU directive on insider trading passed in 1989 and the 1993 ISD[135] required member states to specify a securities supervisory body that would undertake coordination with other member states and participate in a network of regulators. Although

---

[127] Quote, interview senior banker 2; interview, senior exchange official 1.

[128] *Der Spiegel* 7.1.91, *Welt am Sonntag* 3.2.91, *Wirtschaftswoche* 28.6.91, *Frankfurter Allgemeiner Zeitung* 4.7.91, *Handelsblatt* 5.7.91, 14.8.91, 12.9.2001, 10.10.2001, *Rheinischer Merkur* 12.7.91, and the *Wall Street Journal* 21.6.96; interviews senior exchange official 2, senior regulator, and senior banker 2.

[129] Lütz (1998); Rüdiger von Rosen, head of German stock exchanges working party, Georg Wittich, president of Federal Securities Office, BAWe, *Handelsblatt* 27.9.96 and 31.7.98; *Welt am Sonntag* 3.2.91, *Handelsblatt* 14.8.91, 1.10.91, 29.4.92, 27.8.92, 18.6.98, 31.7.98, 28.3.2001, *Die Zeit* 24.1.92, and *Wirtschaftswoche* 28.2.92, *Frankfurter Allgemeiner Zeitung* 18.6.94; interviews senior government official 1, senior exchange official 1 and 2.

[130] *VWD Europa* 29.10.90; Moran (1991).   [131] Lütz (1998: 160).

[132] Lütz (1998: 161–2); cf. Lütz (2000: 157–8); interview senior regulator; cf. interview senior exchange official 2.

[133] Interview senior regulator.

[134] Interviews senior government official 1, senior exchange official 1, and senior regulator; for instance, even the Frankfurt state regulator had only 10 people for stock exchanges.

[135] Council (1989, 1993*a*).

EU directives did not specify the form of such a body reformers claimed that they necessitated a national agency.[136] Hence the second Financial Market Promotion Act 1994 established a new Federal Securities Supervisory Office, the Bundesaufsichtsamt für den Wertpapierhandel—BAWe. The BAWe's responsibilities included surveillance of large share deals, making market conduct rules, enforcement of insider trading rules, and representing Germany at the international level. The BAWe was a first step towards an independent sectoral regulator, but it fell within the jurisdiction of the Ministry of Finance, limiting its independence, and it did not regulate the supervision of markets and trading, which remained within the jurisdiction of the *Länder*.[137]

Further steps came in 2002 under the Fourth Financial Market Promotion Act, in which the federal government increased the powers and independence of the BAWe, which was renamed Bundesanstelt für Finanzdienstleitungsaufsicht (BaFin). The move was strongly influenced by further EU demands that the *Länder* found evermore difficult to fulfil and by the example of Britain creating the FSA, which was seen as successfully bringing together different financial sectors and offering a coordinated approach to regulation.[138] BaFin's responsibilities were greatly widened across the financial sector, following criticism of the separation of responsibilities for regulating financial services among different regulatory organisations.[139] Despite resistance by the *Länder*, BaFin's powers over market behaviour were also widened, notably over money laundering and information.[140] Although BaFin remained within the responsibilities of the Finance Ministry, it was to be financed by market participants (in a manner similar to the FSA) in order to attract good staff by offering better pay than the ordinary civil service and hence be effective both nationally and internationally.[141] Moreover, BaFin's president and vice-president are nominated by the federal government, and its budget approved by an 'administrative council' that includes several representatives of the Federal Finance Ministry, thus underlining the role of the federal government rather than the *Länder*.

BaFin represented a compromise between traditions and the need to 'modernise' to adapt to international standards.[142] Nevertheless, it meant that by 2005, Germany had a federal sectoral regulator for securities trading, which was responsible for much direct supervision of markets, in large measure replacing the *Länder*.

---

[136] Lütz (1998: 158–9, 163); *VWD Europa* 29.10.90, *Welt am Sonntag* 3.2.91, *Wirtschaftswoche* 28.6.91, *Frankfurter Allgemeiner Zeitung* 4.7.91, *Capital* 1.9.91, and *Handelsblatt* 29.4.92, 10.9.2001.

[137] *Handelsblatt* 21.1.93.

[138] Interviews senior banker 2 and senior regulator; Lütz (2002: 247); *Handelsblatt*, 17.10.01, 8.5.01.

[139] Broadly BaFin took over the BAWe's responsibilities for shares, the Bundesaufsichtsamt für Kreditwesen's (BAKred) for banking and the Versicherungswesen's for insurance—*Handelsblatt* 26.5.94, 28.12.94, 7.7.96, 22.3.2000, 18.12.2000, 19.12.2000, the *Financial Times* 10.7.96.

[140] *Handelsblatt* 17.1.2002, 13.3.2002, 21.3.2002 and *Frankfurter Allgemeiner Zeitung* 25.4.2002, 126.4.2002, 16.5.2003.

[141] Interview senior banker 2 and senior government official 1.   [142] Lütz (2002: 246–8).

ITALY

The Process of Reform

In the mid-1980s, Italian stock exchanges were small and fragmented across several cities. Trading on the exchanges was the monopoly of the *Agenti di Cambio*, who were public officials and did business as individuals. But most large share trading took place off the exchanges through the banks.

Reform debates began in mid-1980s. But, the *Agenti* were divided and there was no political will to introduce reform.[143] Only in the 1990s did the position change as new forces began to operate. Although some were domestic (notably the need for a more liquid market due to privatisations and the growth of mutual funds),[144] two international factors provided direct pressures for new institutions. First, policy makers looked at overseas stock exchanges, especially London's Big Bang and subsequent reforms in France.[145] They not only saw examples of new institutions but also enhanced competition for trading shares in large Italian companies.[146] The small size of Italian exchanges became seen as a problem given international competition: the head of Consob pointed out that the value of trades in 1989 was $220 billion in Milan, compared with $469 billion for Paris, $402 billion for Frankfurt, and $1,804 billion for London.[147] Second, EU regulation provided another powerful force for change.[148] It operated directly because the EU's 1993 ISD was transposed into Italian law through the 1996 Eurosim decree no.415/96.[149] More indirectly, transposition provided the occasion for wide-ranging reforms not required under EU law, notably the privatisation of the stock exchange, aided by fears of the competitive pressures on Italian exchanges because of EU liberalisation.

International pressures aided key domestic actors, notably banks, the *Agenti* and the government, to push through reforms despite weak coalition governments and seemingly interminable parliamentary discussions. By 2005, the institutional structure had been radically modified, notably the ownership and concentration of the exchanges and the position of the banks.

---

[143] For an overview, see Ferrarini (1998); *Il sole 24 Ore* 4.1.85, 19.1.85, 27.1.85, 1.5.87, 2.9.89, 4.1.85, 25.7.90.

[144] Interviews senior official, senior practitioner; *Il sole 24 Ore* 2.1.90.

[145] Interview senior official; *Il sole 24 Ore* 7.12.97.

[146] Nardozzi and Vaciago (1994: 15–14) and *Il sole 24 Ore* 31.3.90, 14.6.90.

[147] 18.7.90; interview with Cavazzuti, deputato from the left, 26.11.90; The capitalisation of Italian exchanges was only 16% of GDP in 1993, compared with 38% for France and 124% for Britain, and was lower than that of Madrid or even Amsterdam and Zurich, *Il sole 24 Ore* 18.6.94; 11.5.2001; Arzillo (1999).

[148] Cassese (2000: 262–72); see *Il sole 24 Ore* 14.6.90.

[149] Known as the 'Draghi law' after the then director of the Treasury Maria Draghi; cf. *Il sole 24 Ore* 23.3.96, 16.7.96.

Substantive Reforms

Competition in Securities Trading

Two major related factors weakened Italian stock exchanges in the mid-1980s: the *Agenti di Cambio* were individuals with little capital; the majority of large trades took place outside the exchanges, mostly by the banks, which had financial capital to buy on their own account but were excluded by law from the exchanges.[150] After discussions in the mid-1980s led by the sectoral regulator Consob, the Senate passed a bill altering the position of the *Agenti*. Yet the legislation was held up in the lower house for almost two years, due in large measure to turf battles between Consob, the Banca d'Italia, and the Treasury over the allocation of regulatory responsibilities.[151]

However, by 1990–1, the key domestic actors—the *Agenti*, Treasury, Consob, Banca d'Italia and banks—increased the pressure for change. Indeed, the *Agenti* even went on strike to protest against delays in reform.[152] A key argument was that Italian exchanges faced international competition for business from other European exchanges, especially London's new SEAQ-International exchange. Major Italian companies were quoted on SEAQ-International and by 1990, trading of shares in these companies reached 30% of the levels in Milan.[153] EU regulation (notably the 1993 ISD which was then under discussion), allowing the trading of shares abroad with 'home country control', was argued to greatly increase the competitive threat to Milan.[154] In addition, EU regulation permitted overseas firms to enter the Italian market, including by taking over banks and by remote access to the Italian stock exchanges, created further fears of losing trading to foreign firms.[155]

In the face of these pressures, conflicts over regulatory boundaries were settled[156] and a law was finally passed in 1991.[157] It allowed the formation of companies that could trade on the exchanges (SIMS—società di intermediazione finanzaria) and in which banks could take a share.[158] SIMS were designed to increase the financial capacities of traders and allow the banks to enter the exchanges. They were authorised to trade on their own account, increasing market liquidity. Their activities were also extended well beyond trading quoted shares

---

[150] Interviews senior practitioner; *Il sole 24 Ore* 19.2.90.

[151] Ferrarini (1998); *Il sole 24 Ore* 2.9.89, 3.1.90, 3.3.90,12.6.90, 14.6.90, 2.8.90, 23.11.90, 23.11.90, 7.12.90, 16.12.90.

[152] *Il sole 24 Ore* 3.1.90; 19.10.90, 1.12.90.

[153] *Il sole 24 Ore* 16.6.90; cf. 31.3.90, 14.6.90; cf. 10.5.90, 18.7.90.

[154] Terzo (2000, 2204); *Il sole 24 Ore* 31.3.90, 10.5.90, 14.6.90.

[155] cf. interview, Enzo Berlanda, president of the Consob, *Il sole 24 Ore* 19.10.96.

[156] cf. *Il sole 24 Ore* 23.6.90.

[157] Legge 2 gennaio 1991, n. 1. Disciplina dell'attività di intermediazione mobiliare e disposizioni sull'organizzazione dei mercati mobiliari (SIM); for a critique, see Vaciago (1994).

[158] The law protected the *Agenti* by imposing a lengthy transition period before (2 years), during which time the SIMs could not be majority owned by banks or most other financial institutions.

(e.g. to providing advice). At the same time, the bill imposed a principle of 'concentration', namely an obligation to pass orders through an exchange ('regulated market') unless explicitly authorised by the client and at better prices than offered on the exchange, thereby increasing the incentives for banks to trade on the exchanges. Hence the law greatly strengthened the position of the exchanges.

The Organisation and Ownership of Exchanges

In the mid-1980s, Italy had several stock exchanges, which were controlled by the Chamber of Commerce of the city in which they were located, under legislation dating from 1913. The banks had been pressing for reform since the late 1980s, but without success. However, by the mid-1990s, the *Agenti* and political parties of Left and Right had accepted the need for a single national stock market, computerisation and privatisation.[159]

The most important and direct reason for the acceptance of change was the need to meet international competition from overseas stock exchanges.[160] Migration of share trading to other European exchanges aided by European integration, was particularly underlined.[161] Italy had to create a more innovative and efficient exchange, and increase modernisation. Finally, reform was designed to draw the banks (which were larger and hence better placed to meet overseas competitors) further into securities trading on the exchange.[162] Transformation of the stock exchange into a private company was claimed to be the best way of achieving these aims, as it would provide greater autonomy, incentives for entrepreneurship, and capital for investment.[163]

The law of 1991 began change by transferring control over the exchanges from the city chambers of commerce to a Council, nominated by the Treasury Minister and composed of members chosen by the relevant regulatory organizations, traders and other relevant financial bodies. It also allowed the Consob to insist that all the exchanges be linked by computers, so that trading in fact took place on a single electronic market. But more radical change came when transposition of the EU's ISD provided the occasion for reform through the 1996 Eurosim decree. The decree closed the regional Borse and made the Milan exchange into a company— Borsa Italiana—that was then privatised in 1997 (these changes were of course

[159] Interviews senior regulator 1 and 2, senior practitioner, and senior official; *Il sole 24 Ore* 7.11.92, 17.5.96; for the process, see Ferrarini (36–60).

[160] Draghi (1999) and Cristini (1999); *Il sole 24 Ore* 7.10.96; 10.5.97, article by Francesco Cesarini, president of the Consiglio di Borsa; interview Benito Boschetto, amministratore of Borse Italia, *Il sole 24 Ore* 31.5.97; comments by Carlo Ciampi, then Treasury Minister, *Il sole 24 Ore* 26.6.97; 2.7.97 (comments by Tomaso Padoa-Schioppa head of Consob); *Il sole 24 Ore* 16.7.97; 9.10.97 (interview with Padoa-Schioppa head of Consob).

[161] *Il sole 24 Ore* 7.10.96, 15.1.97 (presentation by Mario Draghi), 7.2.97, 16.7.97.

[162] Cristini (1999) and Arzillo (1999).

[163] *Il sole 24 Ore* 10.5.97, article by Francesco Cesarini, president of the Consiglio di Borsa; 16.7.97; interview Benito Boschetto, amministratore of Borse Italiana 31.5.97; 9.10.97 (interview with Padoa-Schioppa head of Consob).

not required by EU law).[164] The examples of overseas exchanges (such as Deutsche Börse and the LSE) were important in the decision to sell Borsa Italiana as a profit-making company that could attract a wide range of investors, in contrast to earlier plans for a non-profit-making consortium of existing market intermediaries.[165] In 1997 Borsa Italiana was sold by public auction; buyers were overwhelmingly financial institutions, particularly banks and traders (SIMS) who by 1997 were mostly owned by Italian banks.[166] In 2005, planning was well advanced for Borse Italiana to become a listed company, in order to create international alliances.[167]

Thus by 2005, Italy had moved from several small publicly owned exchanges to one private company. The 1990s saw rapid growth in both absolute and relative terms for Borsa Italiana. Its capitalisation rose from 10% of GDP in 1993 to 60% by 2001, and it overtook other European exchanges to become the fourth largest after LSE, Frankfurt and Paris.[168]

Regulatory Organisations

Although the Consob was a long-standing regulator, its main powers concerned information rather than securities trading. It was seen as weak and subject to being bypassed by other public bodies, notably the Banca d'Italia which was the main banking regulator and responsible for ensuring the stability of financial organisations.[169] Yet between 1986 and 2005 Consob was progressively strengthened.[170] Although EU regulation rarely mandated the changes, it gave an impetus to reform.[171] Thus in 1991, as part of the transposition of EU regulation on insider trading, Consob's powers over the provision of information were strengthened. Then the mid-1990s saw major debates on the role of Consob.[172] In particular, financial intermediaries argued that the regulator should become an external regulator, with the exchange itself making most rules for matters such as transparency, settlement, and listing.[173] One reason was to accompany the privatisation of the stock exchange as a profit-making company.[174] However, another reason was that greater competition among exchanges, itself increased by EU regulation, also enhanced pressures for a more efficient and advantageous regulatory system. Policymakers believed that although the EU's 1993 ISD did not impose a particular form of regulatory organisation, its liberalisation measures meant that member states had to adopt attractive, efficient, and low-cost regulatory structures.[175]

---

[164] For analysis, see Morelli (1999); for a concise overview, see Mezzacapo (1999).

[165] Ferrarini (1998: 39–41).

[166] Ferrarini (1998: 51–2) and Cesarini (1998); *Il sole 24 Ore* 6.10.97.

[167] This became possible after the December 2005 law on saving—*La Republicca* 28.12.2005.

[168] *Il sole 24 Ore* 11.5.2001.

[169] cf. Cassese (1986); for battles with the Bank of Italy, over the 1991 SIMS law—*Il sole 24 Ore* 12.6.90, 23.6.90, 2.8.90, 23.11.90.

[170] See Cassese (2000: 262–72).   [171] Cassese (2000: 265).

[172] Ferrarini (1998: 36–46) and Vella (1998).

[173] *Il sole 24 Ore* 1.3.97, article by Francesco Cesarini president of the Consiglio di Borsa *Il sole 24 Ore* 10.5.97.

[174] Interview senior official.   [175] Vella (1998: 481–2).

Following these pressures, and despite Consob's historical weakness, the 1996 law sought to move towards what reformers claimed was the Anglo-Saxon model, namely self-regulation within a statutory framework.[176] Borsa Italia achieved greater 'self-regulation' ('autoregolamentazione'), meaning that it was empowered to set its own rules, notably over listing and codes to ensure that the market functioned properly, instead of the Consob, which now became responsible for approving those rules and ensuring that they were properly enforced.[177] More-over, Consob's powers over market behaviour were strengthened, as well as its autonomy (e.g. through levies to finance its costs and greater freedom over recruitment of personnel).[178]

CONCLUSION

In 1986, France, Germany, and Italy still maintained many of their traditional institutions. Stock exchanges were publicly owned. Trading took place by open cry on their physical floors, often for only a few hours each day. It was the well-established monopoly of publicly appointed traders, who operated as individuals.

Alongside these common features, important differences existed across the three nations. In West Germany and Italy, trading was fragmented across several regional/city exchanges and banks carried out most trading off the exchanges, whereas in France, the Paris Bourse dominated trading. France and Italy had weak national sectoral regulators, whereas in West Germany most regulation was by regional authorities. Each nation had specific rules about types of market—for instance, futures trading was banned in West Germany while France had two markets for the same stocks, and severe restrictions on brokers trading on their own account. These key features are summarised in Table 5.1.

Between 1986 and 2005, these institutional features were greatly altered. The monopoly of individual brokers was ended; instead, entry was allowed for companies, including banks. Stock exchanges were privatised, and became profit-making companies that were quoted (in France and Germany) or planned to be (in Italy). The exchanges sought to internationalise through overseas alliances and mergers. Physical trading floors and limited hours gave way to all-day electronic trading. National specificities such as prohibitions on future markets in Germany or restrictions on brokers dealing on their own account and a free credit market in France were ended. All three countries had national sectoral regulators that had been strengthened over time. Although differences remained in 2005, especially

[176] Ferrarini (1998: 45) and Vella (1998).

[177] Its decisions then being susceptible to review and challenge by Consob—article, Francesco Cesarini, president of Borsa Italia, *Il sole 24 Ore* 10.5.97.

[178] Following domestic scandals (such as the Parmalat shares and Cirio bonds), the Consob was further strengthened by legislation in 2005 (Legge 262 of 28 December 2005) that was primarily designed to transpose the EU's market abuse directive; in particular, Consob gained more powers to ensure disclosure of information by listed companies and over the auditing of listed companies.

Table 5.1. Major institutional features of securities trading in 1986

Institutional feature	France	West Germany	Italy
Organisational position of stock exchanges	Publicly owned trading by *Agents de change*—publicly appointed individuals with personal liability—in Paris Bourse; two markets (*à terme* and *au comptant*)	Publicly owned by regional Chambers of Commerce; trading on exchanges by official brokers (*Kursmakler*) appointed by regional exchange supervisory authorities (*Borsenaufsichtsbehorde*) as individuals with personal liability; domination by banks; no futures market permitted	Publicly owned under control of city chambers of commerce. Trading in exchanges by *Agenti di Cambio*—publicly appointed individuals with personal liability
Competition	Legal monopoly for *Agents de change*	Legal monopoly over trading on exchanges and price setting for official brokers; domination of trading by banks	Legal monopoly for *Agenti di Cambio*, but most trading by banks
Allocation of regulatory powers	Weak sectoral regulator, COB	Regional governments (Länder) responsible for legal supervision of their exchanges; shared powers with federal government	Weak sectoral regulator, Consob

over the centralisation of regulatory powers (between Germany's more decentralised system and the other two countries' single national sectoral regulator), these were less than in 1986. Moreover, differences with institutions found in Britain had greatly diminished (see Chapter 4). The new institutional framework is summarised in Table 5.2.

Reforms were led by domestic actors, notably governments and banks, usually with support from central banks and the leadership of the major stock exchange. They met resistance from traditionally powerful actors, especially brokers, and in Germany, also from the Länder and sometimes the banks. International factors were crucial in the formation, determination, and arguments of domestic reform coalitions and their capacity to drive through and legitimate new institutions. Indeed, decisions such as allowing banks and other financial institutions to take over brokers and enter stock markets or the privatisation of exchanges were part of deliberate policies to encourage the formation of large financial entities that had sufficient capital to compete internationally. Equally, creating and strengthening sectoral regulators were justified in terms of attracting foreign capital by ensuring regulatory frameworks that were recognised as 'respectable' by overseas investors and international bodies.

Table 5.2. Institutional features of securities trading in 2005

Institutional feature	France	West Germany	Italy
Organisational position of stock exchanges	Listed company, part of international group (Euronext)	Dominant exchange, Deutsche Börse, listed company; attempts to take over overseas exchanges	One national exchange, Borse Italia; privately-owned company, listing planned
Competition in trading	Brokers open to take over and entry allowed for companies, including banks	Brokers open to take over and entry allowed for companies, including banks	Brokers open to take over and entry allowed for companies, including banks
Allocation of regulatory powers	Strengthened sectoral regulator, AMF	Strengthened federal sectoral regulator BaFin; significant powers remain with regional governments (Länder)	Strengthened sectoral regulator, Consob

Which forms of internationalisation were important in the institutional transformations? Transnational technological and economic developments continued to put pressures on traditional national economic institutions. Thus increased capital demands for computerisation of exchanges and trading on their own account posed difficulties for brokers operating as single individuals. However, these factors were often in the background in reform debates. Moreover, they had been present since the 1970s and had failed to lead to changes—indeed, an alternative off-exchange bank-led model seemed a possible alternative in Germany and Italy due to ineffective domestic stock markets.

The US offered an alternative example of sectoral arrangements and a potential source of competition for trading. Yet this factor too had limited effects in domestic debates. The US was seen as a distant competitor, not a real threat to securities markets. The SEC and NYSE were examined as examples, but often seen negatively—for instance, in Germany, the SEC was attacked for being over-legalistic.

Instead, a visible and important international factor in domestic debates in all three nations was reform in neighbouring countries, especially Britain. It increased fears of regulatory competition and hence loss of trading, especially in the shares of the largest companies. The transfer of business to London's SEAQ-International market featured prominently in debates in all three nations. Moreover, London's reforms offered an example of how sectoral arrangements could be modified. They redefined what was regarded as possible and beneficial for domestic actors.

The EU also played a significant role. It laid down legal requirements, notably through the 1993 ISD. However, this was of much less importance than two other mechanisms whereby it influenced domestic debates. One was increased fears of regulatory competition arising from EU rules aiding cross-border trading and greater capital mobility. The other was transposition of EU rules, which provided an occasion to reconsider domestic institutional arrangements and legitimated changes that went beyond the requirements of EU law.

For governments and banks, who were the core of the reform coalitions, and to a lesser extent brokers, overseas reforms and EU regulation provided direct impetus for action that applied in the policymaking process. They offered perceptible reasons for change—to avoid loss of business and to implement EU requirements. They altered the institutional arrangements that were seen as appropriate. They aided legitimation of new institutional arrangements, on the grounds of being necessary to meet EU requirements or for survival in the face of overseas threats.

Thus overall, the case of securities regulation in France, Germany, and Italy between 1986 and 2005 underlines the importance of a broad understanding of market internationalisation. While transnational technological and economic developments operated as background factors, overseas reforms (notably in Britain) and supranational regulation by the EU were of greater direct importance for institutional reform. They played crucial roles in the policy process, influencing views of the urgency for action, the possibilities of new institutional arrangements, the benefits of such arrangements and the ways in which reform could be legitimated. They were crucial in the desire and ability of national actors to alter very long-standing institutional features that had resisted transnational technological and economic developments. They contributed to considerable institutional convergence both across the three continental European countries and with their Anglo-Saxon neighbour and rival, Britain.

6

Internationalisation of Telecommunications Markets

In the mid-1960s the telecommunications sector in Europe was a medium-sized industry dominated by one service, voice telephony. It was characterised by relatively slow technological change, low cross-border flows of services and equipment, and weak supranational regulation. By 2005 sweeping internationalisation had taken place that transformed the industry, which had become a 'high-tech sector' and part of the communications revolution, at the core of economic and social life.

This chapter looks at the three most important forms of internationalisation of telecommunications: revolutionary transnational technological and economic developments, and two policy forms, namely reforms in the US and EU regulation. The chapter sets out the three forms and shows how each developed cumulatively and progressively over time. It also argues that all three were beyond the control of policy makers in the four individual countries studied. The first two were clearly exogenous to national policy makers in Europe. EU regulation is more complex, but the chapter argues that it was developed by a partnership between the European Commission and national governments, with all parties making compromises; hence it was beyond the control of any one national government or group of policy makers in a single country. However, the chapter neither seeks to explain why the three forms of internationalisation took place nor provide detailed description of them.

Instead, in keeping with the overall theme of the book, namely how market internationalisation affects domestic institutions, the analysis focuses on how the three forms created pressures to open national markets. In particular, it shows how they each led to challenges to traditional European institutions of monopoly supply, public ownership, and regulation by national governments. Subsequent chapters look at how national policy makers responded to these challenges.

The chapter begins with a brief description of European telecommunications in the mid-1960s, setting out a baseline for later internationalisation. It shows how the sector was stable, nationally segmented, and formed part of government bureaucracy. It then examines each form of internationalisation in turn, underlining its challenges for traditional domestic institutions in European nations.

TELECOMMUNICATIONS IN EUROPE IN THE MID-1960s

In the mid-1960s, telecommunications were dominated by public telecommunications operators (PTOs) such as the Post Office, Direction Générale des Télécommunications, or Deutsche Bundepost.[1] These PTOs had legal monopolies over operating telecommunications networks and the supply of almost all services and terminal equipment. Breaching PTO monopolies was generally a criminal offence. Only manufacturing of equipment fell outside PTO monopolies, mostly being undertaken by privately owned 'national champion' companies such as Siemens in West Germany, Alcatel in France, and GEC and Plessey in Britain.

The PTOs were state owned. Almost all were units within post, telephone, and telegraph ministries, so that they formed part of civil service bureaucracies, and their employees were civil servants. In addition, the supply of telecommunications was linked with postal services. Elected politicians, notably ministers, held most formal regulatory powers, including setting prices, determining standards, and deciding investment.

Transnational technological and economic forces were weak in telecommunications, which were marked by stable and relatively simple technology. The industry was centred on the use of the fixed-line network to supply one service—voice telephony (later labelled POTS—'plain old telephone service'). The industry's technology dated back decades. Thus most signals were transmitted on fixed links using copper wire, the same system as used in the nineteenth and early twentieth centuries.[2] The telephone network had a narrow 'bandwidth'—that is limited transmission capacity. 'Switching' (i.e. routing calls from caller to person called) was undertaken with electro-mechanical switches invented in 1889 and 1916 (the Strowger and Crossbar systems), which involved a mechanical 'arm' making a physical link at exchanges between the line of the caller and the person called. Services other than voice telephony were very small and often unreliable, as the telephone network was designed for voice telephony. Equally, the range of terminal or 'customer premises equipment' was very limited.

Technological features limited the scope for competition. Thus PTOs largely supplied one standard service, which seemed suitable for monopoly supply by a bureaucracy. The combination of low transmission capacity and electro-mechanical switches greatly limited the services that could be provided. In addition, the cost structure discouraged competition: much of the network appeared to be a 'natural monopoly' (i.e. one supplier was more efficient than several competing ones). In particular, setting up a telephone network involved high fixed costs in laying copper cables and establishing exchanges, and it was difficult to interconnect different networks. Strong barriers existed to cross-border trade in equipment and services, notably due to nationally specific standards, so

---

[1] Details of institutional arrangements in Britain, France, (West) Germany, and Italy are provided in following chapters.

[2] Although better coaxial cable was used for trunk and international networks by the 1960s.

that the manufacturing subsector was dominated by the needs of the national infrastructure.

Supranational regulation of telecommunications was very limited. The main organisation, the International Telecommunications Union (ITU) (established in 1865), only dealt with standards and revenue-sharing for cross-border communications.[3] It operated on an intergovernmental basis, lacking powers to impose decisions on members. The European Community played no role in telecommunications.

The US had a somewhat different institutional framework to that in European nations. In particular, the main operator, American Telegraph and Telephone (AT&T), was privately owned and did not hold a legal monopoly. In addition, independent regulatory commissions existed (the Federal Communications Commission (FCC) and separate state-level public utility commissions or boards). However, in practice, the US offered few pressures on European domestic institutions. Many European countries had experimented with private ownership in the late nineteenth and early twentieth centuries but had moved to public ownership due to inefficiencies and the desire of governments to control an important sector.[4] Moreover, although lacking a legal monopoly, AT&T enjoyed a de facto one over much of the sector, appearing to confirm that competition was largely unsustainable in most of the telecommunications market.

TRANSNATIONAL TECHNOLOGICAL AND ECONOMIC FORCES FOR CHANGE

The telecommunications sector was revolutionised by transnational technological and economic forces that began in the mid-1960s.[5] This section briefly summarises these forces, but mainly focuses on how they put pressure on traditional national institutions in Europe.

In the mid-1960s, telecommunications signals were transmitted in analogue form (i.e. as electromagnetic waves) on fixed links using copper wires with low capacity. These technological features were revolutionised by the marriage of telecommunications with microelectronics, which themselves were transformed through remarkable improvements in capacity, miniaturisation, and lower costs.[6]

---

[3] See Savage (1989).   [4] For histories, see Noam (1992) and Schneider (2001a).
[5] cf. Stehman (1995), Thatcher (1999: ch. 3), Schneider (2001a), Lovelock and Ure (2002), Clark et al. (1988), and OECD (1983, 1988a,b).
[6] For instance, 'Moore's law' is that the number of possible circuits on a microchip doubles every 18 months and has held since the mid-1960s—Lovelock and Ure (2002: 151); the cost of an integrated circuit fell by a factor of 10 every five years in the 1970s, while its power rose from 700 bits per circuit in 1970 to 8,000 in 1980—Pigeat and Virol (1980); the cost of processing fell sharply—one estimate was that the cost of 1,700 operations (representing about one million instructions) fell from $0.47 in 1965 to $0.20 in 1975 to $0.07 in 1985—OECD (1988a).

The use of microelectronics allowed the transmission and then the switching of signals to be 'digitalised' (i.e. signals were in 'binary' form); this began in the 1960s and gathered speed in the 1970s and 1980s. Digitalisation offered many advantages—higher quality, the ability to support many services, a larger bandwidth (capacity), and lower costs. A few examples give a flavour: digital transmission in the 1970s using the existing British Post Office trunk network increased capacity from 1.5 million to 120 million bits per second; in the 1980s, digital transmission in France was estimated to reduce costs per 'erlang' of transmission capacity from FF25,580 to FF3,070; digital switches in the early 1980s were estimated to reduce costs per line to $200 from $600 for the previous electromechanical exchanges.[7]

New forms of transmission were also developed or improved from the mid-1960s onwards, such as optical fibre cable, satellites, and microwave networks. They offered lower costs, better quality, and higher transmission capacity. Again, the improvements were dramatic, especially for long-distance transmission. Thus, for instance, in 1980, an optical fibre cable could offer transmission at 100 million bits per second; this had reached 1,000 million bits per second in 1985 and by the late 1990s, a transatlantic cable with a capacity of 30 billion bits per second of data was laid.[8] The cost per voice path of transatlantic cable fell from $23,000 in 1983 to below $2,000 in 1995, while another estimate was that the basic cost of one minute of transmission on a transatlantic cable laid in 1996 was just over one (US) cent.[9] Similarly, the costs of satellite transmission fell dramatically from the 1960s onwards.[10] Then in the late 1990s, microwave systems improved so much that mobile telephones could transmit voice, data, and images, including television.[11]

Digitalisation broke down barriers between telecommunications and other sectors, especially computing and broadcasting, which increasingly shared a common digital technology. Equally, higher transmission capacity and lower costs allowed new services to be developed and commercialised. As a result, telecommunications became a multi-service sector.[12] Thus the second and traditionally smallest telecommunications subsector—advanced services and terminal equipment—grew very rapidly and became very heterogeneous. By the 1990s, everyday examples included fax, email, the Internet, and mobile telephony. In addition there were more specialised services such as electronic commerce, computer-assisted manufacturing, and videotext systems for buying and selling services such as shares or airline tickets. As services multiplied, so did forms of terminal equipment—from different types of mobile phone to fax machines.

---

[7] *The Times* 13.12.74, Chatain and de la Chapelle (1987), and Antonelli (1993).

[8] The *Financial Times* 5.3.98.

[9] The *Financial Times* 27.8.97 and OECD (1998); more generally, the price of optical fibre cable declined rapidly in the 1980s and 1990s: e.g. in 1980 a fibre of 70 million bits per second capacity cost $11.8 per metre; by 1985 cable with a capacity of 900 million bits per second cost $0.35.

[10] OECD (1983, 1988*b*).   [11] cf. Didier and Lorenzi (2002) and Frova (2003).

[12] cf. Lovelock and Ure (2002).

These technological and economic developments were transnational and beyond the control of policy makers in individual European nations. One reason is that they were based on publicly-available scientific knowledge dating from well before the 1970s. They often represented the commercial application of such knowledge.[13] Thus for example, digitalisation was based on research undertaken in the 1940s. A further factor is that European nations accounted for only small shares of world telecommunications and electronics; hence they had little market power over the development of technology internationally.[14] Finally, telecommunications were subject to long-term secular forces concerning the use of information and communication operating across industrialised nations.[15]

Transnational technological and economic developments created strong pressures to open domestic markets and alter traditional sectoral institutions, especially monopolies and supply by state-owned PTOs within posts and telecommunications ministries. Five can be highlighted. First, national monopolies were undermined by entry to markets becoming easier and enforcing monopoly more difficult. Thus for instance, new services and forms of terminal equipment were very heterogeneous and many required very low-fixed investment; hence it became difficult to maintain monopoly supply. The costs of new networks that provided competition (e.g. satellite networks or high-quality urban and international optical fibre networks) fell sharply. To cite just two examples, the charges levied by Intelsat for leasing a satellite circuit per annum in nominal terms alone decreased from $35,000 in 1965 to $5,000 in 1985, and in the 1990s, a basic international 'voice over internet network' could be built for under $100 million.[16] Moreover, bypass of existing networks became simpler. This could take place directly through 'call back' services whereby callers could be rung back if the destination country offered lower tariffs. Equally, it could take place more indirectly by using alternative networks to bypass public switched telephone services—for instance, by providing voice telephony over the Internet or utilising leased lines for both data and voice services. Hence users could find alternatives to the networks run by incumbent PTOs. Finally, firms could relocate telecommunications activities in low-cost countries, thereby avoiding high-cost networks.

The linkage of telecommunications with electronics and broadcasting led to the development of a multitude of services so that telecommunications became economically strategic—that is a host of other industries depend on them, from the finance industry to manufacturing. A couple of examples illustrate the changes.

[13] See e.g. Martin (1971), who offers a prescient forecast of the future of the sector.

[14] In 1982, Europe as a whole only accounted for 17.3% of world semiconductor production; in 1970, shares of total gross investment by network operators in the OECD was 8.1% for Britain in 1970 and 4.3% for France, and in 1980 the figures were 6.3% for Britain and 7.4% for France; see Thatcher (1999: 67–8) and Locksley (1982).

[15] Castells (2002).

[16] The *Financial Times* 27.8.97 quoting ITU figures, *The Economist Telecommunications Survey* 13.9.97, OECD (1983, 1988*b*), and the *Financial Times* 14.1.98, 20.7.98, 28.7.98.

Banking and financial systems now rely on transmission of data electronically—from 'simple' cash cards to complex inter-bank settlement systems. Equally, travel systems have been transformed—from videotext systems that allowed travel agents to view and book flights on special screens in the 1970s and 1980s to direct booking via the Internet from the late 1990s. Finally, telecommunications became central to the social and employment lives of individuals in Europe—by the 1980s, almost every household had a fixed-line connection and by 2005 the vast majority of people had a mobile telephone.

The increasing importance and diversity of telecommunications led in turn to pressures on policy makers to ensure an adequate supply of services and to liberalise supply, rather than protect domestic incumbents. Those pressures were particularly acute in internationally exposed sectors, in which obtaining telecommunications services that matched those of rival nations became important. Moreover, there were powerful actors in the electronics and broadcasting sectors, such as large computer companies or audio-visual conglomerates, who had the political and economic capacity to resist being constrained by the monopolies of telecommunications operators. Hence, as the telecommunications sector lost its clear boundaries, so it became more difficult to prevent competition.

A third pressure on traditional national institutions arose from increased capital requirements for operators. New technologies, such as digital switches or optical fibre cables, offered enormous savings and better quality and made existing equipment obsolete. Also demand for telecommunications increased sharply, from both businesses and residential users. Hence operators needed to invest heavily to expand and modernise their networks. However, obtaining the necessary capital expenditure threatened to increase public expenditure and borrowing as operators were state owned; moreover, large investment to obtain future profits often ran counter to the accounting norms of civil service departments in European nations. It also created a sharp difference with postal services, whose technology remained more stable and which were often unprofitable. These developments made public ownership and linkage of telecommunications with postal services as part of a government department, the standard institutional arrangement in the mid-1960s in Europe, more difficult to sustain.

Changes in costs reduced the advantages of public ownership of PTOs and created a fourth pressure on domestic institutions in Europe. Traditionally, business users cross-subsidised residential ones, who were also voters and hence politically important for governments. This arose because prices for services used heavily by firms were set above cost. In particular, tariffs for long-distance calls (especially international ones) were generally set well above costs and provided a highly disproportionate share of PTOs' revenue and profits.[17] In contrast, prices for

---

[17] For instance, in 1970, international calls represented 0.2% of calls in Britain but 22% of Post Office revenues, with a profit margin of 26.3%; in 1980, profit margins remained at 24.9%; in 1995–6,

connection, line rental, and local charges were held down. However, the costs of international communications fell sharply relative to other services such as local calls.[18] At the same time, technological developments gave large users (especially international ones) greater opportunities and incentives to act against costs that lay above prices: they could bypass the networks or relocate telecommunications operations to low-cost nations. Worse still, large users frequently accounted for a very high proportion of operator revenues and profits.[19] Faced with the danger of losing revenue from large businesses, operators needed to 'rebalance' tariffs by reducing prices for long-distance communications relative to other services. Such changes were unlikely to please residential users and hence made public ownership of PTOs less attractive for governments.

Finally, in some parts of telecommunications, rapid technological change offered not just profits but also involved increased fixed costs. In particular, very high research and development spending was needed. The clearest example came in public switches used in PTOs' public networks: whereas the research and development costs of a traditional electro-mechanical switch were put at £23–£30 million, they were £500–£1,500 million for a digital switch in the 1980s and even higher for optical switches being developed in the 1990s.[20] As a result, the world market share needed for profitability rose: one estimate was that a firm needed 8% of the world market to be profitable for digital switches in the 1980s and 16% for optical switches, while another was that research and development spending on digital switches had reached $6 billion relative to a total world market of $16 billion.[21] Since countries, such as Britain or France, represented 4%–6% of the total world market, equipment manufacturers required international markets. Similarly very high-fixed costs affected 3G ('Third Generation') mobile communications in the late 1990s.[22] Hence strong pressures arose for opening domestic markets and for international standards that allowed firms to supply several national markets.

Overall, transnational technological and economic changes greatly aided cross-border exchanges of services and equipment by weakening national monopolies, altering costs, and increasing demand for international services. They placed strong pressures on traditional sectoral institutions in Europe of monopolies, state-owned PTOs, and provision of telecommunications and postal services by a civil service department.

---

international services accounted for 3.2% of total call minutes but 16% of revenues. Similar figures apply to France—see Thatcher (1999: 275–8).

[18] e.g. the transatlantic cable, TAT 5 (commissioned in 1970) carried 845 voice circuits, while a successor, TAT 7 (commissioned in 1983), carried 4,200 circuits, and costs per circuit declined from $12 for TAT 5 to $2.3 for TAT 7—OECD (1983, 1988*b*).

[19] One estimate in the mid-1980s was that 2,000 firms accounted for 25% of the French operator's revenues and 40% of its profits—Longuet (1988: 31); another is that BT's top 300 clients represented 20% of its income—Cawson et al. (1990: 102).

[20] Ungerer and Costello (1988) and OECD (1988).   [21] OECD (1988).

[22] Ure (2003), Whalley (2004) and Thatcher (2005).

REFORMS IN THE US[23]

For several decades before the 1960s, the US had different regulatory institutions than Western European nations (private ownership of the incumbent AT&T and independent regulatory commissions). However, reforms that ended AT&T's de facto monopoly and broke the firm up greatly increased the contrasts across the Atlantic. Those reforms began in the late 1950s but really gathered pace in the 1970s and early 1980s.

AT&T's monopoly was steadily reduced by the Federal Communications Commission (FCC) and judicial decisions. After liberalisation of certain specific types of terminal equipment in the late 1950s and 1960s, the FCC decided in 1975 that non-AT&T terminal equipment could be directly attached to AT&T's networks. It thereby effectively permitted competition in all terminal equipment. Moreover, AT&T's monopoly over advanced services was also gradually ended, notably in the 1970s.[24] In addition, restrictions on resale of capacity and cost sharing of lines leased from AT&T became permitted, so that it became easier for companies to supply advanced services on lines leased from AT&T or create private networks that bypassed AT&T's public networks. Moreover, competition was allowed in advanced networks such as private microwave networks (1959), public microwave networks (1969), and domestic satellite networks (1972). AT&T attempts to prevent competition to its services were caught by FCC and court decisions; on the contrary, the incumbent found itself obliged to offer interconnection with rival networks such as MCI's private networks.[25] The end result was that by the late 1970s AT&T was left with a sharply reduced monopoly.[26]

The most dramatic changes came in the early 1980s with the breakup of AT&T. The Department of Justice had begun an antitrust case against AT&T in 1974. All attempts by the incumbent to prevent the suit failed, including intensive lobbying of the federal government and Congress. Finally, fearing an adverse court decision, AT&T agreed to be broken up, which was formalised in the Modified Final Judgement of 1984. AT&T kept its international and long-distance services. However, it lost its local operating services which were divested to seven regional Bell operating companies; although known as 'Baby Bells', these were very large companies, often the size of European PTOs.

Competition was greatly increased by the Bell Settlement. It was enforced for all services except those within local areas (the US was divided into 161 local access

---

[23] For analyses, see Black (2002), Brock (1981, 1994), Crandall (1991), Crandall and Waverman (1995), and Horwitz (1989).

[24] In 1956, AT&T and its equipment manufacturer Western Electric had been confined to supplying 'common carrier' services and equipment, thereby excluding data services, settling an antitrust suit begun by the Department of Justice against AT&T; the FCC then greatly extended the definition of data services, so that in principle all 'specialized' or advanced services were open to competition through its 1971 Specialized Common Carrier Decision and 1980 Computer II decision.

[25] Brock (1994: 107–9, 131–45).

[26] Notably transmission on public switched networks and public voice telephony, excluding services involving the processing of data.

and transport areas—'LATAs'), where state regulatory commissions could (but were not obliged to) permit continuing monopoly by the Baby Bells. After 1984, competition spread, not only in long-distance services but also within LATAs. This final monopoly of the Baby Bells within LATAs was ended by the 1996 Telecommunications Act. It made expansion by the Baby Bells beyond intra-LATA services dependent on their local markets being opened to competition.[27]

Reforms in the US provided three sources of potential pressures on traditional European regulatory institutions (cf. Dyson and Humphries 1990). First, they offered a powerful example of institutional change. They showed that monopolies could be ended and very powerful incumbents broken up. They illustrated the power of regulators, courts, and governments. Reformers could point to the advantages of liberalisation, independent regulators, and private ownership, especially as after reforms, prices in the US tended to fall and competition increased, but AT&T did not collapse nor did the network break down. Conversely, for incumbent operators, the US experiences showed the dangers to their apparently well-established positions.

Second, US reforms offered reasons for American firms and policy makers to seek international liberalisation of telecommunications. After breakup, AT&T and the Baby Bells had strong incentives to expand abroad, since they had lost their domestic monopolies. Equally, other US companies grew up such as PanAmSat, MCI, and Worldcom who also sought overseas expansion. American firms were supported by the US government, Congress, and policy makers, who argued that overseas monopolies and public ownership of operators constituted unfair barriers to trade and pressed other nations to open their markets (particularly to US companies).

Third, liberalisation in the US appeared to alter the dynamic of the world telecommunications market. The US accounted for 40%–50% of world revenues from telecommunications services and 25%–45% of total world gross investment by telecommunications operators (compared with 4%–8% for countries such as Britain and France).[28] Competition in the US market seemed to offer opportunities for expansion for European operators and equipment firms, who could now enter the world's largest market. However, American policy makers demanded reciprocity (in the form of liberalisation and privatisation of incumbent PTOs), especially when European PTOs sought to take over US operators.[29] Moreover, reforms in the US placed competitive pressures on European operators. There was direct competition with US-based operators over international services, especially with bypass of international networks. Indirect competition took the form of regulatory competition: if reforms led to better and cheaper telecommunications

---

[27] The Baby Bells had been permitted to offer services within LATAs but not inter-LATA services or information services under the 1984 Settlement; for discussions, see Huber et al. (1996) and Klinger (1997).

[28] For telecommunications services revenues, the US accounted for 48.8% in 1970, 45.6% in 1980, 439% in 1990, and 41.3% in 1995; and for investment, 43.6% in 1970, 41.1% in 1980, and 25.6% in 1990 and 1995—Thatcher (1999: 266–7), based on ITU figures.

[29] See Chapters 8 and 9 for examples.

services for companies in the US (or the belief that they did so), then firms had incentives to relocate their telecommunications operations to the US; moreover, firms based in the US would enjoy competitive advantages relative to those based in Europe. The potential for regulatory competition was greatly increased by the enhanced importance of telecommunications for firms and industries, and by the rapid fall in the costs of long-distance communications, which aided relocation of telecommunications networks from one country to another. Thus US reforms also created competitive pressures for change in European nations.

EUROPEAN UNION REGULATION[30]

Until the late 1980s, EU regulation of telecommunications was extremely limited. When the European Community was created in 1958, the founding members made no mention of telecommunications in the Treaty of Rome.[31] Between 1959 and 1977, the European Community's posts, telecommunications, and telegraph (PTT) ministers met only twice.[32] In the early 1980s, proposals were made to increase the European Community's role in liberalising terminal equipment and setting standards, but these did not result in legislation.[33]

However in 1987 the Commission published a Green Paper that set out a framework for EU legislation, involving liberalisation of terminals and advanced services markets, the possibility of extending competition to voice telephony, and EU re-regulation of competition.[34] It was followed by the gradual development of an increasingly comprehensive and detailed EU framework that was legally binding on member states, beginning with limited segments of the sector (1988–c.1993), then being extended to the entire sector (1993–8), and finally being consolidated with more detailed rules (1998–2005).[35] Four elements of the EU's framework can be analysed: liberalisation, re-regulation (rules governing competition), the application of general competition law, and measures to ensure implementation by national regulatory authorities (NRAs).

Liberalisation took the form of EU legislation that prohibited member states from maintaining monopolies ('special and exclusive rights'). Initially, it was confined to limited segments of the market, notably terminal equipment (such as telephone sets and fax machines), advanced services (such as packet switched

---

[30] The World Trade Organisation became involved in telecommunications regulation, notably with an agreement in February 1997; however, this is not included because it was more limited than EU legislation and hence had almost no implications for institutions in Europe; the term EU is used, although legally decisions have been taken under the European Community pillar of the EU.

[31] Instead they created the Conférence Européenne des Administrations des Postes et des Télécommunications (CEPT), an intergovernmental organisation outside the EU with few powers over its members.

[32] Schneider and Werle (1990: 87).   [33] Sandholtz (1992: 227–56).

[34] Commission (1987).

[35] Notably with the 2002 'regulatory package'—European Parliament and Council (2002a), (2002b), (2002c).

services or videotext), and public procurement of equipment for networks.[36] Its scope was then expanded in the early 1990s to include satellite services, mobile communications, voice telephony, and the infrastructure.[37] In the mid-1990s, EU legislation insisted that competition in the largest segments of the telecommunications market, public voice telephony and the fixed-line public infrastructure, be permitted by 1 January 1998 in member states.[38] Thus, by 1998, EU law insisted that the entire telecommunications sector be open to competition.

EU 're-regulation' involved measures to ensure that competition was 'fair and effective' and prevent member states from protecting their incumbent operators. EU legislation on access to the network for suppliers of services insisted that: conditions imposed by PTOs be based on objective criteria and be non-discriminatory, transparent, and public; tariffs be cost-oriented; and restrictions on access be minimised.[39] Operators, especially those with 'significant market power' (such as incumbents), were obliged to offer interconnection on terms that were 'fair', based on costs, and transparent.[40] Member states could pursue 'social objectives' such as ensuring universal service, but had to use means that avoided distorting competition (such as transparent levies).[41] Equally, EU rules were established for licensing to prevent member states from restricting competition.[42]

Applying general competition law to telecommunications represented the third form of EU regulation. The most important applications concerned the spate of joint ventures, cooperation agreements, and takeovers by incumbent PTOs such as British Telecommunications (BT), France Télécom, Deutsche Telekom, and Telecom Italia that began in the 1990s.[43] These raised significant competition concerns since incumbent PTOs held dominant positions in national markets. The European Commission's Competition Directive (formerly DG IV) investigated the agreements and bids under general competition law; it generally approved them, but subject to conditions, including those relating to domestic institutional arrangements.[44]

---

[36] Commission (1988, 1990*a*) and Council (1990).

[37] Commission (1994, 1995, 1996*a,b*) and Council (1995).

[38] Limited derogations were made, but did not concern the four countries studied here.

[39] Council (1990).   [40] European Parliament and Council (1997*a*, 1997*b*).

[41] Thus for instance, EU legislation (European Parliament and Council 1997*b*) defined the scope of universal service and the mechanisms that member states could establish to finance its costs, but insisted that levies were transparent and did not inhibit competition.

[42] Especially rules that limited the requirement of individual licences—see for instance European Parliament and Council (2002*c*).

[43] Key agreements concerning incumbent PTOs in Britain, France, Germany, and Italy, with date of formal approval by the Commission, included: Concert, an alliance between BT and MCI to supply international advanced services/networks (1994); Atlas, a joint venture and alliance between France Télécom (FT) and Deutsche Telekom (DT) for international cooperation and advanced services (1996); Phoenix, renamed Global One—a joint venture between, FT, DT, and Sprint for international advanced services (1996); BT's unsuccessful bid for MCI (1997); Wind, a joint venture between FT, DT, and Enel to provide full telecommunications services in Italy (1998); a joint venture between BT and AT&T to supply international advanced services (1999); a joint venture between DT, FT, and Energis to build local networks in the UK (1999); cf. Elixmann and Herman (1996) and Gassot et al. (2000).

[44] cf. Blandin-Oberrnesser (1996: 142–7).

EU regulation is implemented by NRAs. These can be independent regulatory authorities but also governments. The EU sought to ensure that NRAs were fair and did not favour certain suppliers. One method was through legally binding EU legislation on liberalisation and re-regulation. Another was through minimal rules on the structure of NRAs. Hence EU directives insisted that NRAs be separate from suppliers. A further method was through Commission monitoring and control over NRAs. Thus for instance, in 2002, a directive (European Parliament and Council 2002) empowered the Commission to order NRAs to withdraw measures that appeared to contravene EU law.

Internationalisation was defined as cross-border forces that are beyond the control of policy makers in any one of the individual countries studied. National policy makers participated in EU decision-making, notably through the EU Telecommunications Council (of Ministers) and the European Parliament. However, no one country controlled EU decisions. On the contrary, different governments had to make important compromises with each other to achieve agreement. Thus for example, France and other 'Mediterranean' states accepted the prohibition of national monopolies, but 'liberal' nations, such as Britain and Germany, were obliged to accept compromises over the timing of competition and also re-regulation over universal service to balance it.[45] Moreover, the European Commission played important roles in expanding EU regulation, notably by putting forward proposals for legislation to the Council and European Parliament, negotiating compromises on legislation, applying general competition law, and sometimes passing its own Commission Directives;[46] its interpretation of its powers was significantly bolstered by legal rulings from the European Court of Justice (ECJ).[47] Hence although EU regulation was not entirely exogenous to policy makers in Britain, France, Germany, and Italy, it was not the product of any one nation nor within the control of policy makers in any one country.

EU regulation had potential direct effects on domestic institutional reforms in Britain, France, Germany, and Italy by creating a set of legally-binding requirements. Thus member states had to transpose EU legislation and ensure that national law met EU requirements—for instance, by ending monopolies, putting in place re-regulation and separating regulation and supply. Traditional national institutions, notably monopoly supply by PTT ministries that combined regulation with supply, were prohibited by EU law. However, it is important to note that the scope of EU legal obligations was limited. Thus, while they covered competition, they did not prohibit public ownership of suppliers—indeed, the Treaty of Rome expressly excludes the EU from determining ownership within member states.[48] Equally, although EU directives required supply and regulation to be undertaken by separate organisations, they did not require regulatory

---

[45] Thatcher (2001).   [46] Under Article 86[ex-90](3).

[47] For a debate on the extent to which EU regulation was led by member states, the Commission and ECJ or a partnership between them, see Sandholtz (1998), Schmidt (1996, 1998), and Thatcher (1999); for analyses combining law and politics, see Scott (1995) and Scott and Audéod (1996).

[48] Article 295 (ex-222) of the Treaty of Rome.

authorities that were independent of governments; indeed, the institutional form of regulators was left to member states.

However, EU regulation also had potential indirect effects on domestic institutional reform in three other ways.[49] First, it offered a 'model' or 'paradigm' of market supply, one far removed from traditional institutional frameworks. The EU model was based on promoting 'fair and effective' competition. It rejected protection of domestic suppliers and ran counter to traditional institutions and norms such as monopoly supply, cross-subsidisation between services, and the combination of regulation and supply within PTT ministries. Second, applying EU regulation (both general competition law and monitoring enforcement of sectoral regulation) offered the EU Commission opportunities to participate directly in domestic decision-making. Thus for example, it could take action against member states for non-compliance with EU law. In addition, its powers over cross-border mergers and takeovers by national suppliers allowed it to bargain with national policy makers, including to demand institutional reforms. Third, EU liberalisation affected the dynamics of telecommunications markets in Europe. In particular, it encouraged cross-border expansion by companies: it ended monopolies in other European markets, while opening the domestic markets of incumbents. Hence it provided opportunities and incentives for suppliers to cease relying on domestic national markets and instead to expand abroad.

CONCLUSION

In the 1960s, internationalisation of telecommunications markets was limited: technology was stable; national markets were largely insulated from each other by national monopolies, public ownership, and country-specific standards; almost all regulatory powers were held by national governments; and supranational regulation was very weak.

Between the mid-1960s and 2005, three powerful international forces developed and transformed the industry. They put pressure on closed markets and traditional national institutions in Europe of monopolies, public ownership, and regulation by governments. Transnational technological and economic factors emerged that fundamentally altered the nature of the sector. They weakened national monopolies, allowed the provision of diverse new services, blurred the boundaries between telecommunications and other sectors such as electronics and broadcasting, and gave incentives for vastly higher investment. They altered the importance of the sector, so that by 2005, telecommunications had become economically strategic. Transnational technological and economic developments posed severe challenges for publicly owned suppliers operating within the public

---

[49] For a discussion of the limits on the direct effects of EU law and the role of other factors, see Schneider (2001*b*) and Thatcher (2004*b*).

sector (and indeed civil service) rules for investment and supply. Equally, they made national monopolies more difficult and costly to uphold, while increasing the difficulties and complexity of regulation by governments.

The US radically reformed its regulatory institutions, especially in the 1970s and early 1980s. It offered an example for European nations of alternative institutional arrangements, notably private ownership of suppliers, breaking up the incumbent operator, allowing competition and regulating through an independent sectoral agency. It also affected the world market for telecommunications, both directly and indirectly through regulatory competition. Hence it altered the incentives for other actors, including European suppliers and governments.

Detailed EU regulation of telecommunications emerged after 1988 and became evermore comprehensive in the 1990s. It provided a set of binding rules that prohibited national monopolies over supply, promoted 'fair and effective' competition, and insisted that regulatory bodies be separate from suppliers. It altered the European telecommunications market, aiding cross-border entry and supply by ending national monopolies. It also offered an alternative model of institutions to the traditional national one in Europe and provided opportunities for the European Commission to enter domestic policymaking.

The three forms emerged gradually and one after another, aiding analysis of their effects through process tracing as well as comparison over time and across countries. Following chapters now examine whether, why, and how these different forms of internationalisation affected domestic decisions about institutional reform in Britain, France, Germany, and Italy.

7

The Force of Inertia: Telecommunications in France, West Germany, and Italy 1965–87

In the mid-1960s, sectoral institutions in telecommunications in France, West Germany, and Italy were well entrenched, often dating back to the nineteenth and early twentieth centuries. They were highly protective of national suppliers and shared many similarities: state-owned public telecommunications operators (PTOs) dominated the sector, thanks to a legal monopoly over almost all networks and services; the PTOs were usually part of the civil service, being units within government postal and telecommunications ministries; the government held most regulatory powers.

In the period until 1987 these arrangements were challenged by powerful international forces. Sweeping technological and economic developments gave rise to economic problems and strong pressures on existing institutional arrangements. Reforms in the US and then in the mid-1980s in Britain (see chapter 8) offered an alternative institutional model for the sector. Several serious debates over reform took place in all three countries.

Yet in the face of these pressures, there was institutional inertia or at most very modest reforms that increased differences across the three nations. The chapter shows how and why this was so. It demonstrates that reform debates remained dominated by domestic actors and that governments failed to build strong coalitions to overcome powerful vested interests led by trade unions and employees, and sometimes political parties. When difficulties arose from increasingly powerful transnational technological and economic developments, alternatives to changing existing institutions were found. These included the addition of new institutions that provided greater flexibility and resources and/or using existing institutions more effectively with greater funding ('layering' and to an extent 'conversion' in Streeck and Thelen's 2005*b* schema). If these both failed, inefficient supply simply continued, tolerated by public policy makers. As for the American example of reform, it was largely rejected.

Thus with respect to the overall argument of the book, the chapter shows that although transnational technological and economic developments contributed to sometimes severe problems in supply and were prominent in reform debates in all three countries, few institutional changes were made. This finding reinforces the similar outcome in securities trading in the three countries between 1965 and 1985, and carries especial weight because the transnational technological and economic developments in telecommunications were so sweeping. By looking at the domestic policy process, the chapter argues that nations can resist pressures arising from such developments, due both to the availability of alternatives to institutional change and to blockages arising from the breadth and resources of coalitions against reform. The chapter also indicates that the ideational power of overseas reforms is often weak, as policy makers were able to reject the US and then British examples of alternative institutional arrangements. Instead, it underlines that if internationalisation fails to influence domestic alliances and aid reformers to justify changes, nations maintain institutional arrangements, even if those arrangements are seen as a cause of serious inefficiencies in supply.

The chapter looks at each country in turn. It sets out the arrangements that existed in the mid-1960s, underlining their longevity and the powerful coalition of interests that benefited from them. It then considers significant attempts at reform in the late 1960s and 1970s, showing difficulties in supply that arose in large measure from the evolving technological and economic features of the industry, and how these were important in domestic debates. It analyses why reform attempts were blocked. For each country, it then looks at the 1980s, when the three countries faced both continuing transnational technological and economic factors and the effects of reforms in the US and then Britain (see Chapters 6 and 8).

FRANCE

Institutional Arrangements in the Mid-1960s[1]

State bodies dominated the telecommunications sector in the mid-1960s. The Posts and Telegraph Ministry ('PTT Ministry'), created in 1879, had a monopoly over the supply of all telecommunications services and public networks derived from a law of 1837 that made it a criminal offence to transmit signals without government authorisation. Only the equipment manufacturers were privately owned and were authorised to supply a few types of advanced terminal equipment. Within the PTT Ministry, a unit, the *direction générale des telecommunications* (DGT) was responsible for running the telephone and telegraph networks. Since the PTT Ministry was a government department, DGT decisions such as price changes or spending were taken, at least formally, by the minister and government. Indeed, most legal powers over the sector (such as licensing of services or equipment) were held by the government. DGT employees were civil servants (*fonctionnaires*) with strong legal rights.

Although the DGT was part of the civil service, it enjoyed special financial arrangements. In particular, after 1923 it enjoyed a separate budget within the annual finance law (the PTT *budget annexe*). The *budget annexe* divided operating income and expenditure from capital spending. It allowed the PTT Ministry to keep surplus revenues and to create reserves for investment. Moreover, the Finance

---

[1] For histories, see Libois (1983) and Bertho (1981, 1991).

Ministry was able to issue bonds repayable over thirty years, to raise funds for capital spending by the DGT.

The institutional arrangements offered advantages for the government and the postal side of the PTT Ministry. The government could use the DGT as an instrument of policy—for example, in regional development or fiscal and industrial policy.[2] At the same time, the *budget annexe* provided the government and DGT with a degree of financial flexibility beyond that of ordinary government departments. Moreover, telecommunications frequently subsidised postal services and provided additional functions for rural post offices and officials. More generally, the postal side of the PTT Ministry had much power over the telecommunications side. On the other hand, the DGT lacked autonomy: although a special elite group of civil servants, telecommunications 'engineers' (the *corps des ingénieurs des télécommunications*) existed, it was weaker than the postal side of the ministry.

Discussions of Institutional Change 1965–80

By the mid-1960s, France faced problems so major that they were dubbed *la crise du téléphone*, arising in large measure from technological and economic developments. Investment failed to match increased demand or new technological opportunities. As demand rose, remarkably long waiting lists developed: from 119,000 in 1961 they reached 377,000 in 1969 and 792,000 in 1972, when the average time to obtain a telephone was 18 months.[3] Call quality fell sharply due to congestion. The French network was technologically backward—for instance, in 1970, 22% of DGT public switches were still manually operated—i.e. DGT personnel physically connected lines at the exchange! France had fallen behind other nations.[4]

The crisis gave rise to sharp pressures for institutional reform in the late 1960s and early 1970s, and in particular, the DGT's *statut*—its organisational position. It was argued that the DGT's *statut* as a unit within the PTT Ministry led to telecommunications not being a priority under the planning process and finding themselves the poor cousin of postal services. In turn, these factors led to lack of investment. The telecommunications side of the PTT Ministry, notably the elite *corps des ingénieurs des télécommunications*, sought two major institutional changes: separation of the DGT from postal services and a new organisational status for the DGT outside the PTT Ministry.[5]

Elected politicians looked seriously at major changes in the DGT's *statut* leading to a series of debates between the late 1960s and early 1970s. In 1967, Valéry Giscard d'Estaing, then head of a major liberal party, suggested that the DGT

---

[2] Aurelle (1986) and Docquiert (1987).   [3] DGT, *Statistique Annuelle*.

[4] See Libois (1983: 96–138); examples included: there were only 9.1 telephones per 100 population in 1961 compared to 39.5 in the US, and 61% of switches were automatic as against 96% in the US.

[5] In particular, the Association des ingénieurs des télécommunications (AIPT)—*Le Monde* 12.10.72, 10.10.72.

should become a state-owned company[6] following the example of Electricité de France (EDF). It would have its own legal personality, management autonomy, and be separated from postal services. In the 1969 presidential elections, Georges Pompidou took up the suggestion and after he took office there was much public discussion of the idea.[7] In 1971, a working party set up by the prime minister examined a proposal that both postal and telecommunications services should be supplied by a state organisation outside the civil service.[8] Nevertheless, no reforms were implemented. The main reason was fierce resistance by from the trade unions; postal workers in particular feared that reform of the DGT's *statut* would threaten unprofitable services and weaken the guarantees provided by civil service employment for their members.

Institutional reform seemed likely with the election of Giscard d'Estaing as president in 1974. During the presidential election campaign, he had argued the DGT should have a separate budget, and suitable structures for an industrial and commercial undertaking.[9] The wide support for change was underlined by a parliamentary report in 1974 on the *crise du téléphone* which recommended that the DGT become an organisation similar to the one that he had proposed in 1967, with its own legal personality and financial autonomy and that it should be managed according to the rules and methods used by industrial and commercial companies.[10] Moreover, after the 1974 presidential election, Gérard Théry (the head of the DGT as Directeur Général des Télécommunications 1974–81) wanted to alter the DGT's institutional position. Nevertheless, this was not attempted during 1974–81. The main factor was fear of trade union opposition. A long postal strike took place from October to December 1974, provoked in large part by fears of a change in the DGT's *statut* and a separation of postal and telecommunications services.[11] It cost the PTT Minister, Pierre Lelong, his post, and almost caused the downfall of the Prime Minister, Jacques Chirac. The strike marked the end of attempts at comprehensive reform of the DGT's *statut*.

Instead, policy makers followed a three-pronged strategy. The first involved providing much greater investment funding through borrowing. In part this was done through existing means, including the Finance Ministry issuing bonds. In part, it was achieved though new financial instruments created in the late 1960s that allowed the DGT to access private capital outside its civil service budget.[12] These instruments allowed the DGT to borrow for investment, with

---

[6] A *compagnie nationale du téléphone*, or an *entreprise nationale*, a status akin to a public corporation in Britain.

[7] *Le Monde* 15.7.69, *Le Figaro* 22.6.70, and *Le Nouveau Journal* 6.2.71.

[8] Libois (1983: 241–2).   [9] *Le Monde* 8.5.74 and 10.5.74.

[10] The precise form was an *Établissement Public et Industriel à Caractère Commercial*, similar to a public corporation in Britain (EPIC)—*Le Monde* 22.6.74 and *La Vie Française* 6.6.74.

[11] Cohen (1992: 55).

[12] Thatcher (1999: 106–7), Bonnetblanc (1985: 152–71), and Touret (1974); one example was the Caisse Nationale des Télécommunications, created in 1967 to allow the DGT to issue bonds in order to finance telecommunications investment. Another example was limited companies created after 1969 to provide capital for telecommunications equipment (*sociétés de financement du téléphone*) on the basis of leasing arrangements whereby the DGT paid only an annual 'rent' for equipment, allowing it

the loans being repaid from future earnings outside the general budget. The second, related strand was to engage in *grands projets*: the DGT led large-scale investment in partnership with privately-owned French manufacturers with the aim of developing world-class technologies.[13] This involved cooperation between the DGT's research centre, the Centre Nationale d'Etudes des Télécommunications (CNET), and the manufacturers. It also allowed the tying of DGT orders to industrial restructuring by the privately owned firms to produce national champion companies such as Alcatel and Thomson. The third prong was to reform the PTT Ministry's internal organisation, notably separating the operation of the postal and telecommunications sides to give the latter greater internal autonomy.

The strategy appeared successful. The DGT invested heavily and grew rapidly, meeting demand. Its *grands projets* strategy bore fruit. Thus in cooperation with French manufacturing 'national champions', the DGT achieved technological advances, notably in digital switching, which France was the first country in the world to introduce.[14] Despite its position as a civil service unit, the DGT appeared able to provide excellent services. The DGT's record of modernisation and innovation in the late 1970s appeared to answer the earlier critics of its organisational position and by the late 1970s there was little discussion of major institutional reform. Instead, a mixture of institutional 'conversion' and 'layering' had been used, such as greater use of existing instruments for borrowing, coordination between the DGT and equipment manufacturers in *grands projets*, and the creation of new financial instruments to access private capital.

French Alternatives to Anglo-American Liberalism 1980–7

Debates on institutional reform re-started in the mid-1980s, led by elected politicians and the DGT's management. They concerned the extent of the DGT's monopoly, its *statut* within the civil service and the creation of a regulatory framework based on competition. The influence of internationalisation was visible, notably transnational technological and economic developments that were blurring boundaries between telecommunications and other sectors and moving the sector towards becoming a multi-service industry, and the example of reforms in the US and Britain.

The DGT's monopoly began to be questioned, notably for services mixing telecommunications with the audio-visual and computing sectors. The most important were 'telematic' services (often known as 'Minitel') that involved data

to repay the capital cost over several years from the extra revenue and profits earned by the expansion of the network: these companies could be owned by private bodies and raised money either from their own share capital or by issuing bonds.

13 Cf. Cawson et al. (1990) and Cohen (1992).
14 See Cohen (1992: 56–74, 86–100), Libois (1983: 158–73), and Le Diberder (1983).

information being transmitted over telecommunications networks, and cable television. The new services involved organisations from outside telecommunications, such as local authorities, the press, computer companies, and large banks. But these new actors refused to accept a DGT monopoly over services.[15] For their part, elected local politicians opposed the extension of the DGT's monopoly into broadcasting and telematics, fearing increased state power over the media.[16] Moreover, by the mid-1980s, economic 'liberals' and the French Right sought to allow competition in parts of telecommunications such as leased lines and specialised services, inspired by 'deregulation' in the US and Britain, the changing nature of the industry, and the desire to reduce the power of the state.[17] In the legislative elections of 1986, the Right's manifesto promised liberalisation, although it was ambiguous over whether competition would be confined to advanced services or apply to the DGT's core network. For its part, by the mid-1980s, the DGT's management accepted that some competition was inevitable due to technological developments and liberalisation abroad, especially in the US.[18]

The DGT's organisational position was also questioned. The DGT had become highly profitable by the 1980s thanks to its modernisation programme. This widened the gap with the loss-making, labour-intensive postal side of the PTT Ministry. However, governments from 1982 began to impose special levies (*prélèvements*) on the DGT for the general state budget, causing much resentment by the DGT's management. Senior DGT staff called for greater autonomy from the government to prepare for competition that was 'inevitable' given technological and economic developments and to prevent government 'raids' on the DGT's finances. Their proposals included the DGT becoming a form of public corporation, with its own legal identity and subject to explicit regulatory rules.[19] The Right, in opposition and in government, promised to make the DGT into a 'public enterprise' to allow it to compete effectively, and to separate supply from regulation and policy.[20]

Yet very few reforms were introduced. The Left governments of 1981–6 avoided reforms of the DGT's *statut*; even separating postal and telecommunications operators, as suggested in a specially commissioned report on postal services in 1984, was not implemented.[21] The only significant change was that limited competition in value-added services was permitted in 1982.[22] Under the Right-led Chirac government 1986–8, although economic liberals' held key ministries,

---

[15] For telematics, see Humphreys (1990); for cable, see Brenac and Payen (1988); for value-added services, *Le Figaro* (21.5.86), *La Tribune de l'Economie* 16.9.86, and *Le Monde* 25.9.87.

[16] *Le Monde* 7.6.84, 6.10.84; Humphreys (1990), and Brenac and Payen (1988).

[17] Darmon (1985), *Le Monde* 16–17.3.86, 15.5.86, and *Le Matin* 22–23.3.86.

[18] *La Vie Française* 4–10.1.85, interview Marcel Roulet (Directeur général des Télécommunications), *Le Monde* 24.9.86.

[19] *Le Monde* 29.11.85, AIT (1985), *La Vie Française* 4–10.11.85, and *Libération* 29.11.85.

[20] *Le Monde* 8.10.85, and *Longuet* (1988).   [21] Chevallier (1984).

[22] Notably telematic services and also planned services on new broadband cable networks.

few changes were made.[23] A consultative document in 1987[24] that suggested the DGT should become a wholly publicly owned 'public telecommunications company' with its own legal identity (similar to Giscard d'Estaing's 1967 proposal) was rapidly abandoned. Equally, additional liberalisation was very modest and subject to conditions that were explicitly designed to prevent large overseas firms such as IBM from achieving market dominance.[25] Plans in the Right's 1987 consultative document to transfer significant powers in telecommunications (such as over licensing, interconnection, and ensuring 'fair competition') to the new independent sectoral regulator for broadcasting, the Commission nationale de la communication et des libertés (CNCL) created in 1986, came to nothing.

There were several reasons for continuing institutional inertia. First, both the Left and many parts of the Right supported the 'French model'. The Left opposed changes that constricted the DGT to unprofitable services; instead it defended the idea of *service public* in which the DGT provided many services, including profitable ones. The Right was divided over the extent to which competition should be allowed; even liberals such as Longuet (PTT minister 1986–8) underlined their attachment to *service public* and protection of the DGT's core monopoly.[26] The DGT accepted competition in services, but had an alternative model: it should have a monopoly over networks, which would be used to support the supply of different services by many organisations. In addition, support for existing institutions was linked to the clear successes of French telecommunications in the early 1980s: the DGT's network was the most modern in the world, with high levels of digitalisation of transmission and switching; rapid technological innovation and new services had been introduced both for residential and for business users, such as the Minitel videotex system and packet-switched network; the *grand projet* model of cooperation between the DGT, political executive, and manufacturers had borne fruit for the public and private suppliers as well as residential and business users.[27]

Second, Anglo-American examples were frequently rejected. The DGT feared and opposed rapid liberalisation of networks and basic services, arguing that experiences of the US and Britain revealed major drawbacks such as the unsustainability of competition and misallocation of resources.[28] Governments rejected 'uncontrolled Anglo-Saxon deregulation' and worried that liberalisation might allow American companies such as IBM, ITT, and EDS to enter the French market

---

[23] Gérard Longuet was PTT Minister 1986–8 while François Léotard was Communications Minister.

[24] PTT Ministry 1988, see Longuet (1988, Annexe 21).

[25] Thus competition was allowed in 'value-added services' but subject to ministerial authorisation and prohibition on use for voice telephony—see Longuet (1988, Annexe 20), and Conruyt (1988), *Le Monde* 3.2.87, 25.9.87, *La Tribune de l'Economie* 24.9.87; only one competitor was allowed in cellular telephony and another in paging, and the companies were French.

[26] *La Tribune de l'Economie* 19.4.86, *Le Quotidien de Paris* 16.5.86, 21.5.86, and *Le Monde* 16–17.3.86, 3.2.87.

[27] Thatcher (1999).   [28] *Le Monde* 15.5.86 and Encaoua and Koebel (1986).

and gain dominant positions.[29] Even liberals on the Right favoured a specifically French strategy of limited, gradual liberalisation accompanied by re-regulation to protect the DGT and public service, and rejected privatisation of the DGT.[30]

Third, reform faced strong opposition. When the Right published its 1987 consultative document that including plans to alter the DGT's *statut*, trade unions led resistance, including a strike: they argued that separation of the postal and telecommunications sides of the PTT Ministry would weaken the former and reduce opportunities for job mobility for PTT employees; removing the DGT from the civil service would mean its employees losing their civil service status and attendant advantages. Reform plans were rapidly abandoned: the prime minister, Jacques Chirac, mindful of the 1974 postal strike that had almost ended his first premiership refused to confront the trade unions.[31]

Finally, potential reformers were unable to establish a strong coalition around a coordinated programme. Liberals sought a move towards a competitive market, but also wished to protect the DGT, which appeared to require changes in the DGT's *statut* to allow it operate as a firm. The DGT was loath to accept greater competition if it did not obtain greater autonomy from the government and the ability to adjust prices to costs. Such changes were not fully implemented between 1986 and 1988, in large measure because of the political controversies they implied (price rebalancing meant higher costs for residential users while alteration of the DGT's organisation position was soon dropped in the face of strong union opposition). Hence the necessary quid pro quo to competition of greater freedom for the DGT was not possible.

WEST GERMANY

The Institutional Position in the Mid-1960s[32]

Telecommunications networks, services, and terminal equipment were supplied by the Deutsche Bundespost (DBP), which enjoyed a monopoly over all networks, services, and terminal equipment, dating from the late nineteenth and early twentieth centuries.[33] Like its predecessor, the Reichpost, the DGP was a federal administration, headed by the minister for postal and telecommunications services and staffed by civil servants. Its status was confirmed under Article 87 of the West German Constitution, so that reform required a constitutional amendment and hence two-thirds majorities in both houses of parliament (the *Bundestag* and the

---

[29] *Les Echos* 31.12.82 and *Le Monde* 3.4.84, 15.5.86, 3.2.87.

[30] *Le Monde* 26.10.85 and *La Tribune de l'Economie* 30.8.86; cf. Longuet (1988).

[31] *Le Quotidien de Paris* 23.6.87 and *Le Monde* 3.7.87.

[32] For a short introductions in English, see Noam (1992: ch. 7); for histories in German, see Werle (1990), and Schneider (2001a).

[33] Notably under the Telegraphengesetz of 1892; the Fernmeldeanlagengesetz of 1928 confirmed that this included terminal equipment.

Bundesrat). Only equipment manufacturers were privately owned, but even so, the DBP set equipment standards.

Although the DBP was a federal administration, special administrative arrangements were made in recognition of its market supply functions. Following the law of 1924 (the Reichspostfinanzgesetz), it was to be managed according to the principles of a business and could borrow monies. It had its own budget (*Sondervermögen*) separated from the general federal budget and administered by the Minister for Posts and Telecommunications. It paid 6% of its revenues to the federal budget instead of taxes. A Postal Administration Council with representatives from the federal parliament, the Länder governments, industry, and the unions, enjoyed significant powers, including approving the DBP's budget, tariffs, and technological choices.[34] Germany had its own 'public service' doctrines: the DBP had to directly serve the general good and hence had to provide services on a universal and affordable basis.[35] At the same time, the DBP was exempt from general competition law (the 1958 law against Restraint of Competition), which prohibited horizontal and vertical cartel agreements, subject only to not abusing its market power.

The institutional framework satisfied most actors in the sector.[36] The government could use the telecommunications side of the DBP to cross-subsidise postal services and as an instrument of macroeconomic and regional policy. Moreover, the federal government received payments from the DBP in lieu of taxes. The DBP's separate budget allowed it to invest and its network was seen as technologically better and larger than other European countries. Employees enjoyed civil service status, with good pay and conditions. Moreover, trade unions, and in particular, the Deutsche Postgewerkschaft (DPG), the postal union that represented 80% of DBP employees, had considerable influence over management decisions, most visibly through the Postal Administration Council. Equipment manufacturers benefited from protection through cartel arrangements, specific German standards, and a large domestic market.

Debates on Institutional Reform 1965–79

From the 1960s onwards, debates on two aspects of institutional arrangements took place: the DBP's organisational position as a federal administration; the extent of its monopoly. Both were strongly linked to technological and economic changes that were altering the nature of the industry, notably increasing demand and the blurring of boundaries between telecommunications, broadcasting, and electronics. Nevertheless, reforms were not undertaken due to the need to obtain agreement from many actors and the failure of discontented parties to build a strong coalition. Instead alternative non-institutional solutions were found to problems.

---

[34] However, it could be overridden by the Cabinet. [35] Steinmetz (1960).
[36] Stehmann (1995: 188–90) and Thimm (1992: 11–27).

In the 1960s, the DBP suffered from financial difficulties.[37] It failed to keep up with increased demand.[38] It faced increased costs (staffing and interest payments), as well as cross-subsidisation of postal services and payments made to the federal government, leading to rising debt. Yet attempts to raise prices met with strong public opposition: for example, an attempt to raise tariffs in 1964 caused public outrage and a boycott of international calls, with the increases being withdrawn before the 1965 elections.

In response to these financial problems, the government and legislature established several commissions of experts. These recommended reforming the DBP's organisational position to increase its autonomy and move towards a commercial entity, and led to the drafting of legislation.[39] Thus a report in 1965 by a commission of seven experts established to examine how the DBP could achieve profitability and improve capital investment recommended that the DBP be made into a public institution led by a Board of Directors and to operate according to market principles.[40] When the centre–left social democrat SPD won the elections of 1969, they announced another commission, the Kommission DBP, comprising twenty-four members from different sectional interests.[41] Following its report, the government drafted legislation to give greater organisational autonomy to the DBP. It envisaged separation of political control and management, with the latter being undertaken by a board of five people who would not be civil servants. The DBP should be managed as if it were a private company, but would also have social obligations. The reforms were supported by the SPD and parts of the liberal party, the FDP, and even elements of the postal union, the DPG. Industry representatives were also in favour but sought greater alterations in the DBP's monopoly. Later, in 1973, the SPD–FDP government prepared another draft postal law (Postverfassungsgesetz).

However, reform proposals were rapidly dropped. Separation of postal and telecommunications services was blocked by opposition from the postal workers' union which was the largest in the DBP and had close links with the Social Democrats.[42] The Postal Ministry was also concerned not to lose its power and control over the DBP. Instead of altering the DBP's organisational position, the government improved its financial situation (e.g. by deferring payment to the federal government and reducing other financial obligations). By the mid-1970s, the DBP had increased investment and its performance was generally very good,

[37] Werle (1990: 128–34).
[38] For instance, in 1965, the Sachverständigenkommission for the DBP estimated a 10% shortfall for existing landlines—Sachverständigenkommission (1966).
[39] For discussions of reform attempts, see Grande (1989: 187–197), Werle (1990: 145–60, 165–7), and Kühn (1971).
[40] It would be *Anstalt des öffentlichen Rechts*, the equivalent of a public corporation in Britain—Sachverständigenkommission (1966).
[41] Noam (1992: 90–2).
[42] Indeed, the postal minister (1974–82), Kurt Gscheidle, was formerly deputy leader of the union.

with rapid growth in the network.[43] As a result, there was little further pressure for modification of its status.

Instead, however, the 1970s saw challenges to the DBP's monopoly.[44] As markets developed for equipment and services that combined telecommunications and electronics such as fax machines and data networks, telecommunications manufacturers and electronics companies such as Nixdorf, pressed for the DBP's monopoly to be limited.[45] The regional governments, the Länder attacked the DBP's monopoly concerning new services that combined telecommunications and broadcasting. Cable television was a particularly sensitive issue because broadcasting was a Länder prerogative whereas telecommunications were a federal matter.

In response, the DBP fiercely opposed any attempts to reduce its monopoly. Indeed, it wished to extend its reach into expanding markets for new terminal equipment. In 1974, it issued a legal order (*Direktrufverordnung*) which stated that the DBP's monopoly covered these markets. The order was challenged by suppliers, but the Constitutional Court ruled in 1977 that the DBP's monopoly did indeed cover the entire telecommunications sector, including terminal equipment and new forms of information transmission.[46] At the same time, the DBP began to develop cable networks that could be used for television and advanced services.

Faced with conflicts over the limits of the DBP's monopoly in an environment of technological change, especially in data processing and cable television, the government established a commission, the KtK (Kommission für den Ausbau des technischen Kommunikationssystems) in 1974 to examine the supply of new services.[47] It was chaired by an economist, Professor Witte, and composed of twenty-two members representing interests such as the Länder, companies, political parties, the unions, the press, and academia. In its 1975 report, the majority called for pilot projects for new services run by the DBP, municipal agencies, and private firms.[48] The DBP would grant authorisations and impose conditions, but would not have the exclusive right to run projects. However, the KtK did not question the DBP's monopoly over terminal equipment or services. Indeed, although discontent by electronics companies and the Länder grew,[49] the outcome of the debates was little change in the DBP's monopoly.

Increasing Debate but no Action 1980–7

The period between 1980 and 1987 saw vigourous debates on the DBP's monopoly and organisational position. They were led by domestic actors, especially political ones, although the European Commission and US firms and officials also played a minor role. The influence of transnational technological factors

---

[43] For figures, see Werle (1990: 214–9).
[44] Noam (1992: ch. 7); Grande (1989: 197–205), Werle (241–306), and Schneider (2001: 241–55).
[45] cf. Thimm (1992: 12) and Grande (1989: 199).   [46] Werle (1990: 163–5).
[47] On the KTK, see Kühn (1986).
[48] KtK (Kommission für den Ausbau des technischen Kommunikationssystems) (1976).
[49] Werle (1990: 310–11).

continued through the growth of services that cut across traditional bound-aries between telecommunications and other sectors, notably broadcasting and electronics. They were also prominent in arguments by economic 'liberals' for greater competition over terminal equipment and advanced services. In addition, reformers used institutional changes in the US and UK as an example and to warn of the dangers to Germany's international competitiveness of failing to follow suit.

The DBP's monopoly came under increasing fire in the 1980s from many sig-nificant actors.[50] The liberal government coalition party, the FDP, the association of German Industry (the BDI), and companies argued that the DBP's monopoly over terminal equipment caused excessive costs, damaged competitiveness, and was unsustainable; frequently they appealed to the examples of other countries which were liberalising such as Britain and the US.[51] A series of reports, notably by the monopolies commission (Monopolkommission) and policy experts, claimed that West Germany had higher tariffs than other countries such as Britain, the US, and Japan and argued for liberalisation.[52] As the DBP developed its own cable television networks, many Länder leaders began to argue that the DBP's monopoly should be limited in order to safeguard their jurisdiction over broadcasting.[53] American companies and public officials lobbied German policy makers for the opening of terminal equipment markets to foreign suppliers.[54] In a rare move, the European Commission threatened to attack the DBP's monopoly over new forms of terminal equipment through court action; it obtained the support of the FDP Economics Minister, Martin Bangemann.[55]

The FDP and certain policy experts also began to criticise the organi-sational structure of the DBP in the mid-1980s. They opposed the use of telecommunications to subsidise loss-making postal services, which resulted in high debt costs.[56] They also argued that in a liberalised market, regulation and

---

[50] See Grande (1989: 206–24).

[51] *Handelsblatt* 11.5.83, 4.5.84; *Frankfurter Allgemeine Zeitung* 17.11.84, 8.12.84, 18.12.84, 26.2.87; *Süddeutsche Zeitung* 17.10.86, 1.2.87, *Wirtschaftswoche* 13.4.84, 28.11.86, *Handelsblatt* 4.5.84, *Blick durch die Wirtschaft* 27.3.86, *Capital* 1.11.86, *Frankfurter Rundschau* 29.1.86, *Süddeutsche Zeitung* 17.2.87, *Frankfurter Allgemeine Zeitung* 26.2.87, comments by Otto Graf Lambsdorf *Frankfurter All-gemeine Zeitung* 11.5.87, *Handelsblatt* 26.6.87, 6.7.87, comments by Dr Tyll Necker, President of the Federal Association of German Industry (Bundesverband der Deutschen Industrie) *Süddeutsche Zeitung* 3.6.87 and *Handelsblatt* 9.7.87, pointing to both overseas experiences and technological developments; Prof Hans-Jürgen Krupp, head of DIW (Deutsches Institut für Wirtschaftsforschung— German Institute for the Study of Economics)—*Der Spiegel* 14.9.87; cf. also comments by the German Chamber of Commerce—*Handelsblatt* 29.2.84.

[52] Monopolkommission (1981) and Knieps et al. (1981); Study by McKinsey commissioned by Witte Commission, urging large-scale liberalisation, *Süddeutsche Zeitung* 27.3.87, 13.4.87, Study by DIW, *Handelsblatt* 4.6.87, Study presented by Institute of German Industry (Institut der deutschen Wirtschaft) attacking the DBP monopoly—*Handelsblatt* 11.8.87, 9.9.87.

[53] *Die Zeit* 27.1.84 and *Handelsblatt* 29.2.84.   [54] *Handelsblatt* 6.12.85 and 31.3.87.

[55] Especially cordless phones—*Süddeutsche Zeitung* 27.7.83, *Frankfurter Allgemeine Zeitung* 8.12.84, 15.1.85, and *Handelsblatt* 15.1.85, 25.1.85.

[56] *Süddeutsche Zeitung* 11.8.83.

supply should be undertaken by separate bodies, and that the provision of the network infrastructure and the competitive supply of services on it should be separated.[57] In these matters, they looked to the examples of the US, and then Britain.[58]

However, ideas of liberalisation and modification of the DBP's organisational position met strong opposition from many major interests, including the DBP itself, trade unions, one of the large government parties the CSU, and the opposition SPD. These actors opposed making the DBP into a public corporation (misleadingly called 'privatisation'), fearing that it would lead to job losses, damage services and prevent it from providing a suitable infrastructure.[59] In addition, the DBP provided useful revenue for the federal government (10% of its profits), which would have had to be replaced with value-added tax that was shared with the Länder if the DPB became a public corporation.[60] Moreover, opponents of reform and the DBP Minister, Schwarz-Schilling, resisted any erosion of the DBP's monopoly over voice telephony and the network.[61] They argued that overseas reforms had led to higher prices (especially for small users) and in any case were inapplicable to Germany. They even opposed liberalisation of terminal equipment on the grounds that standardised equipment was beneficial for users and industry.[62]

Caught between calls for reform and strong opposition, the government did not take a clear position. It introduced only a modest loosening of restrictions on the supply of terminal equipment in 1985. Instead, it decided in 1984 to establish another Commission under Professor Witte (chair of the previous Commission, the 1976 KtK). Its members were drawn from almost every interested domestic party in the sector—the DBP, the four main political parties, employers, and trade unions. It took a year to set up and two years before it reported (1987).

The Commission drew on both German and international experiences. Its members visited the US and Britain.[63] It argued that the British experience was of particular interest for Germany because of similarities in the situation in the two countries, and because separation of telecommunications and postal services in

---

[57] *Süddeutsche Zeitung* 24.1.85, *Die Zeit* 25.1.85, *Frankfurter Allgemeine Zeitung* 25.1.85, *Süddeutsche Zeitung* 28.1.87, 18.2.87, *Die Zeit* 13.3.87.

[58] Knieps et al. (1981), Monopolkommission (1981: 77–90), Monopolkommission (1991), *Blick durch die Wirtschaft* 27.3.1986, *Capital* 1.11.1986, and *Süddeutsche Zeitung* 27.2.1987, 13.4.1987, 3.6.1987.

[59] *Dpa-Meldung* 13.10.86, *Frankfurter Rundschau* 2.2.87, *Frankfurter Allgemeine Zeitung* 13.2.87, 23.5.87, *Die Zeit* 5.6.87, and *Handelsblatt* 5.6.87.

[60] *Capital* 1.1.86.

[61] Kühn (1986), *Süddeutsche Zeitung* 27.7.85, *Wirtschaftswoche* 28.11.86, *Frankfurter Rundschau* 2.2.87, *Süddeutsche Zeitung* 27.3.87 (comments by Postal Ministry rejecting McKinsey study), *Handelsblatt* 11.8.87, and *Der Spiegel* 14.9.87.

[62] *Süddeutsche Zeitung* 27.7.83, *Frankfurter Allgemeine Zeitung* 8.12.84, *Handelsblatt* 9.4.85, and *Süddeutsche Zeitung* 9.5.85.

[63] Witte report 1988 (Regierungskommission Fernmeldewesen (1987: 48–55); for a discussion of how international experiences in Britain and the US influenced debate among experts, see Ritter (2004: 39–40).

Britain had made British Telecom (BT) economically successful and competitive. It also found that privatisation had 'greatly improved' the position of BT, foremost by changing the mentality of employees towards a stronger market orientation, and that the creation of an independent sectoral regulator, Oftel had been effective in lowering tariffs for users. In contrast, its view of the US experience was more mixed, as it believed that private monopolies were not suitable for European markets, while regulation by the FCC did not fit with Europe's legal traditions.

The majority report[64] recommended liberalisation of terminal equipment and of all services except voice telephony. Nevertheless, it argued that Telekom should keep its monopoly over networks, albeit with a review after three years. Supply and regulation should be separated, with the Federal Ministry of Posts and Telecommunications being responsible for the latter. Telecommunications and postal services should be organisationally divided through the creation of a new organisation, Telekom. Within Telekom, different activities should have their own accounts to allow fair competition. However, Telekom would not become a private law company, since that would require a change in Article 87 of the Constitution, and its employees should remain civil servants.

The report was accompanied by much dissent. On the one hand, a minority report supported by the FDP, liberal economists, and some industry associations, argued for greater liberalisation.[65] Technological developments made competition possible, and West Germany should follow reforms overseas to maintain German competitiveness through lower prices and better supply.[66] On the other hand, the trade unions and SPD argued that the majority report went too far.[67] They opposed separation of postal and telecommunications units. They criticised liberalisation of networks, arguing that it would allow entry by foreign companies and that experiences in Britain and the US showed damage to residential and rural consumers and to equipment suppliers. The unions and SPD were supported on some points by the government CSU party and the Länder who feared job losses and diminished regional and parliamentary control over Telekom.[68]

When the government began to prepare legislative proposals in November 1987, the unions organised a strike of 100,000 DBP members.[69] The reformers had failed to build a broad coalition. They faced determined opposition, not just by the trade unions but also several political parties and on liberalisation from the

---

[64] Regierungskommission Fernmeldewesen (1987); for brief summaries and commentaries, see Schmidt (1991: 214–15) and Grande (1989: 210–24).

[65] *Handelsblatt* 11.8.87, 4.9.87, 9.9.87, 10.9.87, Knabbern am Rande eines Monopols, article by Commission member Professor Wernhard Möschel *Frankfurter Allgemeine Zeitung* 26.9.87, and *Süddeutsche Zeitung* 9.9.87, 8.10.87.

[66] *Handelsblatt* 9.7.87, 11.8.87, 9.9.87, 10.9.87, 17.9.87, *Frankfurter Allgemeine Zeitung* 26.9.87 (article by Professor Wernhard Möschel), 19.12.87.

[67] *Frankfurter Allgemeine Zeitung* 4.8.87, 14.8.87, *Süddeutsche Zeitung* 4.8.87, 16.9.87, 3.11.87, 24.11.87, *Handelsblatt* 4.8.87, 10.11.87, and *Die Zeit* 7.8.87.

[68] *Frankfurter Allgemeine Zeitung* 14.8.87, 17.11.87, *Süddeutsche Zeitung* 10.11.87, and Schmidt (1991).

[69] *Frankfurter Allgemeine Zeitung* 19.11.87.

DBP itself. The government had failed to take a clear lead on reform and instead sought consensus, a process that had led to debate but not action.

ITALY

Institutional Arrangements in the Mid-1960s[70]

Although publicly owned operators had a monopoly over the supply of networks, services, and most terminal equipment dating back decades,[71] significant differences also existed between Italy and other European countries such as France and West Germany. First, in Italy, there were four major state-owned network operators, each holding a monopoly in its own domains. The Azienda di Stato per Servici Telefonici (ASST) supplied most services with European and Mediterranean countries and some national services, the Società Italiana per l'esercizio telefonica (SIP) provided local and national trunk services and networks, Italcable offered extra-European services, and Telespazio was responsible for satellite services. Second, the organisational bases and histories of the operators differed. ASST was a unit within the Posts and Telecommunications Ministry, forming part of the civil service and dating from the late nineteenth century. But SIP, Italcable, and Telespazio had their own legal identity and accounts, and their employees were not civil servants. SIP was formed in 1964 from five operators, several of which had been privately owned, operating under concessions dating from 1936.[72] To add confusion, public ownership was not total and took the form of a lengthy chain: SIP, Italcable, and Telespazio were owned by a holding company, Società Torinese Esercizi Telefonici (STET), which only had a majority share holding in SIP. In turn, STET was itself majority owned by the state-holding company Istituto per la Ricostruzione Industriale (IRI), which was under the jurisdiction of the Ministry for State Holdings, not the Posts and Communications Ministry.

The complex state system was known as the *spezzatino* (fragmentation or 'stew'). It had suffered from fragmentation, turf fights among the operators and lack of investment after 1945. In addition, new services such as packet switching or other value-added services caused problems, as the division among the four operators was largely based on concessions granted in 1936.

Institutional Reforms Mid-1960s–1979

From 1964 until the early 1970s, Italy appeared to respond well to increasing demand and the availability of new technology, especially thanks to the creation of

---

[70] For a good overview in English, see Natalicchi (2001).
[71] Notably by laws in 1912 and 1923; for the complex pre-1945 history, see Chiappetta and Napoli (1985: chs. 1 and 2).
[72] For a history, see Bottiglieri (1990: 244–70, 355–7).

SIP in 1964. Investment rose, leading to an expanding network and modernisation (notably automation of switching) that was comparable or better than other European countries.[73] SIP was in good financial shape.[74] Although the fragmentation of Italian telecommunications continued to pose problems, these were eased by an agreement in 1968 on clearer divisions between the networks of ASST and SIP, the two largest operators.[75]

However, the 1970s saw a sharp deterioration in Italy's capacity to respond to technological and economic developments.[76] As macroeconomic and fiscal conditions worsened, telecommunications investment was reduced, and waiting lists rose sharply.[77] SIP's financial position worsened and productivity growth fell. The PTT Minister sought to raise SIP prices sharply, provoking great unpopularity and conflict with the trade unions.[78] Political pressures restrained tariff rises and hence SIP faced problems of worsening debt and even large losses by the late 1970s.[79] Indeed, it was in such financial trouble that it was accused of false accounting.[80]

Reponses to these difficulties were largely focused on financial planning and investment programmes in the 1970s.[81] However, no large-scale institutional reforms were introduced or even seriously considered. Only the trade union confederations and the Communist Party (the PCI) called for change, notably that ASST be given extensive control over STET's telecommunications services as they argued that STET was unaccountable, but this idea was ignored. The key actors in the sector—the political parties, publicly-owned suppliers, and trade unions—all enjoyed benefits from the institutional arrangements.[82] Political parties in government used the sector to provide jobs and financial support to 'clients'. Until the 1980s, the Posts and Telecommunications Minister and senior positions in the IRI firms were always held by Christian Democrats. The suppliers (both ASST and the IRI firms) enjoyed monopolies and state guarantees for borrowing. IRI and the government could also use the sector as part of industrial policy. Employees benefited from the conditions of public sector employment. Trade unions were consulted on policy by the government and represented on the boards of the state-owned companies. In particular, the dominant union, the Confederazione Italiana Sindacati Lavoratori (CISL), worked in close partnership with the Christian Democrats. Thus although Italian telecommunications suffered from high tariffs, poor service, excess demand, low investment, and much turf fighting among the various PTOs during the 1970s, institutional inertia took place.

---

[73] Thus for instance, the number of subscribers rose from 4.22 million in 1964 (8.14 per 100 population) to 6.46 million in 1970 (12 per 100 population)—Bottiglieri (1990: 465–8). By 1970, direct subscriber trunk dialling was available for the entire network, earlier than in Britain or France— Foreman-Peck and Manning (1988: 193); cf. Giacalone and Vergnano (1990: 33–4).

[74] Bottiglieri (1990: 409–13, 469–74).   [75] Bottiglieri (1990: 392–402).

[76] See Pontarollo (1983) and Tedoldi (1977).

[77] From 194,000 in 1970 to reach 828,000 in 1980.   [78] See Tedoldi (1977: 114–62).

[79] 486 billion litre in 1979 and 538 in 1980—Bottiglieri (1990: 468); for a journalistic analysis of political problems, see Giacalone and Vergnono (1990: 41–8).

[80] Giacalone and Vergnono (1990: 41–3).   [81] Richeri (1985: 54–5).

[82] Natallichi (2001: 155–61), Richeri (1985), and Giacalone and Vergnono (1990: 43–7).

1980–7 Increasing Pressure Without Institutional Response

Pressures for institutional reform grew between 1980 and 1987, as failures by operators to cope with technological and economic factors were evident, and domestic actors drew increasingly unfavourable comparisons between Italy and other nations. The publicly-owned PTOs faced increasing demand and rising waiting lists, particularly in big cities.[83] Italy lagged behind other countries in telephone density and policy makers faced arguments that gaps reduced the competitiveness of Italian businesses.[84] At the same time, many tariffs were much higher than in other countries, especially for international calls; they were also unbalanced as rises had been blocked in the late 1970s to provide a *fascia sociale* ('social bandage').[85] Business customers (especially large ones) were dissatisfied over tariffs and the availability and quality of services and criticised them relative to provision abroad.[86] Problems were most acute for new advanced services, which were delayed, often coming into operation years after other countries and which faced difficulties arising from the fragmentation of the network among different PTOs.[87] While Italian firms fell behind, foreign ones developed their own standards and private networks operated without authorisation, creating fear by the publicly owned operators that their networks were being bypassed.[88]

The pressures were particularly strong because the fragmentation of the PTOs created considerable inefficiencies in Italian telecommunications. Government ministers (notably Antonio Gava, Posts and Telegraphs minister in the mid-late 1980s) and the state suppliers—IRI, STET, and SIP—developed plans for ending the fragmentation by taking ASST out of the PT Ministry and merging it with SIP into one 'national pole'; the new operator would be majority owned by IRI, but have a large private shareholding.[89] The companies would be created to reach European standards and to be able to compete internationally.[90] Ministers, publicly owned companies, and businesses justified the need for change by reference to meeting new technological and economic demands and to changes in other countries, notably Britain and the US, as well as France and Japan.[91] The heads of IRI (Romano Prodi) and SIP (Paolo Benzoni) even pressed for partial privatisation

---

[83] For instance, in 1987 there were 300,000 on the 'D' waiting list, with an average delay of 4–5 months for a line; in the big cities, the waiting time was over 7 months—*Il Sole 24 Ore* 22.3.87, 30.3.87.

[84] *Il Sole 24 Ore* 22.2.85, 21.9.85, 15.2.86, 15.12.87.

[85] *Il Sole 24 Ore* 4.9.85, 15.9.85, 25.11.85; for international comparisons, see McDowell (1987).

[86] *Il Sole 24 Ore* 30.10.84, 9.11.84, 16.9.86, 3.10.86, 10.12.87, 15.12.87.

[87] Thus for instance, Fonia-dati the circuit-switched data network was 11 years after the French equivalent, while Italpac, the packet-switched network, began on a trial basis in 1985, 7 years after its French equivalent Transpac and 4 years after BT's equivalent; *Il Sole 24 Ore* 26.1.0.84, 21.9.85, 20.12.86, 2.2.87, 30.3.87.

[88] *Il Sole 24 Ore* 13.11.84, 13.12.84, 20.12.85, 18.7.86.

[89] *Il Sole 24 Ore* 22.2.85, 27.2.85, 28.2.85, 20.6.85, 5.4.86, 17.4.86, 17.4.87.

[90] *Il Sole 24 Ore* 21.9.85, 27.12.87 (article by Francesco Tempestini, sottosegretario alle Poste e Telecomunicazioni).

[91] *Il Sole 24 Ore* 12.4.85, 24.6.85, 4.9.85, 17.9.87.

of SIP in order to increase its capital rather than taking on further debt as part of meeting massive investment plans (the 'Altissimo' plan for 1985–94); they cited the example of BT in making their suggestion.[92]

By the early 1980s, there also seemed considerable agreement on liberalisation of terminal equipment and advanced services.[93] Businesses sought the end of state monopolies to improve supply.[94] Italian suppliers of advanced services and equipment such as Olivetti and Fiat also wished to enjoy a large domestic market to prepare to meet foreign competitors (especially IBM, AT&T, and Siemens) and to expand abroad.[95] The Italian subsidiaries of multinational firms (notably IBM Italia) pressed for competition in advanced services and clearer rules in order to aid their entry into the Italian market.[96] Plans were developed by Gava, PT minister, and the heads of IRI and STET/SIP for significant liberalisation of advanced services and all terminal equipment except the first telephone set.[97] SIP accepted increased competition but looked to the experiences of the US and the UK to argue that liberalisation should not extend to networks, where overseas experiences had shown serious obstacles.[98] The senior managers of the state-owned operators saw liberalisation as the counterpart of organisational consolidation and the freeing and rebalancing of tariffs.[99]

Yet despite the support of ministers, SIP, IRI, and businesses, very few institutional reforms were introduced between 1980 and 1987 due to the workings of the political system. The period saw short-lived coalition governments, which meant that many political parties had to agree to reforms. This was difficult as fragmentation of the operators meant that each operator could be under the influence of a political party (the *lottazione* or form of spoils system).[100] Opposition from several political parties, especially on the left, together with resistance from officials within the Posts and Telecommunications Ministry and concerns from trade unions about reductions in staffing and loss of civil service status for ASST employees meant that ASST was not removed from the PT Ministry nor were SIP or STET partially privatised.[101] Equally, little liberalization was introduced:[102] the unions opposed it and SIP was concerned about losing business in the absence of tariff rebalancing, which was politically difficult due to extra costs imposed on households.[103] Perhaps most important of all, liberalisation depended on altering the organisational position of the operators to allow them to be more efficient and hence compete effectively with new entrants. Thus reform was blocked because

[92] *Il Sole 24 Ore* 24.6.85, 16.9.85.

[93] Pontorollo (1984: 205–6); cf. Commissione Morganti (1983).

[94] They were especially concerned about value-added services and private circuits—*Il Sole 24 Ore* 9.11.84, 21.9.85, 20.12.85, 16.9.86, 3.10.86, 12.11.86.

[95] *Il Sole 24 Ore* 15.11.84, 13.11.84, 25.11.85.   [96] *Il Sole 24 Ore* 18.7.86.

[97] *Il Sole 24 Ore* 28.2.85, 21.9.85.

[98] Article, Paolo Benzoni, Administratore Delegato of SIP, *Il Sole 24 Ore* 18.11.86.

[99] *Il Sole 24 Ore* 25.9.84, 23.10.84, 30.6.85, 15.9.85, 16.9.85, 15.2.86, 17.5.86, 15.12.87.

[100] Natalicchi (2001: 158–61); interview senior lawyer.

[101] *Il Sole 24 Ore* 28.2.85, 31.3.86, 12.11.86, 8.12.86, 1.3.87, 13.5.87; interviews, senior legislator 1, senior telecommunications official 1 and 2.

[102] Only the maintenance of equipment was liberalised.   [103] *Il Sole 24 Ore* 21.9.84, 18.8.86.

liberalisation could not be matched by consolidation and greater independence for the operators. Instead of institutional reform, plans were developed for higher investment, funded by government help and increased borrowing.[104]

CONCLUDING COMMENTS: RESISTANCE TO INTERNATIONALISATION

In the mid-1960s, France, West Germany, and Italy had long-standing institutional arrangements in telecommunications. PTOs were not only publicly owned but were also mostly civil service units within Postal and Telecommunications Ministries. Those PTOs had a monopoly over the bulk of the sector. Only equipment manufacturers were privately owned. Governments held almost all regulatory powers, especially as PTOs were part of the civil service. Cross-national differences also existed, notably between Italy, with its fragmented sector and varied organisational position of its operators, and France and West Germany.

Between the mid-1960s and 1987, transnational technological and economic developments posed major challenges to traditional national institutions. Pressures arose from unmet demand, increased capital requirements for modernisation and the appearance of advanced services and terminal equipment that crossed sectoral boundaries, especially with computing and broadcasting. In addition, reforms took place in the US and then the UK, which offered an example to the three countries.

These international factors played significant roles in the institutional reform debates that took place in all three nations. Those debates centred on separating postal and telecommunications services, taking PTOs out of the civil service to give them greater autonomy from governments, and limiting PTO monopolies over terminal equipment and new services. In Italy there was the additional issue of consolidating the operators. In all three countries, reforms were argued by governments, the telecommunications sides of PTT Ministries, business users and expert reports to be necessary to respond to problems arising from transnational technological and economic developments.

However, proposals for change largely failed. Institutional reform debates remained dominated by domestic actors—notably governments, the management of operators and trade unions. No broad powerful reform coalition was formed among these actors—even government reformers and the senior management of operators failed to cooperate to push through change. In contrast, reform proposals met stiff domestic resistance from a broad and well-mobilised coalition of opponents. PTO employees and unions were a powerful obstacle to removing PTOs from the civil service. Separation of postal and telecommunications

---

[104] Notably the Altimisso plan of 1984, which envisaged investment of 10,000 billion lire cf. *Il sole 24 Ore* 25.9.84, 23.10.84; 24.6.85, 27.12.87; by 1985 the costs of servicing SIP's debt had reached 21% of receipts—*Il sole 24 Ore* 25.9.84, 20.6.85, 24.6.85, 21.9.85, 15.2.86.

services was opposed by postal unions. PTOs resisted greater competition in terminal equipment and advanced services.

Several reasons lay behind the failure to form a powerful coalition for institutional reform. One was that no broad agreement for change involving quid pro quos was developed to offer a basis for such a coalition. In particular, PTOs resisted liberalisation that was not accompanied by greater autonomy for them, which in turn led to politically very controversial issues of altering their organisational basis and structure. Another reason was an unfavourable reaction to reforms in the US and the UK. Finally, rather than formal institutional reforms, countries often choose to allocate greater resources to telecommunications, notably for investment. When these measures succeeded, demand for institutional changes diminished.

As a result, institutional modifications were very limited. In all three countries, the key traditional institutional features of the sector—public ownership, PTO monopolies, strong ministerial controls, and the linkage of postal and telecommunications services within one organisation—remained largely intact despite repeated debates and reform proposals over twenty years. The most important reform—the creation of new financial instruments in France—increased

Table 7.1. The institutional position of telecommunications in 1987 and major changes since 1965

Institutional feature in 1987 and changes since 1965	France	West Germany	Italy
Organisational position of the operator(s)	DGT part of civil service and telecommunications linked to postal services; new financial instruments for capital investment outside government budget	DBP part of civil service; telecommunications linked to postal services;	Several operators (*spezzatino telefonico*); ASST within posts and telecommunications ministry; other operators public corporations, majority-owned by state holding company IRI; some redefinition of division of allocation of services late 1960s
Competition	DGT monopoly; limited liberalisation of advanced services; competition in terminal equipment in early 1980s	DBP monopoly; very limited liberalisation of advanced services; competition in terminal equipment early 1980s	Operators' monopoly; extremely limited liberalisation of terminal equipment in early 1980s
Allocation of regulatory powers	Mostly lay with minister	Mostly lay with minister	Mostly lay with minister, although divided among different ministers

differences across the three nations. Table 7.1 summarises the institutional position in 1987 and the limited reforms made since the mid-1960s.

Thus transnational technological and economic factors and reforms in the US and Britain were significant in creating pressures for change and in reform debates. But the responses were institutional inertia and non-institutional policy changes. In all three countries, even revolutionary changes in the nature of an industry and overseas examples of alternative institutional arrangements were insufficient for modest changes, which were blocked within the domestic policy process. Traditional institutions were maintained.

Telecommunications in France, West Germany, and Italy between 1965 and 1987 underlines the lack of effect of transnational technological and economic factors in altering sectoral institutions, even when combined with reforms in the US. It mirrors the findings of securities trading between 1965 and 1986 (Chapter 3). It shows the power of inertia and vested interests within the domestic policy process to defend institutional arrangements created decades earlier for a very different industry and widely criticised as unsuitable for altered conditions.

8

British Telecommunications: From Laggard to Leader

The case of telecommunications in Britain offers a remarkable example of institutional inertia followed by radical and comprehensive reform. In 1965, sectoral institutions were similar to those in France and West Germany. As in those two countries, transnational technological and economic developments from the mid-1960s onwards caused serious problems of supply. Inadequate domestic institutions were widely blamed in policy debates, leading to serious discussions of reform. However, unlike its Continental neighbours, supply problems in Britain were not resolved through non-institutional mechanisms. At the same time, only limited institutional reforms were made in 1969 and debates on further changes came to nothing. Thus Britain combined failure in supply with institutional inertia.

From the early 1980s onwards, this situation was reversed. Sweeping reforms were introduced, notably privatisation of the incumbent supplier, liberalisation, and the creation of an independent sectoral regulator. These were driven by domestic factors. Nevertheless, internationalisation played a role as US institutions were used to justify change, although they were not studied in depth and many of their features were not copied. The outcome of the reforms was a radical break, not just with previous British institutions but more generally with the 'European model'. In turn, British reforms were largely followed by France, Germany, and Italy, albeit later and for different reasons (see Chapter 9).

The case of telecommunications in Britain serves to support four general arguments concerning market internationalisation and domestic institutional reform. First, it shows that sweeping transnational technological and economic factors can be met with institutional inertia: despite problems in supply and widespread agreement that existing institutions are performing poorly, those institutions can survive. It investigates how and why this occurs, notably the difficulties of forming a powerful reform coalition and the ability of determined groups to block changes. Second, it underlines the role of government in leading reforms: a determined government was able to start change and use overseas reforms to justify it.

Third, the chapter illustrates a distinct 'British' institutional reform process: lack of adjustment to transnational technological and economic developments, even in the face of considerable difficulties in supply; government-led reforms in the 1980s and 1990s; changes mainly driven by domestic factors; the example of institutions in the US used to legitimate change and to provide a palette of possible institutional features; and almost no role for EU regulation. Many of these features were found in reform of stock exchanges (see Chapter 4) and will be seen in airlines and electricity (Chapters 10 and 11).

Finally, the chapter analyses the mechanisms of Americanisation. Reforms in the US were used to as an example to justify change and to provide a source of ideas about possible alternative institutions to those in Britain. At times, the dangers of American firms benefiting from superior institutions in a competitive world market were put forward. But detailed learning or wholesale copying of the US did not occur—British policy makers did not investigate the US in depth and were highly selective as to which US institutions they chose to present as valuable. Hence the major role of the US example was to inspire and aid key reformers to undertake changes that they largely desired for domestic reasons. But, when domestic politics and the US example conflicted, policy makers followed the former not the latter. The role of the US was dependent on its congruence with domestic interests.

The chapter begins with a brief summary of institutional arrangements in the mid-1960s. It then sets out the reforms of the late 1960s, which opened wider debates about sectoral change. Thereafter it traces the increasing difficulties of the sector during the 1970s and the failure of reform attempts. Finally, it looks at changes between 1980 and 2005 that transformed the institutional framework.

INSTITUTIONAL ARRANGEMENTS IN THE MID-1960s

In the mid-1960s, institutional arrangements in Britain largely dated from the nineteenth century.[1] The Post Office (PO) supplied both telecommunications and postal services. It had a monopoly over public telecommunications services, networks, and most terminal equipment, dating from the 1869 Telegraph Act.[2] Although privately owned national champion firms such as GEC and Plessey manufactured equipment, the PO largely controlled supply through its monopsony power and approval of standards.

Since 1840, the PO had been a government department headed by a minister, the Postmaster General. Its budget fell within the government's annual budget, and was subject to Treasury control and parliamentary approval. As part of the civil service, PO investment had to be financed from operating revenue rather than long-term borrowing; no distinction was drawn between capital and current expenditure and any surplus revenue had to be repaid to the Treasury rather than being put aside for future investment.

Between the 1930s and the 1960s, telecommunications in Britain faced problems of excess demand, long waiting lists, under-investment, and inappropriate

---

[1] For histories, see Robinson (1948), Robertson (1947), and Pitt (1980).
[2] With the exception of a municipal operator in Kingston and Hull.

bureaucratic procedures. These were blamed on the institutional framework, notably the PO's income and expenditure being part of the general government budget, the power of the postal side of the PO over telecommunications, excessive ministerial control over the PO, and the application of civil service procedures to an industry.[3] There were several reform proposals to increase the PO's financial autonomy from the government, to allow it to borrow and invest over several years and occasionally to separate the postal and telecommunications sides of the PO.[4]

However, key actors in the sector derived advantages from the institutional framework and were able to block change. Thus the government used the PO, and especially its telecommunications side, to meet short-term fiscal targets. The Treasury wished to keep controls over the PO and government ministers preferred attempts to alter the internal workings of the PO rather than more contentious institutional reforms. The postal side of the PO, which occupied the senior positions in the organisation, opposed losing control over the highly profitable (and rival) telecommunications side, which it used to cross-subsidise postal services. Trade unions, especially those representing postal workers, feared any move that might weaken postal services or remove them from the civil service. They were often joined by the Labour Party (with whom they had strong links). Finally, equipment manufacturers enjoyed a cosy relationship with the PO, including fixed shares of the PO's orders and cost-plus contracts.

PROCESSES OF DECISION-MAKING FOR INSTITUTIONAL REFORM MID-1960s–2005

Four phases of institutional reform can be distinguished between the mid-1960s and 2005: limited reform 1965–69; inertia 1969–79; radical rupture 1980–84; continuing market reform 1985–2005. Despite growing internationalisation, the major participants continued to be domestic actors; only in the late 1990s did overseas firms play a role.

Transnational technological and economic factors were cited frequently in policy debates from the mid-1960s onwards. They sometimes gave rise to very visible pressures—for instance in rising unmet demand, difficulties in introducing new technology or turf battles in the 1990s between telecoms and broadcasting regulators. Reformers argued that institutional structures were inadequate to cope with the evolving nature of the sector. Thus, for example, they cited increased investment needs, the growing heterogeneity of the industry, the blurring of boundaries with other sectors such as electronics, computing, and audio-visual services. Yet, as will be seen, these

---

[3] See Pitt (1980), for the 1960s, see Canes (1966), Shepherd (1968), and Hills (1984: ch. 4 and 1986: ch. 3).

[4] Notably the 1932 Bridgeman report; for an analysis, see Pitt (1980).

pressures and arguments were insufficient on their own for institutional change.

From the late 1970s onwards, regulatory changes in the US were used in British reform debates. On the one hand, reformers presented them as attractive and successful examples of change. On the other hand, they underlined the potential dangers to Britain if it failed to match the US, such as the inability of British telecommunications companies to match their American rivals, missing out on opportunities to expand in the world's largest market, a growing loss of competitiveness of companies in Britain that relied on telecommunications and the transfer abroad of high technology companies. However, learning from the US involved little detailed analysis or studies of the successes or failures of US reforms, being at most confined to rapid fact-finding trips. Moreover, key features of the US sectoral institutions, such as the breakup of the incumbent AT&T or the multi-person regulatory, the Federal Communications Commission, were not copied. The major role of the US was as an example and argument to legitimate changes that were often controversial.

European Union regulation rarely played a role in British debates; indeed, for most of the period from the mid-1980s, Britain was seen as leading Europe towards a liberalised market, against resistance from Continental countries such as France. Only in the late 1990s, were fears of falling behind other European countries and EU regulation used to justify creating a single media regulator. This was, however, the exception rather than the rule.

SIGNIFICANT BUT LIMITED REFORM: THE MID-1960s–1969

In the mid-1960s, the PO faced a recurrence of long-standing problems of rising waiting lists and inadequate investment. As in earlier periods, the PO's management, especially its telecommunications side, pressed for greater autonomy to tackle these. However, unlike the past, the Labour government elected in 1964 seriously examined institutional changes.[5] Moreover, the main trade union for telecommunications engineers, the Post Office Engineering Union (POEU) altered its opposition to reform and began to lobby the government to move the PO out of the civil service. Thus by the late 1960s, widespread agreement existed that the PO's institutional position should be altered.

The main issue became how much additional autonomy should be given to the telecommunications side of the PO. The Union of Postal Workers (UPW) strongly resisted separation of postal and telecommunications services. On the other hand, the Conservative Party and the employers' organisation, the Confederation of

---

[5] The new Postmaster General, Anthony Wedgewood Benn, commissioned a report by the management consultants, McKinseys; in 1965, an Economic Development Committee was established to look at Post Office matters, and in 1967, the Select Committee on Nationalised Industries produced a large report—House of Commons, Select Committee on Nationalized Industries (1967).

British Industry (CBI) argued for separation.[6] They, together with the equipment manufacturers, also urged modest liberalisation in the supply of terminal equipment and a few advanced services.[7] A backbench Conservative MP, Kenneth Baker, even raised the possibility of the injection of private capital into the PO.[8]

The outcome of the debates was the passing by the Labour governments of the 1969 Post Office Act. The Act ended the PO's status as a government department dating from 1840 and offered significant reforms. The PO was transformed into a public corporation, outside the civil service, with its own legal identity.[9] It was no longer headed by a Minister but by a Board, whose members were appointed for fixed terms, and its employees ceased to be civil servants. The PO was to enjoy a degree of operational autonomy—for instance over salaries and its internal organisation. It was given very broad objectives, which mixed social aims and more commercially-oriented duties to break even.[10]

However, more radical reforms were blocked. Public ownership remained. The government retained many powers over the PO, notably appointing its Board and approving its capital spending plans. The PO's budget remained counted within general public expenditure figures, which meant that no distinction was drawn between capital and current spending. Unlike France or West Germany, the PO could not borrow outside general public expenditure nor have its own commercial budget that reflected the characteristics of a capital-intensive industry that yielded long-term returns on investment. Equally, the Act left the PO's monopoly unchanged.

FAILED REFORM ATTEMPTS: THE 1970s

Telecommunications in Britain throughout the 1970s were afflicted with considerable technical and financial problems that arose in significant measure from technological and economic developments.[11] The PO was unable to match rising demand, resulting in lengthy waiting lists.[12] Modernisation stalled as new technologies that offered better quality and greater capacity, especially digital and semi-digital switching, were not introduced. Problems arose over the PO's monopoly, especially over terminal equipment, as users and equipment suppliers complained that the PO was slow to provide new equipment or to approve its supply by private firms.[13]

---

[6] For the complex suggestions of the CBI see PRO [Public Records Office] BT 363/1, notably letter of Stephen Brown to the Paymaster General 27/4/67.

[7] Hills (1984: 17–8) and *The Times* 9.4.69.

[8] *The Times* 23.1.69, 24.1.69, Hansard 26.3.69 col. 1670; see also Canes (1966).

[9] Pitt (1980) and Thatcher (1999: 94–9).   [10] See s9 and s31 of the Act.

[11] cf. Bealey (1976), Pitt (1980), Hills (1984: ch. 4; 1986: ch. 3), and Thatcher (1999: ch. 6).

[12] They rose from 50,000 in 1965 to 108,000 in 1970, 218,000 in 1972, and after a dip in recession to 47,000 in 1976 reached 500,000 in 1980—PRO BT363/5, *The Times* 22.4.70, 11.5.72, 29.7.76, and 15.10.80.

[13] cf. Hills (1984: 117–8); the Post Office allowed private firms to supply advanced equipment such as private automated branch exchanges (PABXs).

The PO met four major difficulties that were linked to its institutional position as a public corporation. First, investment plans were reduced to meet government spending targets or because of short-term falls in demand.[14] Second, government policies over prices, rates of return, and the percentage of investment to be raised from internal financing (mostly profits) were altered at short notice, leading to fluctuations in prices and investment.[15] These two problems were compounded by the fact that not only was the PO's capital expenditure counted as part of the general budget, but also that no distinction was drawn between capital and current spending, so the government budget deficit could easily be reduced by cutting PO investment. Third, the PO was unable to form an effective industrial policy with the national champion suppliers to develop new equipment.[16] Yet any attempts by the PO to introduce new suppliers or increase competition provoked fierce lobbying of the government by existing suppliers. Finally, the application of general government policies on pay and prices caused financial difficulties for the PO and pay disputes with its employees.

These problems gave rise to debates about institutional reform. The central issue was whether and how to alter the organisational position of the PO to allow it to invest and develop new technology. The extent of the PO's monopoly over terminal equipment was also questioned, especially since it could not meet demand.[17] However, the Treasury was reluctant to lose control of PO spending, the PO opposed any reduction of its monopoly, and its postal side feared the loss of the profitable telecommunications business. Perhaps most important of all, the UPW, a large trade union with well-established links to the Labour Party, fought separation of postal and telecommunications services.

The Conservative government of 1970–4 looked briefly at ideas of partial or total privatisation, but rejected them due to fear of union opposition and to the belief that privatisation would merely result in a private monopoly replacing a public one.[18] Equally, they considered reducing the PO's monopoly over terminal equipment and looked at the US example (e.g. the Posts and Telecommunications Minister Christopher Chataway visited the US).[19] However, they accepted the PO's view that competition entailed dangers to the functioning of the network. Hence they left its monopoly untouched.

---

[14] Thus for instance, for the financial year 1974–5, telecommunications capital spending was cut by 20% and further cuts took place in 1975–7—*The Times* 19.12.73, 6.2.74, 12.9.75, 9.11.76, and 11.3.77.

[15] For details, see Thatcher (1999: 121–5).

[16] In particular, Britain's digital switch, 'System X' encountered a series of problems due in large measure to the PO's inability to lead the project—see Cawson et al. (1990); as a result, by 1980s in 1980, 85.3% of the PO's lines were still switched through the old electro-mechanical exchanges and not a single new 'digital exchange' was operating—*British Telecommunications Statistics* (Post Office/BT annual).

[17] Minutes of meeting between the Minister of Posts and Telecommunications and officials PRO TFB/C/4 13.1.72; cf. Public Records Office FV4/64 letter from D. Gottlieb 24.6.71, Public Records Office FV 87/2 letter from Miss J.M. Goose (Private Secretary to Minister of Posts and Telecommunications 17.7.72).

[18] Interview minister.   [19] Speech by Chataway 8.2.72—Public Records Office FV87/1.

In the 1974–5 period, increased criticisms of the PO's performance, waiting lists, and price rises by MPs, trade unions, and the user organisations led the government to establish a public inquiry chaired by Sir Charles Carter to look at the workings and structure of the PO. Submissions to the Carter inquiry showed strong support for alteration of the PO's organisational position, such as separation of postal and telecommunications services. The Carter report strongly criticised the institutional framework governing relations between the PO and the government.[20] It found that their roles were confused, that the government lacked policy analysis capacities and that intervention by ministers was inappropriate. It recommended that the PO be divided into two public corporations for postal and telecommunications services, due to the two being very different businesses, especially concerning capital investment. Drawing on a visit to the US, the Committee examined competition in terminal equipment, but was 'unable to define a new boundary' between the PO's monopoly and liberalised supply, and instead recommended that as an experiment, competition in one type of terminal equipment should be considered.

However, the Labour government rejected most of the Carter Committee's recommendations (Pitt 1980). It feared opposition from the trade unions, especially to separating postal and telecommunications services. It also lacked a parliamentary majority and time. Liberalisation continued to be opposed by the PO. No major reforms were introduced.[21]

RADICAL REFORM 1980–84

Britain faced increasing problems in telecommunications supply in the early 1980s arising in large measure from its failure to cope with technological and economic developments. The PO and then British Telecommunications (BT) were unable to satisfy growing demand, resulting in very long waiting lists even for a fixed telephone line.[22] BT's supply of advanced services and equipment that were needed by firms, notably the powerful financial sector in the City of London, was equally poor.[23] Modernisation of BT's network was slow, especially the introduction of digital switching equipment.[24] BT's capital expenditure met strong financial constraints imposed by the government: maximum borrowing limits and high target rates of return that led to rising prices.[25] At the same

---

[20] Carter Committee (1978).
[21] Except for a temporary and very limited experiment with union representatives on the PO's Board—see Batstone et al. (1983).
[22] The waiting list reached 500,000 in 1980—*The Times* 15.10.80.
[23] Notably private circuits (leased lines), especially digital lines that were needed for advanced services that involved data transmission, and Private Automated Branch Exchanges (PABXs).
[24] In 1984, only 2 of 459 trunk exchanges were digital and only one of 6,292 local exchanges— Vickers and Yarrow (1988).
[25] *The Times* 11.7.80, 1.8.80.

time, BT's national champion equipment suppliers were unable to deliver new equipment.[26]

The Conservative government led by Margaret Thatcher came into office in 1979 without plans for major Conservative reforms. In opposition, the party had only supported limited reforms to separate postal and telecommunications services and to allow competition in terminal equipment. It had not seriously discussed privatisation of telecommunications during its years in opposition (1974–9) and did not mention it in its 1979 election manifesto.

Initially, the government merely implemented its 1979 election promises. It separated postal and telecommunications services by creating BT as a public corporation, wholly publicly owned and separated from the PO, under the 1981 British Telecommunications Act. The change followed the recommendations of the Carter report (Carter 1978). The government obtained the support of the PO Board and unions representing telecommunications engineers; this left only opposition from the postal office union, the UPW, which was insufficient to block the new arrangements.

However, the government announced its intentions to sell shares in BT in July 1982.[27] This decision was very much its initiative. Users did not press for privatisation of BT nor even the ending of its monopoly over the infrastructure.[28] On the contrary, BT's privatisation met fierce parliamentary and extra-parliamentary resistance.[29] Some was predictable, notably from opposition political parties and the trade unions. However, in addition, British equipment manufacturers, who were traditionally core members of the British telecommunications policy community, strongly criticised the sale. Moreover, within the Conservative Party, there were concerns that BT would merely be a private monopoly, that it would abuse its power and that it would withdraw from desirable but 'uneconomic' activities such as providing services in rural areas.

Privatisation was thus driven by the government. Some of its reasons were domestic: privatisation reduced figures for government spending and borrowing, an attraction for the Treasury; it also allowed the Conservatives to claim that they were 'rolling back the State', in contrast with the 'pro-nationalisation' Labour Party. Privatisation was linked to introducing greater competition, as BT's position as a public corporation competing with private companies, but subject to Treasury controls and enjoying a monopoly over the infrastructure, was argued to be incompatible with fair competition.[30] Other reasons arose from frustrations by the Department of Industry over the clash between BT's needs for increased investment to meet demand and introduce new technology on the one hand, and budgetary rules whereby such investment was counted as public spending, which

---

[26] For the failures of System X, Britain's digital exchange, see Cawson et al. (1990).

[27] See Cawson et al. (1990: 95–97), Hills (1986:122–130), and Moon, Richardson, and Smart (1986) for analyses of the privatisation; for details of the sale, see Newman (1986).

[28] cf. Cawson et al. (1990).   [29] See Moon, Richardson, and Smart (1986: 345–9).

[30] The Beesley Report (1981) suggested that BT be freed from price and investment controls in order to be able to compete fairly.

was subject to fiscal restraints, on the other hand.[31] Finally, the US experience of privatised utilities under strong regulation appears to have offered an attractive example to many politicians, including Patrick Jenkin (Secretary of State for Industry 1981–3).[32]

The support of BT's top management appeared vital to privatisation.[33] BT had expressed strong discontent, especially over constraints on its investment, government financial controls, and accounting rules that made no distinction between capital and current expenditure and counted its deficits or surpluses towards public expenditure.[34] Yet it had not sought or suggested privatisation. Indeed, at first, privatisation met strong opposition from BT. The main issue was the break up of the supplier, perhaps into regional companies or separate companies for long-distance transmission and local services, similar to the 1982 breakup of AT&T in the US. This was strongly supported by the Prime Minister[35] and some Conservative backbenchers. The BT Board's main objective was to avoid such a policy, and in informal consultations it threatened to oppose privatisation if it were linked with breakup.[36] In addition, breaking up BT might have reduced sale proceeds, and would have greatly delayed privatisation, as little accounting information was available within the company.[37] Moreover, the Industry Minister (Patrick Jenkin) pointed to higher local charges in the US that he claimed arose from the breakup of AT&T.[38]

Faced with these factors, the government agreed to sell BT as one unit. It was thereby able to form an alliance with BT's management based on a quid pro quo: BT was privatised, competition was introduced into advanced services and terminal equipment and a sectoral regulator was created; on the other hand, BT's management obtained privatisation as a single integrated company and protection from open competition of its core business, namely the infrastructure and voice telephony (see below). The alliance proved an effective one. Privatisation was included in the Conservatives' successful 1983 general election manifesto. Internal Conservative Party opposition was placated by a combination of duties in the subsequent Act and BT's licence conditions notably concerning matters such as rural areas, fair competition, and protection of vulnerable users.[39] The strongest resistance came from the trade unions, notably the POEU, which organised industrial action. However, faced with a newly elected government that had promised privatisation, support by BT's management for the sale and court rulings against industrial action, the POEU was unable to stop the sale.

---

[31] Interview, DoI Minister.

[32] Moon, Richardson, and Smart (1986: 341–3); interview, DoI Minister; *The Financial Times* 23.1.82.

[33] Lawson (1992: 222–3); interview, DoI Minister.

[34] *The Times* 28.11.80; *The Financial Times* 7.3.81, 20.3.81, 7.5.81, and 3.6.81.

[35] Interviews, DoI Minister and DoI/Oftel senior official; cf. Thatcher (1993: 680).

[36] Lawson (1992: 222); interview DoI Minister.   [37] Interviews, DoI Minister and DTI official.

[38] House of Commons Hansard 25.10.82 col. 728.

[39] Moon, Richardson, and Smart (1986: 348).

As a result, the 1984 Telecommunications Act was passed. In November 1984, 50.2% of BT's shares were sold in the largest privatisation ever seen at that time in the world. Moreover, the 1984 Act established a new allocation of regulatory powers. An independent sectoral regulator was created—the Director General of Telecommunications (the DG), appointed by the Secretary of State for a term of up to five years. She or he headed the Office of Telecommunications (Oftel). Responsibilities were divided between the government and the DG. The former issued licences. However, the DG's responsibilities included enforcing licences, keeping public registers of licences, and collecting information. He or she also had powers to modify licences.[40]

Liberalisation ran in parallel with alteration of BT's organisational position. Following its 1979 election manifesto, the Conservative government announced in 1980 that BT's monopoly over most terminal equipment would end over a three-year period. The Secretary of State for Industry (Sir Keith Joseph) stated that 'one of the reasons for America's greater success has been freedom to develop new services and a wide range of equipment.'[41] He also commissioned an economic assessment of liberalisation of advanced services by an academic known for his pro-market views, Professor Michael Beesley. His report (Beesley 1981) recommended that all restrictions on the use of BT's private circuits should be removed, and that BT should be free to set prices and to compete in the supply of all advanced services. However, it went further than its terms of reference: drawing on experiences of competition in the US and new ideas about the shrinking 'natural monopolies' in telecommunications, it recommended that competition should also be allowed in the operation of networks and voice telephony. The report made repeated references to the US, to argue that liberalisation was beneficial and would not endanger BT.[42]

Sir Keith Joseph strongly favoured greater competition, as did Conservative backbench opinion.[43] Moreover, failure in the supply of advanced network and terminal equipment led to considerable discontent by business users and calls for an end to BT's monopoly in these fields.[44] However, BT strongly resisted liberalisation, claiming that it would lead to 'cream-skimming' of profitable services, and hence sharp price rises for residential customers.[45] Faced with powerful opposition, Joseph only pursued one of the Beesley report's recommendations for wider competition, namely proposals for an alternative telecommunications network. The sole response came from 'Mercury', a consortium led by Cable and Wireless,

---

[40] Subject to checks: a licence modification could be agreed by the DG and the licensee, subject to the Secretary of State insisting that the matter be referred to the MMC (Monopolies and Mergers Commission, since 2000, the Competition Commission) or alternatively, the DG could refer a matter to the MMC and if the latter gave a favourable report, could impose a licence modification—for details, see Thatcher (1999: 148–52).

[41] House of Commons Hansard 21.7.1980 col. 29.

[42] Beesley (1981); for references to the US, see e.g. paragraphs 33–37, 40–41, 46–48, and 113–115.

[43] Interview, DoI/Oftel official; The *Financial Times* 15.7.81 and 24.2.82.

[44] The *Financial Times* 15.4.80, 24.4.81, and 1.10.82, *The Times* 15.4.80, 21.4.80, and 15.10.80.

[45] The *Financial Times* 24.4.81, 29.6.81, and 3.7.81.

which Joseph licensed as a second network operator in February 1982.[46] Nevertheless, competition from Mercury was very limited: its 1982 licence was restricted and in practice appeared to primarily concern the supply of leased lines.[47]

The privatisation of BT saw a modest extension of liberalisation. In 1984, the government gave Mercury a new 25-year licence as a public operator, resulting in a duopoly in voice telephony and provision of the infrastructure. Moreover, BT was obliged under its licence to provide interconnection with its network to Mercury and was prohibited from 'undue preference or discrimination', which was vital for competitors. However, wider competition was delayed; in particular, the government promised not to allow unrestricted resale of leased line capacity (i.e. competitors buying capacity from BT and reselling it for public voice telephony) until 1989 nor permit further competition in network operation beyond the BT-Mercury duopoly until 1990. Thus the core of BT's business was protected until for several years.

CONTINUING MARKET REFORM: 1985–2005

After the 1984 Telecommunications Act, reforms towards a competitive regulated market with private suppliers continued, including under the Labour governments elected after 1997.

The government's remaining shares in BT were sold in 1990 and 1993, with almost no comment. The government retained a 'golden share' in the company which it could use to block a takeover. However, when BT sought to take over the American operator MCI in 1997, it faced opposition for the US regulatory authorities on the grounds that it enjoyed state protection from a market takeover. In response, the government decided to end the golden share to aid BT in its bid and hence help its overseas expansion.[48]

Liberalisation was also widened, driven by the government and Oftel, the new sectoral regulator after 1984. The former agreed to extend competition, including in public voice telephony and the infrastructure.[49] The latter made promoting 'effective competition' its highest priority.[50] Thus, in the period between 1984 and 1990, competition was permitted in the supply of almost all advanced services, terminal equipment and mobile and satellite services.[51] In the 1990s, competition was extended to core areas of the sector, including voice telephony and provision of the infrastructure. By 1996, BT had no remaining monopoly. Moreover,

---

[46] The *Financial Times* 3.7.81; the other shareholders later sold their shares to Cable and Wireless.

[47] The licence did not provide for an international switched service and restricted Mercury to 3% of the UK telecommunications market—the *Financial Times* 31.7.84.

[48] The *Financial Times* 16.7.97 and 15.7.97.

[49] See for instance Department of Trade and Industry (1987, 1991, 1997).

[50] See Oftel, *Annual Reports*, especially those of 1984 and 1985; Carsberg (1989, 1991); cf. Hall, Scott, and Hood (2000).

[51] See Thatcher (1999: ch. 10).

a host of re-regulatory rules were developed to try to ensure that competition was fair and effective. These included requirements on BT to provide information to Oftel, to base prices on costs, to separate costs of different services, and to offer interconnection and transmission capacity to rivals at cost-based tariffs.[52]

Sectoral regulation was also altered after 1984, but only when political conditions were propitious. In particular, convergence between telecommunications and broadcasting was discussed throughout the 1990s. The then Conservative government examined the sectoral framework but, being preoccupied with other matters such as the future of the publicly–owned broadcaster, the BBC, took no action.[53] However, this changed after the Labour Party won the general election of 1997. In opposition, it had pledged to create a communications regulator. In government, it appeared initially to backtrack towards merely encouraging cooperation among existing regulators; thereafter, a battle took place to gain priority and parliamentary time.[54] However, an alliance between the ministers for trade and industry and for culture led to the Communications Act 2003.

Several domestic reasons lay behind the passing of the legislation. These included concerns about media pluralism, the perceived weakness of Oftel and worries about the BBC.[55] However, international factors also played an important role in debates. The most-cited factor was technological change, and in particular, 'convergence' between telecommunications and broadcasting.[56] In turn, this was linked to warnings that the existence of several overlapping regulators was inefficient and muddling. Equally, a merged regulator was argued to be necessary to cope with large multinational suppliers that spanned several parts of the communications sectors.[57]

Competition from overseas, and especially the US, was also significant in justifications for reform. The 2001 Communications White Paper argued that Britain needed to be ahead of other nations in creating better institutions.[58] At the same time, it noted that Britain lacked large media companies that could compete internationally. Policy makers feared competition from American media conglomerates, especially after mergers such as America Online and Time Warner (completed 2001). Hence the White Paper argued that Britain needed regulatory structures that helped the creation of multi-sectoral audio-visual firms. However, while it cited such regulatory competition, it offered little analysis of other national structures and made no mention of other combined communications regulators, such as the Autorità per le Garanzie nelle Communicazioni (AGCOM) in Italy. Its major example was the US, where the FCC handles (federal)

---

[52] See Thatcher (1999: ch. 9).
[53] Interview senior DTI official 2; The *Financial Times* 5.12.2000.
[54] The *Financial Times* 18.2.2000, 7.11.2000, and 12.7.2001.
[55] cf. the *Financial Times* 22.9.2000, 14.5.2002, and 20.9.2005.
[56] The *Financial Times* 17.10.2000; DTI/DCMS 2000: 2–3, 11–12.   [57] ITC 2001.
[58] DTI/DCMS 2001: 2, 10; see also BT 2001, the *Financial Times* 17.10.2000.

telecommunications and media issues.[59] Again, however, detailed studies were not undertaken and the new statutory body, Ofcom, was not a close copy of the FCC. Finally, and rarely for Britain, the EU and Europe was cited in reform debates. On the one hand, it was suggested that Oftel had lost previous capacities to influence EU decision-making.[60] On the other hand, the EU was in the process of passing legislation to regulate electronic communications as a whole rather than just telecommunications. Reform allowed Britain to lead other nations in implementing EU legislation.[61]

The 2003 Communications Act created Ofcom, the Office of Communications. It took the powers and place of five previous regulatory bodies, including Oftel and the Independent Television Commission (ITC). Ofcom was established as a statutory corporation. It moved away from the traditional British model of single person regulators. Instead, it was headed by a Board, composed of full-time executive members (including its chief executive) and part-time members, including Ofcom's chairman. Ofcom covered most of the telecommunications and audio-visual sectors.[62]

CONCLUSION

In the mid-1960s, Britain had similar sectoral institutions to those in other European countries such as France and West Germany: a government department, the Post Office, combining telecommunications and postal services, enjoyed a legal monopoly over most of the sector; the government held regulatory powers. Major problems in supply occurred in the 1960s and 1970s that arose in large measure because transnational technological and economic developments met institutionally-related constraints. Yet only modest reforms were made in 1969 and more far-reaching changes were blocked. However, between 1980 and 1984, radical reforms were introduced that reversed century-old institutions; thereafter reform continued towards a liberalised market with a privatised incumbent and an independent sectoral regulator. The main stages of reform are summarised in Table 8.1.

Four general findings concerning internationalisation and institutional reform can be drawn from the history of telecommunications in Britain between 1965 and 2005.

First, the case shows that the political 'market' for institutions responds poorly to economic difficulties. In the 1960s and 1970s, transnational technological and

---

[59] The *Financial Times* 18.2.2000, 17.10.2000, and 12.12.2000, *The Guardian* 3.6.2003, *The Business* 20.1.2002; cf. Select Committee on Culture, Media, and Sport—Fourth Report session (2001–2).

[60] The *Financial Times* 4.9.2000 and 22.9.2000; interview senior DTI official 2; Coen (2005*b*).

[61] The *Financial Times* 17.10.2000, DTI/DCMS (2001: 19).

[62] Although internally, in a manner similar to AGCOM in Italy, there was separation between content and carriage: under the Act, Ofcom was obliged to set up a separate Content Board that would deal with the content of broadcasting, to be chaired by a non-executive member of Ofcom.

Table 8.1. The institutional position of telecommunications in Britain 1965–2005

Institutional feature	1965	1969	1984	2005
Organisational position of the operator(s)	Post Office part of the civil service; posts and telecommunications	Post Office a public corporation; still combined telecommunications and postal services	British Telecom (telecommunications only) majority privately owned	British Telecom entirely privately owned
Competition	Post Office monopoly	Post Office monopoly	Limited competition permitted	Entire telecommunications sector open to competition
Allocation of regulatory powers	Mostly with Minister	Mostly with Minister	Divided between Minister and sectoral IRA, Oftel, some with general competition authority	Divided between Minister and communications IRA, Ofcom, some with general competition authority

economic developments were not dealt with successfully and contributed to major problems such as long waiting lists, failure to modernise the network, and inadequate supply of new services and equipment. Many policy makers, including the government and the telecommunications side of the PO, blamed institutional arrangements. Yet only modest reforms were introduced in 1969. Despite continuing problems and criticisms of the institutional arrangements, no further changes were made.

Second, the British experience illustrates how countries can arrive at similar institutional outcomes for different reasons and through diverse processes. In Britain, reform was largely undertaken for domestic reasons. The most radical reforms came in the 1980s, well before similar changes in the other three nations. Insofar as internationalisation was significant, it was through the influence of the US, whereas Europeanisation played little role. These features stand in contrast to France, Germany, and Italy (analysed in Chapter 9). This distinctly British path is seen in other sectors.

The central role of the government is a third finding. The government often initiated change. It was able to do so even when other actors were not pressing for new institutions. This is best illustrated over privatisation in 1984, which at first was strongly opposed by most sectoral actors. The government was a key source of proposals and impetus for reform.

Finally, the case shows the role of Americanisation in British institutional debates. US regulatory institutions offered examples of alternative arrangements and were used as sources of new ideas—for instance on liberalisation or in designing independent regulatory authorities. Occasionally they were also presented as a source of regulatory competition, as British policy makers worried about keeping upwith the US. However, policy learning from the US was limited: British policy makers did not undertake in-depth studies or analyse the impacts of US reforms. Moreover, when the US example ran into domestic obstacles, it was not followed; thus for instance, the breakup of AT&T was not copied for BT, despite support by Mrs Thatcher as Prime Minister in 1982–3. Thus British policy makers did not import the US model: rather, they looked at the US and selected elements that attracted them and aided the pursuit of interests grounded in domestic politics. The main function of the US example was to legitimate change or present a menu of alternative institutional features from which British policy makers could then select, according to their domestic interests.

9

The European Path to Radical Reform: Telecommunications in France, Germany, and Italy 1988–2005

In 1988, institutional arrangements in France, (West) Germany, and Italy were largely unaltered from the nineteenth and early twentieth centuries. They had remained intact in the face of powerful transnational technological and economic developments and reforms in the US and then Britain. Repeated debates and reform proposals in the 1960s and 1970s had failed. Opposition to change was strong, notably from trade unions, employees of telecommunications operators and some political parties. Radical reform seemed unlikely.

Between 1988 and 2005, debates on institutional modification continued in the three countries. However, in sharp contrast to the preceding periods, reform proposals were implemented. Initially, modest alterations were made in the late 1980s and early 1990s; thereafter, sweeping changes were introduced that transformed sectoral institutions. By 2005, all three countries had broken with previous long-standing sectoral frameworks through privatisation, liberalisation, and delegation of powers to independent regulatory authorities.

Both domestic and international factors were responsible for reform. The chapter focuses on the latter. Transnational technological and economic developments and reforms in the US and Britain, which had been begun before 1988, continued. However, a new factor from 1988 onwards was EU regulation which began slowly but from the mid-1990s offered an evermore comprehensive, detailed, and binding framework for member states (see Chapter 6). The chapter argues that EU regulation was particularly influential; so too, but to a lesser extent, was regulatory competition with Britain. These two policy forms of internationalisation affected the strategies of government and incumbent operators and assisted in creating an alliance between them. EU regulation provided occasions for change and apparently external requirements that offered reformers arguments to legitimate a new institutional framework and overcome opposition. Fear of regulatory competition from Britain became strong in response to international alliances by its main operator BT.

These findings link to three broader arguments about internationalisation and domestic institutional reform. First, they underline the importance of policy forms of internationalisation, particularly EU regulation and reforms in overseas countries, in this case Britain. This is seen in the far-reaching and radical institutional reforms, that differed sharply from the inertia before 1988, when transnational technological and economic developments and US reforms were insufficient for change in the three countries (see Chapter 7). Through detailed process tracing, the chapter shows how and why policy forms of internationalisation were significant in decision-making.

A second argument concerns the carriers and mechanisms of policy forms of internationalisation. EU regulation and reforms in Britain operated through their effects on domestic actors, especially governments and the managements of domestic publicly-owned incumbents who led change. Hence the chapter reinforces the claim that state actors are central as carriers of internationalisation. The two policy forms of internationalisation operated through providing resources to reformers and cementing alliances between them. In particular, EU regulation had effects that went well beyond its legal requirements, as it could be used to legitimate far-reaching changes. Equally, reforms in Britain became significant not because of cross-national admiration, but because of fear of regulatory competition, which had not been present before 1988; the cases underline that the impact of overseas reforms depends heavily on regulatory competition rather than ideational mechanisms. At the same time, the two forms of internationalisation were sufficiently flexible to be used in ways that served the interests of governments and incumbent firms, and provided arguments to justify changes that met fierce opposition. The findings underline the importance of analysing internationalisation as part of domestic policy processes.

Finally, the chapter shows that countries can take diverse paths to similar institutional outcomes. By 2005, France, Germany, and Italy had adopted similar sectoral arrangements to those in Britain, and strong convergence had taken place across the three countries compared with the position in 1988. However, the three countries modified their institutions later and due to different processes and international factors than Britain. Detailed historical process tracing allows important differences in reform paths to be understood that would be missed by looking only at institutional outcomes.

FRANCE

Processes of Reform

In 1988, major institutional reforms seemed unlikely in France. In government, the Right had abandoned its 1987 proposals for limited changes in the face of fierce opposition, including strike action (see Chapter 7). In May 1988, the Left returned to power. The new PTT Minister Paul Quilès stated that altering the organisational position (*statut*) of France Télécom (as the *direction générale des télécommunications* (DGT) had been renamed in 1987) was not on his agenda, criticised deregulation and underlined his support for public service.[1] There was

---

[1] *Le Monde* 20.7.88 and *La Tribune de l'Expansion* 20.7.88.

powerful resistance to change, especially by trade unions, employees, and parts of the political left.

Yet comprehensive reform was introduced by a determined coalition led by the government and France Télécom's management that created a mutually beneficial strategy utilising internationalisation. It took place in three phases: modest changes 1988–90 that largely represented implementation of proposals made in the 1960s; radical alterations 1993–7; and consolidation 1998–2005.

Policy forms of internationalisation played crucial roles, especially reforms in Britain and most important of all, EU regulation. In the period 1988–93, they were additional to domestic factors. Nevertheless, reformers cited not only arguments put forward in the past about the effects of technological and economic developments but also newer ones about competition from large overseas firms such as BT and the effects of the EU's '1992 Single Market' programme.[2] After 1993, international factors became more prominent.[3] France Télécom's management and the government argued that greater competition and privatisation were inevitable and/or necessary due to EU legislation and regulatory competition with other nations (particularly Britain).

They sought international alliances with Deutsche Telekom and a US partner, again justified as essential to meet international competition. They underlined that France Télécom's organisational status had to be altered to prepare for liberalisation at home and abroad and to ensure successful international alliances and expansion. Policy forms of internationalisation aided the formation of the reform coalition and offered it arguments for change.

Substantive Reforms

From Administration to Private Company: Altering France Télécom's Organisational Position

In 1988, France Télécom remained a civil service unit within the PTT Ministry. Many employees, trade unions, and parts of the Left were suspicious of any modification of its organisational position.[4] They feared that employees would lose their civil service status, mobility between the postal and telecommunications branches would end and that reform would lead to privatisation.

Between 1988 and 1990, the Prime Minister Michel Rocard, the PTT Minister Paul Quilès, and eventually President Mitterrand became convinced of the need for institutional reform. Some reasons were domestic.[5] Nevertheless, international

---

[2] Quilès (1989), Chevallier (1989), Leray (a pseudonym for a group of telecommunications engineers based on the name of FT's headquarters) (1994: 115–7), Cohen (1992: 266–7); cf. Prévot (1989: 7–8); interview Prévot Commission.

[3] cf. Chevallier (1996).

[4] For opinions, see Prévot (1989), Leray (1994), *l'Humanité* 20.7.88, 11.4.89, *Le Monde* 13.4.89, *Le Monde* 25.9.93, and *Le Figaro* 12.1.0.93 ; interview Prévot Commission.

[5] Such as Rocard's policy of modernising public service and the desire by France Télécom's management to update employment grades—*Le Monde* 20.9.88; also *Le Monde* 28.1.89.

factors were present, albeit less visible. Reformers argued that France Télécom had to adapt to growing competition and internationalisation, for which its position within the civil service was inappropriate.[6] Rather than being confined to loss-making or declining traditional public service tasks, it should expand into new domains and overseas markets as barriers to entry fell due to technological and economic developments and EU regulation.[7] It should be able to form alliances with overseas firms, to match other rival operators such as BT and AT&T.[8] Nevertheless, the government rejected privatisation, citing negative effects in countries such as Britain and the US.[9]

To reduce opposition, the reform process proceeded slowly and through compromises. The government set up a broadly based commission chaired by a former trade unionist, Hubert Prévot. Following a long debate and report (Prévot 1989), legislation in 1990 sought to strike a balance between greater autonomy for France Télécom, maintenance of the government's role as policy maker and guarantees for staff.[10] From 1 January 1991 France Télécom became an *exploitant public* (a form of public corporation), separated from *La Poste*. It was to enjoy operating and financial autonomy and was headed by its own Board and Chairman. These reforms represented the implementation of ideas put forward since the late 1960s (see Chapter 7). However, in other respects, changes were limited. France Télécom personnel continued to be civil servants. The PTT Minister kept many powers including *tutelle* (formal responsibility) for France Télécom, selection of a third of its Board members and Chairman, and setting its licence conditions.

After 1993, international factors became central for much wider-reaching modifications that involved privatisation.[11] At the national level, the sale of France Télécom offered the government valuable revenue. At a sectoral level, arguments continued about preparing for competition that was presented as inevitable due to technology. But, real impetus came in the early 1990s from two other factors.[12] First, the EU decided in 1993 to end remaining monopolies by 1998. In response, France Télécom's management and the government argued that the company had to become competitive in its home market to meet new entrants, including overseas operators.[13] They claimed it required more autonomy to introduce unpopular decisions such as tariff rebalancing and new working practices that ran counter to civil service rules and traditions.[14] It also meant ending financial burdens

---

[6] Prévot (1989: especially 14–19), Quilès (1989), Roulet (1989), *Le Monde* 28.1.89, *Le Figaro*, 11.4.89, and interview, senior DGT/France Télécom official 1.

[7] *Libération* 14.12.88, 11.4.89, interview, senior France Télécom official 1.

[8] Roulet (1989).   [9] Quilès (1989); cf. Longuet (1989).

[10] Loi du 2 juillet 1990 relative à l'organisation du service public de la Poste et des Télécommunications, and decrees of 12 and 29 December 1990; for summaries, see Bensoussan and Pottier (1991) and Gensollen (1991).

[11] See notably Dandelot (1993) and Roulet (1994).

[12] 01 *Informatique* 1.11.93, *Le Monde* 7.12.93, and Larcher report (1993).

[13] *Le Figaro Economie* 1.3.93, *Le Monde* 21.7.93, 22.3.95, *Libération* 13.10.93, and Chevallier (1996).

[14] For example, in 1992, the government openly blocked tariff changes, in the light of legislative elections in 1993 and in 1994 it was reluctant about tariff rebalancing—*La Tribune Desfossés* 2.9.94.

placed on France Télécom such as levies and obligations to bailout loss-making companies, which other competitors did not face (and which France Télécom's management bitterly resented).[15]

Second, France Télécom's rivals, notably BT, began to form international alliances. Policymakers argued that France Télécom should follow suit (although they did not commission detailed analyses of the results of alliances).[16] The centrepiece of policy became the alliance between France Télécom, Deutsche Telekom, and an American operator designed to capture expanding international services, enter overseas markets, and transform France Télécom's into an 'international champion', a strategy taken up at the highest political level, including by President Mitterrand and Chancellor Kohl.[17] But alliances became linked to privatisation. Thus, alteration of France Télécom's organisational position was almost set as a condition for cooperation by the Germans, given that Deutsche Telekom was to be privatised (see below) and that future cross-holdings between the two operators were envisaged.[18] Equally, France Télécom's attempts to form alliances with privately-owned American operators met obstacles: as a wholly state-owned entity, it was difficult to value France Télécom and hence establish cross-share holdings. In 1993, when France Télécom was beaten by its rival BT in creating an alliance with the US operator MCI, the French operator argued that its failure was due, in large measure, to its institutional position within the public sector.[19] Thereafter, France Télécom sought an alliance with another American operator, Sprint. But the US Federal Communications Commission (FCC) and investors linked approval to regulatory reforms being undertaken in France.[20] Thus privatisation of France Télécom was argued to be essential to meet competition at home and expand abroad.

But change was strongly resisted by trade unions, many France Télécom employees, and the parties of the Left. The result was a lengthy struggle in which arguments about international pressures were central. The first step came on the return to government of the Right in 1993. Gérard Longuet (PTT and Industry Minister) commissioned a report on the future of the telecommunications sector.[21] The report laid strong emphasis on international factors—the need for France Télécom to create alliances with overseas firms, capture the expanding markets for international services, respond to foreign competitors, adapt to markets

---

[15] Notable examples in the early 1990s were the forced purchases of government share in information technology companies such as Thomson and Bull and even two insurance companies (AGF and UAP)—*Le Monde* 25.12.92, 31.1.93, *Les Echos* 1.2.93, and *Le Figaro* 2.2.93.

[16] Interview with Roulet, *Le Monde* 6.7.93 and *Les Echos* 20.7.93.

[17] cf. Chevallier (1996: 912), Hayward (1995), Thatcher (1995), *La Tribune Desfossés* 19.7.93, 2.12.93, 8.12.93, *La Tribune de l'Expansion* 17.9.93, 15.6.94, *Les Echos* 8.11.93, 8.12.93, and *Le Monde* 21.7.93, 22.3.95.

[18] *Le Monde* 21.7.93; comments by Gunter Rexrodt, German Finance Minister, demanding a 'substantial privatisation' of France Télécom—*La Tribune Desfossés* 30.11.93 and *Les Echos* 1.9.94.

[19] Interview with Roulet, *Le Monde* 6.7.93.

[20] *Le Monde* 3.8.94, *La Tribune Desfossés* 18.7.9, and *Le Monde* 22.7.95.

[21] From his former *directeur de cabinet*, Marc Dandelot—Dandelot (1993).

altered by technological and economic developments, and enjoy greater autonomy from government. It claimed that reform was urgent—it had to be implemented at least two years before full liberalisation under EU law in 1998.[22] The report recommended that France Télécom should be transformed into a limited company and partially privatised.

In response, the unions organised a successful one-day strike in October 1993: 74% of France Télécom employees participated. Longuet therefore decided to delay legislation in order to allow a major 'debate' on reform.[23] France Télécom's senior management then launched a new set of 'consultations' and in July 1994, Marcel Roulet, president of France Télécom, published a report setting out the reasons for change, underlining the need to meet international competitors on equal terms and to build alliances with overseas operators such as Deutsche Telekom.[24] However, in the face of continuing union opposition and the forthcoming presidential elections in 1995, the government again postponed a new law.[25]

After 1995, the Right continued in government but the new PTT Minister François Fillon, sought to postpone modification of France Télécom's organisational position, while also pressing ahead with full liberalisation.[26] This led to sharp conflict with France Télécom's management, which used international factors as a key argument for its position. In September 1995, the new publicly designated head of France Télécom, François Henrot, declined the post because of lack of guarantees of rapid reform, which he regarded as essential for the internationalisation strategy, and especially the alliance with Deutsche Telekom.[27] His successor, Michel Bon, repeated the argument, underlining the need for action because of the EU's 1998 date for full liberalisation.[28] On the Right, critics claimed that rapid change was essential for France Télécom to meet international competition and create alliances.[29] Moreover, the head of the FCC linked alteration of France Télécom's *statut* with US regulatory approval of the 'Phoenix' alliance with Deutsche Telekom and the American firm Sprint.[30]

Faced with these powerful pressures, the government made partial privatisation a political priority. It and France Télécom's management campaigned to persuade the public, employees, and unions that reform was essential for France Télécom's future. The central arguments were that making the operator a private company was essential for it to prosper in an internationalised and competitive market by preparing for EU liberalisation in 1998 and forming alliances with other operators.[31] Concessions were made to the unions, notably an early retirement scheme and continued recruitment of civil servants until 2002 even if France Télécom

---

[22] Dandelot (1993: 49).   [23] *Le Monde* 26.11.93.
[24] *La Tribune de l'Expansion* 8.7.94 and Roulet (1994).
[25] *Les Echos* 1.9.94, 9.9.94 and 13.9.94; interview, mission à la réglementation.
[26] *Le Monde* 12.7.95, 13.7.95 and *Les Echos* 13.7.95.
[27] *Le Monde* 10-11.9.95 and *Les Echos* 1.9.95, 11.9.95.
[28] *Le Monde* 4.10.95 and *La Tribune Desfossés* 2.2.96.   [29] cf. Larcher (1996).
[30] *La Tribune Desfossés* 18.7.95 and *Le Monde* 22.9.95.
[31] *Les Echos* 19.3.96, 11.4.96, 30.5.96, *Le Monde* 21.3.96, article by Fillon, PTT Minister, *Le Monde* 7.5.96.

became a limited company.[32] The trade unions were divided and strikes in April and June 1996 mobilised fewer employees and were seen as a failure.[33] The government then passed legislation[34] making France Télécom a 'national company' (*entreprise nationale*) from 31 December 1996; in practice, this meant a limited company operating under private law. Partial privatisation was allowed, as the state had to keep a minimum stake of 51%.[35] In addition, the operator paid the state 37 billion francs to cover pension liabilities, a useful sum for the government that allowed France to meet the Maastricht economic criterion for entry to the Euro. The government retained important powers, such as nominating France Télécom's chairman and specifying its licence conditions.

Alain Juppé's government prepared to sell 30% of France Télécom's shares in May 1997. However, the National Assembly elections of June 1997 saw the return of the Left. During the election campaign, the electoral platform of the Left (the Socialist and Communist parties, the PS and PCF) appeared to rule out even partial privatisation.[36] Yet once in government, the Left faced difficulties over the budget deficit and pressure from France Télécom's senior management, armed with arguments that partial privatisation was needed for internationalisation.[37] The new government rapidly changed tack, citing the same international reasons as its predecessor.[38] It commissioned a report by a former Socialist Minister Michel Delebarre, that supported a partial sale; the main reasons were to permit international alliances, particularly a cross-holding with Deutsche Telekom, and to allow France Télécom to meet international competition.[39] In October 1997, 23.2% of France Télécom's shares were sold.[40]

After 1997, France Télécom engaged in rapid overseas expansion. Paradoxically, its alliance with Deutsche Telekom broke up in 1999. Thereafter, it made acquisitions of overseas companies, notably mobile operators.[41] Since it could not exchange shares, it was obliged to pay cash and take on increased debt. By 2002, it was the most indebted company in the world (debts of €69 billion), had made a loss of €20.7 billion and its share price had fallen from a peak of €150 in 2000 to under €7.[42] With the end of the 'high technology' stock market boom, the operator faced bankruptcy, as banks refused to provide funds and it could not issue further debt.

In response, the government and the company's new head from 2002, Thierry Breton claimed that state majority ownership had been the cause of France

---

[32] *Le Monde* 25.5.96 and *Les Echos* 28.5.96.   [33] *Les Echos* 13.4.96, 25.4.96, and 5.6.96.

[34] La loi no. 96-660 du 26 juillet 1996 rélative à l'entreprise France Télécom, Journal Officiel 27 juillet 1996, p. 11384; for detailed commentaries, see Chevallier (1996) and Boiteau (1996).

[35] 10% of capital was set aside for staff and up to another 39% could be sold in the market.

[36] *Le Monde* 30.5.97, *La Croix* 5.6.97, and *Le Monde* 27.6.97.

[37] *Libération* 5.6.97, *Le Monde* 7.6.97, and *Les Echos* 21.7.96.   [38] *Le Monde* 27.6.97.

[39] Delebarre (1997), *Le Monde* 7-8.9.97, and *Libération* 7.9.96.

[40] 2.5% sold to its staff; after the purchase of the mobile operator Orange in 2000 and increases in capital, the state's share fell to 54.5% by 2003.

[41] Including the German company Mobilcom and British-based company Orange.

[42] Cf. *Le Monde* 6.3.2002.

Télécom's problems.[43] Breton pressed to be allowed to use shares for acquisitions, which necessitated the state holding falling below 51%; he comparing the operator's position with that of overseas companies had which used their shares to make purchases.[44] The government also argued that France Télécom's inability to use its own shares to pay for takeovers was damaging, leading to excessive debt—it was essential to provide France Télécom with fresh capital.[45] It claimed that EU law whereby member states had to allow competition among firms for the provision of 'public services' reduced the need for public ownership.[46] Finally, seizing the occasion of transposing EU directives (the 2002 'package'), it passed legislation in 2003 that made France Télécom a limited company and allowed the state's holding to fall below 51%. Although the trade unions and parts of the political Left attacked the law, they had little impact. Strike action largely failed, as existing France Télécom employees were protected through their civil service status and constant invocation of the lack of choice appeared to have sapped the will to resist; the PS criticised the alteration rather mildly.[47] Thus by end 2003, the government was free to privatise a majority share in France Télécom. This was followed by the sale of 9.5% in 2004 that reduced the state's share to 42% and then the issue of new shares (to fund overseas acquisitions) in September 2005 that diluted the state's share to 33%.

Liberalisation and Regulation

On coming into office in 1988, the new PTT Minister Paul Quilès stated that there would be no 'deregulation'. Nevertheless, liberalisation advanced modestly during the period 1988–92. Competition in advanced services and networks was accepted by the Prévot Commission, the government, and France Télécom's management.[48] One reason was change in international markets and new technology such as private satellite communications.[49] But more directly, policy makers underlined the need to ensure that services matched those available in countries that had liberalised (such as Britain and the US) and to comply with EU legal requirements for liberalisation of services.[50] Indeed, when legislation was passed in 1990, it

[43] *Le Monde* 6.3.2002, 29.5.03 and *Le Monde* 7.10.2003; for the overall strategy see *Les Echos* 11.3.2003.

[44] *Le Figaro Economie* 2.9.2003, *Les Echos* 2.9.2003; a key issue was buying up the subsidiaries Orange and Wanadoo, which generated much cash, but which were outside France Télécom which had only been able to afford to buy a majority stake.

[45] *Les Echos* 31.7.2003, 23.10.2003 and *Le Figaro Economie* 6.12.2003.

[46] *Le Monde* 5.7.2003, 1.8.2003 and *Les Echos* 10.7.2003.

[47] *l'Humanité* 20.10.2003 and *Libération* 22.10.2003.   [48] Prévot (1989: 37–9).

[49] cf. Quilès (1989) and comments in *La Tribune de l'Expansion* 20.7.88, Prévot (1989: especially 75–7), *La Tribune de l'Expansion* 4.1.89 and Roulet (1989), interviews, senior France Télécom officials 1 and 2, Prévot Commission.

[50] cf. Prévot (1989: 18, 32); comments by Quilès on taking office, *Le Figaro* 20.7.88; interview Prévot Commission.

largely followed the EU's directives.[51] It restricted France Télécom's monopoly to the public network infrastructure and 'reserved services', notably voice telephony. Thereafter, some services required a licence issued by the minister, who therefore determined the licence conditions. For some services, he/she could refuse a licence if it was considered to conflict with France Télécom achieving its public service obligations.

Later in the 1990s, France Télécom's remaining monopoly (over fixed networks and voice telephony) was ended with broad consensus, including by France Télécom. In part this was because the incumbent and government believed that competition in networks was inevitable due to technological and economic developments and international competition, notably matching tariffs offered by competitors such as BT or US operators.[52] But the EU was the key factor in the 1990s that provided urgency and justification. The EU's 1998 deadline for full liberalisation provided a discipline and timetable for new legislation.[53] It also weakened a key obstacle to greater competition, namely that France Télécom had historically inherited cross-subsidies that favoured residential users. EU regulation gave the incumbent and ministers the justification to reduce cross-subsidises, by rebalancing tariffs. In particular, EU liberalisation was used to justify raising the costs of local calls and rentals and reducing those of long-distance services, thereby protecting France Télécom from losing revenue and/or market share in a competitive market.[54] More directly, the European Commission linked acceptance of international alliances to domestic liberalisation. Thus it tied approval of the France Télécom–Deutsche Telekom joint venture, 'Atlas' in 1995 to France agreeing to allow competition in non-voice services earlier than required under EU law.[55] The international future of the French incumbent was argued to require liberalisation at home.

By the mid-1990s, there was little direct opposition to the principle of full liberalisation and it was directed as much against the EU, a rather distant target, than the French government.[56] The government passed legislation in 1996 that ended France Télécom's remaining monopolies by 1 January 1998.[57] It specified the services for which individual licences were required and those authorised

---

[51] Loi du 29 décembre sur la Réglementation des Télécommunications, together with the decree of 29 December 1990 on France Télécom's cahier des charges (licence conditions)—see Bensoussan and Pottier (1991) and Gensollen (1991).

[52] *La Tribune Desfossés* 30.5.94, 1.9.95, *Le Figaro* 2.9.94, Dandelot (1993), and *Le Monde* 6.6.96; interviews, senior France Télécom officials 1 and 2.

[53] DGPT (1994); *La Tribune Desfossés* 11.4.95, Fillon (PTT Minister 1995–7), 'Cette réforme concile service public et concurrence', *Le Figaro* 2.10.95, *Le Monde* 1.12.95; interviews, mission à la réglementation, senior France Télécom official 2.

[54] DGPT (1994) and *Le Monde* 10/11.12.95, 10.1.96, 13.5.96.

[55] *Le Figaro Economie* 28.2.95, 18.5.95, *Les Echos* 10.3.95, 1.7.96, *Le Monde* 1.3.95, 22.3.95, and *Libération* 18.5.95.

[56] cf. Hubert Prévot, 'Les télécoms entre le libéralisme débridé et la coopération intergouvernementale', *Le Monde* 12.6.93, Paul Quilès, 'Attention, dérangement', *Le Monde* 4.11.93 and *Les Echos* 9.5.96.

[57] Law no. 96-559 (on liberalisation and competition)—see Chevallier (1996), Berlin (1997), and Maxwell (1996).

under a class licence. It contained detailed provisions to achieve fair and effective competition, such as requirements for interconnection and financial transparency, especially for operators with significant market power. Thus France ended a monopoly begun under a law of 1837, with little opposition.

Creating an Independent Sectoral Regulator

In the mid-1990s, support for an independent sectoral regulator grew among most actors in the telecommunications sector, including experts and officials.[58] Opposition was limited to the Left and some sections of the old Gaullist Right, who wished ministers to keep powers to protect national industrial interests.[59] Supporters of an independent body argued that the government could not be both majority owner of France Télécom and an impartial regulator of competition.[60] However, international factors were also important. Oftel offered a good example of an independent regulator which supporters of an independent agency examined and used to justify an equivalent in France.[61] Perhaps more directly, EU requirements that regulation and supply be separate were used to justify a sectoral body with independence from the government, even though EU law in fact only required independence from suppliers.[62]

The 1996 law on liberalisation and competition therefore established an 'independent administrative authority', the *Autorité de régulation des télécommunications* (ART) from 1 January 1997.[63] The ART was headed by five members, three (including its head) nominated by the government and two by the presidents of the National and Assembly and the Senate, respectively. It was given rather general 'essential objectives', to ensure the good functioning of competition and to preserve the interests of users as a whole together with extensive powers over the regulation of competition, from setting rules to issuing orders and penalties. In 2005 the ART's responsibilities were widened to include postal services and it was renamed the *Autorité de regulation de communications électroniques et des postes*.

GERMANY

Processes of Decision-Making

In 1988 opposition to reform was strong in West Germany. The modest proposals to alter the organisation of the Deutsche Bundespost (DBP) of the 1987 Witte report had met with a well-organised strike (see Chapter 7). Yet after 1988,

---

[58] *Les Echos* 10.1.96 and Lasserre report (1994).

[59] *Les Echos* 28.2.96, 9.5.96 and *Le Monde* 8.5.96.

[60] François Fillon, PTT Minister, 'Notre souci prioritaire est de changer le statut de France Télécom avant 1998', *Les Echos* 18.12.95, and *Les Echos* 9.1.96.

[61] *La Tribune Desfossés* 1.10.93 and *Le Monde* 10.1.96; interview, senior France Télécom official 2.

[62] Interview, mission à la réglementation.   [63] See Lasserre (1997).

sweeping institutional alterations were made, as in France. A first phase involving limited changes, notably legislation in 1989 (the Postreform I); a second phase began after reunification in 1990 and led to the comprehensive restructuring of the sector, notably with the Postreform II legislation (1994) that allowed privatisation of Telekom (renamed Deutsche Telekom); finally, the Postreform III legislation in 1996 ended Deutsche Telekom's monopolies and created a new independent sectoral regulatory agency.

The central actors in the reform process were the government, political parties, and the DBP's management. Overseas firms and regulators, especially from the US, and the European Commission played a limited role. Reform required a lengthy process of compromise and explanation. One reason was (West) Germany's consensual politics and coalition governments. A more specific sectoral factor was that modification of the DBP's position as a federal administration required a two-thirds majority in both houses of Parliament (the *Bundestag* and the *Bundesrat*) to alter Article 87 of the Constitution, which stipulated that the DBP must be a federal administration. Change thus required building broad coalitions and isolating opponents, especially trade unions.

Domestic issues were important in driving change, especially the problems of German reunification. Nevertheless, policy forms of internationalisation were highly significant. Policymakers claimed that institutional reforms matching those overseas (e.g. in Britain) were vital to allow Deutsche Telekom to compete with other operators and to create overseas alliances as its foreign rivals had done. (However, like their French counterparts, German policy makers did not engage in systematic analysis or discussion of the dangers and benefits of such alliances.) EU regulation became increasingly important: it offered an external set of obligations; the need to adapt to the European Single Market was often cited; the European Commission's linkage of domestic liberalisation with approval of overseas alliances provided visible incentives for reform. Moreover, the EU offered a model for reform and aided existing coalitions or 'policy networks' to be reconfigured.[64] Both forms of internationalisation greatly aided in creating consensus and in overcoming Germany's multiple veto points, including in the legislature.

Substantive Reforms

Reforming the Deutsche Bundespost's Organisational Position

Reform of the DBP's organisational position was the central institutional issue after 1988.[65] The first step concerned separation of telecommunications and postal services, an idea dating from the late 1960s and repeated by the 1987 Witte report. It was strongly resisted by the opposition SPD party and the main

---

[64] cf. Schneider and Werle (1991), Grande (1991: 120), Schneider, Dang-Nguyen, and Werle (1994), and Schmidt (1991: 213).

[65] For overviews, see Köbberling (1993), Thimm (1992), Werle (1999: 110–13), and Schneider (2001a: 241–84).

trade union, the DPG, who feared loss of jobs, privatisation, reduction of the DBP's public service task, and the ending of subsidies for postal services.[66] Polls showed that the majority of DBP employees and public opinion were also against change.[67] One of the government coalition parties, the CSU, was cautious, as were the finance and interior ministries, who wished to maintain their control over DBP decisions. Finally, the regions (the Länder) were reluctant to lose their power over telecommunications arising from their parliamentary representatives in the Upper House (the Bundesrat).[68]

Faced with prolonged and vocal resistance, reform involved a lengthy process.[69] Reformers continued to cite domestic reasons for change—for example, reducing cross-subsidisation of postal services by telecommunications and obtaining greater autonomy from the government. However, they also underlined international factors. The most important was the need to prepare the DBP for a competitive market which was presented as inevitable. Hence change was needed to give the DBP greater flexibility.[70] In addition, (West) Germany needed an efficient high quality telecommunications infrastructure, especially in the new European common market; inertia in Germany was contrasted with reforms in other countries, such as Britain or Japan, that had moved public telecommunications operators away from their traditional civil service status.[71] Finally, the DBP had to meet EU law on value-added-tax, which was not levied by traditional government administrations.[72]

After long coalition negotiations and then parliamentary debate, the Postreform I law (the Poststrukturgesetz) was passed in May 1989.[73] It represented a compromise. Three 'public enterprises' were established within the Federal Ministry for Posts and Telecommunications (BMPT)—for telecommunications (DBP Telekom), postal, and financial services. The DBP would be taxed as a normal enterprise from 1992. Senior staff could be recruited from outside the civil service on market salaries. Nevertheless, the changes were limited. The DBP remained within the civil service: the government could not muster a two-thirds majority of both Houses of Parliament to alter Article 87 of the Constitution, under which the DBP was a federal administration. Hence its status as an 'enterprise' was far from clear. Moreover, recruitment of senior staff had to be approved by the minister.[74]

---

[66] *Frankfurter Allgemeine Zeitung* 23.5.87, *Bonner Rundschau* 1.3.88, and *Handelsblatt* 26.6.87, 9.3.88.

[67] *Frankfurter Allgemeine Zeitung* 7.9.88, *Die Welt* 7.9.88, *Handelsblatt* 16.9.88, and *Frankfurter Allgemeine Zeitung* 18.3.89.

[68] *Frankfurter Allgemeine Zeitung* 23.5.87, 17.11.87, *Frankfurter Rundschau* 8.7.88, *Frankfurter Allgemeine Zeitung* 8.7.88, and *Süddeutsche Zeitung* 10.11.87.

[69] *Frankfurter Allgemeine Zeitung* 11.5.88, 8.7.88, 24.2.89, 1.9.88, 13.5.89, *Süddeutsche Zeitung* 11-12.5.88, *Frankfurter Rundschau* 8.7.88, and *Handelsblatt* 1.9.88, 21.4.89.

[70] Interview, Schwarz-Schilling (Posts and Telecommunications Minister) *Die Zeit* 25.9.87.

[71] *Handelsblatt* 23.9.88 and *Frankfurter Allgemeine Zeitung* 10.5.88.

[72] *Handelsblatt* 6.4.87, *Frankfurter Allgemeine Zeitung* 24.11.87, 10.11.89, and *Frankfurter Allgemeine Zeitung* 10.11.89.

[73] For details, see Grande (1991: 230–8), Schmidt (1991: 217–19), and Werle (1990: 332–43).

[74] Ritter (2004: 60) and Werle (1990: 340).

Just after the 1989 law was passed, DBP Telekom faced the shock of German reunification. Integrating East Germany's network created enormous increases in capital spending.[75] In addition, Telekom was engaged in large-scale investment to modernise its network, notably by introducing digital technology, as it feared that alternative high quality networks could lure large business customers away.[76] Yet such expenditure resulted in enormous debts that threatened its financial stability. Thus for instance, by 1993, Telekom had revenues of 54 billion deutschmarks but debts of over 100 billion. Debt servicing costs consumed 12% of income.[77] Moreover, despite its financial burdens, DBP Telekom continued to pay levies towards the federal budget and postal service deficits.[78]

Telecom combined financial vulnerability with international ambitions. Its management and the Telecommunications Minister argued that overseas expansion and alliances were essential to meet foreign competition and to capture expanding markets in international services.[79] In the early/mid-1990s it formed an alliance with France Télécom, through joint ventures; the two operators now wished to engage in cross-share holdings.[80] Both operators also created an international alliance (Phoenix) with the American firm Sprint, and then sought to purchase holdings in Sprint. Telekom's strategy of internationalisation was supported by the government and the opposition party, the SPD: they presented its alliance with France Télécom an example of Franco-German cooperation and expansion in the US as entering the world's largest market.

To deal with the conflict between increasing financial costs and desires for investment and international expansion, Telekom's management and the government turned to privatisation. They argued that a sale of Telekom shares was urgently needed to reduce debts and provide funds for investment.[81] It would also facilitate internationalisation since Telekom shares could be used as capital for acquisitions of overseas companies and joint ventures.[82] Moreover, unit within the

---

[75] By the early 1990s Telekom was spending *c*28 billion deutschmarks per annum, with a long-term aim of spending of 20–22 billion deutschmarks—*Frankfurter Allgemeiner Zeitung* 25.8.93; the 'Telekom 2000' plan of 1991 foresaw expenditure of 50–60 billion deutschmarks by 1998—*Frankfurter Allgemeine Zeitung* 15.8.90, 15.4.91, the *Financial Times* 2.4.91, and *Wirtschaftswoche* 20.9.91.

[76] *Die Zeit* 10.11.95; a key element was the new ISDN—integrated digital services network, which provided digitalisation and much greater bandwidth.

[77] *Frankfurter Allgemeine Zeitung* 25.8.93, the *Financial Times* 26.10.93, and *The Economist* 30.10.93.

[78] Köbberling (1993: 55–6); cf. *Süddeutsche Zeitung* 27.12.90, 7.1.91, 9.1.91, *Handelsblatt* 10.1.91, and *Die Zeit* 26.4.91.

[79] *Frankfurter Allgemeine Zeitung* 26.7.93, 3.2.94, 6.9.94.

[80] In the early 1990s, France Télécom and Deutsche Telekom established several small joint ventures, notably Eutnetcom and Atlas, followed by the more ambitions joint venture (Phoenix)—*Frankfurter Allgemeine Zeitung* 18.9.95; cf. Elixmann and Hermann (1996); after privatisation France Télécom took a 2% stake in Deutsche Telekom which reciprocated with a 2% share in France Télécom—*Tagesspiegel* 21.7.1998; these cross-holdings were ended in 2000.

[81] *Frankfurter Rundschau* 19.11.90, *Die Welt* 19.11.90, *Handelsblatt* 20.11.90, the *Financial Times* 2.4.91, 8.10.91, *Frankfurter Allgemeine Zeitung* 4.4.92, 26.4.93, 25.8.93, 3.2.94, and *Die Zeit* 22.3.96; cf. Werle (1999: 112).

[82] Comments by PTT Minister Wolfgang Bötsch *Frankfurter Allgemeine Zeitung* 3.2.93, article by Helmut Ricke, head of Telekom, *Frankfurter Allgemeine Zeitung* 4.12.91, 6.9.94, *Süddeutsche Zeitung* 9.10.91, and *Frankfurter Allgemeine Zeitung Handelsblatt* 22.10.92.

civil service, Telekom faced legal obstacles to operating overseas. Telekom's management, especially its head, Helmut Ricke, complained that other PTOs in the UK and US did not face the burden of unexpected intervention by ministers and a supervisory board.[83] Finally, German policy makers argued that privatisation was needed to prepare to meet international competitors such as BT or Sprint, especially within a liberalised European market.[84] In addition, privatisation offered much needed funds for the government and the possibility of greater freedom from civil service constraints for Telekom's management.

Privatisation was far from easy, since it required constitutional change and hence support from the opposition SPD. It encountered fierce opposition from the trade unions, who pressed for retaining complete public ownership.[85] However, faced with financial and other pressures, the government entered into lengthy negotiations with the SPD. Initially, the SPD was hostile, but altered its position, having won concessions that the state would keep a majority of Telekom shares for at least five years. It justified its decision in terms of ensuring that Telekom could compete internationally and that Germany should not be disadvantaged relative to other nations in Europe.[86] This left trade unions as isolated opponents of change and their protests were limited and ineffective. As a result, the 'Postreform II' was passed in 1994, altering Article 87 of the constitution. It involved two stages—transforming Telekom into a private law entity as a 'stock corporation'—that is a state-owned company operating under private law (called Deutsche Telekom) in 1995; allowing sale of its shares (confusingly, both stages were termed 'privatisation' in Germany). Twenty-five per cent of Deutsche Telekom shares were sold in 1996, followed by further sales so that by May 2001, only 43% of shares were owned by the public sector.[87] Thus by 2005, Telekom had been transformed from a civil service unit into a majority privately-owned company.

Liberalisation

In the late 1980s, liberalisation remained controversial in Germany. On the one hand, the FDP (a liberal government coalition party), liberal economists, and

---

[83] *Handelsblatt* 27.6.91 and *Stuttgarter Nachrichten* 11.4.92.

[84] *Frankfurter Allgemeine Zeitung* 26.4.93, 29.10.93, *Süddeutsche Zeitung* 23.8.93, and *The Economist* 30.10.93.

[85] *Süddeutsche Zeitung* 11.2.92, *Frankfurter Rundschau* 29.4.92, *Handelsblatt* 24.7.92, *La Tribune de l'Expansion* 28.9.92, *Süddeutsche Zeitung* 26.11.92, and *Die Zeit* 4.12.92.

[86] *Le Monde* 4.2.94; see speeches by SPD members on Postreform II underlining the need to compete internationally and to adapt to EU legislation—e.g. speech by Hans Gottfried Bernrath (SPD), Deutscher Bundestag, Stenographischer Bericht, 208. *Sitzung* 3.2.1994: 17924, speech by Arne Börnsen (SPD) ibid. pp. 17933–17944; speech by Hans Eichel (SPD) on 18.3.1994, Bundesrat 667. *Sitzung* 18.3.1994, Protocol pp. 71–2.

[87] The government's stake fell to 65% in June 1999, 58% in June 2000, and 43% in May 2001; in 2003 the state directly held 20%, a state financial body, the Kreditanstalt für den Wiederaufbau (KFW) held 26%; by December 2005 the state held 15%, and the KfW 22%.

business associations called for extensive liberalisation.[88] After reunification in 1990, those calls for change grew much stronger, as Telekom failed to meet demand and faced problems in financing modernisation.[89] On the other hand, 'deregulation' met considerable criticism from the SPD and trade unions.[90] They feared that jobs and Telekom's financial health would be threatened and that competition would harm domestic consumers.[91]

Gradually, opposition to competition was overcome. International factors played important roles. First, EU regulation operated in several ways. It provided a useful external justification for the government in negotiations with opposition parties (despite the fact that by the mid-1990s, at the EU level, Germany was actively supporting the extension of EU legislation).[92] It also became linked to Deutsche Telekom's strategy of international expansion: the European Commission made regulatory approval of the operator's joint ventures with France Télécom and then with Sprint, dependent on domestic German liberalisation. In addition, new entrants began to turn to the European Commission to make complaints against restrictions on competition within Germany.[93]

Second, US firms and regulators became involved in German liberalisation. In the early 1990s, liberalisation was supported by ministers and equipment manufacturing companies such as Siemens an essential quid pro quo for access to the US market.[94] Then in the mid-1990s the link became explicit because of Deutsche Telekom's international ambitions. American regulatory authorities made easier entry to the German market a condition of approval of Deutsche Telekom's purchase of a stake in Sprint and its attempts at expansion in the US.[95] German policy makers met with bodies such as the FCC and offered rapid domestic liberalisation in the Postreform III in return for regulatory approval of Deutsche Telekom's expansion in the US.[96]

Third, during the 1990s overseas telecommunications operators formed joint ventures with German firms—for instance, BT and Viag, Veba and Cable and Wireless, Thyssen and Bellsouth, AT&T and Mannesman.[97] The new entrants lobbied the government hard for liberalisation and for rules on matters such

---

[88] cf. the minority report from the 1987 Witte Commission; *Handelsblatt* 26.1.88, 9.2.88, *Blick durch die Wirtschaft* 20.7.88, and *Die Zeit* 23.11.90.

[89] *Frankfurter Allgemeine Zeitung* 30.7.90, 20.12.90, *General-Anzeiger* 14.6.91, *Stuttgarter Zeitung* 21.6.90, and *Handelsblatt* 31.7.90.

[90] *Süddeutsche Zeitung* 21.3.90, *Frankfurter Allgemeine Zeitung* 30.7.90, 12.10.90, *Frankfurter Rundschau* 12.10.90, and *Handelsblatt* 31.7.90.

[91] *Stuttgarter Zeitung* 18.1.91.

[92] *Frankfurter Allgemeine Zeitung* 12.9.94, 19.11.94, 27.1.95, 3.8.95; for Postreform I see Thimm (1992: 73, 81).

[93] The *Financial Times* 12.10.96.   [94] *Handelsblatt* 23.9.88 and *Frankfurter Rundschau* 13.3.91.

[95] *Frankfurter Allgemeine Zeitung* 18.2.95, 24.4.95 and the *Financial Times* 22.4.97.

[96] *Frankfurter Allgemeine Zeitung* 18.2.95, 27.4.95, 21.4.97 and *Süddeutsche Zeitung* 4.4.95, 27.4.95.

[97] For a rapid chronology of the often rapidly changing alliances, see *Die Zeit* 18.10.96 and the *Financial Times* 25.1.95, 27.1.95.

as interconnection and licences that allowed effective competition to Deutsche Telekom; they also made legal complaints to the Cartel Office.[98]

Finally, reformers drew on overseas examples and made cross-national comparisons. They claimed that the British and American experiences showed that competition in network operation was possible and beneficial, for instance, leading to lower tariffs.[99] In contrast, Germany had some of the highest tariffs in the Western world and its companies were lagging behind those in other countries.[100] Business users argued that liberalisation was needed to aid German international competitiveness, following in the steps of countries such as the US and Britain.[101] These examples were contested—for example, opponents suggested that in the US and UK, liberalisation had only benefited commercial users and had led to large job losses, or that it would just allow entry by foreign companies into Germany.[102] However, such critiques declined over time and overseas examples provided legitimation for reforms.

In the face of conflicting opinions, the government liberalised gradually. The 1989 Postreform I ended Telekom's monopoly over terminal equipment and advanced services (notably mobile and satellite services) so that approximately 20% of the market was liberalised.[103] Interestingly, after reunification, Telekom was unable to meet demand and the government flirted with the idea of allowing a major foreign company such as AT&T to build a second network.[104] But rapidly this option was abandoned—although the key reason was to protect Telekom, the justification given by the PTT Ministry was that such as step would have gone beyond the requirements of EU law.[105]

Then in 1995, the government undertook a consultation exercise, which revealed that almost all sectoral actors accepted liberalisation, with the exceptions of the SPD and trade unions. However, the SPD's opposition was rapidly overcome thanks to two sets of justifications. First, opening German domestic markets became urgent to obtain regulatory approval of Deutsche Telekom's international expansion by the US, a factor cited as a reason for the SPD accepting liberalisation.[106] Second, the need to introduce new rules to meet EU requirements was underlined.[107] The government and the SPD reached agreement on the Postreform III Bill, passed in 1996, which greatly liberalised the German market. It ended Deutsche Telekom's monopoly over the infrastructure and voice telephony,

---

[98] The *Financial Times* 26.5.94, 13.9.96, 12.1.95 and *Frankfurter Allgemeine Zeitung* 27.1.95, 13.9.96.

[99] *Süddeutsche Zeitung* 21-22.7.89 and *Handesblatt* 27.6.91.

[100] *Wirtschaftswoche* 5.2.88 and *Blick durch die Wirtschaft* 20.7.88.

[101] *Handelsblatt* 14.9.94 and the *Financial Times* 17.5.95, 19.6.96.

[102] *Süddeutsche Zeitung* 7.7.89, 21-22.7.89, *Frankfurter Rundschau* 20.9.88, and *Handelsblatt* 26.6.87, 4.8.87.

[103] For discussions, see Thimm (1992: 75–81), Köbberling (1993: 57–9), and Schmidt (1991).

[104] *Handelsblatt* 20.11.90, 15.3.91 and *Frankfurter Allgemeine Zeitung* 2.9.91.

[105] See Schmidt (1991: 220–1), the *Financial Times* 2.4.91, 8.10.91, *Frankfurter Allgemeine Zeitung* 15.4.91, *Die Zeit* 26.4.91, and Köbberling (1993: 54).

[106] *Süddeutsche Zeitung* 27.4.95 and *Frankfurter Allgemeine Zeitung* 27.4.95.

[107] *Frankfurter Allgemeine Zeitung* 27.1.95, 3.8.95.

and established a licensing regime that aided entry.[108] Moreover, the Act included important provisions to aid competition.[109] Thus in the period between the late 1980s and 1996, Germany had moved from a complete public monopoly to a regulatory framework seeking to maximise competition.

The Allocation of Regulatory Powers

Independent sectoral regulatory agencies have been rare in Germany; instead, ministries and the powerful general competition authority (the Bundeskartellamt) have held most powers.[110] However, in telecommunications, clear international pressures existed to create an independent sectoral body. Overseas entrants, investors, and analysts argued for separation of regulation and supply, and for 'depoliticisation' of the industry; to support their views, they pointed to the examples of the US's FCC and to Oftel.[111] Large companies, including new suppliers, pressed for altered arrangements for competition, and often criticised the government.[112] The latter faced increasing challenges from Deutsche Telekom, including complaints from the European Commission.[113]

In the mid-1990s, the government engaged in an internal debate over whether to make the general competition authority, the highly respected and well-established Bundeskartellamt, the main regulator for telecommunications or to create a sector-specific body. Faced with pressures for a new regulatory system and overseas examples, it decided to create a sectoral agency for telecommunications and postal services, the Regulierungsbehörde für Telekommunikation und Post (RegTP) in Postreform III. The RegTP enjoyed a degree of independence from the government[114] and represented an exception in Germany's traditional administrative structures which rarely offered such autonomy.[115] One major reason given for its creation was EU law: EU legislation was interpreted as requiring a regulatory body separate from the government, or at least offering a strong model for such as body. In addition, the British regulator Oftel was taken as an example worth following. Thus internationalisation was significant in breaking with German administrative traditions.

---

[108] Licences were only necessary under certain conditions, such as when they involved the supply of public services; in principle, the number of licences was unlimited, but if technical factors prevented this (e.g. for some mobile networks), licences were to be granted by tender or auction.

[109] For instance, obligations on the dominant PTO to provide access to competitors on a non-discriminatory basis, including 'unbundled access'—Werle (1999: 115–7).

[110] cf. Döhler (2002), Eberlein and Grande (2000), Eberlein (2000), and Lodge (2002).

[111] *Frankfurter Rundschau* 7.11.92, the *Herald Tribune* 10.5.95, and the *Financial Times* 7.2.95, 29.12.95, 19.6.96.

[112] *Frankfurter Allgemeine Zeitung* 27.1.95, 13.9.96, 30.1.97, the *Herald Tribune* 10.5.95, and the *Financial Times* 29.12.95, 27.6.96, 13.9.96, 14.3.97.

[113] The *Financial Times* 12.3.96, 12.10.96.

[114] Although formally under the supervision of the Economics Ministry, the RegTP had a court-like structure of decision-making 'chambers', and implicitly a degree of autonomy from ministerial instructions—see Böllhoff (2005: 55–7) and *Frankfurter Allgemeine Zeitung* 29.1.96, 7.6.96.

[115] Döhler (2002).

ITALY

Processes of Decision-Making

In 1988 Italian telecommunications remained fragmented, with no fewer than five operators under diverse forms of public ownership. The institutional framework was widely recognised as economically inefficient and serious attempts at reform began. But they faced powerful actors with strong interests in the existing arrangements, notably political parties who divided influence over different operators among themselves in a form of 'spoils system'. Since there were coalition governments, political parties could often block decisions.

Yet between 1992 and 1997, the government formed an alliance with new actors in the sector—the Anti-Trust Authority (created in 1990) and the European Commission—to introduce comprehensive changes that ran counter to decades of history. The various operators were consolidated into one, Telecom Italia, which was then privatised; liberalisation was introduced; an independent communications authority was created.

These reforms were remarkable for Italy in their swiftness and extent, ending years of institutional logjams. However, they were fiercely contested. Privatisation faced opposition from Rifondazione Communista, an important component of the centre-left government after 1996. The new sectoral authority faced hostility, notably from two opposition parties, the Lega Nord and Silvio Berlusconi's Forza Italia, since it concerned the extremely politically sensitive broadcasting sector. In addition, covert opposition came from other political parties which stood to lose political patronage, officials in the PTT Ministry and for some changes, the management of Telecom Italia.

Although dissatisfaction with supply and domestic political developments were important (notably the fall of the First Republic in 1992, fiscal problems, and the creation of the Anti-Trust Authority in 1990), international factors were crucial in overcoming strenuous resistance to change. In particular, the EU was a visible and important source of impetus and legitimacy. The European Commission played a direct role in pressing governments to meet EU legal requirements, sometimes taking legal action. It also linked domestic regulatory reform to other decisions, gaining leverage over the Italian government. More indirectly, the Commission cooperated with the Anti-Trust Authority, which used EU law to pursue its strategies. The external force of the EU was central in breaking through resistance to reforms and aiding the adoption of reforms that were similar to those seen in France and Germany.

SUBSTANTIVE REFORMS

Consolidation of PTOs and Privatisation

In 1988, Italy had a complex and unreformed organisational structure of suppliers. The *spezzatino* (stew) comprised ASST ((l'Azienda di Stato per Servici Telefonici), which formed part of the civil service within the Posts and Telecommunications Ministry, and four operators that were public corporations (SIP, Telespazio, STET, and Italcable). To make matters even worse, STET was a holding company that owned shares in the other three operators, but was itself majority owned by the state holding firm IRI. To add further complexity, there were minority private holdings in SIP and STET and their shares were publicly traded.

There were long-standing reasons to reform the structure of the operators arising from the fragmentation of the network into several PTOs: inefficiencies from inter-operator quarrels; problems of raising private capital and increasing debt for STET and SIP; and inefficiencies and inadequate investment by ASST.[116] However, policy forms of internationalisation also played a central role. Overseas examples provided policy makers and users with evidence to underline Italy's backwardness compared to other European nations in terms of telephone penetration, new services, and investment; in 1988, a five-year investment plan was established (the 'Piano Europa') to reduce the gap with other European nations, but this also increased the financial pressures on the operators.[117] Reformers contrasted the Italian anomaly of fragmented PTOs with powerful overseas PTOs, especially BT and AT&T.[118] They argued that Italian PTOs had to be consolidated to be able to form alliances and/or to compete with overseas PTOs, and signalled the danger of losing customers through entry by new suppliers and bypass of existing networks.[119]

However the EU was the central factor for change. '1992' (the European Single Market) was a recurrent theme used to justify the urgent need for institutional reform. Reformers claimed that organisational changes in telecommunications were needed to enhance Italian competitiveness in the new single market.[120] In the early 1990s, an additional factor gave urgency for change: IRI, the owner of most shares in STET, faced severe financial difficulties. The Italian government wished to inject money into IRI to save it from bankruptcy. However, such state aid was only approved by the European Commission on terms agreed in 1993 by the Commissioner for Competition, Karel Van Miert, and the then Foreign Minister Beniamino Andreatta. Those terms included the privatisation of IRI's telecommunications businesses.

The first steps in reform were to transfer ASST from the Posts and Telecommunications Ministry to IRI and merge the different operators into one operator,

---

[116] Morganti (1990); interviews, senior telecommunications official 1 and 2; *Il Sole 24 Ore* 29.3.88, 24.2.90, 11.8.90, 27.12.90, 19.8.92.

[117] Interviews, senior telecommunications official 1 and 2, senior telecommunications official 3; *Il Sole 24 Ore* 24.2.88, 26.2.88, 27.1.89, 10.5.90, 12.5.90, 4.1.91, 8.4.91, 19.8.92, Morganti (1990) and Giacalone and Vergnano (1990) for comparative data showing poor Italian performance, see Pontarollo and Costa (1992) and Giacalone (1992).

[118] Interview, senior telecommunications official 3; *Il Sole 24 Ore* 11.8.90, 8.10.91, 22.5.92.

[119] Interviews, senior telecommunications official 1 and 2; *Il Sole 24 Ore* 6.5.88, 17.12.88, 5.10.89, 20.7.90, 26.4.91, 8.10.91; indeed, STET entered into an 'alliance' with BT and Telefonica in 1988, while BT established offices in Rome with the express intention of capturing Italian clients.

[120] *Il Sole 24 Ore* 17.2.88, 6.5.88, 9.6.88, 29.9.88, 17.11.88 (interview with Minister Mammi), 31.3.90; interview, senior telecommunications official 3.

often known as 'super-STET'. From 1988, Posts and Telecommunications Minister Mammi, and his successors, made the rapid creation of super-STET a priority.[121] Senior managers at IRI, STET, and SIP also pressed continuously for change.[122] Industry representatives, particularly Confindustria (the employers' organisation), and large users called for reorganisation.[123] Broad agreement on the creation of a super-STET appeared to exist.

However, in fact, powerful opposition continued.[124] It took the form of passive resistance, but was all the more effective for this, since with unstable short-term governments and a multiplicity of political parties, reform proposals ran into the sands of Italian politics. Obstruction was led by the Socialist Party (PSI), part of the Christian Democrat Party and the CISL trade union.[125] The elected politicians pointed out practical difficulties (such as valuing SIP and ASST), but also feared loss of party patronage, particularly since mergers would reduce the number of posts available for the spoils system.[126] The CISL trade union feared losing its dominant position within the ASST if the latter were transferred to IRI and SIP.[127]

Given opposition, the reform process was lengthy. Only after prolonged negotiations and intervention by the Prime Minister (De Mita), did the Council of Ministers approve proposed legislation whereby ASST would be transferred to IRI by spring 1989.[128] Then, although the Bill was put before the Chamber of Deputies in April 1989, it fell victim to parliamentary obstruction, especially over whether ASST would retain a separate identity within IRI (and hence be available as a distinct organisation for the spoils system).[129] Despite 'ultimatums' from ministers concerned,[130] the Bill remained stalled until early 1992, when it was finally passed (law no. 58/1992) but at the cost of compromise: ASST was transferred to IRI in December 1992 but the difficult decision of whether it would be merged with the other operators was put off into the future.[131]

After 1992, this matter was finally resolved by an alliance led by Giuliano Amato (Prime Minister 1992–3) and Romano Prodi (then head of IRI).[132] One reason was the political crisis following the end of the First Republic which gravely weakened the power of existing political parties. However, unlike the earlier period, reform was given added impetus by international factors. First, consolidation was important to allow privatisation and raise revenue and hence meet the conditions

---

[121] Giacalone and Vergnano 1990; *Il Sole 24 Ore* 20.1.88, 29.7.88, 9.9.88, 12.2.89.

[122] Notably Romano Prodi (head of IRI until 1990 and again 1993–4), Paolo Benzoni head of SIP and later Italcable, and Giuliano Graziosi (head of STET 1984–90)—*Il Sole 24 Ore* 29.3.88, 29.10.88, 12.3.91.

[123] *Il Sole 24 Ore* 25.2.88, 29.9.88, 17.11.88, 11.11.89, 31.3.90; see Morganti (1990), report commissioned by Confindustria; interview, senior telecommunications official 3.

[124] See Giacalone and Vergagno (1990).

[125] *Il Sole 24 Ore* 30.3.88, 11.2.89; interview, senior telecommunications official 1 and 2.

[126] *Il Sole 24 Ore* 29.10.88, Giacalone and Vergagno (1990); interview, senior lawyer.

[127] *Il Sole 24 Ore* 29.10.88, 3.11.88.   [128] *Il Sole 24 Ore* 5.8.88, 3.12.88, 2.3.89, 3.3.89.

[129] *Il Sole 24 Ore* 4.8.89, 12.9.89, 24.9.89, 1.12.89, 27.12.89, 4.2.91.

[130] *Il Sole 24 Ore* 2.3.90.   [131] *Il Sole 24 Ore* 4.2.91, 17.1.92.

[132] *Il Sole 24 Ore* 22.5.92, 19.11.92.

agreed with the European Commission for refinancing IRI.[133] Second, the creation of international alliances by BT, Deutsche Telekom, and France Télécom increased pressures to establish a powerful Italian PTO. Prodi and other reformers argued that consolidation was needed to match overseas operators, because markets were increasingly international and being opened by EU regulation.[134] More visibly, alliances of overseas operators led to falls in the stock market values of the Italian PTOs (STET, SIP, and Italcable) that were majority state owned (by IRI) but quoted on stock exchanges.[135] By 1994, opposition was overcome by these strong pressures and the different PTOs, including SIP and ASST, were merged to create Telecom Italia, which was then fused with STET in 1997.[136] At last Italy had one large incumbent operator.

The next step was privatisation of Telecom Italia. This gained the support of centre and centre-left governments after 1994, notably those led by Amato and Prodi (1996–8). One reason was their desire to liberalise telecommunications. But other, more urgent reasons were linked to the EU. Privatisation was driven by the need to comply with the 1993 agreement with the European Commission, as well as raising funds to meet the Maastricht criterion for a single currency; the Commission provided an external justification for change.[137] In addition, privatisation was seen as a response to internationalisation by overseas rivals (given added urgency by EU liberalisation), since it would aid Telecom Italia to expand abroad and form alliances with foreign firms.[138] In the 1990s, Telecom Italia's management also favoured privatisation to gain greater autonomy from the government. At home it wished to be free to rebalance tariffs without government hindrance to meet competition arising from liberalisation (itself driven by the EU). Internationally, it wished to form alliances with IBM in services and with AT&T. The trade unions did not oppose privatisation, accepting the argument that it was essential for competitiveness.[139]

Nevertheless, the far-left Rifondazione Communista Party, whose support was essential for the centre-left governments of 1996–2001, fiercely resisted privatisation. It blocked change for many months, in alliance with the centre-Right. As the process slipped into the moving sands of inter- and intra-party bargaining in 1995–6, the European Commission exerted visible pressure and urgency: the Competition Commissioner Van Miert set deadlines for his 1993 accord to be respected and pressed for action; in addition, the agreement provided an external justification for privatisation.[140] In 1997, Rifondazione Communista finally gave

---

[133] Fragmentation lowered the value of IRI's telecommunications businesses; when the formation of TI was announced, STET's value rose—*Il Sole 24 Ore* 12.11.93.

[134] *Il Sole 24 Ore* 23.6.93, 11.10.93, 10.11.93, 12.11.93, 3.12.93, 11.1.94, 20.3.94, 27.11.96, 6.12.96, 15.2.97 (interview with amministratore delegato of STET, Tomaso Tommasi).

[135] *Il Sole 24 Ore* 10.11.93, 12.11.93.

[136] The mobile operator TIM and the space communications company Telespazio were floated as separate companies with majority Telecom Italia shareholdings.

[137] Interviews, senior lawyer, senior legislator 1, minister 1.

[138] *Il Sole 24 Ore* 28.7.94, 10.10.94, 16.11.94, 9.2.95, 28.3.96, 6.7.96, 19.10.96, 27.11.96.

[139] Interviews, ministers 1 and 2.

[140] *Il Sole 24 Ore* 3.2.96, 6.7.96, 19.7.96, 11.9.96, 5.10.96; interviews, ministers 1 and 2.

way (in return for keeping majority public ownership in other areas such as electricity), and 96.5% of shares in Telecom Italia were sold.[141] In 2002, the state decided to sell its remaining shares and end its 'golden share'.

Liberalisation

After 1988, policy makers increasingly accepted the need for competition. Large firms and the employers' association Confindustria called for liberalisation of advanced services and networks.[142] The Anti-Trust Authority made competition in telecommunications one of its priorities after 1990.[143] Officially, the government also supported liberalisation, which would benefit users and increase investment.[144] Even Telecom Italia/STET's management accepted that competition was inevitable and indeed beneficial, since it would allow greater freedom to set tariffs to meet international competition.[145]

International factors played a clear role in increasing acceptance of competition. Ministers, SIP/Telecom Italia, and users looked at liberalisation of advanced services and terminal equipment in other countries such as Britain, France, Germany, and the US, finding that it aided users and did not harm PTOs, whereas prices were higher in Italy for services and equipment.[146] Overseas companies, such as Bell Atlantic, Racal, and Salomon Brothers, sought to create partnerships with Italian firms in order to enter new markets, especially mobiles.[147] Policy makers underlined that EU regulation insisted on liberalisation.[148]

In practice, however, competition met many obstacles, including failures to alter legislation, delays in issuing licences and anti-competitive conditions over vital matters such as licence costs and interconnection.[149] Telecom Italia and Posts and Telecommunications Ministry officials offered covert resistance, so liberalisation was 'a continuous struggle'.[150] Thus for example, in 1989 a 'regulatory plan' published by Posts and Telecommunications Minister Mammi foresaw the reduction of SIP's monopoly to 'basic services', such as email, but only very modest liberalisation was introduced (for terminal equipment).[151] Equally, attempts to

---

[141] The Treasury retained 3% and the Bank of Italy 0.5%.

[142] *Il Sole 24 Ore* 25.2.88, 29.9.88.   [143] *Il Sole 24 Ore* 12.8.94.

[144] Interviews, senior minister/regulator, ministers 1 and 2.

[145] *Il Sole 24 Ore* 5.7.95, 18.7.95; interviews, senior ministry official 1, senior telecommunications official 3.

[146] Interview, senior telecommunications official 3, senior advisor; *Il Sole 24 Ore* 24.4.90, 26.4.90, 8.11.90, 8.10.91, 18.1.92; 30.6.94, 26.2.95; and Morganti (1990).

[147] Notably Olivetti with Bell Atlantic and other American firms, and Fiat with Racal; Salomon Brothers proposed establishing a separate mobile subsidiary to STET Giacalone and Vergangno (1990: 22–3, 8.10.91).

[148] *Il Sole 24 Ore* 24.2.88, 6.5.88, 29.9.88, 2.3.90, 24.4.90, 4.1.91, 12.3.91, 29.8.91.

[149] *Il Sole 24 Ore* 13.9.96.

[150] Interviews, senior lawyer, senior minister/regulator, senior regulator 1, senior ministry official 1.

[151] *Il Sole 24 Ore* 15.7.89; competition was extended to the maintenance and supply of most terminal equipment—e.g. telex machines and modems *Il Sole 24 Ore* 8.7.88, mobile telephones *Il Sole 24 Ore* 28.2.90.

introduce competition in mobile telephony and advanced networks were impeded by SIP/STET.[152]

The EU played important and new roles in the struggle for liberalisation in the 1990s.[153] First, Italy had to transpose EU directives. When it failed to do so, the European Commission initially publicised the matter and then began an infringement procedure.[154] It also threatened to refuse to authorise international alliances by Telecom Italia's if the Italian market was not fully liberalised.[155] Second, the European Commission acted directly against barriers to competition.[156] It threatened and sometimes began infringement proceedings against the Italian government over anti-competitive practices. The most public examples concerned mobile communications.[157] Its role was particularly important because the sectoral regulator AGCOM (see below) did not fully begin work until 1999–2000 and Telecom Italia resisted liberalisation in practice, protected by its links with political parties and PT Ministry officials.[158] Third, EU law offered additional weapons for liberalisers against opponents within Italy.[159] In particular, the Anti-Trust Authority successfully argued that EU directives had direct effect and hence were 'self-executing'.[160] It was thus able to threaten to use EU law regardless of whether the government had passed domestic legislation transposing EU liberalisation directives.[161]

The result of these pressures, especially by the EU, was that Italy ended Telecom Italia's monopolies, first in advanced services and networks and then in fixed line telephony and networks. It also licensed three mobile operators and established rules designed to ensure fair competition,[162] such as 'roaming' rights between mobile operators, local loop unbundling, and application of the general competition law prohibiting of abuse of a dominant position.[163] In 2001, it allocated no fewer than five licences for the new 3G mobile networks.

The Allocation of Regulatory Powers

By the early 1990s, policy makers such as Romani Prodi and Giuliano Amato and economic 'liberals' such as Senator Franco Debenedetti believed that a strong

---

[152] *Il Sole 24 Ore* 8.2.92; Giacalone and Vergnano (1992: 23–4); interviews, senior telecommunications official 1 and 2, senior legislator 1.

[153] Interviews, senior minister/regulator, senior legislator 1, senior ministry official 1, senior lawyer, senior regulator 1, adviser, minister 2, and senior telecommunications official 3.

[154] *Il Sole 24 Ore* 18.7.95, 6.11.97 and Noam (1992).   [155] *Il Sole 24 Ore* 27.5.97, 19.12.97.

[156] Interviews, senior lawyer, senior regulator 1, adviser.

[157] For mobiles see Cassese (2001: 623–31); *Il Sole 24 Ore* 1.4.95, 18.7.95, 11.9.96, 24.1.97, 24.6.97, 9.10.97; interviews, senior minister/regulator, senior lawyer, senior regulators 1 and 2.

[158] Interviews, senior ministry official 1, senior lawyer.

[159] Interviews, senior minister/regulator, senior regulator 1, senior lawyer.

[160] cf. *Il Sole 24 Ore* 22.7.94, decision of the Anti-Trust Authority in the Telecom Italia–Telesystems case *Il Sole 24 Ore* 12.1.95.

[161] *Il Sole 24 Ore* 12.1.95, 6.2.95, 6.5.97; interview, senior regulator 1.

[162] For a critique of the application of such rules, see Perez (2002).

[163] Cf. Perez (2002: 66–97).

independent authority was needed to regulate a privatised operator and a liberalised market, and that it would reassure investors; they drew on overseas experiences, notably that of Britain and the US.[164] However, the government also pressed for a regulator to cover both telecommunications and broadcasting. There were important domestic reasons for this (particularly Silvio Berlusconi's extensive media ownership), but also international ones: the FCC in the US provided an example, in addition to arguments that technological and economic developments were lowering barriers between telecommunications and broadcasting; the EU Green Paper on convergence inspired work on an audio-visual regulator.[165]

Unlike in the other three countries, the creation of an independent sectoral regulator was visibly controversial.[166] One reason was its linkage to privatisation: the law of 1994 which made the sale of STET conditional on the creation of an authority.[167] Other factors were its coverage of broadcasting and reticence by many officials in the PT Ministry about losing powers.[168] The controversies surrounding the creation of AGCOM and Rifondazione Communista's obstruction resulted in a lengthy legislative process lasting from 1994 until July 1997, when law 249/97 was finally passed to allow privatisation of Telecom Italia to proceed. A compromise was agreed on AGCOM's institutional form: within AGCOM there were two commissions (for the infrastructure and networks, and for services); the president was chosen by the prime minister,[169] while each division had four members, two elected by the Senate and Chamber of Deputies, thus ensuring that the main government party and opposition would have one each.[170] Nevertheless, AGCOM represented considerable innovation, as it was the first telecommunications and broadcasting regulator among EU member states.[171]

CONCLUSION

In the period between 1988 and 2005 the formal institutions of telecommunications in France, Germany, and Italy were greatly reformed. Initially (from 1988 to *c*.1993), changes were modest, involving separation of posts and telecommunications, limited moves away from civil service status for the operator and a small degree of liberalisation. However, from the mid-1990s reforms were radical. All three countries privatised incumbent operators, ended monopolies across the sector, and established independent sectoral regulators. Well-established institutional

---

[164] *Il Sole 24 Ore* 5.2.93, 1.8.94, 8.3.95, 3.4.95, 8.4.95, 10.11.95, 7.4.96, 7.8.96.

[165] *Il Sole 24 Ore* 3.5.95, 15.6.96, 26.6.96, 18.10.96; interviews, senior regulator 2, senior legislator, adviser.

[166] For a history of the creation of the sectoral regulator, see *Il Sole 24 Ore* 10.11.95, and more generally see Giraudi and Righettini (2001), Cassese and Franchini (1996), Martinelli (2000), Perez (1996, 2002), and Gobbo and Zanetti (2000); in fact, law 481 of 1995 formally created an authority, but it was only implemented with the law of 1997; interviews, senior regulator 1, minister.

[167] Law 474 of 1994.   [168] Interviews, senior minister/regulator, senior lawyer.

[169] In agreement with the Minister for Communications and formally nominated by the president.

[170] For details, see Perez (2002: 107–12).

[171] Switzerland established a combined telecommunications and media regulator in 1992.

Table 9.1. Institutional frameworks in 1988

Institutional feature	France	West Germany	Italy
Organisational position of the operator(s)	DGT part of civil service and telecommunications linked to postal services; financial instruments for capital investment outside the budget	DBP part of civil service; telecommunications linked to postal services;	Several operators (*spezzatino telefonico*); ASST within Posts and Telecommunications Ministry; other operators public corporations within state holding company IRI
Competition	DGT monopoly; limited liberalisation of advanced services and terminal equipment	DBP monopoly; competition in terminal equipment and for some advanced services	Operators' monopoly; extremely limited liberalisation of terminal equipment
Allocation of regulatory powers	Mostly lay with minister	Mostly lay with minister	Mostly lay with minister, although divided among different ministers

features often dating from the nineteenth century, such as public ownership, linkage of posts and telecommunications within government ministries, and public monopolies, were ended. As a result, by the end of 2005, formal institutional structures in the three countries had strongly converged both with each other and with Britain (see Chapter 8).[172] Tables 9.1 and 9.2 summarise the position in 1988 and 2005, with dates of major changes.

Table 9.2. Institutional frameworks in 2005

Institutional characteristic and changes since 1988	France	West Germany	Italy
Organisational position of operator(s)	France Télécom limited company and shares publicly traded (1997); majority privately owned (2004); minority public stake	Deutsche Telekom limited company and shares publicly traded; majority privately owned (2001); minority public stake	Telecom Italia completely privately owned (majority since 1997)
Competition	All monopolies ended; rules for fair and effective competition	All monopolies ended; rules for fair and effective competition	All monopolies ended; rules for fair and effective competition
Allocation of regulatory powers	Independent telecommunications regulator (1996)	Independent telecommunications and postal services regulator (1996)	Independent media and communications regulator (1997)

---

172 For a similar finding of convergence, see also Schneider (2001*a*).

Reforms in France, Germany, and Italy were introduced by coalitions of domestic actors, with governments and the managements of incumbents at its core. Overseas companies (usually in alliance with domestic new entrants) and the European Commission sometimes played a role, but nevertheless, the dominant actors were domestic. Reform coalitions had to overcome strong opposition that involved trade unions, employees, and sometimes political parties.

Although reform coalitions were mainly domestic, internationalisation played significant roles that were clearly seen in debates and decisions to modify institutions. Reformers argued that powerful technological and economic factors such as higher demand and the development evermore advanced services and terminal equipment necessitated institutional changes. These factors had already been at work for some time before 1988. However, unlike previous periods, reformers also gave greater attention to regulatory comparisons and competition, especially with Britain. They saw Britain both as an example and as a source of competition, although they did not engage in in-depth studies of the British case. More directly, they were concerned about rival foreign operators, such as BT and AT&T, who were creating international alliances and were presented as a threat in increasingly competitive markets.

However, the most important international factor was the EU. It affected domestic reform debates in several ways. First, it provided an external set of legal requirements, especially concerning liberalisation. Second, introducing EU legislation provided occasions for wider reforms such as privatisation or creating new regulatory authorities. Third, the European Commission linked domestic regulatory reform to approval of international alliances that operators and governments claimed were essential to compete with overseas operators (claims that were not based on detailed studies or waiting for the results of such alliances). Finally, the EU provided ammunition for domestic reformers. Sometimes this took the form of legal powers and rights that could be used to attack existing institutions. But often its more important role was to offer arguments that countries had to prepare for a liberalised European market and that this necessitated institutional reforms not required by EU legislation such as privatisation.

Telecommunications in France, Germany, and Italy after 1988 can be used to sustain three central arguments about internationalisation and domestic regulatory reform. First, the cases underline the importance of policy forms of internationalisation. Whereas before 1988, transnational technological and economic factors had been met with institutional inertia, thereafter policy forms of internationalisation—overseas reforms and supranational regulation—played significant roles in comprehensive and radical reforms that ended very long-standing institutions.

A second issue concerns the carriers and mechanisms whereby internationalisation operated. Particular forms of internationalisation influenced the strategies, coalitions, and resources of domestic actors in the policymaking process. In particular, they affected the desire and ability of governments to create reform coalitions with the leaders of publicly owned incumbents, pointing to the importance of state actors in internationalisation. Overseas firms were rarely major participants in decision-making. Moreover, policy forms of internationalisation influenced domestic decision-making because they offered reformers directly useful reasons and arguments. Thus, for instance, EU regulation was used to legitimise changes that were not legally required such as privatisation and creating independent regulatory authorities. Regulatory competition with Britain operated through claims about 'keeping up', fear of BT in international alliances and presenting Britain as an attractive example. However, cross-national learning was limited: in-depth studies of matters such as the success of international alliances or new institutional arrangements in Britain were not undertaken, indicating that the role of overseas examples lays more in legitimating change than learning about new institutional arrangements.

Finally, the cases show a continental European 'reform path' that contrasts with that in Britain, and was also seen in stock exchanges, and will be set out for electricity and airlines (Chapters 5, 10, and 11). However, in Britain reforms were largely driven by domestic factors; the most important international factor was the US example and the EU played little role. In contrast, in the three other nations, international factors were central. Moreover, the most relevant overseas example and source of regulatory competition was Britain more than the US. Finally, the most important form of internationalisation was EU regulation. Thus similar outcomes arose later and through different processes and factors than in Britain. Nevertheless, by 2005, France, Germany, and Italy had adopted similar sectoral institutions to those in Britain and, compared with 1988, much convergence had occurred across the four countries.

10

Power Politics: Electricity Supply in Europe

Electricity, like telecommunications and securities trading, is a strategic sector for industrialised economies, affecting many other domains. Moreover, historically in Western Europe, its economic institutions were very similar to the two other sectors: supply to users was a monopoly, and was usually undertaken by publicly-owned suppliers; regulatory powers were held by governments (national or sub-national) and sometimes also business associations. Furthermore, from the 1960s onwards, the sector has been subject to transnational technological and economic developments, followed by reforms in the US and then Britain, and, finally, growing EU regulation.

However, the occurrence and potential impact of the three forms of internationalisation have differed from securities trading and telecommunications, providing useful variation. Transnational technological and economic developments mostly took place in the 1970s and 1980s but became weaker thereafter. In contrast, policy forms of internationalisation became more significant from the late 1990s, especially EU regulation. Moreover, in electricity, the potential for international regulatory competition is much weaker than for securities trading or even telecommunications: most users cannot relocate rapidly; cross-border supply is limited in Europe;[1] switching of new investments to low-cost electricity countries is often slow and difficult; electricity supply is vital but its cost can be of limited immediate significance for many users for whom electricity is a small component of total costs.

The electricity supply industry thus helps to test and refine the general arguments about internationalisation developed from the cases of securities trading and telecommunications. First, it provides another case to briefly test the effects of transnational technological and economic developments on institutions, by rapidly examining the period between the mid-1960s and the mid-1980s when these developments were at their most powerful.

Second, the case enables examination of the role of policy forms of internationalisation in the relative absence of transnational technological and economic forces. Whereas in securities trading and telecommunications, all three forms of internationalisation were combined, in electricity, only the policy forms were strong in the late 1980s and 1990s. Hence the sector allows testing of whether

---

[1] Indeed, in 1990 only 7% of EU member states' electricity needs were imported, from EU and non-EU sources—McGowan (1990: 45); one reason is lack of cross-border transmission capacity.

the effects of policy forms of internationalisation on institutional change are independent of transnational technological and economic developments.

Third, the sector permits deeper investigation of the effects of overseas reforms on national institutions. Such reforms can operate in two ways: through regulatory competition, by attracting business abroad and/or aiding overseas suppliers to become more competitive; ideationally, acting as an example that can be followed. Both mechanisms worked in securities trading and telecommunications. However, regulatory competition in electricity is weak. Hence the main route for overseas reforms to influence domestic decisions about institutional change is through cross-national learning or examples (at least in the short to medium term). Thus the 'ideational' impacts of overseas reforms are much more exposed.

The chapter puts forward four central arguments utilising the sector's characteristics. First, it shows that there was institutional inertia when transnational technological and economic developments took place in the absence of policy forms of internationalisation. This confirms findings from earlier chapters on securities trading and telecommunications.

Second, it shows that policy forms of internationalisation are important even in the absence of powerful transnational technological and economic developments. In particular, EU regulation was significant in France, Germany, and Italy from the 1990s onwards. It provided political impetus for reform by offering occasions for reconsidering existing institutions and for EU-level policy learning. It also provided arguments for change based on opportunities for overseas expansion in a liberalised European market and fears of domestic incumbents being disadvantaged if national institutions were not altered. Thus the impacts of policy forms of internationalisation do not depend on favourable transnational technological and economic conditions (this finding is confirmed by the cases of airlines and postal services in Chapters 11 and 12).

Third, the chapter argues that without potential regulatory competition, overseas examples played little role in domestic debates. Even Britain failed to pay serious attention to US reforms or seek to copy them. Thus when overseas examples do not offer potential competition, they are of limited interest to national policy makers and their ideational role is weak. This finding suggests that only when overseas examples are linked to the material interests of actors in the domestic policy process do they become influential in institutional reform: cross-national learning, even if superficial, or use of overseas reforms to legitimate change, is highly dependent on an apparent threat from those overseas nations.

Finally, the chapter shows that Britain followed a different path from the other three countries, acting earlier and mainly for domestic reasons, whereas reforms came later in France, Germany, and Italy and international reasons were more significant. This follows the findings of other sectors.

The chapter begins with a brief overview of sectoral institutions in the mid-1960s. It then looks at the three forms of market internationalisation, underlining the growth of the EU's regulatory framework. Reforms in Britain are considered first and separately. Thereafter France, Germany, and Italy are analysed, showing the role of EU regulation in institutional change. The conclusion draws out broader findings for internationalisation.

Table 10.1. Economic institutions in the mid-1960s

	Britain	France	West Germany	Italy
Organisational position of incumbent(s)	Public corporations—CEGB for generation and transmission; twelve area boards for distribution	EDF—fully state-owned, covering almost entire industry	Mixture of private ownership and municipal/regional ownership; no national supplier; large number of suppliers	ENEL—publicly owned, covering almost entire industry
Competition	Monopoly over transmission and supply; a few independent generators	Monopoly over transmission and supply; a few independent generators	Competition avoided through use of concessions and industry agreements	Monopoly over transmission and supply; a few independent generators
Allocation of regulatory powers	Government	Government	Municipalities and Länder governments; strong role for industry associations	Government

SECTORAL ECONOMIC INSTITUTIONS IN THE MID-1960s[2]

The electricity supply sector can be divided into three activities: generation, transmission on a grid, and then distribution or supply from the grid to users. In the mid-1960s, publicly-owned and vertically-integrated suppliers in Britain, France, and Italy dominated all three activities: they were responsible for the vast majority of the generation of electricity[3] and held legal or virtual monopolies over its transmission and its distribution to users. There were no independent regulators and most formal powers were held by governments and suppliers.

However, significant cross-national diversity also existed in the degree of concentration and organisational position of suppliers.[4] In France and Italy, a single publicly owned national supplier dominated the sector—Electricité de France (EDF) and Ente Nazionale per l'Energia Elettrica (ENEL). In contrast, in West Germany there was no national supplier; instead, suppliers were regional or municipal, with some being privately owned and operating under locally allocated contracts or concessions. Britain (England and Wales)[5] was an intermediate case, with a single generating and transmission company, the Central Electricity Generating Board (CEGB) and twelve regional Area Electricity Boards; all were public corporations. Table 10.1 summarises the institutional framework in each country.

---

[2] For overviews, see McGowan (1995) and Midttun (1997).
[3] For figures showing the decline of non-utility generation, see McGowan (1993: 10).
[4] McGowan (1993: ch.1).
[5] Separate arrangements existed in Scotland and Northern Ireland; for simplicity, these are excluded.

INTERNATIONALISATION AND ELECTRICITY SUPPLY

Significant transnational technological and economic developments occurred in the electricity sector between the 1960s and the 1980s. Generation increasingly moved from coal to oil and nuclear power. International oil prices gyrated, rising sharply in 1973–4 and 1979–80, but falling in the 1980s. Nuclear power was developed in the 1960s and 1970s, but then suffered major setbacks in the 1980s, especially after the Three Mile Island and Chernobyl accidents of 1979 and 1986. At the same time, demand for electricity grew sharply.

However, the strength of transnational technological and economic forces for change abated in the period from *c*. 1990 to 2005 for developed nations and in cross-sectoral perspective were much weaker than in telecommunications or securities trading.[6] International oil prices became more stable (until 2004–5), while nuclear power generation stagnated.[7] Demand for electricity grew only slowly.[8] Moreover, the grid remained a natural monopoly throughout the period, in contrast to telecommunications where rival infrastructures became economically feasible in the 1980s and 1990s as their costs fell. Thus pressures on existing sectoral institutions from rapid rises in demand, major new technologies requiring large-scale investment, and oil price rises were much less important in the 1990s than in earlier periods.

The US offered a further source of internationalisation by providing an example of alternative institutions. Most generation was in the hands of private suppliers at the state level, although a significant minority of suppliers was undertaken by public agencies.[9] The prices, quality, and activities of suppliers were regulated by state-level public utilities commissions as well as the Federal Power Commission (replaced in 1977 by the Federal Energy Regulatory Commission). Divergence between American and European sectoral institutions grew from the late 1970s as competition was increasingly permitted in the US. The 1978 Public Utility Regulatory Policies Act (PURPA) required utilities to purchase power from other generators if the latter were cheaper, and hence encouraged competition in electricity generation.[10] Liberalisation was extended in the 1980s and especially the 1990s as some states began to allow competition in supply, so that users could contract directly with generators and new firms could enter the market. The most notable example was California, which passed legislation in 1996, although this became a 'negative example' after 2000 when

---

[6] cf. Bartle (2002) for a comparison with telecommunications.

[7] The averages for crude oil in dollars per barrel rose from $1.26 in 1970 to $36.01 in 1980 to reach $22.49 in 1990, but between 1990 and 2003 they remained between $22.49 and $30.50; only in 2004 and 2005 did they rise sharply (to $52.93)—source: International Energy Authority, 'Crude Oil Spot Prices'; the main transnational technological and economic change from the 1980s onwards was the development of smaller units for generation, notably 'combined cycle gas turbines' using gas to generate electricity, but this concerned only a minority of generation—cf. Thomas (1997: 64) and Gallon (2000).

[8] One figure was 2% per annum—Gallon (2000).

[9] Private firms accounted for over 70% of generation by 1970—Gomez-Ibanez (2003: 112).

[10] Palast, Oppenheim, and MacGregor (2003: 119).

competition in the wholesale market was followed by prices shooting up ten-fold and the state's largest private utility going bankrupt. Overall, the US could influence (positively or negatively) decisions in Europe through learning and mimetism.

The development of a comprehensive EU regulatory framework provided the third and most important form of internationalisation in electricity.[11] Until the late 1980s, the EU played almost no role in electricity supply, but thereafter its role expanded.[12] Initially, EU liberalisation was controversial. Thus Commission proposals in the early 1990s that competition should be permitted for all con-sumers and that generators and distributors should have access to transmission grids (known as 'third-party access') aroused fierce opposition from almost all member states, with only Britain and Ireland supporting the Commission.[13] However, from the mid-1990s onwards, the positions of member states evolved. They gradually accepted the need for EU regulation to create a market open to competition.[14] By the early 2000s, even the French government altered its position and accepted competition throughout the sector.[15] EU-level debates concerned the timing of reform and matters such as separation of monopoly infrastructures from other parts of the sector and objectives set for national regulatory authorities rather than the principle of liberalisation.

As a result, significant EU legislation was passed from the mid-1990s onwards.[16] It had many similarities with that in telecommunications: it ended member states' rights to maintain monopolies, insisted on separation of regulation and supply, and introduced rules designed to ensure that competition was 'fair and effective'. However, in contrast to telecommunications, EU directives were passed by the Council of energy ministers and the European Parliament rather than the Commission acting alone.[17]

The first major legislative development was the 1996 directive on electricity.[18] It obliged member states to allow competition in generation. It liberalised supply to large final users, so that 25%–33% of distribution would be open to competition by 2003.[19] It also provided access to the monopoly grid for all suppliers so that competition could occur in generation and distribution. Moreover, to deal with vertically-integrated operators who combined control of the monopoly grid with generation and distribution, the directive included provisions on access to the grid

---

[11] For analyses, see Matlary (1997), Eising (2002), Cameron (2005), Geneste (1997), and Desama (2003).

[12] For an analysis, see McGowan (1993: ch. 4).

[13] Eising (2002: 92–5) and Desama (2003); cf. Schmidt (1996), Padgett (1992), and Matlary (1997).

[14] Eising (2002); see also Padgett (2003).

[15] Turmes (2003); see Desama (2003); cf. Nicole Fontaine (then junior industry minister)—Fontaine (2003).

[16] For a complete analysis, see Cameron (2002, 2005).

[17] i.e. using co-decision procedures rather than under Article 86 [ex-90](3); the Commission had originally threatened to use the latter.

[18] European Parliament and Council (1996).

[19] European Parliament and Council (1996); cf. Eising (2002).

to ensure that competition in other parts of the sector was fair.[20] EU legislation required member states to create dispute settlement authorities that were independent of the parties and able to resolve conflicts over access to the electricity network.

However the 1996 directive left considerable room for choice for member states.[21] In generation, they could implement competition either by issuing licences, so that any licensed company could produce electricity, or by introducing a system of competitive bidding for generation, a system less likely to aid entry. With respect to the vital matter of access to the grid, the directive allowed three forms of third-party access: negotiations between new entrants and the grid operator; regulated third-party access in which the grid operators publish prices; a 'single buyer' in which there is a single wholesale buyer of electricity. The last was a concession to countries led by France and represented a less-liberalised approach. Moreover, the directive did not require sweeping changes such as structural 'unbundling'—that is obliging vertically-integrated companies to place their generation, transmission, and distribution activities in separate companies to aid fair competition. Nor did it insist that regulators be independent of governments or be sectoral authorities. Finally, in another concession to opponents of unregulated competition, it permitted member states to impose various public service obligations on suppliers, including those concerning security, continuity and quality of supply, and protection of the environment. The latitude of the legislation resulted in 'a patchwork of uneven implementation'.[22]

More extensive legislation followed. In particular, the electricity directive of 2003 greatly extended competition.[23] It obliged member states to end monopolies over distribution to all users, including residential ones by 2007. It removed the single buyer option of supply and that of bidding for generation capacity, usually seen as less competitive models than third-party access and licensing of generators. Rules to ensure fair competition were set out, notably greater separation of the monopoly grid from generation and distribution activities that were subject to competition. The directive insisted that national regulatory authorities be independent of suppliers and that they be capable of carrying out their duties efficiently but did not require independence from the government. As a counterpart to liberalisation, important provisions for public service were included but did not require independence from the government.[24] Finally, in 2003 the EU also issued a regulation to aid cross-border trade.[25] Thus by 2005, electricity supply in Europe faced an increasingly comprehensive and detailed EU regulatory framework centred on aiding competition.

---

[20] For instance, the principle of non-discrimination in access to the grid, and the requirement that within operators, accounts, and management of the grid should be separated from other activities.

[21] Cameron (2002) and Padgett (2003).   [22] Cameron (2005: 9).

[23] European Parliament and Council (2003*a*); for an analysis, see Cameron (2005).

[24] For instance to protect consumers via price transparency and fair contractual terms or special measures for vulnerable users.

[25] European Parliament and Council (2003*b*); it established inter-network compensation mechanisms, encouraged consistent charging for access to networks, and set out measures to deal with allocation of transmission capacity; see Cameron (2005: 28–9).

REFORM IN BRITAIN

As in telecommunications and securities trading, Britain reformed its electricity sector before other European nations.[26] The Conservative government led by Margaret Thatcher introduced comprehensive reforms, beginning with the 1989 Electricity Act. Unlike other network industries, it broke up the main generator and owner of the grid, the CEGB, into three generating companies (National Power, PowerGen, and Nuclear Electric) and a company for the transmission network (National Grid). It then progressively privatised these companies and the twelve distribution companies, the Regional Electricity Companies (RECs) between 1990 and 1996.[27] It also extensively liberalised. Competition in distribution was allowed for larger users and then progressively extended so that by 1998 all consumers—industrial and residential—could choose any licensed supplier.[28] Competition in electricity generation was ensured through a 'spot market' in which generators offered electricity, and suppliers had to buy at the lowest price. An independent regulatory body, Offer (The Office of Electricity Supply) was created in 1989, strongly modelled on Oftel in telecommunications; it was merged with its counterpart for gas in 2000 to form the Office of Gas and Electricity Markets (Ofgem). Far from 'deregulation', Offer/Ofgem created a complex regulatory framework designed to aid and govern competition.[29]

The reform of electricity supply in Britain owed little to international factors. The industry was profitable and did not face problems in raising capital for new technology or international competition, unlike stock exchanges or telecommunications operators. Although policy makers were aware of the US model,[30] it played little role in British reforms, which in any case went much further than those in the US. British decisions came before EU legislation and were driven by domestic factors, notably the attraction of raising revenue from privatisation, the desire to increase competition and the aim of reducing the power of the coal miners, whose strikes endangered governments.[31] Policy makers also drew strongly on the experience of reforming other network industries in Britain, notably telecommunications and gas, to conclude that privatisation was possible, that a regulatory agency was needed and that selling vertically-integrated incumbents impeded competition.[32] Finally, in sharp contrast to the three European countries analysed below, change was driven through despite strong opposition from the senior managers of the industry: the CEGB's chairman, Lord Marshall, fought hard to

---

[26] For analyses, see Surrey (1996), Newbery and Green (1996), and Thomas (1997).

[27] Majority stakes in the RECs were sold in 1990, in National Power and Powergen in 1991 and in the nuclear generators—consolidated as British Energy—in 1996; the National Grid Company was sold as a separate firm by the RECs in 1995—Thomas (1996).

[28] In 1990, the threshold was 1 MW; by 1994 it was 100 kW; by April 1998 it applied to all users, including domestic ones.

[29] Notably price caps on services in which competition was regarded as insufficient, and also rules over access to the electricity grid and for wholesale trading of electricity from the generation 'pool'.

[30] cf. Littlechild (1993: 120–1).

[31] Thomas (1996: 50–54); for memoirs of key policy makers, see Lawson (1992: 176–80, 234–40) and Parkinson (1992: 260–80).   [32] Thatcher (1993: 680–5).

prevent its breakup.[33] Hence the British case shows the role of domestic inter-sectoral isomorphism rather than international institutional isomorphism.[34]

INSTITUTIONAL REFORMS IN FRANCE, GERMANY, AND ITALY

In 1990, existing regulatory institutions in France, Germany, and Italy dated back several decades and appeared strongly entrenched.[35] Attempts at change between the mid-1960s and 1990s had been rare and few had succeeded.[36] There were several important obstacles to reform. A 'political and economic cartel' (Mez 2003: 193) benefited from institutional arrangements such as monopoly and public ownership. The managers of electricity suppliers could engage in expansion and technological projects, notably nuclear power. Governments used the highly profitable suppliers for their own ends such as raising revenues, providing employment, or underpinning active industrial policies.[37] Employees and trade unions enjoyed employment protection and rights to participate in decision-making. Finally, suppliers such as EDF or German utilities were regarded as highly successful by the general public, and in any case, electricity was argued to be a natural monopoly.[38]

Yet from the mid-1990s onwards, policy makers in all three nations, particu-larly governments, the senior managers of incumbents, and (when established) independent regulators, began to embrace and introduce reforms. The most far-reaching modifications were in Italy, which offer a surprise given the many obsta-cles to change, including short-term divided governments, political support for protecting ENEL, the state-owned dominant supplier, and strong cross-subsidies designed by politicians to benefit certain groups.[39] Nevertheless, in 1992, ENEL was transformed from a public enterprise into a private law company. Privatisa-tion by sale of tranches of shares then followed. Initially, only 31.8% were sold in 1999, but then a further 35.6% were sold between 1999 and 2005.[40] Thus by 2005, the state owned approximately one-third of ENEL's shares. Liberalisation took place, as Italy passed legislation in 1999, 2001 and 2004[41] that transposed EU directives. The market for distribution was opened to competition, first for

---

[33] Parkinson (1992: 269–70) and Thatcher (1993: 683).

[34] For a discussion of similar patterns of isomorphism in railways, see Lodge (2002).

[35] Thus the major legislation in West Germany was the Energy Business Act 1935 and in France that of nationalisation in 1948; Italian institutions were more recent, with nationalisation to create ENEL dating from 1962—for cross-national histories, see Mittun (1997) and Glancher and Finon (2003).

[36] McGowan (1993: ch. 2); thus for instance, ideas of greater competition or establishing a federal regulator were put forward in West Germany in the 1970s, but no action was taken—Eising (1999: 221) and Mez (2003: 201).

[37] Nationally, or in West Germany at the Land and municipal levels.

[38] cf. De Paoli (2004), Lorenzoni (2003), Batail (1997), and Poppe and Cauret (1997: 202–4, 213–7).

[39] For overviews, see Di Porto and Silva (2005) and Lorenzoni (2003).

[40] Another 10% were sold to the Cassa Depositi e Prestiti, a company largely owned by the govern-ment.

[41] The 'Bersani decree' no. 79/99 and the 'Marzano' Law no. 239 of 23 August 2004.

large users, reaching 70% of the market by 2004, and then by 2007, for all users.[42] Competition in generation was encouraged: entry was permitted, with a licensing procedure; a 'power exchange' was eventually established in 2004 that offered a virtual marketplace for the spot trading of electricity by producers and consumers; no company was allowed to produce or import more than 50% of electricity in Italy from 2003.[43] Moreover, ENEL was partially broken up: under the 1999 decree, it was constituted as separate companies for different activities.[44] Management of the grid was given to a new company (TERNA) from 1999, albeit that ENEL retained ownership; under the 2004 law, the grid is to become a separate company that will be privatised, with ENEL's stake limited to a maximum 20%. ENEL was also obliged to sell-off generating capacity, resulting in three new generating companies being established. Finally, in 1995, an independent regulatory authority was created for energy, the Autorità per l'Energia Elettrica ed il Gas (AEEG);[45] its goals included promoting competition.[46]

Regulatory institutions in Germany at the end of the 1980s were very different from those in the three other nations, particularly due to the higher degree of fragmentation of the industry among many regional and municipal producers, and between public and private suppliers. However, the period thereafter saw the emergence of a small number of large private firms, thanks to takeovers and mergers.[47] As a result, by 2005, Germany had two very large vertically-integrated suppliers (now called EON and RWE) as well as four main grid providers,[48] thereby reducing fragmentation. Public policy makers were deeply involved in consolidation: mergers were approved by the Federal Cartel Office and were aided by the Länder and municipalities selling their stakes in electricity supply companies.[49]

Rules governing competition were also radically altered to aid entry.[50] The 1998 law on the Energy Industry[51] allowed competition in distribution for all users, including residential ones. Thus it went well beyond the EU's legal requirements (notably the 1996 electricity directive). However, entrants still faced obstacles. In particular, key rules governing access to the transmission grid were made through 'association agreements' negotiated between peak associations of electricity suppliers, which gave powerful incumbents incentives and opportunities

---

[42] Cameron (2002: 255). [43] Caiazzo (2005: 237–8).
[44] Generation, sales to liberalised markets, sales to remaining monopoly markets, ownership of the grid and decommissioning of nuclear plans.
[45] It was headed by a Board of 3 members (increased to 5 in 2004) and appointed for 7 years.
[46] cf. Ranci (2003) and Caiazzo (2005).
[47] In particular, the three large suppliers that existed in 1990—VIAG, RWE, and VEBA took over a series of other regional and municipal suppliers (generators and distributors); moreover, in 1999, a merger between VEBA and VIAG was announced, together with one between RWE and another of the largest large firms which controlled the grid, VEW; e.g. see Mez (2003: 203–8) and Eberlein (2000: 87–9).
[48] RWE, E.On, Vattenfall Europe, and EnBW.
[49] For instance, Bavaria's sale of shares in Bayenwerk in 1994, Hamburg's sale of shares in HEW in 1999 or Berlin's sale of shares in BEWAG in 1997—Mez (2003: 204).
[50] See Börner (2001). [51] Gesetz zur Neuregelung des Energiewirtschaftsrechts.

to limit entry.[52] Moreover, unlike the other three countries, no sectoral independent regulatory authority was established. Instead, liberalisation depended on the application of general competition rules by the federal competition authority, the Bundeskartellamt, rather than detailed sectoral rules. But the Bundeskartellamt had very limited resources and sector-specific expertise in energy, and in any case, acted after anti-competitive behaviour had taken place ('ex post regulation'). Following many criticisms of these barriers to competition, including by the European Commission[53] and despite much resistance by incumbent suppliers and their associations, a new law was passed in 2005 to transpose the 2003 EU electricity directive.[54] It established a sector-specific energy regulator.[55] Moreover, to aid competition, conditions for third-party access to the grid were introduced instead of negotiated access, together with provisions for non-discrimination. To ensure a degree of separation between the monopoly grid on the one hand, and distribution and generation that were open to competition on the other hand, vertically-integrated suppliers were also obliged to place their transmission activities into separate companies; again, the aim was to assist entry. Hence by 2005, Germany had considerably strengthened sectoral institutional arrangements for a regulated competitive market in a manner similar to the other three nations.

France seemed the least likely candidate for reform in electricity. Until the late 1990s, French policy makers strongly resisted alteration of sectoral economic institutions for electricity. Domestically, change was seen as unnecessary since EDF was regarded as highly successful.[56] There was powerful support for EDF's *statut* (organisational position) as a public law company that dated from nationalisation in 1946.[57] Unions were strong in EDF and opposed reform, including with strike action.[58] Given these features, France missed the deadline of 1999 for transposing the EU's 1996 directive into law and only acted after an ECJ ruling.[59] When it did so, liberalisation was limited: market segments opened to competition went no further than required by EU law; within EDF, monopoly elements such as running the running the grid and distribution system were not separated from other activities through the creation of different entities; strong restrictions were laid down for exchanges that allowed trading of electricity.[60]

Yet after 1999, French policy makers began to embrace institutional reform. The 2000 Electricity Law[61] not only implemented EU requirements but also created an independent sectoral regulator, the Commission de Régulation de l'Electricité (CRE).[62] It opened 70% of the French market to competition by 2004, with

[52] Coen (2005 : 112–17), Coen and Héritier (2002: 11–14), and Eberlein (2000: 92–3).

[53] See e.g. European Commission (2003); cf. Cameron (2002: 316–19).

[54] Pritasche and Klauer (2005).

[55] By adding responsibility for energy to the telecommunications and postal regulator, to form a federal agency for network regulation, the Bundesnetzagentur.

[56] Finon (2003: 257, 259).   [57] It was an Etablissement public industriel et commercial (EPIC).

[58] Lauriol (2005: 124).   [59] Lauriol (2005: 123–4).   [60] Finon (2003: 260–2).

[61] Loi no 2000—108 du 10 février 2000 relative à la modernisation du service public de l'électricité.

[62] Extended to gas in 2003 when it became the Commission de Régulation de l'Energie.

complete opening to occur by 2007.[63] Moreover, despite having fought hard in EU negotiations for the option of using single buyer arrangements in the 1996 electricity directive, France failed to make use of it, and instead implemented the third-party access model that was more favourable to competition. In 2004, the pace of change quickened with the law on Public Service in Electricity and Gas which transposed the EU's 2003 directives on electricity and gas.[64] In keeping with EU obligations, the 2003 law obliged EDF to create an independent legal entity for the grid. However, it also went beyond EU requirements by transferring some assets for local distribution networks to local authorities and allowing the small non-EDF suppliers to operate outside their previously strictly limited geographical limits. The two decisions increased the potential for competition. Most radically, EDF's *statut* was radically altered: it was made into a private law limited liability company and the government was authorised to sell up to 30% of the shares (13% were sold in November 2005). Overall, the reforms meant that by 2005, France had moved a considerable way towards the formal institutions of a regulated competitive market, in stark contrast to the position in 1990.

Thus by 2005, considerable institutional convergence had taken place across the three nations, as all moved towards partially or majority privately-owned incumbents, markets opened to competition, the establishment of rules to ensure that entry was not blocked by incumbents, and independent sectoral regulatory authorities. National peculiarities, notably high fragmentation and subnational ownership of suppliers and regulation by the general competition authority in Germany had been reduced or ended. Moreover, the institutions had moved considerably towards those in Britain. Table 10.2 summarises the position in 2005.

Internationalisation and Domestic Reform in France, Germany, and Italy

International factors were significant in the reform of sectoral institutions in France, Germany, and Italy, working alongside domestic factors.[65] However, the three forms of internationalisation enjoyed unequal roles. Transnational technological and economic factors were not prominent in domestic policy debates. Reform in the US was also largely absent from reform decisions; indeed, the example of California together with power failures in the US were seen as warnings of the dangers of liberalisation.[66] The British example played a minor role, especially in Germany, where it had a 'demonstration effect', showing that competition did not endanger security of supply, and was used by expert commissions to justify

---

[63] Lauriol (2005: 131).

[64] Loi no 2004—803 du 9 août 2004 sur le service public de l'électricité et le gaz—see Richer (2004) and Lauriol (2005).

[65] The latter included raising revenue from privatising suppliers, reducing high electricity prices in Germany and Italy or weakening the constraints of public ownership and powerful trade unions; e.g. of these factors, see *Il Sole 24 Ore* 3.4.95, De Paoli (2004), Lorenzoni (2003), and Eberlein (2000: 89).

[66] Poniatowski and Revol (2003) and De Paoli (2004).

Table 10.2. Economic institutions in electricity in 2005

	France	Germany	Italy
Organisational position of incumbent	EDF—private law company, to be partially privatised (30%)	Private law companies, most privately owned notably two largest suppliers EON and RWE; some smaller suppliers still owned by Länder or municipalities	ENEL—majority privately owned (66%)
Competition	70% by 2004, all by 2007; some sale of capacity and transfer of some distribution networks to municipalities; grid owned by EDF but in independent legal entity	Entire market opened to competition; four regional grid companies; several smaller generation and distribution companies	Entire market opened to competition; sale of part of ENEL's generating capacity to 3 firms; grid to be placed in separate company with maximum 20% ENEL share
Allocation of regulatory powers	Independent sectoral regulator for energy—CRE	Independent regulator for network sectors—energy, posts, telecommunications, and railways	Independent sectoral regulator for energy—AEEG

'deregulation'.[67] But it was insufficient to overcome opposition to liberalisation in the early 1990s, especially from sub-national governments.[68]

The key international factor in reform in all three nations was EU regulation.[69] It had direct effects by obliging member states to alter institutional arrangements, notably to liberalise and to unbundle the grid from other activities, and to separate regulation from supply. When member states failed to transpose EU legal obligations, the EU Commission began legal action against them.[70] It also had indirect effects that contributed to domestic reforms going much further than those required to meet EU obligations. Thus privatisation and the creation of sectoral independent regulatory agencies (IRAs) were not mandated by EU law

---

[67] Eising (1999: 220), Eising (2000: 274), and Pfaffenberger (1992).

[68] Mez (1997: 250) and Di Porto and Silva (2005: 20–21).

[69] For clear statements on the importance of the EU, see: for Germany, Eising (1999, 2000) and Eberlein (2000); for Italy, Di Porto (2003: 215), Di Porto and Silva (2005: 20–1), and Lorenzoni (2003: 316); for France: Finon (2003: 257), De Minicault (2003), Poniatowski and Revol (2003), Syrota (president of the French regulator the CRE) (2003), and Chevallier (2003).

[70] Thus for instance, the Commission conducted infringement procedures against France regarding non-implementation and against Germany for incomplete implementation in 2001 (European Commission 2001).

and on several occasions, countries went beyond EU directives on liberalisation and restructuring of incumbents.[71]

Five indirect effects of EU regulation can be analysed. First, it provided occasions for reform. In all three countries, passing legislation to transpose EU directives provided opportunities for wider reviews of institutions and recasting sectoral arrangements. Examples included the creation of IRAs in France in 2000 and Germany in 2005, modification of EDF's organisational position (its *statut*) in 2004 or the sale of ENEL generating capacity decided in 1999.

Second, discussion and negotiations at the EU level contributed to learning by domestic actors, as they interacted with overseas colleagues and Brussels officials and reconsidered their preferences.[72] Moreover, they affected structure of domestic interest groups, shifting power within them to more internationally-minded elements.[73]

A third and important effect of EU regulation was to put pressures on decision-makers through fear of being disadvantaged. Policy makers in Italy and Germany feared the entry of large overseas suppliers, especially EDF.[74] This was a strong reason for German policy makers to allow the creation of large, vertically-integrated suppliers, which were then seen as capable of 'taking on' EDF. In Italy, fear of EDF and the need to deal with the country's dependence on imports (which account for *c.* 35% of Italian electricity needs), especially from France, were important in the liberalisation of generation and the privatisation of ENEL. More indirectly, the EU Commission put pressure on countries to move towards privately-owned suppliers and sectoral regulators. Thus for instance, it took legal action against France for illegal state aid because EDF's debts were guaranteed by the government, allowing the company to borrow more cheaply than 'commercial' (i.e. private sector) rates. Germany's decision to create a sectoral regulator for networks in 2005 followed pressure by the Commission and worries that its lack of a sector-specific body led to disadvantages in EU discussions and European 'networks of national regulators' in electricity.[75]

However, EU regulation also offered opportunities for incumbents to expand abroad, providing a fourth and perhaps the most important route for EU influence. EDF is the clearest example.[76] Thanks to nuclear power stations, it had a large electricity surplus to export and also low variable costs. Moreover, it pursued a strategy of expansion abroad and buying up overseas firms—for instance EnBW in Germany or Montedison in Italy. By 2000, 19% of its turnover came from other European nations.[77] German and Italian electricity companies such

---

[71] For instance Germany in introducing competition through the sector in 1998 or even France in increasing the freedom of local producers and the distribution assets of local authorities in the 2004 law.

[72] For an extensive discussion, see Eising (1999, 2002).

[73] Cf. Eising (1999, 2002) for German interest associations.

[74] *Il Sole 24 Ore* 17.10.02, 6.12.02, 20.3.2003, and 22.3.2003.

[75] *Handelsblatt* 17.02.2003, 27.03.2003, 01.04.2003, and 12.05.2003.

[76] Gallon (2000), Chevallier (2003), Batail (1997), and Lautier (2003).

[77] Lautier (2003: 281).

as RWE, EON, and ENEL also increasingly sought overseas expansion.[78] But overseas takeovers and mergers frequently required approval under general EU competition law from the European Commission (and especially its Competition Directorate),[79] which often imposed conditions involving domestic liberalisation. Thus for instance, the Commission made approval of EDF's acquisition of a stake in the German supplier EnBW conditional on selling generating capacity, while it used the merger between VEBA and VIAG to insist that Germany establish detailed rules to govern access to the grid and take measures to ensure unbundling of different activities by vertically-integrated suppliers.[80] The overseas ambitions of national champion incumbent firms were sometimes dependent on Commission support against foreign governments. The most obvious example was EDF's takeover of the Italian company Montedison. In the 2004 electricity law, Italy placed limits on ownership of shares by companies from other countries who did not offer reciprocal market access. This provision was known as the 'anti-EDF' law, since it was designed to limit EDF's voting share in the Italian company Montedison in which it had taken a large hostile stake in 2001.[81] EDF's bargaining position was greatly strengthened by the Commission taking legal action against the Italian law.[82] In turn, the Commission's attitude was linked to France transposing the 2003 directives and liberalising its home market.[83] Thus the counterpart to international expansion by incumbents was often domestic liberalisation, a point recognised by French and German policy makers and which helps to account for their apparently surprising acceptance of EU liberalisation.[84]

Finally, EU regulation offered justifications for changes that were frequently controversial and met resistance from several sources: trade unionists and employees (especially in EDF), sub-national authorities (e.g. in Germany), some political parties (e.g. in Italy and France) and public opinion which feared that privatisation and liberalisation would damage an industry that was seen as efficient, successful and serving the public interest. EU regulation aided legitimation of new institutions.[85] Thus policy makers argued that privatisation was essential to match overseas competitors and succeed in a liberalised European market. Hence for instance, in Italy, the centre-left government in the late 1990s was able to claim that the system needed to be 'modernised' to prepare for competition (whereas in fact a key reason for privatisation was to meet fiscal targets).[86] The best example came in France, where the EU Commission's action against 'state aid' for EDF

---

[78] Chevallier (2003), Poppe and Cauret (1997); *Il Sole 24 Ore* 16.10.97, 17.10.02, 1.3.2003, and 1.5.2003.

[79] Under the 1989 Regulation whereby large cross-border mergers needed Commission approval.

[80] Eberlein (2000) and Mez (2003).   [81] *Il Sole 24 Ore* 17.7.2003 and 29.9.2003.

[82] *Il Sole 24 Ore* 10.7.2003.

[83] The matter was settled by Italian policy makers seeking a share of the French electricity market for ENEL in exchange for accepting ENEL control over Montedison. *Il Sole 24 Ore* 22.7.2003.

[84] Chevallier (2003), Batail (1997), Poniatowski and Revol (2003), and Eberlein (2000).

[85] Aided by a raft of public service obligations which could be used to argue that the EU was not just 'deregulating' electricity.

[86] *Il Sole 24 Ore* 6.12.93, 2.1.97, interview with under-Secretary for Industry Umberto Carpi *Il Sole 24 Ore* 24.2.97.

was used to justify alteration of EDF's *statut*, although the legal basis for the Commission's case was very shaky; in fact, the main motivation for policy makers was partially to privatise EDF and to provide EDF with funds to expand through acquisitions.[87] Thus domestically, EU regulation was used by governments to transform institutional design questions from political choices into matters of 'implementation' of EU law, over which they claimed to have little choice.[88]

CONCLUSION

The case of electricity supply supports and develops the conclusions drawn from analysis of securities trading and telecommunications. Four major arguments can be put forward. First, strong transnational technological and economic developments from the mid-1960s until the mid-1980s were met with little change in domestic economic institutions. This finding mirrors the evidence in other sectors such as securities trading, telecommunications, and airlines (see Chapter 11).

A second conclusion is that the four countries took diverse routes to similar institutional frameworks. As in securities trading and telecommunications, Britain stands out as an exception. It reformed before Continental nations. It did so primarily for domestic reasons, and was strongly influenced by its own experiences in telecommunications—that is cross-sectoral isomorphism was important. In terms of internationalisation, Britain remained an island. In contrast, international factors were significant in France, Germany, and Italy.

Third, the case of electricity allows more detailed analysis of the effects of reforms in overseas nations. Regulatory competition across nations was relatively weak compared to securities trading and telecommunications. Hence the main potential mechanism for overseas reforms was ideational—through providing an example to be copied or learnt from. The cases show that although policy makers did look at overseas examples, these played little role in domestic debates. The US example was not prominent in Britain and in the other three countries it was either ignored or seen in a negative light following problems with liberalisation after 2000. Equally, policy makers in Germany looked at the British example in the early 1990s, but it was insufficient to overcome interests that opposed liberalisation. Copying or modelling or even citing overseas examples was weak in the absence of those examples affecting the material interests of domestic actors through regulatory competition.

Finally, the case of electricity underlines the importance of EU regulation for institutional reforms in France, Germany, and Italy. It played significant roles in the 1990s, despite weak transnational technological and economic pressures for change. It provided a set of legal obligations for member states. EU negotiations aided in altering the preferences of domestic actors through learning and

---

[87] Cf. Cheneroy-Gueriand (2004), Richter (2004) and Katz (2003).
[88] cf. Eising (1999) for Germany.

changes in their internal distributions of power. Transposition of EU directives created occasions for reform and debate. EU regulation increased pressures on governments and incumbents, mainly through fear of being disadvantaged by less effective institutions in a liberalised European market. It also provided legitimation for reforms that were desired for both international and domestic reasons. But most important of all, it offered national incumbent suppliers opportunities for overseas expansion. Thus, overall, EU regulation aided governments and the managements of incumbents to overcome domestic resistance to change. It offered them both pressures to adapt to competition, but also the alluring prospect of creating international champions operating across several previously closed national markets in Europe.

With respect to the overall argument of the study, the case of electricity illustrates the value of a policy analysis approach to internationalisation. The chapter has shown that policy forms of internationalisation influence domestic reform decisions even if transnational technological and economic factors are weak. It also underlines that cross-national policy learning must be linked to the interests and strategies of actors in the domestic policy process: when potential regulatory competition is weak, they pay little attention to overseas reforms. On the other hand, as the cases of securities trading and airlines (Chapter 11) and to a lesser extent telecommunications show, when direct or indirect competition is strong, policy makers pay careful attention to reforms in nations seen as rivals.

11

Changing Course: Airlines in Europe

In the mid-1960s, economic institutions for airline transportation in European nations resembled those in telecommunications, electricity, and sometimes stock exchanges—state ownership of suppliers, limited competition, and regulation by governments.[1] Thereafter, the three forms of internationalisation of markets examined in earlier chapters also arose. But variations in the occurrence of those forms allow testing and development of the arguments constructed in earlier cases.

Transnational technological and economic developments in airlines were much more subdued in the 1990s than in the 1970s and 1980s. But the US undertook sweeping reforms in the 1970s and 1980s that liberalised its market and altered the overseas strategies of its airlines and policy makers. Finally, the EU developed an increasingly wide regulatory framework from the late 1980s onwards. Hence in the 1990–2005 period the effects of policy forms of internationalisation (US reforms and EU regulation) on domestic institutional reform can be studied when transnational technological and economic developments did not operate very strongly (unlike securities trading and telecommunications, in which all three forms cumulated). In this respect, the airline sector is similar to electricity, offering a second case of its kind.

At the same time, other important differences between the two sectors allow us to delve more deeply into the effects of reforms in overseas nations. Unlike electricity, potential direct international competition is high in airline transportation: the majority of revenues and profits arise from overseas flights, especially outside Europe, rather than domestic routes. Reforms in the US or Britain therefore offered the direct risk of loss of revenues and profits for incumbent carriers. Thus the case allows examination of overseas reforms that could operate through both ideational' and competitive mechanisms, whereas in electricity, only the former was strong.

The chapter focuses on the period between the 1980s and 2005. It puts forward three claims that are important for the book's overall themes. First, it argues that despite weak transnational technological and economic developments, policy forms of internationalisation aided domestic institutional reforms. These forms of internationalisation can operate independently of technological and economic ones. This confirms the findings of the case of electricity.

[1] The chapter looks at the scheduled commercial transport of passengers, for reasons of space it omits cargo and military air transport and charter flights; equally, given its focus on economic institutions, it does not look at air traffic control and safety.

Second, the airlines sector underlines that overseas reforms operate through regulatory competition rather than mimetism. In particular, changes in American domestic institutions altered the competitive advantages of US airlines, creating pressures on institutions in Europe and representing a significant factor in reform. Conversely, when the American example clashed with domestic interests, it was not followed. Thus the ideational power of overseas reforms is less important than fears of loss of competitive advantage. The international character of the airline industry allows the effects of overseas reforms to be particularly exposed.

Third, the case confirms findings of earlier chapters that Britain followed a different reform path to France, Germany, and Italy in terms of timing and the factors driving change. US reforms were important as they offered both a source of competition and an example. But even Britain failed to copy the US model when it clashed with the interests of the incumbent national carrier, British Airways (BA).

The chapter begins by briefly outlining the key economic institutions in Europe in the mid-1960s, showing significant similarities among Britain, France, West Germany, and Italy. It then looks at internationalisation of the sector, underlining the role of competition from US carriers in the world market and the growth of EU regulation from the 1990s. Thereafter it studies reforms in Britain, before examining changes in the other three countries, for which it emphases the importance of EU regulation and competition from British suppliers. More general conclusions are set out in the final section.

ECONOMIC INSTITUTIONS FOR AIRLINES IN THE MID-1960s IN EUROPE

In the mid-1960s, Britain, France, West Germany, and Italy each had one main state-owned 'flag carrier'—BA, Air France, Lufthansa, and Alitalia. These airlines had usually been created by state-led mergers of several companies.[2] Governments held most powers, notably to license airlines, determine sharing of capacity on routes and approve fares. In practice, the 'flag carriers' held a monopoly over domestic flights and were the sole national airline for most international routes.

International flights were regulated by the 1944 Chicago convention and bilateral agreements between governments. They were very much an 'administered market': for most routes, each country nominated just one airline, thereby creating duopolies. Moreover, each pair of governments agreed capacity sharing (i.e. a set division between designated national carriers), fares and sometimes a guaranteed allocation of landing slots for overseas carriers. Designated airlines

---

[2] Doganis (1991) and Dienel and Lyth (1998).

had to be licensed and owned by nationals of the country. Thus competition was extremely limited.

AIRLINES AND INTERNATIONALISATION

As in electricity, the most significant transnational technological and economic developments took place in the period before the 1990s.[3] Airlines faced major cost pressures, especially from higher fuel prices following the oil price shocks of 1973–4 and 1979–80. They also needed to invest in the new generations of aircraft that were developed, such as Boeing 747s in the late 1960s.[4] Demand for air travel rose sharply from the 1960s onwards, although it was sensitive to world recessions (e.g. falling temporarily during the 1990 Iraq war). However, over the 1990–2005 period, transnational technological and economic changes greatly diminished. Oil prices were stable or falling and demand rose steadily. The most important technological features of the industry, such as wide-bodied jets, were largely established.[5] Hence airlines, unlike stock exchanges and telecommunications, were not revolutionised by transnational technological and economic changes after the 1980s.

The US is a major, if not the predominant, force in the airline sector. It accounts for approximately 40% of the global market for airline transportation, a figure similar to telecommunications and securities trading. Moreover, international non-European flights, especially to the US, have accounted for a high percentage of European airline revenues and profits.[6]

The US traditionally had different institutional arrangements to those in Western Europe: there were several airlines, all privately owned; federal regulation took place through an independent regulatory commission, the Civil Aviation Board (CAB).[7] However, as in Europe, competition was limited. The CAB sought to protect existing airlines by preventing entry and setting fares at levels that ensured profitability.

As in telecommunications and securities, major reforms were undertaken in the 1970s and 1980s (notably the 1978 Airline Deregulation Act). They increased the scope for competition by ending restrictions on fares and entry, and abolishing the CAB (in 1985); they allowed carriers, notably new ones, much greater freedom over tariffs and routes. Following liberalisation, the nature of the US airline

---

3 Jönsson (1987: ch. 3) and Doganis (1991: ch. 1).   4 Staniland (2003*a*: 169).

5 The most significant transnational technological and economic development in the 1990–2005 period development was the appearance of the Internet which aided electronic booking by passengers instead of relying on the telephone or travel agents, but this only grew rapidly after 2000.

6 For instance, by 1992, extra-European flights represented 58% of BA's revenues, 50% of Air France's, and 44% of Alitalia; transatlantic flights accounted for 31% of BA's revenues, and 17% of Air France's and Alitalia's revenues, Staniland (2003*b*).

7 For overviews of the development of US airline regulation, see Morrison and Winston (2000), Sinha (2001: chs. 6–8), and Pickrell (1991).

industry altered. Fares fell sharply and usage rose. The structure of airline services was modified, with the increasing use of 'hub and spoke' systems, in which each large airline had a hub airport, which it served with 'spokes'— that is flights from other regional airports. New entrants appeared and capacity increased, leading to fierce competition. After the mid-1980s, the industry underwent successive waves of consolidation, as airlines merged and several major carriers met severe financial difficulties, going bankrupt (e.g. PanAm and TWA) or filing for protection from creditors ('Chapter 11 protection') (e.g. in 2005, Delta and Northwestern).

Reforms in the US had implications for airlines in Europe.[8] First, they altered competition in the world market. The US offers a large domestic base for airlines, with consequent competitive advantages in an industry with high fixed costs (such as jets). Moreover, following domestic liberalisation, US airlines cut costs and increased their efficiency. Financial problems made them desperate for business and lowered costs as bankrupt airlines were bought at low prices and could avoid certain payments (notably to creditors thanks to Chapter 11 protection offered to firms on the edge of bankruptcy). They led to consolidation of the US industry around three big airlines in the 1990s (American, Delta, and United), which were formidable competitors for European flag carriers. Perhaps most important of all, the new hub and spokes system aided US airlines in competition for international flights: it cut costs; it made control of domestic American 'spokes' vital for competitive advantage in the transatlantic market, since passengers could take the same airline to and from a hub and then take a connecting international flight without off-loading their luggage, saving time, trouble, and money. In contrast, European airlines were not permitted 'cabotage' rights (i.e. the ability to fly domestic US routes) nor to own a US airline. They faced a choice between maintaining their traditional services to many US regional airports, which was costly and limited the number of flights per day, or also focusing on hub airports, thereby obliging their passengers to buy tickets on US airlines to reach 'spokes' airports, which was inconvenient and costly. To avoid this unpleasant choice, there were strong incentives for European airlines to form alliances with US carriers and obtain access to hub airports.

A second effect of US domestic reform was increased pressure by US airlines and policy makers on other countries to allow competition in airline services, to compensate for lost revenues and profits at home and to open new opportunities for 'hungry' expansionist US airlines. The US challenged the traditional Chicago convention agreements and sought to make bilateral 'open skies' agreements with other nations that allowed greater competition.

A third effect was that US reforms offered a powerful illustration of the advantages of liberalisation. Competition seemed to greatly benefit consumers through lower fares and more choice; yet it was also followed by rapid growth for the industry as a whole (even if not for incumbent airlines). The US offered an

---

[8] See Staniland (2003*b*).

example of reform and a force for modification of the international regulatory regime, in ways similar to telecommunications.

As in the other network industries examined in this book, the EU was unimportant in the regulation of air transport until the late 1980s; indeed, the sector was omitted from many competition rules. However, the position changed in the late 1980s.[9] Britain began to press hard for liberalisation. The European Commission also sought to expand its activities, helped by European Court of Justice rulings that general competition law did apply to air transport.[10] Initially EU regulation was strongly opposed by many member states. However, Germany altered its position, as eventually did the foremost foe of liberalisation, namely France. As a result, considerable legislation was passed, particularly in three regulatory 'packages' in 1987, 1990, and 1992.

EU legislation greatly increased the scope for competition.[11] Airlines were freed to set their own tariffs.[12] Capacity sharing was ended. Airlines with licences from an EU member state could complete on all international routes within the EU from 1992, and on domestic routes within other member states (cabotage) from 1997.[13] A 1993 regulation required member states to give priority in the allocation of available landing slots to new entrants, although it did not fully open up access to the infrastructure—i.e. take-off and landing rights.[14] EU rules for ownership, airworthiness, and economic standing were designed to prevent member states from granting licences only to favoured national carriers.[15] The measures offered a significant framework for domestic and European flights. Moreover, general competition law was applied to airlines, notably rules on mergers and acquisitions, cooperation agreements, and state aid. These were important from the late 1980s onwards as incumbents sought to create international alliances, but also met severe financial difficulties. The main gap in EU regulation concerned international agreements (such as with the US), which continued to be made by member states—only in 2003 did the Council give the Commission the power to negotiate on behalf of the EU.

Overall, European economic institutions in airline transportation faced a changing combination of forms of internationalisation: after an upsurge in the 1960s and 1970s, transnational technological and economic changes slowed in the 1990s. In contrast, strong pressures arose from US reforms from the 1970s onwards and an EU regulatory framework grew from the late 1980s onwards that sought to promote competition.

---

[9] For analyses of EU regulation, see Stevens (2004: ch. 7), Travis (2001), Kassim (1996), O'Reilly and Stone Sweet (1998), and Button (2004: Annex 1).

[10] Notably the 1986 Nouvelles Frontières case, see Stone Sweet and O'Reilly (1998).

[11] For a list of legislative measures until 2002, see Stevens (2004: 148–9).

[12] See Council (1992*a*).   [13] See Council (1992*b*).

[14] Instead, member states were allowed to keep 'grandfather clauses' in which airlines which used slots for 80% of the time could keep them without auction or challenge, Council (1993*b*); in 2004 the Commission issued a Consultation paper on introducing slot trading, but no legislation to end grandfather rights, AGCM (2005: 89–90).

[15] Council (1992*c*).

BRITAIN[16]

Analysis of the British experience is interesting because it exposes national choices when the example of the US clashes with the interests of the domestic incumbent. Hence the limits of the ideational mechanism of overseas reform are shown, as well as the importance of competitive mechanisms that directly affect interests in the domestic policy process.

Britain began to move away from traditional institutions by promoting limited competition between two British carriers (BA and British Caledonian) from the mid-1960s onwards and creating an independent economic regulator, the Civil Aviation Authority, in 1971.[17] Nevertheless, it continued to protect British Caledonian and the state-owned incumbent BA, especially for transatlantic flights.[18] But as in other network industries, radical change began in the 1980s. The Thatcher government pursued twin policies of privatisation and liberalisation. The sale of BA was planned in 1979, but was delayed because the airline was making losses and then faced legal action in the US.[19] During the early 1980s BA was made profitable (notably through cost cutting) and the legal action was settled. BA was then entirely privatised in 1987.

Liberalisation also became official policy from the early 1980s. The 1980 Civil Aviation Act made the interests of users equal to those of airlines in licence hearings. In 1984, government policy was altered, allowing the CAA to license airlines to run routes wherever they wished and at whatever price they chose. Initially, liberalisation was timid, due to the overriding aim of preparing BA for sale and then protecting its success.[20] Nevertheless, once BA was securely privatised and profitable, liberalisation gradually grew for domestic and European flights.[21] Britain began to sign forms of 'open skies' agreements with other European countries, beginning with the Netherlands in 1984; these typically ended price controls and capacity sharing, and opened access to airports, aiding more carriers to fly between the countries. From the late 1980s, new entrants such as British Midland began operating. However, the major change came in the 1990s as 'no frills' low-cost airlines such as Ryanair, Easyjet, or Go were licensed and encouraged to operate from 'second-tier' airports such as Stansted, Luton, and Gatwick.[22] By 2005, these had taken a substantial share of UK domestic and European markets.[23]

---

[16] For histories, see Lyth (1998), Dobson (1995), and Staniland (2003a: ch. 8).

[17] Baldwin (1985).

[18] Notably through the 'Bermuda 2' agreement of 1978 which severely restricted competition in US–UK flights, see Dobson (1995).

[19] It was sued by Laker airways over alleged anti-competitive practices on transatlantic routes, Lawson (1992: 226–8).

[20] In 1988, BA was even allowed to take over British Caledonian, eliminating its main British competitor.

[21] Dobson (1995: 179–86).

[22] For details, see Williams (2002: 93–113) and Button (2004: 57–64).

[23] In June 2003, EasyJet had a 18.6% of the UK domestic market, Flybe British European 14.7% and Ryanair 4.1%, while for the intra-European market, Ryanair had 17.5% and EasyJet 10.4%, Baccelli

BA had only a minority share of domestic flight capacity and faced at least six other significant competitors.[24]

Changes in Britain had implications for other flag carriers in Europe, both in terms of competition and as an example of the effects of liberalisation. Traffic from Britain accounted for perhaps 70% of the total European no frills airline market in 2003.[25] The number of international routes flown from Britain rose from 357 in 1989 to 439 in 2000, while the number of outbound seats increased by 201%.[26]

Although European flights are important, the transatlantic market is more significant for British carriers. The UK-transatlantic market is the UK's largest international aviation market outside the EU, with 18 million passengers in 1999.[27] Moreover, London is Europe's largest hub for international flights accounting for no less than 32% of the total flights of the largest 9 European airports.[28] Liberalisation of transatlantic flights was much more limited than for domestic and European ones. The most sensitive issue was BA's slots at Heathrow Airport, which was large and profitable, being a 'hub' airport. In the 1990s, some opening took place as slots were given to a second UK airline (Virgin Atlantic), several US airlines entered (using the slots of bankrupt airlines such as PanAm) and certain restrictions were lifted (e.g. on setting ticket prices). Nevertheless, despite several years of talks, no open skies agreement was reached between Britain and the US.[29] The British government was not prepared to reallocate slots without major concessions from the US, and faced facing strong pressure from BA and Virgin. Hence by 2005, only two major British airlines (BA and Virgin Atlantic) flew transatlantic flights from the key airport of Heathrow and accounted for approximately 60% of bilateral traffic.[30]

Thus reform in Britain presents a mixed picture: privatisation and liberalisation of domestic and European markets took place in the 1980s and 1990s, but change in the important transatlantic routes was much more limited.

The Role of Internationalisation in British Institutional Reform

Privatisation was strongly driven by domestic factors rather than international ones. It formed part of the Thatcher government's attack on nationalised industries and was planned immediately after the 1979 election. It was not necessary to

and Senn (2004: 17, 26); Williams (2002) offers examples of market share in 2000 for 'no-frills' airlines of an estimated 33% of the London–Glasgow market and 17% of the London–Frankfurt routes.

[24] In June 2003 BA was estimated to account for 36.7% and 47.9% of European flights going to and from the UK, Baccelli and Senn (2004: 14–26).

[25] Button (2004).   [26] Williams (2002: 10–11).

[27] House of Commons Environment, Transport and Regional Affairs Committee (2000).

[28] Baccelli and Senn (2004: 70–74).   [29] Chang and Williams (2002: 138) and Dobson (1995).

[30] Williams (2002: 154).

meet transnational technological and economic demands—on the contrary, BA was profitable by 1987 and did not face pressures to raise capital. Equally, greater competition in British and European routes was undertaken mostly for domestic reasons. It was aided by favourable factors such as low oil prices and the spread of the Internet which reduced costs (especially for new 'no frills' entrants), but the key factors were government policies of licensing low-cost airlines and allowing access to second-tier airports. EU regulation was seen as important in ensuring that the new entrants had rights to fly to other EU member states but not for British policies on low-cost airlines.[31]

In contrast, regulatory reforms in the US played an important but paradoxical role in the lack of liberalisation for transatlantic services.[32] On the one hand, the apparently beneficial effects of 'deregulation' in the US attracted British policy makers, especially as it fitted with the Conservative government's general policy of promoting competition. On the other hand, policy makers feared that competition in transatlantic services would disadvantage BA relative to US airlines. Transatlantic traffic was vital for BA—for example, 60–80% of its profits in 1989–91 came from routes to the Americas.[33] But BA was not allowed cabotage in the US (i.e. the right to fly to destinations within the US) or to own a US airline.[34] This was important in the new hub and spoke method of operating flights in the US because BA could not offer connecting flights within the US, whereas its US rivals could do so.[35] Moreover, liberalisation in the US caused several major airlines to make huge losses and go into chapter 11 protection against creditors, which BA believed enabled them to unfairly lower fares since they were insulated from requirements to make profits or pay debts. Thus reforms in the US created competitive disadvantages for BA.

When British policy makers confronted a conflict between the ideational attraction of US liberalisation and the dangers from competition by US carriers, the latter largely won out. Faced with BA's fears, the British government resisted strong pressure from US policy makers and airlines for greater access to British airports and the entry of new carriers. As a result, liberalisation of transatlantic routes was very limited and slow.

Air transport regulation in the UK offers a curious case for the effects of internationalisation. Change was strongly driven by domestic policies. Internationalisation permitted and aided change in European and domestic markets, but overall impeded it in flights with the US. When forced to choose between the ideational attraction of US-style liberalisation and protection of BA against the dangers of competition from the US, British policy makers mostly plumped for the latter.

---

[31] See for instance, the *Financial Times* 20.9.1989 (article by Christopher Tugendhat, chairman of the CAA), 30.11.91, 9.12.1992.

[32] See Dobson (1995: 188–91).   [33] Dobson (1995: 190).

[34] This altered somewhat in 1993 when BA made a deal with US Air.

[35] cf. Williams (2002: 153–4).

FRANCE, GERMANY, AND ITALY[36]

Analysis of institutional reform in France, Germany, and Italy confirms the 'continental' European path to change. Reforms in the US were important as a competitive pressure, although not as an attractive example—that is, their ideational power was weak. However, the crucial and most visible forces for change in domestic policy debates were the threat of competition from BA and EU regulation.

After the Second World War, all three Continental countries had national flag carriers that were private law companies but majority publicly owned.[37] The incumbents did not hold legal monopolies over flights, but in practice, governments made them the sole carrier for most routes. Small privately-owned carriers existed, but they rarely competed with the incumbent and instead flew routes that the latter did not serve.[38]

The incumbent airlines frequently made large losses, especially after recessions in 1973–4 and 1990. Yet ideas of reform met fierce opposition, notably by trade unions and employees, and sometimes by political parties to which airlines had strong links. Thus, for example, the possibility of selling the state's share of Lufthansa was brought up in the mid-1980s as part of the Kohl government's general privatisation programme but met strong opposition from one of the three government coalition parties and hence made little progress.[39] Equally, Air France was on the list of companies open to privatisation in the privatisation law of 19 July 1993, passed when the Right returned to government. It was in poor financial shape (suffering from high operating deficits and debt) after the 1990 Gulf War. Yet attempts at cutting costs and altering working practices met with a major strike in 1993, the resignation of the head of Air France, Bernard Attali and the abandonment of the original privatisation plans. Similarly, Alitalia made large losses, especially after oil price rises and subsequent recessions in 1973, 1979–80, and 1990, but proposals to reform labour relations and reduce costs were frequently met with effective strikes.

Liberalisation made little headway in continental Europe in the 1980s and early 1990s. The US example of deregulation was not welcomed. Instead, incumbents resisted attempts by new entrants to gain market share by using their political influence and through strategies of buying potential domestic rivals or sometimes

---

[36] For an overview of Air France's history, see Neiertz (1998); for West Germany, see Dienel (1998); for Italy, see overview see Mantegazza (1998); for Germany and France, see Staniland (2003a: chs. 10 and 11).

[37] The French nationalisation law of 16 June 1948 required a minimum state ownership of 55% of Air France; by the late 1980s, a tiny proportion of shares remained in private hands. West Germany's Lufthansa was re-established in 1953 as a private law company and was partially privately owned; by 1987 the state share was 65%. Alitalia, was majority state-owned and in 1994, the state-holding company IRI held almost 90% of voting shares.

[38] Thus, e.g., Lufthansa had a monopoly over regular services; other companies could operate 'occasional services', but only if Lufthansa did not lay claim to them. In France, some routes were given to Union de Transports Aériens (UTA) and domestic flights were undertaken by Air Inter, but Air France held a large minority stake in the latter.

[39] *Handelsblatt* 13.3.86, 4.4.86, 27.4.87, 6.7.87, 1.10.87, and 2.8.88.

driving them out of business. Thus in France, Air France and the government rejected US-style 'deregulation' both domestically and at the EU level.[40] Airline transport was argued to be a natural monopoly and entry by new carriers was strongly discouraged, aided by Air France's considerable political clout.[41] Indeed, concentration increased as Air France bought up other domestic rivals.[42] Similarly in West Germany, Lufthansa prevented the emergence of any new rival carriers and bought new competitors.[43] In Italy, attempts at entry were rare and rapidly failed.[44]

Major change in sectoral institutions in France, Germany, and Italy only took place from the mid-1990s onwards. The most far-reaching was privatisation. Germany acted first. The state's share in Lufthansa was reduced from 51% to 36% in 1994 and the airline was fully privatised in October 1997. However, to comply with international rules that routes must be assigned to 'nationally owned' carriers, legislation in 1997 (the Luftverkehrsnachweis-Sicherungsgesetz) required a majority of shares to be held by German entities. In France, after the bitter 1993 strike over cost reductions, shares were given to employees in 1994 to obtain staff assent to a new recovery package. Under the centre-left government of Lionel Jospin, Air France's capital was 'opened' (the word privatisation was carefully avoided) in 1999 and again in 2001 (the state's share fell from 94% in 1998 to 56% by 2001). Further major changes occurred in 2004 when Air France merged with the Dutch company KLM. One of the conditions was that the French state should reduce its share from 56% to 44.7% and possibly to 20% (in December 2004 the French government agreed to reduce its stake to 25%). Alitalia made large losses between 1991 and 2005. It received over €2.5 billion (c£1.67 billion) in 'recapitalisation' (in reality, forms of subsidy) from its public sector owners in the period 1991–2002 and then faced a further financial crisis in 2004.[45] In contrast to the earlier period, the response was partial privatisation, so that by 2003, the state shareholding was 62% and December 2005, it fell the Treasury's share fell to 49.9%.[46] Thus by 2005, state shareholdings had been greatly reduced.

Competition also grew from the mid or late 1990s onwards.[47] All three countries signed open skies agreements with the US that allowed airlines much greater freedom to compete over fares, capacity, and flights.[48] They licensed new airlines.

---

[40] For a good example by a head of Air France, see Attali (1994); for a polemical argument, see Perri (1994).

[41] For a polemical account, see Belhassine (1997); cf. Autier, Corcos, and Trépo (2001: 136–9, 170, 178).

[42] It took a 35% stake in a small private rival, TAT, in 1989 and then in 1990, bought its major domestic rivals, UTA and Air Inter so that it controlled 98% of scheduled flights by French airlines, Lecat (2002: 419).

[43] Dienel (1998: 113–14).   [44] Mantegazza (1998: 166, 189).

[45] Baccelli and Senn (2004: 13).   [46] *La Repubblica* 17.12.2005 and 28.12.2005.

[47] For details, see Baccelli and Senn (2004: 23–27, 43–45), Williams (2002: chs. 2, 4, and 5), and Seifert (2001).

[48] For instance by allowing airlines to set prices unless both governments agreed to overrule them, and ending restrictions on numbers of designated airlines, capacity, frequency of flights, and types of

New entrants emerged for intra-European flights and domestic flights, including 'no frills airlines' such as Volare, Ryanair, and Easyjet. Established overseas airlines took stakes in domestic carriers.[49] As new entrants emerged, so the incumbents' share of capacity fell, so that by 2003 they only supplied a minority of capacity for international flights within Europe.[50] Although incumbents continued to supply most of their domestic markets, their share of this market also fell slightly.[51] Thus significant liberalisation had taken place compared with the situation in the late 1980s when incumbents had a de facto monopoly; by 2005 the most significant blockages concerned slot allocation for important 'hub' airports, notably Frankfurt and Paris Charles de Gaulle.

The main difference between institutional reform in airlines and the other sectors examined is the absence of sectoral economic regulators. None was created in the three countries.

The Role of Internationalisation in Institutional Reform

Governments in France, Germany, and Italy had domestic reasons for privatisation and liberalisation. In particular, the state-owned airlines were often making large losses. However, governments had met such deficits in the past without altering sectoral institutions. Moreover, reforms in the 1990s still met determined resistance, especially by trade unions and employees.[52] Yet the major difference with the earlier period, when such resistance large prevented reform, was that international factors played a more prominent role. Two were crucial: competition with overseas airlines; EU regulation. Both became linked to privatisation and liberalisation, as part of new strategies of international alliances and cutting costs.

Policy makers in France, Germany, and Italy became increasingly concerned about strengthened competition from US airlines and very importantly, BA. The former were becoming increasingly dangerous rivals thanks to lower costs and their advantages from the 'hub and spokes' systems. Thus for instance, US airlines increased their market share of US–French traffic from 48% in 1980 to 68% by 1992, and for US–Germany traffic from 46% in 1980 to 57% in 1992.[53] The US

aircraft; agreements signed by Italy in 1999, Germany's successive agreements in 1989, 1996, and 2000, and for France a partial agreement in 1998 and a full one in 2002.

[49] For example, British Airways bought a stake in a small private rival to Air France, TAT in 1994, and then in 1996 purchased a stake in another private carrier, Air Europe; these were later sold.

[50] By 2003, Air France supplied only 38% of the market for European flights to and from France, Alitalia had only 21.6% market share of intra-European flights to and from Italy, and Lufthansa's only 29% of European services to and from Germany, Baccelli and Senn (2004: 24–5).

[51] Thus by 2003, Air France still held 85% of the market for French domestic flights, Lufthansa had 73% of the domestic market capacity and Alitalia 49.4% of Italian flights, Baccelli and Senn (2004: 15–16).

[52] Thus, e.g., despite Alitalia being on the verge of bankruptcy in 2004, a lengthy strike took place against privatisation. Similarly, a cost-cutting programme in Air France in 1998 designed to encourage private investors was met by a pilots' strike, Autier, Corcos, and Trépo (2001: 300–1).

[53] Button (2000: 324).

carrier Delta even established a network of routes from Germany to the US, taking a large share of transatlantic traffic and undermining Lufthansa's market share and revenues.[54] The other major competitor, BA, enjoyed lower costs and pursued a strategy of becoming a 'global airline'.[55] It began to form a 'strategic alliance' with US carriers to have access to the US market, while using Heathrow as its European hub.[56]

In response to foreign competition and to gain access to overseas gateways (especially in the US), the flag carriers of the three Continental countries sought to form their own strategic alliances and reduce costs. But public ownership and closed national markets soon became obstacles to these aims. US airlines were wary of alliances with state-owned airlines and the price of anti-trust immunity in the US for such alliances or partial takeovers of American carriers was an 'open skies agreement' with the US to allow greater competition in the transatlantic market. Cost-cutting too faced difficulties, especially lack of political support in the face of industrial action by airline staff. As a result, airline managements and governments began to argue that privatisation and liberalisation were needed to cope with greater international competition.[57]

These factors were seen in privatisation in Germany and then France. In the 1990s, as Lufthansa made large losses following the 1990 recession, its management and the government argued that full privatisation was essential to raise capital, compete internationally and engage in international alliances with other privately-owned airlines; the example of the recently privatised BA was cited as an important factor.[58] Similarly, policy makers in France feared that Air France was isolated due to its ownership.[59] Much attention was focused on BA, seen as a dangerous competitor due to its lower costs, international alliances, overseas acquisitions, and access to private investment capital.[60] Air France's management began pressing for change, arguing that it was essential to enable it to form international alliances to compete with privately-owned overseas carriers, including BA, Lufthansa, and US airlines.[61] The argument of privatisation as essential for Air France to form international alliances was taken up by the center-left government, including the Communist Transport Minister Jean-Claude Gayssot, to justify partial privatisation in 1999 and 2001. Then in 2004, an essential part of the merger between Air France and KLM in 2004 was a sharp reduction in the state's share.

Policymakers in France and Germany also 'traded' open skies agreements with the US in return for international alliances for their incumbents. Thus a key reason

---

[54] Staniland (2003a: 234).   [55] Seristo (1993: 173–5).

[56] In the early 1990s, it allied itself with USAir; later it became a member of the Oneworld alliance, which included American Airlines.

[57] Cf. Staniland (2003a: 186).   [58] *Handelsblatt* 13.5.93, 28.7.94, 16.9.94, and 25.1.96.

[59] Neiertz (1998: 44) and Autier, Corcos, and Trépo (2001: 295).

[60] See Attali (1994) and Perri (1994: 103–4, 115–16).

[61] Attali (1994), Autier, Corcos, and Trépo (2001: 276–80), and Staniland (2003a: 239); indeed, lack of government response led to the resignation of the airline's head, Christian Blanc (a move that mirrors the departure of France Télécom's head and then his designated replacement in 1995 due to the failure to achieve government support for rapid privatisation; see Chapter 9).

for Germany signing an open skies agreement with the US was to allow Lufthansa to obtain anti-trust immunity for its alliance with the large US carrier, United Airlines.[62] When Air France sought to obtain immunity from US anti-trust rules in order to enter an alliance with Delta Airlines, American policy makers linked approval to an open skies agreement.[63] With Air France facing major financial difficulties and seeking to win back international passengers, France signed a limited open skies agreement with the US in 1998 and a full agreement in 2001.[64]

The second major international factor in reform was EU regulation, especially in France and Italy. It operated in at least two major ways. First, sectoral rules on liberalisation were important in opening up European and domestic routes to competition. Thus in France, EU rules aided much greater entry, especially by smaller charter companies running scheduled flights and low-cost airlines using regional airports.[65] In Italy, liberalisation only began in earnest after the 1997 deadline of the third liberalisation package: until that date, competition was very limited, especially from overseas carriers.[66]

A second mechanism was the European Commission's use of general competition law to aid reforms. In return for authorising mergers and state aid to loss-making carriers, the Commission demanded greater liberalisation and promises of privatisation. Thus it accepted Air France's takeover of the French carriers UTA and Air Inter in 1990 on condition that Air France sold its 35% share in the French airline TAT and that a second carrier be designated for some routes. Equally, in 2004 it approved Air France's alliance with KLM which led to a merger between the two companies but insisted that the former gave up 47 pairs of landing slots.[67] The Commission approved Air France's recapitalisation in 1994 under conditions designed to make the carrier operate as if it were a commercial enterprise, and a promise by the French government to move towards privatisation when the carrier was restored to financial health.[68] Similarly, Commission approval of recapitalisation of Alitalia in 1997 and 2004 was linked to other reforms such as further liberalisation, privatisation (through a recapitalisation that would reduce the state holding below 50%) and ending anti-competitive practices by Alitalia.[69] When recapitalisation and the lowering of the state share seemed in danger in 2005, the Commission threatened to reopen the state aid case.[70] Hence again, French and Italian national policy makers traded liberalisation and privatisation in return for the Commission ratifying state aid and the creation of more powerful incumbents through mergers and takeovers. More generally, EU rules meant that state protection for national flag carriers from competition was diminished and

---

[62] Chang and Williams (2002: 137–8).

[63] Subsequently Air France formed part of the 'Sky Team' alliance.

[64] Espérou (1999) and Chang and Williams (2002: 138).

[65] Autier, Corcos, and Trépo (2001: 170).   [66] cf. *Il Sole 24 Ore* 2.1.97 and AGCM (2005: 73–5).

[67] AGCM (2005: 83); for details of the merger, see Baccelli and Senn (2004: 79–81).

[68] Conditions included no further state aid, ensuring that Air France became profitable and making the relationship between state and airline one of commercial arms-length investor.

[69] The *Financial Times* 24.4.97, 11.7.97, 27.11.97 and *The Guardian* 8.6.2005.

[70] *La Repubblica* 15.9.2005 citing EU transport Commissioner Jacques Barrot, 17.12.2005, 28.12.2005.

Table 11.1. Economic institutions for airline transportation in 1987

	Britain	France	West Germany	Italy
Position of main incumbent	BA fully privatised 1987	Air France almost totally majority state-owned	Lufthansa majority state-owned	Alitalia almost totally state-owned
Competition in scheduled flights[72]	Duopoly policy with British Caledonian; modest liberalisation on domestic and European routes	Air France sole French carrier for most foreign flights (some given to UTA); domestic flights, near monopoly of Air Inter	Lufthansa sole German carrier for most foreign flights; near monopoly for domestic flights	Alitalia sole Italian carrier for most foreign flights and near-monopoly for domestic flights
Allocation of economic regulatory powers[73]	Independent regulatory authority (Civil Aviation Authority, est 1971)	Government department	Government department	Government department

that airlines had to be managed on a commercial basis, making privatisation more of a 'necessity'.[71]

CONCLUSION

In the mid-1960s, economic institutions for airline transportation in Britain, France, West Germany, and Italy were similar to those in other network industries: suppliers were publicly owned, there was little competition and regulatory powers were held by governments. These national institutions were largely maintained until the late 1980s in the three latter countries. However, Britain engaged in modest reforms in the late 1960s and early 1970s, and then in the late 1980s, privatised its incumbent and engaged in liberalisation of domestic and European flights. It did so mostly for domestic reasons. Thus in 1987, just before EU regulation started, there were important diffrences between Britain and the other three countries which had largely maintained post-war institutions (see Table 11.1).

After 1988 and especially from the mid-1990s onwards, significant reforms of privatisation and liberalisation were undertaken in France, Germany, and Italy. These were driven by governments and airline managements despite considerable domestic opposition, especially from trade unions and employees. The result is that in 2005, the position had altered, towards a regulated competitive market of privatised suppliers, with considerable similarities across the four nations (Table 11.2).

[71] Saissi (1997). [72] Charter flights are excluded from this chapter.
[73] Powers over air traffic control and safety are excluded from this chapter.

Table 11.2. Economic institutions for airline transportation in 2005

	Britain	France	West Germany	Italy
Position of main incumbent	BA fully privatised 1987	Air France state minority share (44.7% with promise to reduce to 25%)	Lufthansa fully privatised	Alitalia state minority share (49.9%)
Competition in scheduled flights[74]	Several carriers on European and domestic routes; two major British carriers for US routes	Several carriers on European routes; dominance of Air France for domestic routes; open skies agreement with US	Several carriers on European routes; dominance of Lufthansa for domestic routes; open skies agreement with US	Several carriers on European routes; dominance of Alitalia for domestic routes; open skies agreement with US
Allocation of economic regulatory powers[75]	Independent regulatory authority (Civil Aviation Authority, est 1971)	Government department	Government department but independent regulator planned	Government department

The airline transportation sector allows development or confirmation of three general arguments that arise from previous chapters. First, like electricity, it shows that transnational technological and economic factors are not a necessary condition for policy forms of internationalisation to be significant in decision-making nor for sectoral institutional reform. Indeed, the major changes came after the mid-1990s when the airline market was technologically and economically relatively stable. Conversely, despite the internationalised nature of airline transportation, major transnational technological and economic developments in the 1970s and 1980s such as oil price shocks in 1973–4, 1979, and 1990, large airline losses and the need to invest in new aircraft, were met with major institutional inertia in the decades before 1990.

The airline sector allows development of a second line of argument, namely that overseas reforms operate through regulatory competition rather than being copied. US deregulation of airlines in the late 1970s was followed by lower fares, expansion of the industry and greater efficiency. Nevertheless, policy makers in France, Germany, and Italy largely rejected the US example. Interestingly, US reforms also had limited ideational effects in Britain: although the US offered an attractive example for British policy makers, when American institutions or policies conflicted with domestic interests, Britain did not follow the US example or succumb to pressure from US policy makers, but chose to protect the incumbent, BA.

---

[74] Charter flights are excluded from this chapter.
[75] Powers over air traffic control and safety are excluded from this chapter.

In contrast, regulatory reforms in the US increased the international competitiveness of US airlines (e.g. the hub and spoke organisation of the vast US industry is financially bankrupt through still flying airlines). Britain feared such competition and acted to respond to it. In turn, policy makers in France, Germany, and Italy feared regulatory competition from overseas, especially from airlines in Britain; they worried that BA's privatisation, cost-cutting and international alliances threatened their own flag carriers. Although concerned about competition from US airlines, they also saw opportunities to create international alliances with them. Thus, as in other sectors, Britain acted as a Trojan horse for liberalisation in Europe.

A third and related finding is that Britain followed a different reform path to France, Germany, and Italy. It reformed earlier and mainly for domestic reasons. Insofar as international factors played a part, it was through looking at the US as a source of competition as much as an example. In contrast, the other three nations modified their institutions later, and for both domestic and international reasons. The latter included regulatory competition from Britain and EU regulation. The EU acted both through sectoral legislation and application of general competition law, whereby governments traded Commission approval of mergers and takeovers by incumbents' airlines and state aid to those airlines in return for liberalisation and privatisation. More generally, the EU both altered the environment of airline transportation, making continuation of subsidies and protection more difficult, and was used in domestic debates to legitimate change.

The chapter thus confirms three findings from previous cases: policy forms of internationalisation have effects independent of transnational technological and economic developments; US reforms operate through inspiring and legitimating change in Britain (but not wholesale copying) and through regulatory competition; Britain followed its own reform path that differed from that of France, Germany, and Italy but also then influenced those three countries through fear of regulatory competition.

12

Liberalising the Letter: The Reform of Postal Services

Postal services seem a most unlikely case for internationalisation. Postal institutions have deep national roots. State-owned postal services date back centuries, sometimes to the Middle Ages, and their monopolies predate even those in telecommunications. They employ large numbers of people (1.7 million in the EU in 1992) and are generally strongly unionised.[1] They offer essential services, notably for vulnerable social groups, such as low-cost banking, payment of welfare benefits, and provision of vital state documents. Post offices are present in every city and town and are frequently a focal point for rural communities. Most state post organisations enjoy significant national symbolism.

At the same time, few transnational technological and economic developments have taken place in the sector. Unlike the other cases studied, neither the US nor Britain deregulated or even privatised their state-owned post offices. Thus France, Germany, and Italy did not face examples from the two Anglo-American liberal economies. Moreover, the scope for international regulatory competition is low, since 93% of all postal traffic in Europe is national.[2] Instead, the main form of internationalisation has been EU regulation between the mid-1990s and 2005.

Thus postal services offer a 'low tech' sector with strong domestic historical, political, and symbolic roots faced with only one major form of policy internationalisation. It allows a further test of the importance of EU regulation for domestic regulatory reform. It offers a particularly 'hard case' for policy forms of internationalisation to influence institutional choices.

The central findings are that only limited reform took place before the mid-1990s, including in Britain (in sharp contrast to other sectors). Change met determined and successful resistance, particularly from trade unions and employees, supported by public opinion. However, from the late 1990s, significant institutional alterations were made, as postal operators became more commercial organisations and expanded overseas. EU regulation provided both pressure for change and justifications for it. Thus the case of postal services allows two general arguments about internationalisation to be made. First, it underlines the role of policy forms of internationalisation, and in particular the influence of EU regulation, even in the absence of transnational technological and economic

---

[1] European Commission (1992).   [2] European Commission (1992).

pressures or prior reforms in the US or Britain. It shows how EU regulation had both direct effects, through its legal requirements, and also indirect ones that went beyond these requirements, through opening up apparent opportunities and threats for national incumbent postal operators. Indeed, EU regulation had important impacts through being used by actors in the domestic policy processes despite legal requirements that were more limited than in the other sectors studied. Postal services offer a notable case for the role of EU regulation given deeply entrenched domestic institutions and low levels of cross-border trade.

Second, postal services underline that Britain follows a different reform path to its Continental neighbours. Unlike the other sectors examined in this book, Britain did not privatise or liberalise in the 1980s. Modifications of traditional institutions in the 1990s were in part due to EU legislation, as well as other reasons. Yet the EU was not significant in debates, which centred on domestic factors. Thus even when Britain introduced reforms to meet EU regulation, policy makers used other factors to justify change. The case of postal services underlines the extent to which the EU is not accepted as a good reason for institutional alteration in Britain. In contrast, EU legislation was much more explicitly visible in changes in France, Germany, and Italy.

The chapter begins by examining internationalisation in the sector, especially EU regulation. It then looks at reform at Britain between the late 1980s and 2005, before turning to the three other countries.

INTERNATIONALISATION OF THE POSTAL SECTOR

Two of the three forms of internationalisation examined in this book were very weak in postal services in the period from the mid-1960s until 2005. The technology of postal services remained stable, especially for collection and delivery. These two functions have high fixed-costs and hence are likely to be natural monopolies; in particular, delivery accounts for 65% of postal service expenses and its costs fall in direct proportion to customer density and volume, making entry very difficult.[3] The scope for international competition seems limited, given that most deliveries are national and that 'remailing' (sending post abroad for re-delivery domestically) depends on a wide gap between transborder costs and domestic prices. Technological change and with it possible competition have been confined to mail sorting or tracking items electronically, and to certain advanced 'valued added' services such as hybrid email, or accelerated/express delivery services, which account for only a small proportion of total traffic.[4] The most significant technological and economic developments arise from the use of email and the

---

[3] Pilley (2001: 14), quoting European Commission and OECD data.
[4] For an overview, see Anderloni and Pilley (2001).

Internet, but these were available only to a minority of the population until after 2000.

In sharp contrast to other networks, the US has a state-owned postal service, the USPS (US Postal Service) that enjoys a monopoly over standard mail.[5] Before 1970, the USPS strongly resembled traditional European institutions: it was a government department headed by a postmaster general, appointed by the president and its employees were civil servants. The 1970 Postal Reform Act made the USPS into a public corporation, headed by a Board, with its own employees; moreover, a federal regulatory agency was established, the Postal Rate Commission, to ensure that postal prices were justified. Nevertheless, central traditional features of the USPS remained—especially federal ownership, monopoly, and national tariffs. Thus the US did not offer an example of liberalisation or private ownership.

Until recent years, the EU played almost no role in postal services. The first significant attempts to establish EU legislation came in the early 1990s. They followed a similar path to that in telecommunications in the late 1980s, but unlike the latter, were rather unsuccessful.[6] A Commission Green Paper in 1992[7] suggested that a clear division across the EU be made between 'reserved services' (i.e. those kept under monopolies) and others which should be open to competition. The Commission then drafted a directive to be passed under Article 86[ex-90] (3), which empowers it to legislate to enforce general competition law for public enterprises without the approval of the Council of Ministers or European Parliament.[8] In addition, the European Court of Justice (ECJ) ruled that postal organisations were covered by Article 86[90], thereby providing a legal base for the Commission.[9] But the draft directive met such fierce opposition from national governments and incumbent postal operators, including Britain, that the Commission withdrew it.[10] In addition, throughout the 1990s, the Commission refused to take active measures through general competition law, even when faced with complaints that incumbents were extending their monopolies beyond their legitimate boundaries and also illegally competing with new entrants.[11]

Despite these unpropitious beginnings, the Commission moved forward in the mid-1990s. It decided to act using ordinary Council directives covered by co-decision procedures (i.e. legislation that required the consent of the Council of Ministers and European Parliament). It obtained agreement from member states, leading to a first step, the 1997 Postal Services Directive, which represented a rather modest move towards a regulated competitive market.

The legislation required limited liberalisation. It restricted national monopolies to reserved services—that is those over which member states could choose to maintain a monopoly. All non-reserved services had to be opened to competition and monopolies were to be maintained only insofar as to ensure the maintenance

---

5 For overviews and critiques, see Sherman (1991) and Oster (1995).
6 Derenne and Stockford (2002: 149). 7 European Commission (1992).
8 A similar process had taken place in telecommunications in the late 1980s—see Chapter 6.
9 In *Corbeau* 1993—Case C-320/91 Corbeau [1993] ECR I-2533.
10 Campbell (2002: 266) and McGowan (2002: 337). 11 Derenne and Stockford (2002).

of universal service, which was defined legally.[12] However, reserved services were defined rather broadly and accounted for the bulk of the sector.[13]

The 1997 directive also sought to aid competition. The key issues were usage of the incumbents' network of post boxes, sorting, and delivery systems, together with subsidies paid for provision of losses due to ensuring universal service. The directive stated that access to the postal network was to be made available to new entrants on transparent and non-discriminatory conditions. It obliged universal service providers to keep separate internal accounts for reserved and non-reserved services, and to use 'analytical accounting' by 2000, in order to ensure clarity about cross-subsidisation between services opened to competition and those left under their monopoly. It also stated that 'terminal dues' (i.e. prices paid for delivering an item) were to be related to costs, and to be fair and transparent. These fees are particularly important for remails, when mail is sent from one country to another to be posted back to that country. Remail allows price competition between countries if prices for overseas mail are lower in one nation than prices for domestic mail within another country—for instance, if prices for mail from Holland to Germany are lower than for mail within Germany. But, at the same time, the directive allowed member states to establish compensation funds paid by all operators to support universal service, whose costs were determined by national regulatory authorities (NRAs) not the European Commission. This provided potential for member states to subsidise incumbents. Moreover, conditions for access to the existing postal network were not specified in detail, allowing scope for incumbents to block new entrants.

As in other sectors, the directive insisted that NRAs be legally separate from, and operationally independent of, postal operators. However, it did not specify their institutional form (notably whether a sectoral regulator was needed or whether it had to be independent from elected politicians).

Overall, the 1997 Postal Directive balanced partial competition with protection of postal operators. On the one hand, it limited national monopolies and set some rules for incumbent suppliers. On the other hand, it permitted continuing monopolies for the majority of the postal sector and its rules allowed considerable scope for national governments to restrict competition to their state-owned incumbents.

After this first step, the European Commission and the ECJ continued to be very restrained in pressing liberalisation in the period between 1997 and 2001.[14] But after 2001, the Commission began to take a more decisive role.

---

[12] It included collection and delivery once a day from every home or premises for postal items up to 2 kg, packages up to 10 kg, and services for registered and ensured items.

[13] Reserved services were items priced less than five times the public tariff for such as item and under 350 g, including normal mail (domestic and cross-border), direct mail and 'accelerated' mail (i.e. fast delivery services). One estimate (albeit by a biased source, namely the express mail industry) was that the directive opened a further 3% of the market above that already practised by member states, Geradin and Humpe (2002: 101).

[14] For specific cases, see Geradin and Humpe (2002: 97–9, 109–10) and Derenne and Stockford (2002: 163–4).

It started legal action against postal ministries that were both regulators and owners of postal administrations, contrary to the 1997 directive's requirement that regulators be independent of suppliers.[15] It sought to increase the scope for international remail.[16] It attacked cross-subsidisation of services opened to competition, striking at practices such as incumbents running loss-making services or offering 'fidelty rebates'.[17] It tightened the definition of reserved services to exclude hybrid services that mixed traditional courier and new electronic services.[18] Most important of all, it proposed new legislation in 2000 to increase competition.

The result was a further postal services directive in 2002.[19] This sharply reduced the services over which member states could maintain monopolies (the 'reserved area').[20] It also sought to prevent incumbents from using their remaining monopolies to restrict fair competition in liberalised services. In particular, it prohibited cross-subsidisation of non-reserved services (which were open to competition) out of revenues from services in the monopoly reserved sector, except to the extent to which it is shown to be strictly necessary to fulfil specific universal service obligations imposed in the competitive area. Finally, the Commission was to submit a report by December 2006 confirming 2009 as the date for 'full accomplishment of the postal internal market', thereby foreshadowing further liberalisation.

Thus EU legislation had grown by 2005; nevertheless, it fell far short of full liberalisation. Moreover, it was much less detailed than in other sectors such as telecommunications or electricity, especially concerning re-regulation to aid new entrants faced with powerful incumbents with well-established networks.

BRITAIN[21]

From the nineteenth century until 1969, the Post Office (PO) was a government department headed by a minister, the Postmaster General. It enjoyed a monopoly over mail and indeed the 'penny post' had begun in 1840. In the late nineteenth century, telecommunications were added to the PO's responsibilities.

---

[15] In 2001 it formally requested Belgium to alter its arrangements and began an investigation against other member states including France and Italy—Derenne and Stockford (2002: 153) and Geradin and Humpe (2002: 116).

[16] Notably in its decision in 2001 following a complaint by Consignia against Deutsche Post concerning mail sent from Britain to Germany but containing reply envelopes addressed to Germany—Derenne and Stockford (2002: 169–70).

[17] Commission decision against Deutsche Post following a complaint by UPS—see Derenne and Stockford (2002: 171–2).

[18] Commission decision against Italy—Derenne and Stockford (2002: 173–4).

[19] European Parliament and Council (2002*d*).

[20] From letters of 350 g and 5 times the basic postal tariff to 100 g and 3 times the basic tariff in 2003, with a further reduction in 2006 to 50 g and 2.5 times the basic tariff in 2006.

[21] For good historical overviews, see Campbell (2002) and McGowan (2002).

The organisational position of the PO was modified after the late 1960s, but this was mainly due to policies concerning telecommunications (see Chapter 9). Thus in 1969 it was taken out of the civil service and made into a public corporation, headed by a Board, with its own legal identity and employees. Then in 1981, telecommunications were removed from the PO. Moreover, the PO's monopoly was set at items priced at under £1, while the minister was given powers to license competitors.

Strong pressures for more sweeping changes existed between the 1970s and the early 1990s. There were several lengthy strikes (e.g. in 1971 and 1996), during which the PO's monopoly was suspended. For its part, the PO's management complained that the government left it too little managerial and financial autonomy; indeed, tight 'external financing limits' not only constrained investment but also meant payments to the government, constituting a kind of 'stamp tax'. The PO's monopoly was reviewed by the Monopolies and Mergers Commission (MMC) in 1979 and 1984, although it concluded that the monopoly was justified to maintain universal services and services to rural and regional areas.

Nevertheless, in stark contrast to other network industries, significant reforms such as privatisation or liberalisation were not undertaken before the late 1990s. Indeed, even Margaret Thatcher promised in the 1987 general election that the PO would not be privatised. After 1990, the Conservative government under John Major envisaged introducing greater competition, and a Green Paper in 1994 proposed privatisation of the PO and reducing its monopoly. But these plans were rapidly shelved as the postal workers had a strong trade union (the Union of Communication Workers) that ran a successful anti-privatisation campaign. Although similar obstacles had been overcome in other industries such as telecommunications, privatisation was also unpopular with public opinion and there were strong concerns (by the public and Conservatives MPs) that competition would damage the PO's service, especially in rural areas.

Serious reforms in sectoral institutions only began in the late 1990s.[22] They were driven by both domestic and international factors. The former included dissatisfaction by the PO's management over government financial limits and poor industrial relations. The latter involved a new strategy by the PO's management of preparing for overseas competition and ensuring international expansion. Although EU regulation barely featured in British debates, in practice it played significant roles. First, transposition of the EU's 1997 postal directive required liberalisation and offered an occasion for other reform steps. Second and more importantly, EU regulation opened up continental European markets for competition, while also providing overseas operators with opportunities to expand in Britain, and reasons to do so given that their comfortable domestic markets were being undermined. The PO's management and the government were concerned that the PO could not compete with international rivals who were expanding in the British market; major examples include Deutsche Post or DHL. Third, EU regulation justified the wish by PO senior managers to expand abroad; the POs

---

[22] See especially McGowan (2002).

then chief executive officer, John Roberts, claimed that a 'superleague' of three or four post offices would emerge in Europe, with a few more viable at the global level.[23]

A first step was taken in July 1999, when the Postal Services Regulation implemented the 1997 EU Postal Directive. Competition was allowed, but only insofar as required by the directive.[24] Moreover, the Regulation went beyond the directive in three significant ways: it insisted that tariffs be uniform across the country, it made the PO responsible for the universal service obligation, and it established a sectoral regulator, albeit initially advisory, the Postal Services Commission.

The most controversial issue was privatisation. There was fierce union and employee opposition to even partial privatisation. In contrast, the PO's management argued that it was essential for the creation of an internationally competitive PO. One of its key justifications was to open the way for international alliances through joint ventures or at the very least, overseas acquisitions (indeed, the PO had already made 20 purchases in 1998–9 alone). Faced with these rival views, the newly-elected Labour government commissioned a review in 1997 which was inconclusive, exposing divisions between those seeking different forms of privatisation (partial or through a 'partnership' with the private sector) and opponents of any sale of PO shares.

As a result, legislation was introduced—the 2000 Postal Services Act—which represented a compromise between traditional arrangements and a privatised company operated in a regulated competitive market. The Act converted the PO from a public corporation into a public limited company. Its shares were owned by the government and any disposal required further primary legislation. But the new legal form allowed sale of shares and the legislation permitted privatisation through share swaps as part of a commercial alliance. Hence partial privatisation was made legally possible. The Act also transformed the Postal Services Commission (PSC) into an independent regulatory agency. The PSC's primary duty was to ensure provision of the universal service obligation, wherever possible by promoting competition, and it was responsible for issuing licences, including to the PO. Yet unlike other sectoral regulators, the PSC was not given general competition law powers.

By 2005, the PO was seeking to transform itself from a British mail service to an international competitor in the transport of mail, documents, parcels, home shopping, advertising, and financial services. International expansion and meeting overseas competitors in the domestic market were the centrepiece of arguments by the PO management and government for privatisation. Although EU regulation was largely unmentioned, it provided good reasons for the PO's strategy. The traditional institutional framework had been considerably altered, but strong opposition had blocked a full move to a completely liberalised market with a privatised incumbent, the model adopted in other network industries.

---

[23] Quoted in Campbell (2002: 362–3).
[24] For instance, over the thresholds of letters up to 2 kg and packets up to 20 kg.

FRANCE, GERMANY, AND ITALY

As in Britain, postal operators in France, West Germany, and Italy—La Poste, the Deutsche Bundespost (DBP), and Le Poste Italiane—were state-owned in the late 1980s. They usually had long historical roots dating back decades and often centuries—for instance, La Poste traces its roots back to the Middle Ages. They were also part of the civil service and linked with telecommunications, as units within PTT Ministries. They enjoyed wide monopolies.

Institutional reform seemed difficult. Post offices were seen as a crucial part of the social and economic fabric of the nation, especially in rural areas. The operators had very close links to governments and were often used as instruments of regional and employment policies. They made large losses, often subsidised by their telecommunications and financial services. Most important of all, they provided secure employment to large numbers of civil servants, who were well unionised and ready to defend their position. The difficulties of change are best illustrated in France, where serious discussions of separating postal and telecommunications services and converting them into forms of public corporation during the 1970s and 1980s met fierce and successful trade union opposition.[25] Thus plans for change in 1974 were met by a lengthy postal strike that almost cost the then Prime Minister Jacques Chirac his post; further strikes took place in 1987 and 1988.

Yet between the late 1980s and 2005, postal institutions were greatly changed. Two phases can be distinguished: modest alterations between the late 1980s and 1996 that largely arose from modifying the position of the telecommunications sides of PTT Ministries; after 1997, when EU regulation played an increasing role.

Modest and Diverse Reforms 1989–96

Between c. 1989 and 1996, modest reforms were made in France, Italy, and especially Germany. The most important concerned the organisational position of the operator. This was strongly related to the desire to reform the telecommunications side of PTT Ministries and reduce postal service deficits.[26] In addition to domestic factors, EU regulation played a significant role in two ways. The first and most important was indirect, through its influence on the establishment of telecommunications operators as separate bodies outside PTT Ministries (see Chapter 9). Modification of telecommunications had implications for postal services, especially because losses by postal operators had often been cross-subsidised by telecommunications sides of PTT Ministries. Second, the 1992 European Commission Postal Green Paper and discussions about a postal directive offered

---

[25] Thatcher (1999: 107–9) and Libois (1983: 241–2); in the 1980s, an official report on La Poste called for reform—Chevallier (1984).

[26] For Germany, see Heinen (2002) and Büchner (1995); for France, Barreau (1995: 41–9); and for Italy, Valsecchi (2004: 7–8).

the prospect of liberalisation, and hence both the danger of competition in home markets and opportunities for expansion abroad.

However, modifications were modest and differed considerably across the three nations. Germany went furthest, with successive reforms (Postreforms) in 1989, 1994, and 1996 that altered the organisational position of the operator, its monopoly and the allocation of regulatory powers. It undertook change both as part of alterations in telecommunications and with an eye on the anticipated EU liberalisation of postal services in the mid-1990s, seeking to make Deutsche Post an international company, ready to expand abroad.[27] At the same time, policy makers worried about other European competitors, especially the Dutch operator TPG, which was made into a public corporation and then majority privatised between 1994 and 1996.[28]

Under the first 'Postreform' (the 1989 Poststrukturgesetz), the Posts and Telecommunications Ministry was divided into three units—for postal services, telecommunications, and banking. The postal unit was renamed Deutsche Bundespost (DBP). Under the second Postreform in 1994, the Constitution was altered to allow all three corporations to become limited companies operating under private law and to permit private undertakings to supply postal (and telecommunications) services.[29] Although mainly driven by the needs of telecommunications, the same constitutional article applied to postal services. The federal government was the sole shareholder of DBP and was obliged to own a majority of shares for five years, a similar position to that in telecommunications.

Following the second Postreform, competition was allowed in courier, express and parcel services, and some bulk and advertising mail. The new constitutional provisions stated that provision of basic services should be ensured through regulation of competitive supply but also allowed the posts and telecommunications minister to award monopoly rights to DBP for a provisional period.[30] The third Postreform in 1996 extended competition, by stating that no licences were required for services for items of over 1 kg. It provided Deutsche Post with a statutory monopoly that was smaller than that allowed under the 1997 EU Postal Directive.[31] More radically, the monopoly was to end in December 2002, when licences were to be sold to establish a compensation fund for any universal service obligations which would not be met by market competition.

The allocation of regulatory powers was also gradually altered. In the second Postreform (1994), the federal government, not Deutsche Post, became responsible for ensuring appropriate 'basic' postal services. The third Postreform (1996) created a sector-specific independent regulatory body for both postal services and telecommunications, the (RegTp). It was given important re-regulatory powers, notably to set rates for licensed services provided by undertakings with a dominant position in a market, as well as ensuring that universal service obligations (set by

---

[27] Campbell (2002: 76–8, 107–9).   [28] Arnaboldi and Bauer (2002).
[29] Büchner (1995).   [30] Notably Articles 87f and 143b.
[31] Only 200 g instead of 350 g in weight; moreover, competition was allowed in direct mail services, for more than 50 items, weighing more than 50 g.

the Ministry of Economics) were met. The RegTP issued licences for those areas opened to competition but which required authorisation.[32]

Change was rather more modest in France and Italy in the period 1989–96. In the former, after a long process of discussion under the centre-left government of Michel Rocard, the postal and telecommunications administrations were made into two separate *exploitants publics* (a form of public corporation) as part of reform of France Télécom in 1990. Nevertheless, their staff remained civil servants and the government kept many powers over La Poste.[33] A broad consensus remained in the early 1990s against corporatisation or privatisation of La Poste and against liberalisation.[34] In Italy, the postal administration became Ente Poste Italiane, a state agency structurally separated from the civil service in 1994 but still subject to many government controls. However, in neither country did significant liberalisation take place, leaving substantial contrasts in monopolies across the three nations.[35] Nor was reallocation or redefinition of regulatory powers undertaken, so PTT ministers remained the main regulators.

Significant Reforms 1997–2005

After EU legislation in 1997 and 2002, institutional reform grew as the three countries moved towards a new framework in which postal operators were companies (with majority public ownership except in Germany) and their monopolies were reduced but not entirely ended. In France and Germany, regulatory powers were given to sectoral agencies. This common trend involved considerable change for France and Italy, but paradoxically, a slowing down of alterations planned in Germany.

Germany continued along its reform route, with the sale in 2000 of 29% of its incumbent, renamed Deutsche Post World Net. After further rules, a majority of shares was privately owned by the end of 2005. The 1996 Postreform had planned that Deutsche Post's monopoly would end in 2002. After further sales, a majority of shares were privately owned by 2005. But planned liberalisation was not fully implemented.[36] Thus although the 1996 Postreform had stated that Deustche Post's monopoly licence over reserved services was renewed until 2007; instead, its monopoly was reduced in line with EU requirements.[37] In 2005, the RegTP

---

[32] Addressed items between 200 g and 2 kg, and unaddressed mail over 50 g; for a summary, see Schwarz-Schilling (2002).

[33] cf. Barreau (1995) and Chevallier (1990).   [34] Campbell (2002: ch. 7, and 268).

[35] In France, La Poste had a monopoly for all items up to 1 kg; Poste Italiane had a monopoly over all closed mail items and parcels up to 20 kg; however, competition was allowed in 'open items' such as commercial invoices and press articles. Thus content was the basis for monopoly. In addition, concessions had been given to some private operators, notably for express delivery services and corporate bodies in certain cities. Legally, these concessions did not end the state's monopoly but transferred it (and the state's obligations) to the private operator for a fixed number of years.

[36] Notably the Monopoly Commission (1999) and the sectoral regulator, the RegTP—*Handelsblatt* 7.12.2001.

[37] To 100 g on 1 January 2003 and then 50 g by 2006.

was absorbed within the new 'network regulator', the Bundesnetzagentur, linking postal services evermore closely to other network sectors.

Poste Italiane became a limited company operating under private law in 1998 although its shares remained publicly owned. In February 2005, the Italian Prime Minister announced that the government was considering a partial privatisation of Poste Italiane.[38] Liberalisation also occurred, largely in line with the requirements of EU law. A decree in 1999 transposing the EU's 1997 Postal Directive adopted the minimum opening required by the directive and ended the traditional distinction between open and closed items (with competition being allowed in the former but not the latter). The 1999 decree also defined universal service provision, following the EU directive, and set up a 'compensation fund' to pay for it. Licences were required to supply non-reserved services and included an obligation to contribute to the universal service fund. Liberalisation was broadened as the 2002 directive was implemented by decree in December 2003. However, no independent regulatory authority was established: the ministry continued to regulate the sector (although 2005, plans were made for postal services to be given to the communications regulator AGCOM).[39]

Reform was most difficult in France. It transposed the 1997 EU Postal Directive in 1999 (a year late) through a one article amendment of unrelated law; only in 2001 was full legislative transposition undertaken.[40] The modifications in 1999 allowed greater competition, but went no further than EU requirements. Moreover, France's transposition was open to criticisms, notably over whether it was allowing full and fair competition while leaving too many opportunities to unfairly subsidise La Poste. Thus for instance, the French legislation applied a broader notion of public service than the EU's universal service and placed the responsibility (and ability to justify tariffs) for universal service on La Poste rather than calculating its cost and setting up a compensation fund for it. It failed to establish a licensing system, making entry difficult. It left the PTT minister in the position of both having many controls over La Poste, and also being the regulator for the postal sector, contrary to the directive's insistence that supply and regulation be separated.[41]

Following the EU's 2002 Postal Directive, further reforms were introduced in France. Competition was extended in 2003 to meet EU requirements. A new postal Act was passed in 2005.[42] It transposed EU liberalisation so that the weight limit for the reserved area was reduced to 50 g. It also defined the notion of

---

[38] European Commission (2005: 157).

[39] In 2006, a group of academics close to the centre-left political coalition proposed transferring the ministry's responsibilities to AGCOM, the independent Communications regulator—De Vincenti and Vigneri (2006) and in February 2007, a bill to do so was announced.

[40] In 1999 it was part of a law on national and regional development; the legislation in 2001 was needed because Members of the Parliament opposed the use of secondary legislation given the importance of the subject matter—Rodrigues (2002: 241).

[41] Menéndez Sebastiàn (2004: 191–203).

[42] Loi rélative à la régulation des activités postales du 20 mai 2005; for an overview, see Delion and Durupty (2005).

universal service and set up a compensation fund to which all service providers would contribute. In addition, it extended the Autorité de régulation des télécommunications' responsibilities to include postal services, transforming it into the Autorité de régulation des communications électroniques et des postes, and hence avoiding the problem of the ministry being effectively regulator and controller of the incumbent supplier.

Alteration of postal institutions in France and Italy faced significant obstacles. In Italy, Poste Italiane was much less efficient than its foreign counterparts, both in terms of quality and labour productivity;[43] reform exposed it to competition and threatened cuts in its employment. In France, postal reform remained politically very sensitive. La Poste enjoyed high support as a public entity. Its employees had considerable strike capacity. Most importantly, it was seen as vital in rural development. Thus for instance, in 2001 and 2004–5, the closure of rural post offices provoked sharp political debate and considerable pressure from elected politicians at local and national levels. Thus, overall, there was little enthusiasm in either nation for liberalisation or privatisation.

EU regulation was central to overcoming opposition in France and Italy. First, liberalisation and re-regulatory rules in France and Italy were undertaken to transpose the 1997 Postal Directive. The Commission put pressure on member states to correctly transpose directives. Thus after complaints that the French state was abusing its dominant position since it both fixed postal tariffs and supervised La Poste, the European Commission opened an enquiry and proceedings against France. It began proceedings against member states (beginning with Belgium) over the lack of separation of postal services and regulation, placing pressure on France to alter the allocation of regulatory powers and triggering reform in 2005 (although EU law did not require the creation of a sectoral independent regulatory agency).[44] The Commission also took action against Italy, arguing that the 1999 decree failed to completely transpose the 1997 Postal Directive.[45] A Commission Decision in 2000 led Italy to alter domestic legislation to reduce Poste Italiane's monopoly.[46]

Second, EU regulation set the pace of liberalisation. For France and Italy, this occurred as they only liberalised when required to do so by EU law. For Germany, the effect was the converse, slowing up reform. The 1996 Third Postreform planned to introduce full competition in 2002. However, the Social Democratic-Green government that came into office in 1998 sought to protect Deutsche Post's domestic position. (It should be noted that historically there were close links between the Social Democrats and the postal workers union.) The government was able to justify its refusal to extend liberalisation by the fear that

---

[43] For international comparisons, see Anderloni and Pilley (2002: 60–7) and European Commission (2005).

[44] Hanne (2004: 30–1), Rodrigues (2002: 251), and European Commission (2005).

[45] Since it appeared to include a number of hybrid services (mixing mail and electronics) in Poste Italiane's reserved area.

[46] Notably by excluding such hybrid services from the reserved area—Perrazzelli and Fratini (2002: 292–7).

other European suppliers would enter the German market but that without EU regulation, the same would not be available to Deutsche Post.[47] Germany should not 'go alone' and instead should be in step with its European neighbours such as France.[48] Instead, the government decided to follow the EU's timetable for liberalisation, and hence delayed the end of Deutsche Post's monopoly from 2002 until 2007.

A third effect of EU liberalisation was to increase pressures and opportunities for change which were often desired both because of EU regulation and for other reasons. With respect to the latter, traditional postal services were growing slowly by the 1990s and faced competition from other cheaper telephone and electronic communications. In addition, postal organisations faced the weight of historically-imposed high labour costs. Their senior managers sought to make them more efficient and to diversify into fast-growing markets such as financial services and email. EU regulation provided justifications and increased incentives for new strategies based on more efficient working practices, reducing labour costs and international expansion. Overseas growth became central to many postal operators.[49] Thus for instance, German policy makers sought to make Deutsche Post an international company, in part to take advantage of EU-driven opening of national markets.[50] Privatization was designed to make Deutsche Post more efficient and aid it to become the leading European mail supplier.[51] Indeed, after corporatisation and privatisation, Deutsche Post not only changed its name to underline its international ambitions (to Deutsche Post WorldNet) but also expanded abroad, buying up foreign firms and setting up subsidiaries. The most spectacular acquisition was a majority stake in the international rapid delivery company DHL between 1998 and 2001, but this was one of a host of overseas purchases.[52] By 2000, no less than 29% of its turnover came from abroad.[53] Similar patterns were seen in France and even Italy. La Poste began to expand abroad through acquisitions, joint ventures and international alliances, usually by using private law subsidiaries.[54] The new EU context gave rise to major efforts to alter Poste Italiane's organisation and increase its efficiency.[55] It also played an important role in Poste Italiane to become an international group, preparing to compete with the likes of Deutsche Post, through international acquisitions and joint ventures.[56] Thus EU regulation aided a switch in strategies of policy makers towards making postal operators commercial and internationally-competitive organisations, through transformation into corporations and privatisation.

---

[47] Smith (2001a, 2001b).

[48] *Handelsblatt* 28.3.2001, 14.5.2001, and 7.12.2001; Campbell (2002: 81).

[49] For new postal strategies, see Anderloni and Pilley (2002), for France, see Campbell (2002: ch. 7), for Italy, see Valsecchi (2004), for Germany, see Campbell (2002: ch. 2) and Maschke (2002).

[51] Arnaboldi and Bauer (2002: 106) and Campbell (2002: 76–8).

[50] Campbell (2002: 76–8, 107–9).   [52] See Campbell (2002: 101–5).

[53] Campbell (2002: 105).   [54] Campbell: 264–7.

[55] cf. Valsecchi (2004: 7,10) and Passera (2000) (CEO of Poste Italiane).

[56] Valsecchi (2004: 50–6).

CONCLUSION

Postal services appear an unlikely candidate for internationalisation and alteration of sectoral economic institutions. On the one hand, there have been domestic obstacles to reform. These include the very long historical roots of post offices, the power of their numerous employees and their considerable national symbolism. On the other hand, internationalisation pressures have been limited. Transnational technological and economic developments have been minor compared with those in telecommunications or securities trading. Unlike the other sectors, the US has not provided an example of reform, but instead has retained public ownership. The main form of internationalisation has been EU regulation, which developed from the early 1990s onwards, albeit that it remains less comprehensive or detailed than in telecommunications, electricity, or securities trading.

Yet despite these unpropitious factors, significant reform occurred in all four countries. Before 1997, change differed across the four. Initially, Britain led the way, making the PO a public corporation in 1969 and then separating it from telecommunications in 1981. Similar changes took place partially and later in the other three nations between 1989 and 1994. However, in the 1990s, it was Germany that moved furthest, transforming Deutsche Post into a private law limited company and planning its privatisation, liberalising services and creating a sectoral regulator. Interestingly, Britain did not transfer the privatisation and liberalisation of other network sectors into postal services—privatisation was ruled out by Mrs Thatcher in the 1980s and then blocked in the early 1990s. Thus cross-sectoral institutional isomorphism within Britain failed to operate. The result was that considerable divergence across the four countries developed. Tables 12.1 and 12.2 compare the institutional positions in 1985 and 1996.

Table 12.1. Sectoral institutions in 1985*

	Britain	France	Germany	Italy
Position of incumbent	Public corporation, 100% state owned	Part of Posts and Telecommunications Ministry; employees were civil servants; close links to telecommunications	Part of Posts and Telecommunications Ministry; employees were civil servants; close links to telecommunications	Part of Posts and Telecommunications Ministry; employees were civil servants
Competition	Limited (only items over £1)	Limited (only items over 1 kg)	Limited	Limited but competition in letters over 2 kg, open items (commercial invoices and press articles) and some concessions (local monopolies) to private companies
Allocation of regulatory powers	Government	Government	Government	Government

* Hortsmann (1997) derived from official sources.

Table 12.2. Sectoral regulatory institutions in 1996*

	Britain	France	Germany	Italy
Position of incumbent	Public corporation, 100% state owned	Public law, établissement public (form of public corporation, but not a limited company); 100% state owned; employees were civil servants; close links to telecommunications	Private law limited company; privatisation allowed after five years	Publicly-owned state corporation
Competition	Limited (only items over £1)	Limited (only items over 1 kg)	Significant (courier, express, parcel, some bulk/advertising mail up to 100 g; items over 1 kg)	Limited but competition in letters over 2 kg, 'open items' (commercial invoices and press articles) and some 'concessions' (local monopolies) to private companies
Allocation of regulatory powers	Government	Government	Independent sectoral regulatory for posts and telecommunications— RegTP	Government

* Hortsmann (1997) derived from official sources.

After 1997, reform spread and cross-national differences diminished, notably concerning liberalisation and to a lesser extent the existence of a sectoral regulator. Thus by 2005, sectoral institutions had been considerably altered compared to 1996 and several cross-national differences in the degree of competition had been ended (Table 12.3).

Table 12.3. Sectoral regulatory institutions in 2005

	Britain	France	Germany	Italy
Position of incumbent	public corporation—100% publicly owned	Public law, établissement public (form of public corporation, but not a limited company); 100% state-owned; employees are civil servants	Majority privately owned limited company	Public corporation 100% publicly owned
Competition	Yes—main reserved area is post under 100 g and costing less than 80 p	Yes—main reserved area is post under 100 g	Yes—main reserved area is post under 50 g	Yes—main reserved area is post under 100 g
Allocation of regulatory powers	Sectoral independent regulatory authority	Sectoral independent regulatory authority	Cross-sectoral independent regulatory authority	Government

Several factors were at work in the reforms, including the desire to reduce postal losses. However, EU legal requirements were important. Thus EU directives set the pace of liberalisation, and Britain, France, and Italy all followed EU requirements, the last two somewhat reluctantly. Germany had planned to open its markets further and earlier than EU requirements, but after 2001 held back to match the EU's pace of change, not wishing to go it alone. The Commission pressured recalcitrant member states—France and Italy—to transpose its directive correctly, an important factor given their lack of enthusiasm for liberalisation.

But the effects of EU regulation went further than its legal requirements. It offered occasions for reform, as member states needed to transpose EU directives. It provided justifications for moving postal operators towards being enterprises ready for competition. By liberalising postal markets, it offered reasons for overseas expansion by previously national operators. It could also be used as a threat, through entry of more efficient suppliers. Thus EU regulation provided incentives and threats for postal operators that contributed to a broad rethinking of postal institutions.

Postal services appear to be staid and stable, far removed from the rapidly internationalised sectors such as telecommunications. Yet by 2005, postal operators had moved from being civil service administrations to corporations, with new ambitions to become international firms. A novel regulatory framework of liberalisation, rules governing competition, and sectoral regulators was in place.

The chapter thus shows the power of EU regulation in sectoral institutional reform. Despite the absence of major technological and economic changes or the US as an example and pressure, the EU played a significant role in the development of a new institutional framework that overturned very deeply-rooted features. At the same time, its role varied. In France and Italy, its influence was visible, as it was used to justify change. In Germany, it led to slower liberalisation than planned, as the EU timetable for competition was adopted. However, in Britain, although changes were made to meet EU requirements, as well as for other reasons, they were not legitimated by reference to the EU. Thus as in other sectors, the receptiveness of Britain to EU regulation remained low. Nevertheless, the outcome by 2005 was that the four countries had adopted similar reforms and moved towards a liberalised regulated market.

13

Conclusion: Internationalisation
through Policy

The theme of this study has been the effect of internationalisation of markets on national economic institutions. The key questions have been: What does internationalisation of markets mean? Who are its carriers within domestic institutional reform debates? Through which mechanisms does it operate in those debates? What are the comparative institutional outcomes in the face of different forms of internationalisation?

In response to these questions, the book has distinguished three forms of internationalisation: transnational technological and economic developments; then two policy forms, namely regulatory reforms in important overseas nations (the US) and supranational regulation (by the EU). It has examined key institutions in five economically and politically strategic sectors. In two—securities trading and telecommunications—all three forms of internationalisation developed over the period between the mid-1960s and 2005. In the other three sectors—electricity, airlines, and postal services—one or both policy forms were strong by the 1990s, whereas transnational technological and economic internationalisation was weak. The three additional cases allow greater investigation and testing of the impacts of policy forms of internationalisation.

The effects of internationalisation have been compared across four European nations that represent different forms of capitalism, namely Britain, France, Germany, and Italy. Process tracing over extended periods of time has allowed actors' strategies and coalitions to be studied. Thus internationalisation has been analysed historically and comparatively across countries and sectors.

This concluding chapter relates the findings of the book back to broader themes. It begins by briefly summarising the central empirical arguments. Then, building on the analytical starting point for the study, namely the second image reversed (SIR) and comparative institutionalist literatures analysed in Chapter 1, it offers a policy analysis approach to internationalisation and institutional reform. Thereafter, it looks at how the arguments could be tested elsewhere and generalised. Finally, the chapter relates its findings on cross-national diffusion of institutions and analyses of Europeanisation.

CENTRAL EMPIRICAL FINDINGS

In the mid-1960s, there were strong similarities in European network industries concerning three key economic institutions, namely the organisation of suppliers, rules governing competition, and the allocation of regulatory powers. Suppliers of services were generally publicly owned and enjoyed monopolies over services. Governments held almost all regulatory powers—there were virtually no independent sectoral regulators. The institutional framework in Europe stood in sharp contrast to that in the US, where there were often privately-owned suppliers and independent regulatory commissions.

Yet significant national and sectoral exceptions to this general picture existed in the four countries. The extent of centralisation of supply and the allocation of regulatory powers differed, as did the role of privately ownership. Thus for example, Britain had private ownership and self-regulation of the London Stock Exchange (LSE). In contrast, Germany and Italy had substantial decentralisation in the organisation and regulation of stock exchanges. France had one dominant exchange, but complex rules for dual prices of securities. In electricity, there were many suppliers in West Germany, comprising a mixture of public and private, and regional and municipal organisations. Italian telecommunications were fragmented. The key common features and exceptions are presented in Table 13.1.[1]

Internationalisation—defined as factors that put pressures on nations to open their markets, operate across borders and are outside the control of any one national government—created strong pressures on traditional European institutions in all five sectors. However, the impacts varied according to the type of internationalisation.

Revolutionary transnational technological and economic developments took place in securities trading and telecommunications from the mid-1960s onwards. They created tremendous challenges to traditional institutions through higher demand, greater capital requirements, increased potential for cross-border flows, and a weakening of natural monopoly. They contributed to serious problems for national suppliers and were regularly cited in domestic debates on institutional reform. In response, governments attempted to alter long-standing institutions, which were widely criticised as inefficient.

Yet in all four countries, institutional inertia was the main response to technological and economic internationalisation. Insofar as institutional reforms were undertaken, they were modest, differed across the countries and were introduced in the late 1960s and early 1970s before the full force of technological and economic pressures was felt. Inertia arose for several reasons. Governments were unable to forge broad reform coalitions, whereas trade unions, the employees of suppliers, and political parties strongly and successfully opposed change.

---

[1] Further exceptions, such as whether suppliers, were part of the civil service or public corporations, and if the latter, which form of public corporation, are not noted here, although they are set out in chapters.

Table 13.1. Sectoral institutions in 1965

	Common features across Britain, France, West Germany, and Italy	Distinctive national features (by sector)
Organisation of suppliers	Public ownership; one dominant national supplier	(i) **Securities trading:** *Britain:* London Stock Exchange a privately-owned club; *West Germany and Italy:* several strong regional stock exchanges (ii) **Telecommunications.** *Italy:* fragmentation of suppliers (iii) **Electricity.** *West Germany:* regional and municipal, and mixture of public and private electricity suppliers
Rules governing competition	Monopoly	(i) **Securities trading:** *Britain:* separation of wholesaler and retail traders (jobbers and brokers) and de facto not legal monopoly for securities trading; *France:* dual markets (ii) **Airlines:** *Britain:* duopoly
Formal allocation of regulatory powers	Held by governments	(i) **Securities trading:** *Britain:* reliance on informal norms and self-regulation; *West Germany:* strong powers for associations and Länder; *Italy:* strong powers for associations and cities (ii) **Electricity.** *West Germany:* municipalities and Länder governments; strong role for industry associations

Moreover, policies that did not require major institutional modifications were pursued, such as increasing funding or using existing institutions diversely. Finally, inefficient supply was accepted or at least allowed to continue.

In contrast, policy forms of internationalisation, namely reforms in significant overseas countries (the US and then Britain), and EU regulation, played significant roles in sweeping reforms in securities trading and telecommunications in the 1980s and 1990s. They were also important in electricity, airlines, and postal services in the period between the 1990s and 2005, despite transnational technological and economic internationalisation being relatively weak. The two policy forms influenced the strategies and coalitions of key domestic actors. In particular, they aided the formation of strong reform coalitions led by governments and the management of incumbent suppliers, and weakened the previous coalition of opponents of change.

The mechanisms through which policy forms of internationalisation affected domestic decisions were various. One was international regulatory competition. Regulatory reforms in the US and then Britain led policy makers in other nations to worry that their domestic suppliers would be disadvantaged in international competition if they too were not reformed. Equally, new institutional frameworks abroad were used in domestic debates to legitimate change. As for EU regulation, its influence went well beyond its legal requirements: it increased fears of regulatory competition by liberalising markets; it provided legitimation for changes; transposition of EU legislation into national law offered occasions for wider reforms.

Domestic debates in the 1980s–2005 period led to sweeping institutional reforms, in sharp contrast to the experiences of the 1960s and 1970s. In securities trading and telecommunications, all four countries adopted a single powerful privatised supplier, replaced monopolies with rules designed to allow competition and delegated powers to independent regulatory authorities. National specificities were ended.[2] Similar modifications were seen in electricity and airlines, and even postal services. Their significance is especially noteworthy in these three sectors because transnational technological and economic developments were weak and indeed in airlines and electricity, were greatly diminished compared to the 1960s and 1970s. By 2005, a new European institutional framework centred on majority privately owned or at least corporatised suppliers, competition and independent sectoral regulators had emerged in all four nations. National exceptions were rare (Table 13.2).

Table 13.2. Key sectoral institutions in 2005

	Key institutional features	National differences (by sector)
Organisation of suppliers	Stock exchanges, telecommunications, airlines, electricity: majority private ownership of dominant incumbent; Postal services: publicly-owned corporations	(i) Electricity: EDF majority state-owned; mix of public and private, regional and city suppliers in Germany although concentration around few dominant private suppliers (ii) Postal services: Deutschepost majority privately-owned
Rules governing competition	Competition	(i) Electricity: full liberalisation in Britain, to be introduced in other three countries by 2007 (ii) Airlines: no Open Skies agreement between Britain and US
Allocation of regulatory powers	Shared between governments and sectoral independent regulatory authorities except in airlines	(i) Airlines: independent economic regulator in Britain (ii) Postal services: no independent regulator in Italy

[2] Such as dual pricing in French securities trading or the existence of several powerful regional stock exchanges in Germany and Italy or self-regulation in British securities trading.

Yet adoption of similar institutional forms was combined with different reform routes. In particular, the role of internationalisation, the timing of change, the countries seen as valuable examples and the role of supranational regulation varied between Britain on the one hand and France, Germany, and Italy on the other.

Reforms were undertaken earlier in Britain than in the other three countries. Domestic factors were central to initiating changes, which were pushed through by determined governments; often policy makers looked to the US to legitimate change and seek lessons for institutional design only after they already decided to undertake reform. EU regulation played almost no role and indeed was often viewed with suspicion.

International factors were more significant in France, Germany, and Italy than in Britain. They played significant roles both in decisions to begin reform and in their implementation. Policy makers looked at overseas experiences, but more at Britain than the US, since the former was seen as a source of regulatory competition and as an example. But perhaps the greatest contrast with Britain lay in the role of EU regulation, which was central in the three countries to creating strong reform alliances and providing powerful legitimating arguments to overcome determined resistance by a broad coalition of interests defending the status quo.

It is worth stating briefly the lines of argument or inquiry that were not pursued in the study. The book did not show that internationalisation was the sole cause of institutional reform, but rather that it played significant roles in domestic decisions. Equally, it does not claim that adoption of a similar institutional framework across the four countries ended all differences. Thus, for instance, in some countries, minority public ownership of incumbents remained. Moreover, certain features of sectoral regulatory authorities such the scope of agency responsibilities and the method of appointment of their members also varied across the four nations. However, the book also does show that these are variations within a new general institutional framework that is similar in having majority private ownership of suppliers, competition in supply and regulation by independent sectoral agencies. Finally, and most importantly, the study does not claim that similar institutional forms led to convergence of behaviour.[3] Instead, it has focused on the role of different forms of internationalisation and has noted the adoption of similar forms concerning three key formal sectoral institutions.

Overall, the central findings are that policy forms of internationalisation influenced the reform of national economic institutions whereas transnational technological developments had little impact. Policy forms played a significant role because of their effects on domestic actors within national policy processes. The four nations adopted similar sectoral institutions, but did so through different routes that reflected their diverse domestic politics.

---

[3] For a discussion of contrasts in strategies towards Europeanisation and relationships between governments, regulatory agencies, and suppliers despite common moves towards privatisation, liberalisation, and independent sectoral regulators in network industries in Europe, see Thatcher (2007), Bartle (2002), and Coen (2005a, 2005b).

A POLICY ANALYSIS OF INTERNATIONALISATION AND ECONOMIC INSTITUTIONS

The analytical starting point of the book was two literatures that deal directly with internationalisation of markets and national institutions, namely the SIR approach and comparative institutionalism.[4] Although they have different *foci*, both predict dissimilarities in national responses to economic internationalisation. The SIR literature examines how exogenous shocks or reductions in barriers to trade affect domestic decision-making. It argues that responses depend on conflicts arising from the distributional consequences of internationalisation, as mediated by diverse national institutions. Those institutions are usually taken as fixed, or at most prone to different reforms, so that national responses to common international changes also vary. Comparative institutionalist studies have given great weight to analysing how existing institutions operate and mould decision-making. They argue that institutional change is highly bounded by existing institutions, which affect the interests, coalitions, and ideas of domestic policy makers. In particular, historical institutionalist works claim that existing national institutions both differ and endure in the face of international economic pressures; more recent varieties of capitalism models suggest that in the face of increased capital flows, nations reform their institutions but in diverse ways, in order to protect the efficiency of national firms.

The case studies point to the strengths of the two literatures. As the SIR approach suggests, international factors often played significant roles in domestic decisions. They influenced the strategies and coalitions of policy makers. Yet they did so through existing national actors in the domestic policy process, supporting the focus of comparative institutionalist studies on domestic decision-making. Empirically, even revolutionary transnational technological and economic developments were met with institutional inertia or diverse reforms. Equally, national reform routes differed in terms of timing and process. These findings are consistent with the empirical predictions of SIR and comparative institutionalist models.

Yet the limits of both approaches are also exposed. They use a narrow definition of internationalisation, centred on trade and capital flows, but underplay other forms that also affect markets. Equally, they give great attention to socio-economic actors, but too little to governments. As a result, their analyses risk being over-dominated by economic efficiency and distributional consequences, leaving too little scope for public policy processes. Moreover, they overstate institutional stability and cross-national differences and cannot explain either the dramatic changes seen in the sectors studied or the adoption of similar sectoral institutions by four nations despite their contrasting histories and macro-level institutions.

Given the foregoing critique, this section suggests the benefits of seeing the SIR and comparative institutionalist models as complementary. It draws on both

---

[4] For a review, see Chapter 1.

but also seeks to remedy their *lacunae* in order to develop a policy analysis of internationalisation and sectoral institutional change. The SIR model aids in identifying sources of internationalisation and their effects on socio-economic actors. The comparative institutionalist approach aids analysis of how internationalisation plays out in decisions about national institutions. However, the framework applied in the present study looks directly at how internationalisation arises from decisions of policy makers and then affects national policy processes. Hence it gives greater place than current SIR and comparative institutionalist models to public actors such as governments, regulators and political parties, and to political mechanisms that involve legitimation and argument. It studies how and why internationalisation provides scope for countries to adopt similar sectoral institutions despite diverse macro-level ones. At the same time, by examining the interaction between internationalisation and domestic politics, it remains sensitive to specific national reform routes. It relates internationalisation to broader political debates and struggles that include but also go beyond socio-economic actors and economic efficiency.

Four elements of a policy analysis approach can be set out here, concerning: the nature of internationalisation of markets, carriers, mechanisms, and patterns of institutional change. They respond to the questions set out at the start of the chapter. First, internationalisation of markets should include policy forms such as the regulatory decisions of powerful overseas nations and international organisations, as well as trade and capital flows. Although the SIR literature often focuses on the latter two, it accepts that a change in the costs of international economic transactions can arise from government policies (cf. Frieden and Rogowski 1996). This must be explicitly integrated into analysis. The case studies suggest that policies pursued by other nations affect markets. Equally, supranational regulation can do so, for as Fligstein (2001) points out, markets are constituted by rules, and hence altering those rules matters. Internationalisation need not be a *deus ex economia*, or inevitable 'force of markets' beyond the control of policy makers. Instead, it can arise from the decisions of governments—be these from supranational bodies to which they have collectively delegated or from decisions of powerful overseas governments. A broader view of internationalisation offers a better understanding of how markets can be altered.

A second aspect concerns the carriers of internationalisation within nations. The case studies suggest that these are likely to be domestic actors who continue to dominate decision-making about institutions. Internationalisation affects their strategies and coalitions. Thus, it operates through 'indirect penetration' rather than entry of overseas actors into national policymaking (Kahler 1985). Moreover, while the SIR and varieties of capitalism literatures valuably point to the effects of internationalisation on socio-economic interests, the case studies show that the role of public policy makers, such as governments, regulators, and political parties, is also crucial. In particular, governments do not just respond passively to internationalisation or socio-economic interests; indeed, the cases show that they initiate and lead change, form reform coalitions and sometimes impose new arrangements on socio-economic interests.[5] Hence the resources, strategies, and relationships of governments must be considered.

A third element concerns the mechanisms whereby internationalisation influences domestic decision making. Using DiMaggio and Powell (1991), chapter 1 divided mechanisms into efficiency (driving competitive isomorphism) on the one hand, and then mechanisms of coercion, mimetism and normative processes (responsible for institutional isomorphism) on the other hand. The cases examined in the book suggest that the importance of different mechanisms of internationalisation depends strongly on their insertion into the policy process. Although the mechanisms found empirically do not always map neatly onto DiMaggio and Powell's typology, three were particularly important: an efficiency mechanism through regulatory competition; the use of legally-binding EU measures (coercion) to provide political impetus for wider reforms; selective cross-national mimetism or learning.

Absolute economic efficiency appears inadequate on its own to result in reform. The examples of securities trading and telecommunications in the 1960s-1980s show that institutions that were widely regarded as 'inefficient' (for governments and users) survived reform attempts by government and were tolerated. In contrast, economic efficiency through cross-national regulatory competition with other nations considered by domestic policy makers as rivals for markets was much more effective. Thus for instance, after long periods of stability, policy makers in France, Germany and Italy responded to the Big Bang in London or privatisation of British Telecom and British Airways, fearing that their suppliers would be disadvantaged. Regulatory competition was important because it provided a visible source of pressure that was used by policy makers (especially governments and incumbents) within domestic policy processes to justify reform.

As for coercion, mimetism and normative processes, these mechanisms are powerful if they become linked with other processes and interests within domestic policy making by providing occasions and legitimation for reforms desired both to respond to market internationalisation and for other reasons (often domestic). Thus although EU regulation offered coercion through its legally-binding rules on member states, its significance lay more in its non-coercive functions linked to the domestic policy process. In particular, when EU regulation had to be transposed into domestic law, the occasion was used for comprehensive reconsideration of institutional frameworks. Equally, EU regulation was used by policy makers to claim that they had little choice over undertaking broad institutional reforms, even though these went beyond those legally required by the EU. As regards mimetism, policy makers pointed to overseas examples when it aided them in domestic struggles and to deal with fears of overseas regulatory competition. Equally, they imported overseas institutional features selectively when it fitted with their domestic strategies.

---

[5] Hence the analysis agrees with Linda Weiss's attack on the 'myth of the powerless state', Weiss (1998).

In contrast, when mechanisms were not linked with domestic actors and issues but operated alone or contrary to other interests of domestic policy makers, they were much less important. Thus cross-national mimetism was very limited when it ran counter to the interests of powerful domestic actors such as incumbent suppliers. Equally, cross-national learning was very superficial, with little analysis of how well and why overseas institutions performed. As for normative processes, international epistemic communities played little direct role in institutional decisions, which remained dominated by domestic actors.

Hence a policy analysis involves going beyond legal frameworks to understand that the importance of overseas reforms of internationalisation and supranational regulation often lies in their utility for domestic makers in providing political impetus and legitimating changes. But such utility can only be judged by looking into domestic policy struggles.

In terms of institutional outcomes, the book offers three cross-national claims that are directly linked to its policy analysis approach. First, it suggests that transnational technological and economic forms of internationalisation have little impact on domestic sectoral institutions. Using the cases studied, it argues that institutional inertia was the dominant outcome and insofar as reforms were introduced, they were modest and differed across nations. Transnational technological and economic forms of internationalisation can give rise to problems such as inadequate supply or pressures on monopolies. However, the existence of such problems is insufficient for an institutional response, because governments need resources that they can use in the policy process to overcome opposition from powerful existing domestic actors who enjoy benefits from existing institutions and have formed powerful coalitions to prevent reform, even if institutions are performing badly.[6] Moreover, as shown, non-institutional responses may be an appealing alternative for policy makers to modifying institutions. The book contends that technological and economic developments are neither a sufficient nor a necessary condition for institutional modifications.

A second claim is that policy forms of internationalisation can undermine long-standing sectoral institutions, even if these have lasted for decades or centuries, as was the case for public ownership and monopolies in the five sectors. They can operate even in nations where reform is difficult due, for instance, to multiple veto points and players.[7] A third argument is that policy internationalisation aids international isomorphism, as very different nations with diverse macro-level political and economic institutions and histories can adopt similar sectoral economic institutions. Both these claims run counter to predictions derived from the SIR and comparative institutionalist literatures. They may arise in part because the book looks at sectoral institutions rather than macro-level ones. But they are also due to a different view of internationalisation, and especially its integration into domestic policy-making processes.

---

[6] This supports similar arguments by historical institutionalists at a macro-level, see for instance, Hall (1986).

[7] Such as Germany and Italy — cf. Tsebelis (1995, 2002).

Policy forms of internationalisation have considerable scope to contribute to change and to aid the spread of similar sectoral institutions across diverse nations because they affect the strategies, resources and coalitions of policy makers within domestic political struggles. Through the mechanisms of regulatory competition, the use of legally-binding supra-national measures to provide political impetus for wider reforms and selective cross-national mimetism or learning, they play a role in key domestic actors altering their institutional strategies and preferences. Equally, they aid governments to create powerful reform coalitions, especially with incumbent suppliers, and to weaken coalitions supporting the status quo. They provide justifications for decisions imposed on opponents of reform.

At the same time, policy makers can derive considerable advantages from policy forms of internationalisation. They can link 'problems', such as apparent threats from overseas competitors or 'imposed' EU regulation to institutional 'solutions' desired for other, domestic reasons; one example is privatisation, which governments often seek for fiscal reasons but justify in terms of responding to internationalisation.[8] They can use overseas examples selectively, ignoring those that run counter to domestic interests. [9] They have considerable scope for choice in institutional design in implementing supranational regulation. Hence policy forms of internationalisation are especially influential because they are flexible and can be married to other unrelated reasons for reform.

However, a policy analysis of internationalisation does not exclude cross-national differences. On the contrary, it involves examining the interactions between internationalisation and domestic policy processes. These can differ from one nation to another. Thus for instance, in Britain, reform came earlier, and internationalisation played a more secondary role to domestic factors, than in France, Germany, and Italy. Moreover, whereas the US example had a resonance in Britain and EU regulation did not, in the other three nations, it was a combination of EU regulation and the British example that was significant. These contrasts reflect differences in domestic politics and policy processes, but did not prevent the emergence of similar formal institutions.

Thus overall, the policy analysis approach used in the study offers a broader view of internationalisation and relates it to the domestic policy process. It gives greater prominence to the scope for public policy makers to mould institutions and to lead change. It also seeks to integrate political mechanisms involving argument and legitimation as well as material interests and distributional conflicts. It sees institutional reform as a part of a policy process in which internationalisation plays a significant role.

TESTING THE ARGUMENTS IN OTHER CASES

How can the arguments developed from the sectoral cases in Europe be tested to see whether they hold more broadly? Three avenues seem open. First,

---

[8] Cf. March and Olsen 1972.
[9] See for instance, how Britain 'learnt' from the US in telecommunications or airlines.

internationalisation could be examined in other industries in Europe. These might be network industries that have experienced different combinations of forms of internationalisation, thereby producing further cases. One example is the railway sector.[10] Here, as in electricity and airlines, transnational technological and economic developments such as high-speed trains, mostly occurred before the 1990s. However, unlike those sectors, EU regulation developed much more slowly. Moreover, the scope for regulatory competition is much lower. Finally, although Britain introduced reforms in the 1990s, these were widely seen as unsuccessful. The policy approach to internationalisation would predict that changes in Britain were driven by domestic factors and that policy makers only looked abroad after initial decisions had been taken. It would also suggest that institutional modifications only took place in continental European nations when EU regulation grew. Another interesting case in Europe would be the water industry. EU regulation has concerned the environment rather than liberalisation of supply and regulatory competition is very limited, but Britain undertook privatisation of water suppliers in the late 1980s and created a sectoral regulator. The policy analysis developed in the present study would predict that since ideational factors are weak, continental European nations would fail to follow Britain's example unless and until EU regulation of competition develops.

A second avenue is to examine non-network industries in Europe. Thus for instance, chemicals, pharmaceuticals, insurance, cars, steel and coal, biotechnology and agriculture have all been subject to various forms of EU regulation, some sector-specific but others arising from general competition law. Several have experienced revolutionary transnational technological and economic changes (e.g. chemicals, pharmaceuticals, or bio-technology). The scope for regulatory competition also varies. These industries would allow examination of the importance of regulatory competition and whether EU regulation serves the purposes of legitimating reform. They would also test whether governments are crucial in initiating and leading change and forming alliances with producers.

A third avenue for expanding the range of cases is to look at network industries outside Europe. The US does not seem a good case, because the study found no evidence that its decisions to alter its institutions and regulatory policies were influenced by competitive pressures or examples from other countries.[11] However, sectoral institutions in the five industries studied in the present work have been reformed in many other areas of the world, including Latin America and Asia.[12] Did internationalisation play similar roles as in Europe? In particular, what was the impact of overseas examples such as the US and Britain? Did supranational regulation, notably by the World Trade Organisation, play a part in aiding the creation of reform coalitions and offering political impetus for new institutions?

---

[10] For cross-national studies, see for instance Lodge (2002) and Héritier (2005).
[11] Hence reforms in the US were treated as an independent variable in this study.
[12] See, for instance, Murillo (2002), Levi-Faur (2003), and Meseguer (2004).

RELATING THE CASES TO DEBATES ON
CROSS-NATIONAL DIFFUSION

An increasing large literature explains the spread of similar policies and institutions across nations through processes of 'diffusion' or 'policy transfer'.[13] These processes arise from interdependence, so that the adoption of a new institution or policy in one country affects its adoption by other nations. Simmons and Elkins (2004) divide these processes into two groups. First, those that alter pay-offs of decisions—i.e. their costs and benefits. They may alter material pay-offs through mechanisms such as changes in one country altering relative competitive advantages. They can affect reputational pay-offs, as new norms lead to punishment of countries that make 'deviant' choices. Second, diffusion processes can arise from the spread of new information due to learning. New information can be gathered from successful nations, communication through transnational networks or from cultural reference groups. A key issue is the role and importance of these two sets of cross-national diffusion processes.

Diffusion approaches have been applied to the three types of economic institution examined here. Thus for instance, the spread of privatisation has been ascribed to learning, emulation or 'policy bandwaggoning' (Ikenberry 1990; Meseguer 2004), as countries followed the lead of Britain and the US. Liberalisation of telecommunications and electricity in Latin America has been argued to result in part from policy learning (Levy-Faur 2003). The spread of IRAs has been ascribed, among other factors, to a process of emulation (Gilardi 2005).

Although the present study was not designed around the diffusion literature, the cases provide strong evidence of cross-national diffusion. Regulatory competition, or at least fear of it, was important in domestic decision-making. It increased the desires of governments and incumbent firms to reform domestic institutions to avoid loss of competitive advantage, representing an example of altered pay-offs. With respect to Simmons and Elkins' second category of processes, information spread cross-nationally as national policy makers looked abroad at overseas examples.

The evidence found can be used to put forward two major points about diffusion processes. First, it reveals the nature and purpose of learning, which Simmons and Elkins (2004) categorise under the heading of gathering of new information. Cross-national policy learning does indeed offer an important possible diffusion process. However, it can take many forms, from deep 'social learning' to emulation or just 'modelling' national changes on overseas policies or institutions.[14] The cases suggest that most cross-national policy learning was superficial rather than deep. Thus for instance, British policy makers frequently looked at institutions in

---

[13] For important general work on diffusion of policy and innovation see for instance, Rogers (2003), Walker (1969), and Berry and Berry (1999); for policy transfer, see Dolowitz and Marsh (1996, 2000).

[14] Among the vast literature, see Rose (1993), Hansen and King (2001), Blyth (2002), Bennett (1997), Bleich (2003), Campbell, (1998), Dolowitz and Marsh (1996), Goldstein and Keohane (1993), Hall (1989), and Page (2004).

the US (in all the sectors except postal services), while policy makers in the other three nations looked abroad, especially to Britain. But there were few serious studies that examined how well institutional changes in the US or Britain performed; instead, learning was often confined to knowledge of the broad outlines of reforms overseas and sometimes a few visits. Even in securities trading, a domain with very high capital mobility, learning was skin-deep: as one senior British policy maker put it, 'we looked at the US but not comprehensively', and undertook little research since 'I knew enough about the US'.[15]

Superficiality of cross-national learning was related to its main functions in the policy process: to legitimate new institutional arrangements and offer possible institutional designs from which domestic decision-makers could pick as and when they chose. These functions can be seen by looking at three features of cross-national learning in the cases: its dependence on other factors; selective learning (if not 'mis-learning'); the unimportance of overseas examples when they conflicted with domestic interests.

Learning often entered the decision-making process after policy makers had already decided to introduce reforms for other reasons. Thus for many years, British policy makers paid little attention to the US institutional frameworks for securities trading and telecommunications, rejecting them as inferior to their existing institutions; however, when domestic actors such as the Office of Fair Trading, the government, and the Bank of England wanted to justify change in the 1980s and 1990s (largely arising from domestic factors), they presented the US in a much more positive light.[16] Similarly, during the mid-1980s, policy makers in France, Germany, and Italy refused to follow Britain's path of privatisation and liberalisation; but then in the 1990s, they sought to use Britain as an example to support reforms that were driven by fear of regulatory competition, EU regulation and domestic factors. Cross-sectoral comparisons reinforce the argument that cross-national policy learning depends on other factors. In particular, learning was much greater when international regulatory competition appeared strong. Thus for example, significant learning and indeed copying occurred in securities trading in the 1980s as continental European nations followed London's 'Big Bang', but they were much weaker in electricity, where regulatory competition was limited.[17]

Learning was highly selective. It often involved only limited investigation and little emulation. Thus for instance, the French securities regulator, the COB (established in 1967), was supposedly modelled on the US SEC, but it was very different in its structure, independence, and powers.[18] Similarly, British policy makers cited the virtues of liberalisation of telecommunications in the US, but failed to investigate in depth or follow the American decision to break up the incumbent, AT&T.[19]

Furthermore, when overseas examples conflicted with domestic interests, they were not followed. Hence for example, in the airlines sector, even the supposedly liberal Thatcher government of the 1980s refused to follow the US route of

---

[15] Interview, senior financial regulator 3.   [16] See Chapter 4.   [17] See Chapters 5 and 10.
[18] See Chapter 3.   [19] See Chapter 8.

'deregulation' in order to protect the incumbent, BA.[20] Similarly, in telecommunications, it failed to follow the US example of the breakup of the incumbent operator, as this would have delayed privatisation of BT.[21]

Hence cross-national learning seems both superficial and instrumental, undertaken to legitimate change and to provide a palette of institutional designs which are then used selectively. It is dependent on being congruent with the pre-existing interests of policy makers (themselves shaped by other forms of internationalisation and domestic factors). The decision to 'learn' from abroad, the interpretation of overseas experiences, and choices over which overseas examples to follow must be analysed as part of domestic policy processes.

A second contribution to the diffusion debate concerns cross-national paths of change. The cases show that different diffusion processes led to common outcomes. They reveal a clear pattern that differed between Britain and the continental European countries. Privatisation, liberalisation, and delegation to independent agencies in Britain were strongly driven by domestic factors. Even in the one partial exception, securities trading, where strong regulatory competition was important, the 1986 Big Bang was largely initiated for domestic reasons. Internationalisation offered an additional factor, especially for justifying reform: only after British policy makers had decided to introduce reforms, did they look seriously to the US as a potential competitor and/or a source of ideas. In contrast, the adoption in France, Germany, and Italy of similar economic institutions to those introduced in Britain was highly driven by international factors, notably a combination of fear of regulatory competition from Britain and most important of all, EU regulation. Moreover, policy makers in the three countries paid most attention to the British example and largely ignored or rejected the US one. Thus for example, Germany policy makers in securities trading regarded the US as backward, but took great interest in London's institutions.[22]

The cases thus suggest that examining outcomes is insufficient to understand diffusion processes. The spread of similar institutional forms does not mean that common explanations necessarily apply. There is the well-known problem of 'spurious diffusion' when non-diffusion processes (such as domestic factors) give rise to similar outcomes. However, the cases also underline how different international diffusion processes can give rise to similar institutions. Detailed process tracing and case studies can identify causal mechanisms, processes, and diffusion paths, offering a valuable complement to quantitative analyses. Finally, the cases show how supranational regulation can play an important role in diffusion. Yet such regulation sits uneasily in a cross-national diffusion framework. Unless an extreme 'intergovermentalist' position is taken, decisions by supranational organisations are unlikely to merely reflect national preferences, but are also likely to be influenced by the preferences and strategies of those organisations themselves. Moreover, decisions are the result of bargaining among several nations, including the nation whose reforms are being investigated. The importance of EU regulation

[20] See Chapter 11.   [21] See Chapter 8.   [22] See Chapter 5.

in continental Europe points to the need to look at another literature, namely that on 'Europeanisation'.

SUPRANATIONAL POLICY: EU REGULATION AND EUROPEANISATION

The book has examined supranational policy as a form of internationalisation of markets, and taken EU regulation as an example. The case studies show that in all five sectors, EU sectoral regulation grew from being almost non-existent between the mid-1960s and late 1980s into a detailed regulatory framework. That framework ran counter to traditional national institutions, notably monopolies for suppliers and governments that were both suppliers and regulators. Hence EU regulation offers valuable material for investigating the effects of supranational policy across time, different sectors and four diverse countries.

One question is why EU regulation grew. This has been the subject of intense debate, both generally and specifically in telecommunications and energy.[23] Since the present study focuses on the domestic level, it does not seek to enter that debate, although the chapters on internationalisation do point out that EU sectoral regulation grew progressively and was agreed (sometimes after lengthy debate) by national governments acting in the Council of Ministers.

A different question concerns the effects of EU regulation on politics within member states. Literature on Europeanisation has been growing rapidly.[24] Initial studies focused on adaptation pressures on national institutions arising from the goodness-of-fit—the extent to which existing national arrangements meet new EU requirements (Green Cowles et al. 2001). The lower the goodness-of-fit, the stronger the adaptation pressures that arise. These are in turn mediated by national factors such as veto points, cultures, and administrative structures.[25] However, more recent studies have argued that European integration may have broader effects than producing adaptation pressures.[26] It may affect cross-national

[23] For general debates between 'neofunctionalists' and 'inter-governmentalists', see Sandholtz and Stone Sweet (1998), Moravcsik (1998); for an analysis of the weaknesses of EU rule-making, see Vibert (2001); for specific debates in telecommunications and electricity over whether the Commission imposed its preferences on national governments, or the latter altered their preferences towards greater EU regulation through learning, or whether national governments (and with them their national champion incumbent suppliers) acted in partnership with the Commission to create jointly an EU regulatory framework, see Schmidt (1996, 1998), Sandholtz (1993, 1998), Scott (1995), Eising (2002), and Thatcher (2001).

[24] 'Europeanisation' is itself used in many different senses; sometimes it includes European integration (e.g. Lawton 1999), sometimes it just refers to the effects of European integration on decision-making at the national level (Green Cowles, Caporaso, and Risse 2001); here it is used in this latter, more specific sense.

[25] cf. Schmidt (2002), Green Cowles, Caporaso, and Risse (2001), Ladrech (1994), Héritier et al. (2001), and Haverland (2000).

[26] Featherstone and Radaelli (2003), Knill and Lemkuhl (2002), Knill and Lenschow (2005), and Schmidt (2002, 2006).

learning and policy networks.[27] It may also influence policymaking through its effects on discourse.[28] It may give rise to cross-national mimetism, thereby producing isomorphism.[29]

The cases show that EU regulation was significant in domestic institutional decisions in France, Germany, and Italy, and indeed was often the most important form of internationalisation. In contrast, it played almost no role in Britain. The evidence can be used to throw light on how and why Europeanisation can sometimes have effects well beyond goodness-of-fit, by linking it directly to winners and losers in the domestic policy process.[30]

In Britain, there was a very high goodness-of-fit between domestic institutions and EU regulation, since reforms in Britain preceded EU legislation. Yet even in those rare cases when this was not the case (e.g. liberalisation of postal services in the late 1990s), the EU was not used in domestic discussions. Governments did not need to justify reforms by reference to the EU. Indeed, EU legislation was sometimes treated with suspicion (e.g. in securities trading), even though it offered opportunities for overseas expansion by firms based in Britain. The outcome is a paradox: EU regulation often followed that in Britain, yet it was not welcomed. But the key reason is that it did not aid governments or incumbent firms in domestic reforms. Truly Britain was an 'awkward partner' in Europe.[31]

France, Germany, and Italy had a lower goodness-of-fit with EU regulation than Britain. Hence they had to alter their institutions to comply with EU legal requirements, notably over liberalisation, separation of regulation and supply and ending illegal state aid. Moreover, EU regulation created wider pressures beyond its legal requirements. It ran counter to traditional industrial and social policies such as cross-subsidising services, state funding of *grands projets* that have broad social and economic benefits but make losses, or policies favouring domestic equipment suppliers.[32] It increased the perils (or fears) of regulatory competition, as domestic incumbents worried that overseas firms enjoying superior institutional positions would be able to enter domestic markets. Thus for instance, in telecommunications and airlines, policy makers in continental Europe became alarmed that the privately owned and competition-hardened BT and BA were more efficient than their domestic incumbents and were better able to create international alliances. Equally, German and Italian policy makers in electricity were concerned about entry to their home markets by the French giant EDF.

However, EU regulation also offered opportunities as well as pressures for governments and the managements of domestic incumbent suppliers.[33] Both sets of actors were able to craft a strategy to respond to EU regulation. One element of that strategy was to ensure large, internationally-competitive firms. Hence when suppliers were fragmented (e.g. in Italian telecommunications or German electricity), concentration took place. Another element was privatisation, in which

27 Radaelli (2003) and Bomberg and Peterson (2000).
28 Radaelli and Schmidt (2004) and Schmidt (2002*a*, 2002*b*, 2006).
29 Radaelli (2000).   30 Cf. Thatcher (2004*b*) for telecommunications.
31 cf. George (1998).   32 cf. Hayward (1995).   33 See Chapters 5, 9, and 10–12.

competing in a liberalised EU market was used as a major argument for change. A third element was internationalisation of suppliers through alliances, mergers and takeovers, seen in all five sectors. A further element was delegation of powers to independent sectoral regulatory agencies, which were responsible in large measure for detailed implementation of EU regulation.

These changes not only offered a response to EU regulation but also provided considerable advantages to governments and incumbent firms. For governments, privatisation offered substantial revenue; indeed, sales of network industries were crucial elements of fiscal policy from the 1990s onwards in all three Continental countries. Moreover, EU regulation was used by governments to justify delegating unpopular and increasingly complex issues to independent regulatory agencies (IRAs), such as rebalancing of tariffs, interconnection of rival networks or dealing with increased costs in electricity. Finally, within the overall framework of EU regulation, governments have kept much freedom over institutional design. Thus for example, they choose key aspects of IRAs, such as which powers are delegated to them (and which are retained by governments), the number of regulators, and who nominates them. Equally, they determine the form, timing, and target revenues from privatisation.

For incumbent suppliers, privatisation and concentration of domestic firms, which were justified by the needs to respond to pressures arising from EU regulation, also offered benefits. The changes increased their capacity to become 'international champions' by expanding abroad. They also aided in updating internal structures and working practices, which were justified by the need to meet foreign competition in domestic markets. These aims were vigorously pursued from the 1990s onwards by companies such as EDF, France Télécom, EON, Deustche Telekom, Deutsche Börse, Deutschepost, Euronext (the Paris-based grouping of stock exchanges), and incumbent airlines. Expansion and internal reorganisation offered the prospects of higher profits and increased remuneration for senior managers, as well as interesting work. Moreover, EU 'imposed' liberalisation offered good reasons to rebalance tariffs to match costs, especially for residential users, an unpopular policy that had previously often been blocked by governments.

Indeed, the institutional reforms offered the best of both worlds for incumbent suppliers. While enjoying the benefits of privatisation, international expansion, and concentration, they maintained long-standing linkages with elected politicians. They became private international champions. Hence for instance, French companies such as EDF or Air France, were promoted by national policy makers; France Télécom was rescued by the government from near bankruptcy in 2001; Italian electricity producers were protected by governments from takeovers by EDF and Alitalia received state funding on several occasions to avoid bankruptcy.[34] Finally, independent regulatory agencies offered advantages for firms, notably in terms of consistency and predictability compared with elected politicians and through their acceptance of unwinding expensive and increasingly vulnerable cross-subsidies.

---

[34] See for instance Chapters 11 and 12.

Thus privatisation, liberalisation, and delegation to independent regulatory agencies (IRAs) both represented responses to EU regulation and also offered other benefits for governments and incumbent national suppliers. Yet these institutional reforms (especially privatisation) were often opposed by trade unions, employees and sometimes subnational governments. EU regulation offered powerful arguments to justify them. Transposition of EU directives offered occasions for reconsideration of entire institutional frameworks. Reformers argued that not just liberalisation but also delegation to IRAs and sometimes even privatisation were required by EU law, yet in fact, neither were legally mandated and privatisation only entered discussions when governments in France or Italy 'bargained' with the European Commission to allow state aid in return for promises of later sales of government shares. Equally, reformers claimed that in a liberalised European market, national incumbents faced dangerous overseas competitors, especially privatised British firms such as BT or BA, and hence needed to be privatised to compete with these foreign rivals. A third argument was that EU liberalisation increased opportunities for international expansion, through takeovers, mergers and alliances, which in turn necessitated privatisation and acceptance of domestic liberalisation; this was seen in all sectors, including ones subject to little regulatory competition such as postal services.

Overall, the cases underline that the importance of supranational regulation lies as much in its wider indirect effects on domestic policy processes than on its direct legal requirements or goodness-of-fit with existing formal institutions. They show how Europeanisation involves opening up national policymaking to 'external' EU policies that become part of domestic calculations and strategies. The mechanisms of Europeanisation go well beyond producing legal adaptation pressures to include claimed imposition, fears of enhanced regulatory competition, and occasions for wider reforms. However, to appreciate fully how and why EU regulation was so powerful within policy processes, one must also examine the winners and losers from Europeanisation. For governments and incumbent suppliers, it offered both a source of pressure and of opportunities. It helped to create or reinforce coalitions between them for institutional changes and weakened their opponents, notably trade unions and employees. It offered opportunities and arguments for reforms that both responded to international developments and also provided unrelated domestic benefits. Thus a broader analysis of Europeanisation beyond 'goodness of fit' is needed due to its linkages with processes of legitimation and reconsideration of institutional structures.

CONCLUDING COMMENTS

Internationalisation represents an important force for institutional change. Powerful transnational technological and economic developments are transforming many sectors, putting pressures on existing institutions and closed national markets. Rival nations frequently alter their domestic institutions, offering sources of regulatory competition and examples of alternative institutional arrangements.

Supranational regulation is growing, not only by the EU but also other organisations such as the WTO. The second image reversal and comparative institutional models underline the need to integrate international factors into studies of domestic politics. The present study follows them, but argues that rather than treating international factors as external pressures that are mediated by diverse domestic settings, analyses should study how and why different forms of internationalisation can change those institutional settings. It suggests that internationalisation should be seen as part of the policy process: at the international level, where overseas decisions and supranational regulation are important forms of internationalisation; at the national level, where these forms become part of domestic policymaking concerning reform of economic institutions.

Interviews

Britain

Sir Kenneth Berrill, Chairman Securities and Investment Board 1986–92, Chairman of Vickers Da Costa, 1981–5.

Lord Borrie, Director General of Fair Trading 1976–92.

Rt. Hon. Christopher Chataway, Minister of Posts and Telecommunications 1970–2, Minister of State, Department of Trade and Industry 1972–4.

Sir Howard Davies, Chairman Financial Services Authority 1998–2002 Deputy Chairman Bank of England 1996–8.

Sir Nicholas Goodison, Chairman London Stock Exchange 1976–88.

Lord Patrick Jenkin, Secretary of State for Industry 1981–3.

Mr Paul Kirby, senior Department of Trade and Industry official.

Sir Andrew Large, Chairman of the Securities and Investments Board 1992–7 and Chairman of The Securities Association (TSA) 1987–8.

Sir David Walker, Executive Director Bank of England 1981–96, Chairman Securities and Investment Board 1988–92.

Mr Bill Wrigglesworth, senior civil servant, telecommunications matters, Department of Industry/Department of Trade and Industry, 1978–84, then Oftel Deputy Director General 1984–92, Oftel Director General 1992–3.

France

Mr Philip Auberger, Député and, Rapporteur général de la Commission des Finances, de l'Economie et du Plan à l'Assemblée Nationale 1993–7.

Mr Fabrice Demarigny, secrétaire général, Committee of European Securities Regulators (CESR).

Mr Alain Ferri, Agent de Change 1975, Président société de Bourse Ferri 1978–96, premier adjoint Chambre des Syndicat des Agents 1984–7, Président Association Française des Sociétés de Bourse and then l'Association Française des entreprises d'investissement 1993–6.

Mr Pierre Fleuriot, Chef du Service des études et du développement du marché Ministry of Finance 1986–91, Directeur Général of the Commission des Opérations de Bourse 1991–6, Président AMBRO Securities 2000.

Mr Bruno Lasserre, Délégué aux affaires juridiques de la direction générale des télécommunications 1986–9, Directeur de la réglementation générale au ministère des postes et télécommunications 1989–93, Directeur général des postes et télécommunications 1993–7, mission à la réglementation.

Mr Jean-François Lepetit, Conseil des Marchés Financiers 1996–2002 (président 1998–2002), président de la Commission des Opérations de Bourse (COB) 2002–3.

Senator Philippe Marini, Rapporteur Général de la commission des finances, Sénat.

Mr Gérard Moine, senior posts France Télécom 1992–2000, directeur de cabinet de Paul Quiles, Ministre de la Poste, des Télécommunications et de l'Espace, 1988–91, 1991–2 directeur de cabinet of Edith Cresson (Prime Minister).

Mr Michel Prada, président, Commission des Opération de la Bourse (COB) 1995–2002 and président, Autorité des Marchés Financiers (AMF) 2003–.

Mr Hubert Prévot, head, Prévot Commission 1988–9.

Mr Marcel Roulet, Directeur Général France Télécom 1986–95.

Mr Jean-François Théodore, directeur général de la Société des Bourses Françaises 1990–2000 (président-directeur général), and président-directeur général Euronext 2000–today.

Germany

Dr Rolf Breuer, Board member Deutsche Bank 1985–2002, spokesman of the board 1997–2002, president of the supervisory board 2002–2006, president of German Banking Association 2001–2006.

Dr Karl-Burkhard Caspari, Vice President BaFin.

Dr Gernot Ernst, former President Berlin Stock Exchange, President of ARGE (Arbeitsgemeinschaft der deutschen Wertpapierbörsen) 1986–93.

Dr Jörg Francke, Frankfurt stock exchange (Manager DTB) 1988, General Manager, Berlin Stock Exchange 1989.

Dr Werner Kerkloh, Federal Finance Ministry (Head of Unit for Securities and Stock Exchanges 2005).

Dr Andor Korwitz, head of Berlin Stock Exchange.

Mr Kübel-Sorger, Head of Frankfurt Stock Exchange 1989–93.

Mr Frederich von Metzler, Partner Metzler Bank 1971–today; Chairman Executive Board Frankfurter Wertpapierbörse 1989–93, Chairman Supervisory Board Frankfurter Wertpapierbörse/Deutsche Börse AG 1989–93, Member Supervisory Board Deutsche Börse AG 1993.

Dr Rüdiger von Rosen, Centre for Financial Studies Bundesbank 1986–95.

Italy

Professor Giuliano Amato, head of Autorità Garante della Concurrenza e del Mercato (AGCM) 1994–7; Prime Minister 1992–3, 2000–1.

Mr Salvatore Bragantini, member Consob 1996–2001.

Dr Reno Caiazzo, senior lawyer.

Mr Michele Calzolari, Agente di Cambio, head of a SIM and presdent Assosim 1998 (association of intermediaries, Associazione Italiana Intermediari Mobiliari).

Professor Filippo Cavazzuti, Under-Secretary, Treasury Ministry 1996–8.

Professor Enzo Cheli, President Autorità per le Garanzie nelle Communicazioni (AGCOM) 1998–2004.

Senator Franco Debenedetti.

Professor Mario Draghi, Director General of the Italian Treasury from 1991 to 2001.

Dr Guiliano Graziosi, 1984–90, Amministratore Delegato (head) STET.

Mr De Iulio, senior manager, Telecom Italia Mobile.

Senator Michele Lauria, Minister, Posts and Telecommunications 1996–8.

Dr Luigi Parcu, senior official, Autorità Garante della Concurrenza e del Mercato (AGCM).

Mr Pepe Rao, senior government adviser 1996–2001.

Cons Guido Salerno- senior official (Permanent Secretary) Postal and Telecommunication ministry.

Dr Franco Sircana, IRI 1963–81 and 1983–90.

Professor Luigi Spaventa, President Commissione Nazionale per le Società e la Borsa (CONSOB) 1998–2003.

References

AGCM [Autorità Garante della Concurrenza e del Mercato] (2005). *IC 24 Dinamiche Tariffarie del Trasporto Aereo Passeggeri*. Rome: Autorità Garante della Concurrenza e del Mercato.

Aguilar, J.-P. (2000). 'Frank Exchanges', *The Banker*, March: 96–7.

Albert, M. (1993). *Capitalism Against Capitalism*. London: Whurr.

Allen, H., Hawkins, J., and Sato, S. (2002). 'Electronic Trading and Its Implications for Financial Systems', in M. Balling, F. Lierman, and A. Mullineux (eds.), *Technology and Finance*. London: Routledge, pp. 204–39.

Almond, G. A. (1989). 'Review Article: The International-National Connection'. *British Journal of Political Science*, 19/2: 237–59.

Anderloni, L. and Pilley, O. (2001). 'Changing Context for Postal Systems in Europe', in R. Ruozi and L. Anderloni (eds.), *Modernisation and Privatisation of Postal Systems in Europe*. Berlin: Springer, pp. 9–72.

Andrews, D. M. (1994). 'Capital Mobility and State Autonomy: Toward a Structural Theory of International Monetary Relations', *International Studies Quarterly*, 38: 193–218.

Antonelli, C. (1993). 'The Dynamics of Technological Interrelatedness: The Case of Informations and Communications Technologies', in D. Foray and C. Freeman (eds.), *Technology and the Wealth of Nations*. London: Pinter, pp. 194–207.

Arnaboldi, F. and Bauer, E. (2002). 'The Experience of Flotation: The Cases of TNT-Post Group and Deutsche Post AG', in R. Ruozi and L. Anderloni (eds.), *Modernisation and Privatisation of Postal Systems in Europe*. Berlin: Springer, 73–126.

Arnold, T., Hersch, P., Mulherin, H., and Netter, J. (1999). 'Merging Markets', *The Journal of Finance*, 3: 1083–107.

Arzillo, F. (1999). 'Il sistema dell'intermediazione mobilare e la direttiva Eurosim', in G. Morelli (ed.), *La riforma dei mercati mobiliari italiani*. Rome: Bancaria.

Attali, B. (1994). *Les Guerre du Ciel. Cinq ans aux commandes d'Air France*. Paris: Fayard.

Aurelle, B. (1986). *Les télécommunications*. Paris: La Découverte.

Autier, F., Corcos, G., and Trépo, G. (2001). *Air France. Des années héroïques à la refondation*. Paris: Vuibert.

Autin, J.-L. (1989). 'La réforme de la COB. La consecration d'une instance régulatrice', *La Semaine Juridique, Cahiers de droit de l'entreprise*, March: 2–10.

Baccelli, O. and Senn, L. (2004). *Il trasporto aereo in Italia*. Milan: Egea.

Baldwin, R. (1985). *Regulating the Airline*. Oxford: Oxford University Press.

Barreau, J. (1995). *La Réforme des PTT*. Paris: La Découverte.

Bartle, I. (2002). 'When Institutions No Longer Matter: Reform of Telecommunications and Electricity in Germany, France, and Britain', *Journal of Public Policy*, 22/1: 1–27.

Batail, J. (1997). 'Le "marché intérieur de l'électricité', *Economies et Sociétés, Economie de l'Energie*, 7/5-6: 117–35.

Batstone, E., Ferner, A., and Terry, M. (1983). *Unions on the Board: An Experiment in Industrial Democracy*. Oxford: Blackwell.

Bealey, F. (1976). *The Post Office Engineering Union*. London: Bachman and Turner.

Beesley, M. (1981). *Liberalisation of the Use of British Telecommunications Network*. London: HMSO.

Belcredi, M. (1994). 'Regolamentazione e supervisione dell'attività di intermediazione finanziaria', in G. Nardozzi and G. Vaciago (eds.), *La Riforma della Consob nella prospettiva del mercato mobilaire europeo*. Bologna: Il Mulino.

Belhassine, L. (1997). *Le Ciel Confisqué*. Paris: Albin Michel.

Bennett, C. J. (1991). 'How States Utilize Foreign Evidence', *Journal of Public Policy*, 11/1: 31–54.

Benoit, R. (1989). 'La Commission des opérations de Bourse après la réforme d'août 1989', *Regards sur l'actualité*, 147: 147–56.

Bensoussan, A. and Pottier, I. (1991). 'Réglementation et concurrence', *Communications et Stratégies*, 2: 154–71.

Berger, S. and Dore, R. (eds.) (1996). *National Diversity and Global Capitalism*. Ithaca, NY: Cornell University Press.

Berry, F. and Berry, W. (1999). 'Innovation and Diffusion Models in Policy Research', in P. Sabatier (ed.), *Theories of the Policy Process*. Boulder, CO: Westview Press.

Bertho, C. (1981). *Télégraphes et téléphones: de Valmy au microprocesseur*. Paris: Le Livre de Poche.

——(ed.) (1991). *L'Etat et les Télécommunications en France et à l'étranger*. Geneva: Droz.

Beyer-Fehling, H. and Bock, A. (1975). *Die deutsche Börsenreform und Kommentar zur Börsengesetznovelle*. Frankfurt am Main. Knapp.

Bézard, P. (1989). 'Le Nouveau visage de la Commission des Opérations de Bourse', *Revue Internationale de Droit Comparé*, 41/4: 929–57.

Black, J. (1997). *Rules and Regulators*. Oxford: Clarendon Press.

Black, S. (2002). *Telecommunications Law in the Internet Age*. San Francisco, CA: Morgan Kaufmann.

Blair, M., Mingella, L., Taylor, M., and Threipland, M. (2000). *Blackstone's Guide to the Financial Services and Markets Act 2000*. Oxford: Oxford University Press.

Blanden, M. (1974). 'Ariel's Contentious Start', *The Banker*, January: 29–32.

Blandin-Oberrnesser, A. (1996). *Le Régime juridique communautaire des services des télécommunications*. Paris: Masson/Armand Collin/CNET-ENST.

Bleich, E. (2003). *Race Politics in Britain and France: Ideas and Policymaking Since the 1960s*. Cambridge: Cambridge University Press.

Blomquist, R. (1970). 'The Banking Year', *The Banker*, November: 1227–33.

Blyth, M. (2002). *Great Transformations: Economic Ideas and Institutional Change in the Twentieth Century*. New York: Cambridge University Press.

Boiteau, C. (1996). 'L'entreprise nationale France Télécom', *La Semaine Juridique*, 41: 379–84.

Böllhoff, D. (2005). *The Regulatory Capacities of Agencies*. Berlin: Berliner Wissenschafts-Verlag.

Boltho, A. (1996). 'Has France Converged on Germany? Policies and Institutions since 1958', in S. Berger and R. Dore (eds.), *National Diversity and Global Capitalism*. Ithaca, NY: Cornell University Press, pp. 89–104.

Bomberg, E. and Peterson, J. (2000). 'Policy Transfer and Europeanization: Passing the Heineken Test?', London: Political Studies Conference.

Bonnetblanc, G. (1985). *Les Télécommunications françaises. Quelle statut pour quelle entreprise?* Paris: La Documentation Française.

Börner, A.-R. (2001). 'Country Report: Germany', in D. Geradin (ed.), *The Liberalization of Electricity and Natural Gas in the European Union*. The Hague: Klewer, 155–68.

Borrie, G. (1986). 'Restrictive Practices Control in the United Kingdom', *The Journal of Business Law*, September: 358–71.

Bottiglieri, B. (1990). *SIP: Impresa, Tecnologia E Stato Nelle Telecomunicazioni Italiane*. Milan: Franco Angeli.

Boyer, R. (1996). 'The Convergence Hypothesis Revisited: Globalization but Still the Century of Nations?' in S. Berger and R. Dore (eds.), *National Diversity and Global Capitalism*. Ithaca, NY: Cornell University Press, pp. 29–59.

Braithwaite, J. and Drahos, P. (2000). *Global Business Regulation*. Cambridge: Cambridge University Press.

Bremer, H. (ed.) (1976). *Die Börsensachverständigenkommission 1968–1975. Aufgaben und Ergebnisse*. Berlin: Walter de Gruyter.

Brenac, E. and Payen, G. (1988). *Une politique en Dérive. La DGT et le Plan Câble*. Grenoble: Université de Grenoble.

Brock, G. W. (1981). *The Telecommunications Industry: The Dynamics of Market Structure*. Cambridge, MA. and London: Harvard University Press.

——(1994). *Telecommunications Policy for the Information Age: From Monopoly to Competition*. Cambridge, MA: Harvard University Press.

Brown, P. (1996). 'The Politics of the EU Single Market for Investment Services', in G. Underhill (ed.), *The New World Order in International Finance*. Houndmills, UK: MacMillan, pp. 124–43.

Büchner, L. M. (1995). 'The German Postal Reform of 1994', *Annals of Public and Cooperative Economics*, 66/4: 457–77.

Burgard, J.-J. (1972). 'La Commission des Opérations de Bourse', *Banque* 311: 861–70.

Button, K. (2000). 'Ownership and Regulation of International Airlines', in W. Bradshaw and H. Lawton Smith (eds.), *Privatisation and Deregulation of Transport*. Basingstoke: Palgrave: Macmillan, 307–34.

——(2004). *Wings Across Europe*. Aldershot: Ashgate.

Caiazzo, R. (2005). 'Italy', in P. Cameron (ed.), *Legal Aspects of EU Energy Regulation: Implementing the New Directives on Electricity and Gas across Europe*. Oxford: Oxford University Press, pp. 225–54.

Cameron, P. (2002). *Competition in Energy Markets*. Oxford: Oxford University Press.

——(2005). 'Completing the Internal Market in Energy', in P. Cameron (ed.), *Legal Aspects of EU Energy Regulation: Implementing the New Directives on Electricity and Gas across Europe*. Oxford: Oxford University Press, pp. 7–39.

Campbell, J. L. (1998). 'Institutional Analysis and the Role of Ideas in Political Economy', *Theory and Society*, 27/4: 377–409.

Campbell, R. M. (2002). *The Politics of Postal Transformation: Modernizing Postal Systems in the Electronic and Global World*. Montreal: McGill-Queen's University Press.

Campi, C. (1968). 'Osservazioni sul progretto di riforma della legislazione sulle borse valori', *Rivista delle Società*, 13: 771–98.

Canal, C. (1974). 'Foreign Banks under Fire', *The Banker*, September: 1108–11.

Canes, M. (1966). *Telephones—Public or Private?* London: Institute for Economic Affairs.

Caplain, M. (1971). *Rapport sure le marché des actions*. Paris: Commissariat du Plan.

Carsberg, B. (1989). 'Injecting Competition into Telecommunications', in C. Veljanovski (ed.), *Privatisation and Competition*. London: Institute for Economic Affairs, pp. 81–95.

——(1991). 'Office of Telecommunications: Competition and the Duopoly Review', in C. Veljanovski (ed.), *Regulators and the Market*. London: Institute for Economic Affairs, pp. 98–106.

Carter Committee (1978). *Report of the Post Office Review Committee, Cmnd 6850*. London: HMSO.

Cassese, S. (1976). *L'Amministrazione dello Stato*. Milan: Giuffrè.

—— (1986). 'I poteri della Consob per l'informazione del mercato', *Bancaria*, 10: 77–80.

—— (2000). *La nuova costituzione economica*. Rome: Laterza.

—— (2001). 'L'arena pubblica: Nuovi Paradigmi per lo Stato', *Rivista trimestrale di diritto pubblico*, 3: 601–50.

—— and Franchini, C. (eds.) (1996). *I garanti delle regole*. Bologna, Italy: Il Mulino.

Castells, M. (2002). *The Rise of the Network Society*, 2nd edn. Oxford: Blackwell.

Cawson, A., Holmes, P., Webber, D., Morgan, K., and Stevens, A. (1990). *Hostile Brothers*. Oxford: Clarendon Press.

Cerny, P. (1989). 'The "Little Big Bang" in Paris: Financial Market Deregulation in a Dirigiste System', *European Journal of Political Research*, 17/2: 169–92.

Cesarini, F. (1998). 'Il Processo di evoluzione delle borse in Italia e in Europa', *Bancaria*, 54/2: 89–93.

Chang, Y.-C. and Williams, G. (2002). 'European Major Airlines's Strategic Reactions to the Third Package', *Transport Policy*, 9: 129–42.

Chapman, C. (2002). *How the Stock Markets Work: A Guide to International Markets*. London: Random House Business.

Chatain, D. and de la Chapelle, J. (1987). 'Le réseau interurbain à l'aube de l'an 2000', *Revue Française des Télécommunications*, 63: 24–33.

Chenevoy-Gueriaud, M. (2004). 'L'Etablissement public industrial et commercial face au droit communautaire: la decision du 16 octobre 2002 de la Commission Européenne relative aux aides d'Etat à Electricité de France', *Revue de Recherche Juridique*, 3: 1955–90.

Chevallier, J. (1984). *L'Avenir de la Poste*. Paris: La Documentation Française.

—— (1989). 'Les enjeux juridiques: l'adaptation du service public des télécommunications', *Revue Française d'Administration Publique*, 52: 37–52.

—— (1990). 'La mutation des postes et télécommunications', *Actualité Juridique—Droit Administratif*, October: 667–87.

—— (1996). 'La nouvelle réforme des télécommunications: ruptures et continuités', *Revue Française de Droit Administratif*, 12/5: 909–51.

—— (2003). 'Quelle politique de l'énergie en France et en Europe', *Revue Politique et Parlementaire*, 1026: 26–38.

Chiappetta, F. and Napoli, S. (1985). *Le telecomunicazioni in Italia*. Rome: Bulzoni.

Choinel, A. (1990). *Le Marché Financier: Structures Et Acteurs*. Paris: La Banque.

Clark, J., McLoughlin, I., Rose, H., and King, R. (1988). *The Process of Technological Change*. Cambridge: Cambridge University Press.

Clark, R. and Sherrington, M. (1980). 'Telecommunications and Financial Markets', *The Banker*, March: 95–101.

Clarke, W. (1979). *Inside the City: A guide to London as a Financial Centre*. London: Allen and Unwin.

Clifton, J., Comín, F., and Díaz Fuentes, D. (2006). 'Privatizing public enterprises in the European Union 1960-2002: ideological, pragmatic, inevitable?', *Journal of European Public Policy*, 13/5: 736–56.

Coen, D. (2005*a*). 'Changing Business-Regulator Relations in Germany and the UK', in D. Coen and A. Héritier (eds.), *Refining Regulatory Regimes: Utilities in Europe*. Cheltenham: Edward Elgar, pp. 91–119.

—— (2005*b*). 'Managing the Political Life Cycle of Regulation in the UK and German Telecommunication Sectors', *Annals of Public and Cooperative Economics*, 76/1: 59–84.

────── and Böllhoff, D. (2002) *Regulating the Utilities: Business and Regulator Perspectives in the UK and Germany*, Berlin: Anglo-German Foundation.

────── (eds.) (2005). *Refining Regulatory Regimes*. Cheltenham: Edward Elgar.

────── and Thatcher, M. (eds.) (2001). *Utilities Reform in Europe*. Huntington, WV: Nova Science.

────── (2005). 'The New Governance of Markets', special issue, *Governance*, 18/3.

Cohen, E. (1992). *Le colbertisme 'high tech'*. Paris: Hachette.

Coleman, W. and Underhill, R. (1995). 'Globalization, Regionalism and the Regulation of Securities Markets', *Journal of European Public Policy*, 2/3: 488–513.

Commission of the European Communities (1987). *Towards a Dynamic European Economy—Green Paper on the Development of the Common Market for Telecommunications Services and Equipment* COM(87) 290, 30 June 1987.

────── (1988). *Commission Directive of 16 May 1988 on Competition in the Markets in Telecommunications Terminal Equipment* 88/301/EEC OJ L 131/73, 27.5.88.

────── (1990). *Commission Directive of 28 June 1990 on Competition in the Markets for Telecommunications Services* 90/388/EEC, OJ L 192/10, 24.7.90.

────── (1994), *Commission Directive 94/46/EC of 13 October 1994 amending Directive 88/301/EEC and Directive 90/388/EEC in particular with regard to satellite communications* OJ L268/15.

────── (1995), *Commission Directive of 18 October 1995 amending Directive 90/388/EEC with regard to the abolition of the restrictions on the use of cable television networks for the provision of already liberalised telecommunications networks*, OJ L 256/49, 26.10.95.

────── (1996a), *Commission Directive 96/2/EC of 16 January 1996 amending Directive 90/388/EEC with regard to mobile and personal communications*, OJ 1996 L20/59.

────── (1996b), *Commission Directive of 28 February 1996 amending Directive 90/388/EEC regarding the implementation of full competition in telecommunications markets*, Directive 96/19/EC, OJ L 74/13, 22.3.96.

Commissione Morganti (1983). *Rapporto al Presidente del Consiglio sulle Telecomunicazioni*. Milan: Franco Angeli.

Conac, P.-H. (2002). *La Régulation des marchés boursiers pas la Commission des Opérations de Bourse (COB) et la Securities and Exchange Commission*. Paris: LGDJ.

Conruyt, P. (1988). 'Reseaux à valeur ajoutée: une demande évolutive', *Revue Française des Télécommunications*, 65: 70–77.

Conseil d'État (2000). *Rapport Public 2001*. Paris: La documentation Française.

Coquelet, M.-L. (2004). 'Recours contre les décisions de l'AMF' in H. de Vauplane and J. Daigre (eds.), *Droit Bancaire et Financier: Mélanges AEDBF-France IV*. Paris: Banque.

Cortell, A. P. and Peterson, S. (1999). 'Altered States: Explaining Domestic Institutional Change', *British Journal of Political Science*, 29: 177–203.

Council of the European Communities (1989). *Council Directive 89/592/EEC of 13 November 1989 coordinating regulations on insider dealing*. OJ L 334 , 18.11.89.

────── (1990). *Council Directive 90/387/EEC of 28 June 1990 on the Establishment of the Internal Market for Telecommunications Services through the Implementation of Open Network Provision*. OJ L 192/1, 24.07.90.

────── (1992a). *Council Regulation (EEC) no. 2409/92 of 23 July 1992 on Fares and Rates for Air Services*. OJ L240, 24.8.1992, p. 15.

────── (1992b). *Council Regulation (EEC) no. 2408/92 of 23 July 1992 on Access for Community Air Carriers to Intra-Community Air Routes*. OJ L240, 24.8.1992: p. 8.

Council of the European Communities (1992c). *Council Regulation (EEC) no. 2408/92 of 23 July 1992 on Licensing of Air Carriers.* OJ L240, 24.8.1992, p. 1.

——(1993a), *Council Directive 93/22/EEC of 10 May 1993 on investment services in the securities field.* OJ L 141, 11.6.199.

——(1993b). *Council Regulation (EEC) no. 95/93 of 18 January 1993 on Common Rules for the Allocation of Slots at Community Airports.* OJ L14, 22.1.1993, p. 1.

——(1995). *Council Directive 95/62/EC of 13 December 1995 on the Application of Open Network Provision (ONP) to Voice Telephony.* OJ L 321/6, 30.12.95.

Courbis, B. and Dupuy, C. (1989). 'Paris et Londres face à la mondialisation', *Revue d'Economie Financière,* 10: 138–50.

Couret, A. (1988). 'Le Big-Bang français', *Bulletin Joly,* February: 1–149.

—— Martin, D., and Faugérolas, L. (1989). 'Sécurité et transparence du marché financier', *Bulletin Joly,* 11bis: 1–141.

Crandall, R. W. (1991). *After the Breakup: U.S. Telecommunications in a More Competitive Era.* Washington, DC: Brookings Institute.

—— and Waverman, L. (1995). *Talk Is Cheap: The Promise of Regulatory Reform in North American Telecommunications.* Washington, DC: Brookings Institute.

Cristini, G. (1999). 'Nuovi assetti istituzionali e operative aperti dal decreto Eurosim', in G. Morelli (ed.), *La riforma dei mercati mobiliari italiani.* Rome: Bancaria.

Crouch, C. and Streeck, W. (eds.) (1997). *Political Economy of Modern Capitalism: Mapping Convergence and Diversity.* London: Sage.

Czada, R. (ed.) (2000). *Von der Bonner zur Berliner Republik: 10 Jahre Deutsche Einheit.* Wiesbaden: Westdeutscher Verlag.

Dandelot, M. (1993). *Le secteur des Télécommunications en France: Rapport au Ministre de l'Industrie, des Postes et Télécommunications et du Commerce Extérieur.* Paris: PTT Ministry.

Darmon, J. (1985). *Le Grand Dérangement.* Paris: Lattes.

De la Serre, R. (1991). *'L'Avenir de l'Intermédiation Bousière en France.* Paris: Conseil des Bourses de Valeurs.

De Witt, F. (1985), 'Paris place financière', *L'Expansion,* 19.4.85.

Decoopman, N. (1979). *La Commission des opérations de bourse et le droit des sociétés.* Paris: Economica.

——(2003). 'La Nouvelle Architecture des Autorités Financières', *Doctrine,* 42: 1817–22.

Deeg, R. (2005). 'Change from Within. German and Italian Finance in the 1990s', in W. Streeck and K. Thelen (eds.), *Beyond Continuity. Institutional Change in Advanced Political Economies.* Oxford: Oxford University Press, pp. 169–202.

—— and Lütz, S. (2000). 'Internationalization and Financial Federalism', *Comparative Political Studies,* 33/3: 374–405.

Degryse, H. and Achter, A. van (2002). 'Alternative Trading Systems and Liquidity', in M. Balling, F. Lierman, and A. Mullineux (eds.), *Technology and Finance.* London: Routledge, pp. 171–89.

Delebarre, M. (1997). *Les enjeux d'avenir pour France Télécom.* Paris: PTE Ministry.

Delion, A. and Durupty, M. (2005). 'La loi de regulation postale et l'évolution de la Poste', *Revue Française d'Administration Publique,* 114: 352–4.

Department of Trade and Industry (1987). *Class Licence for the Running of Telecommunications Systems Providing Value Added and Data Services.* London: Department of Trade and Industry.

——(1991). *Competition and Choice: Telecommunications Policy for the 1990s, Cmnd 1461.* London: HMSO.

Department of Trade and Industry (1997). *Telecommunications Liberalisation in the* U.K. London: Department of Trade and Industry.

Derenne, J. and Stockford, C. (2002). 'Abuse of Market Power in Postal Services', in D. Geradin (ed.), *The Liberalization of Postal Services in the European Union*. The Hague: Klewer.

Desema, C. (2003). '1990–2003: heures et malheurs de la libéralisation du marché de l'électricité', *Revue Politique et Parlementaire*, 1026: 80–4.

DGPT, (1994) *Quelle réglementation pour les télécommunications françaises?* Paris: Ministère de l'Industrie, des Postes et des Télécommunications et du Commerce Extérieur.

DGT (Direction Générale des Télécommunications), *Statistique Annuelle*. Paris: DGT/France Télécom, annual.

Di Porto, F. and Silva, F. (2005). 'Rimformare le utilities è difficile: il caso elettrico italiano', *Mercato, Concorrenza, Regole*, 7/1: 11–50.

Didier, M. and Lorenzi, J.-H. (2002). *Enjeux économiques de l'UMTS*. Paris: La Documentation Française.

Dienel, H.-L. (1988). 'Lufthansa: Two German Airlines', in H.-L. Dienel and P. Lyth (eds.), *Flying the Flag. European Commercial Air Transport since 1945*. Basingstoke: Macmillan, pp. 87–125.

——— and Lyth, P. (eds.) (1988). *Flying the Flag. European Commercial Air Transport since 1945*. Basingstoke: Macmillan.

DiMaggio, P. J. and Powell, W. W. (1991). 'Institutional Isomorphism and Collective Rationality', in W. W. Powell and P. J. DiMaggio (eds.), *The New Institutionalism in Organizational Analysis*. Chicago, IL: University of Chicago Press, pp. 63–82.

Djelic, M.-L. (1998). *Exporting the American Model: the Postwar Transformation of European Business*. Oxford: Oxford University Press.

Dobbin, F. (1994). *Forging Industrial Policy. The United States, Britain, and France in the Railway Age*. Cambridge: Cambridge University Press.

Dobson, A. P. (1995). *Flying in the Face of Competition: the Policies and Diplomacy of Airline Regulatory Reform in Britain, the USA and the European Community*. Aldershot: Ashgate.

Docquiert, H. (1987). *SOCOTEL: Expérience de coopération Etat-Industrie*. Paris: Socotel.

Doganis, R. (1991). *Flying Off Course*. London: Routledge.

Döhler, M. (2002). 'Institutional Choice and Bureaucratic Autonomy in Germany', *West European Politics*, 25(1): 101–24.

Dolowitz, D. and Marsh, D. (1996). 'Who Learns What from Whom? A Review of the Policy Transfer Literature', *Political Studies*, 44/2: 343–57.

——— ——— (2000). 'Learning from Abroad: The Role of Policy Transfer in Contemporary Policy-Making', *Governance*, 13/1: 5–24.

Domowitz, I. and Steil, B. (2002). 'Securities Trading', in B. Steil, D. G. Victor, and R. R. Nelson (eds.), *Technological Innovation and Economic Performance*. Princeton, NJ: Princeton University Press, pp. 314–26.

Donnedieu de Vabres, J. (1980). 'La COB : Une administration de mission', *Revue Administrative*, 195: 237–41.

Donnell, E. (1970). 'Subsidiary Activities—the Reasons Why', *The Banker*, November 1970: 1235–38.

Draghi, M. (1999). 'Il mercato finanziario ad una svolta', in G. Morelli (ed.), *La riforma dei mercati mobiliari italiani*. Rome: Bancaria.

Dupont, X. (1986). 'Bourse de Paris: le défi de la mondialisation', *Politique Internationale*, 31: 89–95.

Dyson, K. and Humphreys, P. (eds.) (1990). *The Political Economy of Telecommunications.* London and New York: Routledge.

Eberlein, B. (2000). 'Institutional Change and Continuity in German Infrastructure Management: The Case of Electricity Reform', *German Politics*, 9/3: 81–104.

——and Grande, E. (2000). 'Regulation and Infrastructure Management: German Regulatory Regimes and the EU Framework', *German Policy Studies*, 1/1: 39–66.

——(2005). 'Beyond delegation: transnational regulatory regimes and the EU regulatory state'. *Journal of European Public Policy* 12/1: 89–112.

——and Kerwer, D. (2004). 'New Governance in the European Union: A Theoretical Perspective', *Journal of Common Market Studies*, 42/1: 121–42.

Eising, R. (1999). 'Reshuffling power. The liberalisation of the EU electricity markets and its impact on the German governance regime.' in B. Kohler-Koch and R. Eising (eds.), *The Transformation of Governance in the European Union.* London, New York: 1999, pp. 208–28.

——(2000). *Liberalisierung und Europäisierung: Die regulative Reform der Elektrizitätsversorgung in Großbritannien, der Europäischen Gemeinschaft und der Bundesrepublik Deutschland.* Opladen: Leske and Budrich.

——(2002). 'Policy Learning in Embedded Negotiations: Explaining EU Electricity Liberalization', *International Organization*, 56/1: 85–120.

——and Jabko, N. (2001). 'Moving Targets: National Interests and Electricity Liberalization in the European Union', *Comparative Political Studies*, 34/7: 742–67.

Elixmann, D. and Hermann, H. (1996). 'Strategic Alliances in the Telecommunications Service Sector: Challenges for Corporate Strategy', *Communications et Stratégies*, 24: 57–88.

Encaoua, D. and Koebel, P. (1986). *Réglementation et Déréglementation des Télécommunications: Leçons Anglo-Saxonnes et Perspectives d'Evolution en France.* Paris: Direction de la Prévision.

Espérou, R. (1999). 'Bilateral Relations between France and the United States. The Air Transport Agreement of 18 June 1998 Seen in Perspective', *ITA Studies and Reports*, 48: 17–20.

European Commission (1992). *Green Paper on the Development of the Single Market for Postal Service.* COM/91/476.

——(1999). *Commission Communication on Implementing the Framework for Financial Markets: Action Plan,* COM 232. Brussels: Commission of the European Communities.

——(1999). *Financial Services: Implementing the Framework for Financial Markets: Action Plan Communication from the Commission.* COM 232, 11.05.99.

——(2000). *Communication on Upgrading the Investment Directive.* (93/22/EC), COM(2000)729.

European Commission (2001). *First Benchmarking Report on the Implmentation of the Internal Electricity and Gas Market.* Commission Staff Working Paper, SEC 1957, 3.12.2001.

——(2003). *Second Benchmarking Report on the Implementation of the Internal Electricity and Gas Market.* Commission Staff Working Paper SEC 448, 7.4.2003.

——(2005). *Development of Competition in the European Postal Sector.* MARKT/2004/03/C, Annex II.

European Council (1977). *Directive 77/780/EEC on the Coordination of Laws, Regulations and Administrative Procedures Relating to the Taking-Up and Pursuit of the Business of Credit Institutions* [First Banking Coordination Directive], OJ L322/30.

_____ (1979). *Directive 79/279/EEC Coordinating the Conditions for the Admission of Securities to Official Stock Exchange Listing* [Admission Directive]. OJ L66/21.

European Parliament and Council (1997a). *Directive 97/13/EC on a Common Framework for General Authorizations and Individual Licences in the Field of Telecommunications Services.* OJ L 117/15, 7.5.97.

_____ (1997b). *Directive 97/51/EC of the European Parliament and of the Council Amending Council Directives 90/387/EEC and 92/44/EEC for the Purpose of Adaptation to a Competitive Environment.* OJ L 295/23, 29.10.97.

_____ (1997c). *Directive 97/33/EC of the European Parliament and of the Council on Interconnection in Telecommunications with Regard to Ensuring Universal Service and Interoperability through Application of the Principles of Open Network Provision (ONP).* OJ L199/32, 29.10.97.

_____ (2002a). *Directive of the European Parliament and of the Council on a Common Regulatory Framework for Electronic Communications of Networks and Services (Framework Directive).* OJ L 108, 24.4.2002, p. 33.

_____ (2002b). *Directive of the European Parliament and of the Council on Access to, and Interconnection of, Electronic Communications Networks and Associated Facilities (Access Directive).* OJ L 108, 24.4.2002, p. 7.

_____ (2002c). *Directive of the European Parliament and of the Council on the Authorisation of Electronic Communications Networks and Services (Authorisation Directive).* OJ L 108, 24.4.2002, p. 21.

_____ (2002d). *Directive 2002/39/EC of the European Parliament and of the Council of 10 June 2002 Amending Directive 97/67/EC with Regard to the Further Opening to Competition of Community Postal Services.* OJ L 176, 05/07/2002: 21–25.

_____ (2003a). *Directive 2003/54/EC of the European Parliament and Council Concerning Common Rules for the Internal Market in Electricity.* OJ L176/37, 15 July.

_____ (2003b). *Regulation No. 1228/2003 of the European Parliament and of the Council of 26 June 2003 on Conditions for Access to the Network for Cross-Border Exchanges in Electricity.* OJ l176/1, 15.7.2003.

European Parliament and Council (2003c). *Directive2003/6/EC of the European Parliament and of the Council of 28 January 2003 on insider dealing and market manipulation (market abuse).* O.J. L 96 12.04.2003.

_____ (2004). *Directive 2004/39/EC of the European Parliament and of the Council of 21 April 2004 on Markets in Financial Instruments Amending Council Directives 85/611/EEC and 93/6/EEC and Directive 2000/12/EC of the European Parliament and of the Council and Repealing Council Directive 93/22/EEC.* OJ L 145, 30.04.2004 P. 0001–0044.

Evans, P. B., Jacobson, H. K., and Putnam, R. D. (eds.) (1993). *Double-Edged Diplomacy. International Bargaining and Domestic Politics.* Berkeley, CA: University of California Press.

Featherstone, K. and Radaelli, C. (2003). *The Politics of Europeanisation.* Oxford: Oxford University Press.

Feigenbaum, H., Henig, J., and Hamnett, C. (1999). *Shrinking the State: The Political Underpinnings of Privatization.* Cambridge: Cambridge University Press.

Ferrarini, G. (1998). 'La riforma dei mercati finanziari e il testo unico', in G. Ferrarini and P. Marchetti (eds.), *La Riforma dei mercati finanziari.* Rome: Edibank.

Finon, D. (2003). 'Introducing Competition in the French Electricity Supply Industry', in J.-M. Glanchant and D. Finon (eds.), *Competition in European Electricity Markets.* Cheltenham: Edward Elgar, pp. 257–84.

Fligstein, N. (2001). *The Architecture of Markets: An Economic Sociology of Twenty-First Century Capitalist Societies*. Princeton, NJ: Princeton University Press.

Fontaine, N. (2003). 'L'avenir érnergetique européen et le modèle français', *Revue Politique et Parlementaire*, 1026: 14–7.

Foreman-Peck, J. and Manning, D. (1988). 'Telecommunciations in Italy', in J. Foreman-Peck and J. Müller (eds.), *European Telecommunications Organisation*. Baden-Baden: Nomos, pp. 181–201.

Franke, G. (2001). *Deutsche Finanzmarktregulierung nach dem Zweiten Weltkrieg zwischen Risikoschutz und Wettebwerbssicherung Bankhistorisches Archiv, Beiheft*, 39, Regulierung zwischen Risikoschutz und Wettbewerbssicherung, pp. 66–87.

Fraser, D. and Rose, P. S. (eds.) (1980). *Financial Institutions and Markets in a Changing World*. Dallas, TX: Business Publications.

Frieden, J. A. and Rogowski, R. (1996). 'The Impact of the International Political Economy on National Policies', in R. O. Keohane and H. Milner (eds.), *Internationalization and Domestic Politics*. Cambridge: Cambridge University Press, pp. 25–47.

Frison-Roche, A.-M. (2004). 'Les contours de l'Autorité des marchés financiers', in H. de Vauplane and J. Daigre (eds.), *Droit Bancaire et Financier. Mélanges AEDBF-France IV*. Paris: Banque.

Frova, S. (2003). *UMTS: Protagonisti, tecnologia, finanza e regolamentazione*. Milan: EGEA.

Fry, R. (1969). 'Financial Centers of the World', *The Banker*, July: 617–24.

Gallon, S. (2000). 'La fin du monopole d'EDF en France et la concurrence sur le marché européen de l'électricité', *Regards sur l'Actualité*, 263: 3–25.

Garrett, G. (1995). 'Capital Mobility, Trade, and the Domestic Politics of Economic Policy', *International Organization*, 49/4: 657–87.

—— (1998). *Partisan politics in the global economy*. Cambridge and New York: Cambridge University Press.

Garrett, G. and Lange, P. (1996). Internationalization, Institutions, and Political Change', in R. O. Keohane and H. Milner (eds.), *Internationalization and Domestic Politics*. Cambridge: Cambridge University Press, pp. 48–78.

Gart, A. (1994). *Regulation, Deregulation, and Reregulation*. New York: John Wiley & Sons.

Gassot, Y., Pouillet, D., and Balcon, L. (2000). The Merger and Acquisition Frenzy', *Communications et Stratégies*, 38: 159–96.

Geneste, B. [Bernard] (1997). 'La libéralisation du marché de l'électricité', *Revue des affaires européennes-Law and European Affaires*, 2: 146–56.

Gensollen, M. (1991). 'Les réformes institutionelles et réglementaires des télécommunications en 1990', *Communications et Stratégies*, 3: 17–34.

George, A. L. and Bennett, A. (2004). *Case Studies and Theory Development in the Social Sciences*. Cambridge, MA: MIT Press.

George, S. (1998). *An Awkward Partner: Britain in the European Community*. Oxford: Oxford University Press.

Geradin, D. and Humpe, C. (2002). 'The Liberalisation of Postal Services in the European Union', in D. Geradin (ed.), *The Liberalization of Postal Services in the European Union*. The Hague: Kluwer, 91–109.

Gerring, J. (2004). 'What Is a Case Study and What Is It Good For?', *American Political Science Review*, 98/2: 341–54.

Giacalone, D. (1992). *Italia Chiama Europa: Politica e telecomunicazioni*. Rome: DEA Editrice.

—— and Vergnano, F. (1990). *La Guerra del Telefono*. Milan: Il Sole 24 Ore.

Giddens, A. (2000). *Runaway World*. New York: Routledge.

Gilardi, F. (2005). 'The Institutional Foundations of Regulatory Capitalism: The Diffusion of Independent Regulatory Agencies in Western Europe', *The Annals of the American Academy of Political and Social Science*, 598: 84–101.

Giraudi, G. and Righettini, M. (2001). *Le autorità amministrative independenti*. Rome: Laterza.

Giurisprudenza Commerciale (1975). 'Dibattiti: problemi attuali delle borse volori' [Presentations by several speakers, including U. Aletti and F. Caffé, S. Cassese, F. Cesarini, G. Castellano, G. Minervini, G. Tagi].

Glancher, J.-M. and Finon, D. (2003). *Competition in European Electricity Markets: A Cross-Country Comparison*. Cheltenham: Edward Elgar.

Gobbo F. and Zanetti G. (2000). 'Istituziozioni e mercato: il ruolo delle Autorità nell'economia italiana', *L'Industria*, 21/4.

Goldstein, J. and Keohane, R. O. (eds.) (1993). *Ideas and Foreign Policy: Beliefs, Institutions, and Political Change*. Ithaca, NY: Cornell University Press.

Gomez-Ibanez, J. (2003). *Regulating Infrastructure*. Cambridge, MA: Harvard University Press.

Goodison, N. (1988). 'London's Place in the Global Securities Market', *International Affairs*, 64/4: 575–83.

Goodman, J. B. and Pauly L. B. (1993). 'The Obsolescence of Capital Controls? Economic Management in an Age of Global Markets', *World Politics*, 46/1: 50–82.

Goulard, F. (2003). *Sécurité financière*. Paris: Assemblée Nationale.

Gourevitch, P. (1978). 'The Second Image Reversed: The International Sources of Domestic Politics', *International Organization*, 32/4, 881–912.

—— (1986). *Politics in Hard Times: Comparative Responses to International Economic Crises*. Ithaca, NY: Cornell University Press.

Gower, L. C. B. (1984). *Review of investor protection: report part 1*. Cmnd.9125. London: HMSO.

—— (1988). ' "Big Bang" and City Regulation', *Modern Law Review*, 51/1: 1–22.

Grabar, N. (1988). La Commission des operations de Bourse à la lumière de l'expérience américaine', *Le Débat*, 52: 67–75.

Grande, E. (1989). *Vom Monopol zum Wettbewerb? Die neokonservative Reform der Telekommunikation in Großbritannien und der Bundesrepublik Deutschland*. Wiesbaden: Deutscher Universitätsverlag.

Grazia, V. de (2005). *Irresistible Empire*. Cambridge, MA: Harvard University Press.

Green Cowles, M., Caporaso J., Risse, T., and Héritier, R. (eds.) (2001). *Transforming Europe*. Ithaca, NY: Cornell University Press.

Greene, M. (1981). 'Automation of Foreign Exchange and Other Trading Operations', *The Banker*, April: 119–23.

Grundfest, J. A. (1990). 'Internationalization of the World's Securities Markets: Economic Causes and Regulatory Consequences'. *Journal of Financial Services Research* 4: 349–378.

Guillaume-Hofnung, M. (1982). 'Réflexions sur la nature juridique de la Commission des opérations de Bourse', *Revue du droit public* 98: 1343–82.

Haas, P. (1992). 'Introduction: Epistemic Communities and International Policy Coordination', *International Organization*, 46/1: 1–35.

Hadding, W. and Schneider, U. H. (eds.) (1987). *Beiträge zum Börsenrecht*. Frankfurt am Main: Knapp.

Haggard, S. (1990). *Pathways from the Periphery: The Politics of Growth in the Newly Industrializing Countries*, Ithaca, NY: Cornell University Press.

Hall, C., Scott, C., and Hood, C. (2000). *Telecommunications Regulation; Culture, Chaos, and Interdependence Inside the Regulatory Process*. London: Routledge.

Hall, P. A. (1986). *Governing the Economy*. Cambridge: Polity Press.

——(ed.) (1989). *The Political Power of Economic Ideas: Keynesianism across Nations*. Princeton, NJ: Princeton University Press.

——(1993). Policy Paradigms, Social Learning, and the State', *Comparative Politics*, 25/3: 275–96.

——and Soskice, D. (eds.) (2001a). *Varieties of Capitalism. The Institutional Foundations of Comparative Advantage*. Oxford: Oxford University Press.

————(2001b). 'An Introduction to Varieties of Capitalism', in P. A. Hall and D. Soskice (eds.), *Varieties of Capitalism. The Institutional Foundations of Comparative Advantage*. Oxford: Oxford University Press, pp. 1–68.

——(2007). 'The Evolution of Varieties of Capitalism in Europe' in In B. Hancke, M Rhodes and M Thatcher (eds.), *Beyond Varieties of Capitalism*. Oxford: Oxford University Press, pp. 39–86.

Hallerberg, M. and Basinger, S. (1998). 'Internationalization and Changes in Tax Policy in OECD Countries. The Importance of Domestic Veto Players', *Comparative Political Studies* 31/3: 321–52.

Hamilton, A. (1986). *The Financial Revolution*. New York: Free Press.

Haney, S. (1985). 'Deregulation: Plugging in for the "Big Bang" ', *The Banker*, November: 85–8.

Hancher, L. and Moran, M. (eds.) (1989). *Capitalism, Culture and Economic Regulation*. Oxford: Clarendon Press.

Hancké, B. (2001). 'Revisiting the French Model: Coordination and Restructuring in French Industry', in P. A. Hall and D. Soskice (eds.), *Varieties of Capitalism. The Institutional Foundations of Comparative Advantage*. Oxford: Oxford University Press, pp. 307–34.

Hanne, H. (2004). 'La libéralisation des télécommunications et de la poste en France', *Regards sur l'actualité*, 306: 19–31.

Hansen, R. and King, D. (2001). 'Eugenic Ideas, Political Interests, and Policy Variance,' *World Politics*, 53: 237–63.

Harington, H. (1993). 'Welders at the Ready', *The Banker*, December: 48–51.

Haverland, M. (2000). 'National Adaptation to European Integration: The Importance of Institutional Veto Points'. *Journal of Public Policy* 20/1: 83–103.

Hayward, J. E. S. (1976). 'Institutional Inertia and Political Impetus in France and Britain'. *European Journal of Political Research* 4: 341–59.

—— (ed.) (1995). *Industrial Enterprise and European Integration. From National to Internationalized Champions: Firms and Governments in the West European Economy*. Oxford: Oxford University Press.

Heinen, A. (2002). 'Germany', in D. Geradin (ed.), *The Liberalization of Postal Services in the European Union*. The Hague: Kluwer, pp. 225–78.

Held, D., McGrew, A., Goldblatt, D., and Perraton, J. (1999). *Global Transformations: Politics, Economics, and Culture*. Cambridge: Polity Press.

Helleiner, E. (1994). *States and the Reemergence of Global Finance*. Ithaca, NY: Cornell University Press.

Héritier, A., Kerwer, D., Knill, C., Lehmkuhl, D., Teutsch, M., and Douillet, A. (eds.) (2001). *Differential Europe: The European Union Impact on National Policymaking*. Lanham, MD: Rowman and Littlefield.

—— (2005). 'Managing Regulatory Developments in Rail', in D. Coen and A. Héritier (eds.), *Refining Regulatory Regimes: Utilities in Europe*. Cheltenham: Edward Elgar, pp. 120–44.

Hill, M. (1997). *The policy process in the modern state* (3rd ed.). London: Prentice Hall.

Hills, J. (1984). *Information Technology and Industrial Policy*. London and Canberra: Croom Helm.

—— (1986). *Deregulating Telecoms: Competition and Control in the United States, Japan, and Britain*. London: Pinter.

Hirst, D. and Thompson, G. (1999). *Globalization in Question*. Cambridge: Polity Press.

Hiscox, M. (2002). 'Commerce, Coalitions, and Factor Mobility: Evidence from Congressional Votes on Trade Legislation', *American Political Science Review*, 96/3: 593–608.

Hollingsworth, J. R. and Boyer, R. (eds.) (1997). *Contemporary Capitalism: The Embeddedness of Institutions*. New York: Cambridge University Press.

Horstmann, W. (1997). 'Postal Monopolies in Industrialized Countries: A Case for Dergulation', *Zeitschrift für Wirtshaftspolitik*, 46/3: 302–23.

Horwitz, R. B. (1989). *The Irony of Regulatory Reform: The Deregulation of American Telecommunications*. New York and Oxford: Oxford University Press.

House of Commons Environment, Transport and Regional Affairs Committee (2000). *Eighteenth Report*. London: HMSO.

Houthakker, H.S. and Williamson. P. J. (1996). *The economics of financial markets*. New York: Oxford University Press.

Huber, P. W., Kellog, M. K., and Thorne, J. (1996). *The Telecommunications Act of 1996*. New York: Little Brown.

Humphreys, G. (1986). 'Paris Brokers Give Up Their Quill Pens', *Euromoney*, October: 42–7.

Ikenberry, J. (1990). 'The International Spread of Privatization Policies: Inducements, Learning, and "Policy Bandwagoning"', in E. Sulieman and J. Waterbury (eds.), *The Political Economy of Public Sector Reform and Privatization*. Boulder, CO: Westview Press, pp. 88–108.

Immergut, E. M. (1992). *Health Politics: Interests and Institutions in Western Europe*. Cambridge: Cambridge University Press.

Institute of Contemporary British History (1999). 'Witness Seminar: "Big Bang"', *Contemporary British History*, 13/1: 100–32.

ITC (Independent Television Commission) (2001). *ITC Welcomes Double Dividend*. London: ITC Press Release.

Jaeger, P. G. (1985). 'La Legge n281 ed I nuovi poteri della Consob', *Jurisprudenza commerciale*, I: 946–58.

James, H. (1998). 'Die Reichsbank 1876 bis 1945', in Deutsche Bundesbank (ed.), *Fünfzig Jahre Deutsche Mark*. Munich: Deutsche Bundesbank, pp. 29–89.

James, O. and Lodge, M. (2003). 'The Limitations of "Policy Transfer" and "Lesson Drawing" for Public Policy Research', *Political Studies Review*, 1/2: 179–93.

James, P. (ed.) (2001). *The Financial Services and Markets Act, A Practical Legal Guide*. London: Sweet and Maxwell.

Jenkins, W. I. (1978). *Policy analysis: a political and organisational perspective*. London: Martin Robertson.

John, P. (1998). *Analysing public policy*. London: Pinter.

Jönsson, C. (1987). *International Aviation and the Politics of Regime Change*. London: Pinter.

Kahler, M. (1984). *Decolonization in Britain and France: the domestic consequences of international relations*. Princeton, NJ: Princeton University Press

Kassim, H. (1996). 'Air Transport', in H. Kassim and A. Menon (eds.), *The European Union and National Industrial Policy*. London: Routledge.

Katz, D. (2003). 'La Commission européenne conteste le statut d'établissement public industriel et commercial d'EDF au regard du regime des aides d'Etat', *La Semaine Juridique Administrations et Collectivités territoriales*, 43: 1378–9.

Katzenstein, P. (1978). *Between Power and Plenty: Foreign Economic Policies of Advanced Industrial States*. Madison, WI: University of Madison Press.

――― (1985). *Small States in World Markets: Industrial Policy in Europe*. Ithaca, NY: Cornell University Press.

Keegan, W. (2004). *The Prudence of Mr. Gordon Brown*. Chichester: John Wiley & Sons.

Keohane, R. O. and Milner, H. (eds.) (1996). *Internationalization and Domestic Politics*. Cambridge: Cambridge University Press.

Kindleberger, C. P. (1993). *A Financial History of Western Europe*, 2nd edn. New York: Oxford University Press.

King, D. S. (1992). 'The Establishment of Work-Welfare Programmes in the United States and Britain: Politics, Ideas, and Institutions', in S. Steinmo, K. Thelen, and F. Longstreth (eds.), *Structuring politics. Historical Institutionalism in Comparative Analysis*. Cambridge: Cambridge University Press, pp. 217–50.

――― (1999). *In the Name of Liberalism: Illiberal Social Policy in the USA and Britain*. Oxford: Oxford University Press.

Kitschelt, H., Lange, P., Marks, G., and Stephens J. D. (eds.) (1999). *Continuity and Change in Contemporary Capitalism*. Cambridge: Cambridge University Press.

Klinger, R. (1997). *The New Information Industry: Regulatory Challenges and the First Amendment*. Washington, DC: Brookings Institute.

Knieps, G., Müller, J., and von Weizsäcker, C. C. (1981). *Die Rolle des Wettbewerbs im Fernmeldewesen*. Baden-Baden, Germany: Nomos Verlagsgesellschaft.

Knill, C. and Lemkuhl, D. (2002). 'The National Impact of European Union Regulatory Policy: Three Europeanization Mechanisms', *European Journal of Political Research*, 41: 255–80.

――― and Lenschow, A. (2005). 'Compliance, Competition, and Communication: Different Approaches of European Governance and Their Impact on National Institutions', *Journal of Common Market Studies*, 43/3: 583–606.

Köbberling, U. (1993). 'The Limits of National Governance. Regulatory Reform of Telecommunications in Canada and Germany', *International Journal of Political Economy*, 23: 49–82.

Kommission für den Ausbau des technischen Kommunikationssystems (KtK) (1976). *Telekommunikationsbericht*. Bad Godesberg: Heger.

Krasner, S. (1984). 'Approaches to the State. Alternative Conceptions and Historical Dynamics', *Comparative Politics*, 16: 223–46.

KtK [Kommission für den Ausbau des Technischen Kommunikationssystems] (1976). *Bedürfnisse und Bedarf für Telekommunikation*. Bonn, Germany: Hans Heger Verlag.

Kühn, D. (1971). 'Die neue Unternehmensverfassung der Deutschen Bundespost', *Jahrbuch des Postwesens, Bad Windsheim*, pp. 17–71.

Kuhn, E. (1986). 'Überblick über die Entwicklung der ordnungspolitischen Diskussion im Bereich der Telekommunikation', *Zeitschrift für öffentliche und gemeinwirtschaftliche Unternehmen*, 9/2: 169–85.

Kynaston, D. (2001). *The City of London: A Club no More, 1945–2000*. London: Chatto and Windus.

Ladrech, R. (1994). 'Europeanisation of Domestic Politics and Institutions: The Case of France', *Journal of Common Market Studies*, 32/1: 69–88.

Landi, G. (1975). 'Consob', *Revista delle società*, 20/1: 1–37.

Larcher, G. (1996). *L'avenir de France Télécom: un défi national, rapport du Sénat no. 260*. Paris: Sénat.

Lascoumes, P. (1985). 'La COB : Entre Magistrature économique et gestion du droit des affaires', *Déviance et Société*, 9/1: 1–30.

—— (1997). 'L'autorité de régulation des télécommunications (ART)', *l'Actualité Juridique Droit Administratif*, 3: 224–28.

Laurence, H. (2001). 'Money Rules', in *The New Politics of Finance in Britain and Japan*. Ithaca, NY and London: Cornell University Press.

Lauriol, T. (2005). 'France', in P. Cameron (ed.), *Legal Aspects of EU Energy Regulation: Implementing the New Directives on Electricity and Gas across Europe*. Oxford: Oxford University Press, pp. 123–43.

Lautier, D. (2003). 'Les performances des enterprises électriques européennes', *Economies et Sociétés*, 9/2–3: 257–87.

Lawrence, H. (1996). 'Regulatory Competition and the Politics of Financial Market Reform in Britain and Japan', *Governance*, 9/3: 311–41.

Lawton, T. (1999), 'Governing the Skies: Conditions for the Europeanisation of Airline Policy', *Journal of Public Policy* 19/1: 91–112.

Lawson, N. (1992). *The View from No.11*. London: Corgi.

Le Diberder, A. (1983). *La Modernisation des reseaux de telecommunications*. Paris.

Le Portz, Y. (1988). *Commission de Reflexion sur les marchés financiers à terme*. Paris: COB.

Lecat, J.-J. (2002). 'La propriété et le contrôle des companies aériennes. Le Cas d'Air France', *Revue International du Droit Comparé*, 2 (IIID): 415–40.

Lee, R. (1998). *What Is an Exchange?* Oxford: Oxford University Press.

Lehmann, P.-J. (1997). *Histoire de la Bourse de Paris*. Paris: Presses Universitaires de France.

Leper, R. (1979). 'Our Foreign Guests', *The Banker*, February: 55–64.

Leray, A. [pseudonym for group of France Telecom employees] (1994). *Les Télécoms en questions. Privatisation ou service public*. Paris: Les éditions de l'Atelier.

Levi-Faur, D. (2003). 'The Politics of Liberalisation: Privatisation and Regulation-for-Competition in Europe's and Latin America's Telecoms and Electricity Industries', *European Journal of Political Research*, 42/5: 705–40.

Levy, B. and Spiller, P. (1996). *Regulation, Institutions, and Commitment*. Cambridge: Cambridge University Press.

Libois, L.-J. (1983). *Genèse et Croissance des Télécommunications*. Paris: Masson.

Lieberman, E. S. (2001). 'Causal Inference in Historical Institutional Analysis: A Specification of Periodization Stategies. *Comparative Political Studies*, 34/9: 1011–35.

Littlechild, S. (1993). 'New Developments in Electricity Regulation', in Institute for Economic Affairs, *Major Issues in Regulation*. London: Institute for Economic Affairs, pp. 119–40.

Locke, R. (1995). *Remaking the Italian Economy*. Ithaca, NY: Cornell University Press.

Locksley, G. (1982). *The EEC Telecommunications Industry. Competition, Concentration, and Competitiveness*. Brussels: Commission of the European Communities.

Lodge, M. (2002). *On Different Tracks: Institutions and Railway Regulation in Britain and Germany*, Westport, CT: Praeger.

Longuet, G. (1988). *Télécoms. La Conquête de Nouveaux Espaces.* Paris: Dunod.

——(1989). 'Dix questions à M. Gérard Longuet', *Revue Française d'Administration Publique*, 52: 17–24.

Lorenzoni, A. (2003). 'Institutional and Organizational Reform in the Italian Electricity Supply Industry', in J.-M. Glachant and D. Finon (eds.), *Competition in European Electricity Markets.* Cheltenham: Edward Elgar, pp. 331–26.

Loriaux, M. (1991). *France after hegemony: international change and financial reform.* Ithaca: Cornell University Press.

Lovelock, P. and Ure, J. (2002). 'The New Economy: Internet Telecommunications and Electronic Commerce?', in L. Lievrouw and S. Livingstone (eds.), *Handbook of New Media: Social Shaping and Consequences of ICTs.* London: Sage.

LSE (London Stock Exchange) (1978). *Evidence to the Committee to Review the Functioning of Financial Institutions* [the 'Wilson Committee']. London: LSE.

Lütz, S. (1996). *The Revival of the Nation-State? Stock Exchange Regulation in an Era of International Financial Markets.* Cologne: Max Planck Institute.

——(1997). 'Die Rückkehr des Nationalstaates? Kapitalmarktregulierung im Zeichen der Internationalisierung von Finanzmärkten', *Politische Vierteljahresschrift*, 38/3: 475–98.

——(1998). 'The Revival of the Nation State? Stock Exchange Regulation in an Era of Globalized Finance', *Journal of European Public Policy*, 5/1: 153–68.

——(2000). 'Vom koordinierten zum marktorientierten Kapitalismus?', in R. Czada (ed.), *Von der Bonner zur Berliner Republik: 10 Jahre Deutsche Einheit.* Wiesbaden: Westdeutscher Verlag, pp. 651–70.

——(2002). *Der Staat und die Globalisierung von Finanzmärkten. Regulative Politik in Deutschland, Großbritannien und den USA.* Frankfurt am Main: Campus Verlag.

Lyth, P. (1998). 'Chosen Instruments: The Evolution of British Airways', in H.-L. Dienel and P. Lyth (eds.), *Flying the Flag. European Commercial Air Transport since 1945.* Basingstoke: Macmillan, pp. 50–86.

Mahoney, J. and Rueschemeyer, D. (2003). *Comparative Historical Analysis in the Social Sciences.* Cambridge: Cambridge University Press.

Majone, G. (1991). 'Cross-National Sources of Regulatory Policymaking in Europe and the United States', *Journal of Public Policy*, 11/1: 79–106.

——(ed.) (1996). *Regulating Europe.* London: Routledge.

Mantegazza, A. (1998). 'Alitalia and Commercial Aviation in Italy', in H.-L. Dienel and P. Lyth (eds.), *Flying the Flag. European Commercial Air Transport since 1945.* Basingstoke: Macmillan, pp. 159–94.

Marchetti, P. (1987). 'La Consob e gli ordinamenti speciali', *Amministrare*, 17/1: 5–21.

Marini, P. (1994). *Rapport d'Information au nom de la commission des Finance.* Paris: Sénat.

Martin, J. (1971). *Future Developments in Telecommunications.* Englewood Cliffs, NJ: Prentice-Hall International.

Martinelli, E. (2000). 'Autorità independenti e politica', *Amministrare*, 30/1–2: 127–46.

Maschke, W. (2002). 'Transformation at Deutsche Post World Net Using the Example of Socially Compatible Workforce Adjustment' in M. A. Crew and R. R. Kleindorfer (eds.), *Postal and Delivery Services.* Boston, MA: Kluwer, pp. 303–20.

Matlary, J. (1997). *Energy Policy in the European Union.* Basingstoke, UK: Macmillan.

Maxfield, S. (1997). *Gatekeepers of Growth: The International Political Economy of Central Banking in Developing Countries.* Princeton, NJ: Princeton University Press.

McDougall, R. (1990). 'Smoothing the Continental Shelf', *The Banker*, May: 10–14.

McDowell, M. E. (1987). *Oftel Working Paper no. 2, International Comparison of Telephone Charges.* London: Oftel.

McGowan, F. (1993). *The Struggle for Power in Europe*. London: Royal Institute for International Affairs.

—— (1995). 'The European Electricity Industry and EC Regulatory Reform', in J.E.S Hayward (ed.), *Industrial Enetrprises and European Integration*. Oxford: Oxford University Press, pp.125–57.

—— (2002). 'British Postal Reform in the Context of European Changes-Lagging Behind, Catching Up or Leading the Way?', in D. Geradin (ed.), *The Liberalization of Postal Services in the European Union*. The Hague: Kluwer, pp. 329–52.

McNamara, K. (1998). *The currency of ideas: monetary politics in the European Union*. Ithaca, N.Y.: Cornell University Press.

McRae, H. and Cairncross, F. (1984). *Capital City: London as a Financial Centre*. London: Methuen.

Menéndez Sebastiàn, E. V. (2004). *La liberalizacioìn del servicio postal en la Unioìn Europea: los ejemplos de EspanÞa, Francia, Suecia, Italia y Alemania*. Cizur Menor, Navarra, Spain: Aranzadi Editorial.

Meseguer, C. (2004). 'What Role for Learning? The Diffusion of Privatisation in OECD and Latin American Countries', *Journal of Public Policy*, 24/3: 299–325.

Mez, L. (2003). 'New Corporate Strategies in the German Electricity Supply Industry, in J.-M. Glachant and D. Finon (eds.), *Competition in European Electricity Markets: A Cross-Country Comparison*. Cheltenham: Edward Elgar, 193–216.

Mezzacapo, V. (1999). 'Spunti sistematici sulla disciplina dei mercati nel Testo Unico della finanza', in G. Morelli (ed.), *La riforma dei mercati mobiliari italiani*. Rome: Bancaria.

Michie, R. (1999). *The London Stock Exchange: A History*. Oxford: Oxford University Press.

Midttun, A. (ed.) (1997). *European Electricity Systems in Transition*. Oxford: Elsevier.

Mignoli, A. (1991). 'Nuove leggi e nuova Consob', *Revista delle società*, 60: 953–62.

Milner, H. V. (1988). *Resisting Protectionism: Global Industries and the Politics of International Trade*. Princeton, NJ: Princeton University Press.

—— and Keohane, R. O. (1996a). 'Internationalization and Domestic Politics: An Introduction', in R. O. Keohane and H. Milner (eds.), *Internationalization and Domestic Politics*. Cambridge: Cambridge University Press, pp. 3–24.

Ministère de l'Economie et Finances (1972). *La Réforme de la Bourse de Paris*. Paris: Service de l'Information, Ministère de l'Economie et Finances [Bauumgartner Report].

Moloney, N. (2002). *EC Securities Regulation*. Oxford: Oxford University Press.

Monicault, F. de (2003). 'L'europe de l'énergie: photographie d'une révolution', *Revue Politiqiue et Parlementaire*, 1026: 5–11.

Monopolkommission (1981). *Die Rolle der Deutschen Bundespost im FernmedleWesen Sondergutachten*, vol. 9. Baden-Baden: Monos.

—— (1991). *Zur Neuordnung der Telekommunikation. Sondergutachten*, vol. 20. Baden-Baden: Nomos.

—— (1999). *Wettbewerb auf Telekommunikations und Postmärkten?*

Moon, J., Richardson, J. J., and Smart, P. (1986). 'The Privatisation of British Telecom: A Case Study of the Extended Process of Legislation', *European Journal of Political Research*, 14: 339–55.

Moran, M. (1989). 'A state of inaction: the state and stock exchange reform in the federal republic of Germany' in S. Bulmer (ed.), *Changing Agenda of West German Public Policy*. Aldershot: Dartmouth, pp.110–27.

—— (1991). *The Politics of the Financial Services Revolution: The USA, UK, and Japan*. Basingstoke: Macmillan.

Moran, M. (1992). 'Regulatory Change in German Financial Markets', in K. Dyson (ed.), *The Politics of German regulation*. Aldershot: Dartmouth, pp. 137–58.

――― (1994). 'The State and the Financial Services Revolution: A Comparative Analysis', *West European Politics*, 17/3: 158–77.

――― (2003). *The British regulatory state: high modernism and hyper-innovation*. Oxford: Oxford University Press.

Moravcsik, A. (1998). *The Choice for Europe: Social Purpose and State Power from Messina to Maastricht*. Ithaca, NY: Cornell University Press.

Morelli, G. (ed.) (1999). *La riforma dei mercati mobiliari italiani*. Rome: Bancaria.

Morgan, E. V. and Thomas, W. A. (1962). *Stock Exchange*. London: Elek Books.

Morgan, G. Whitley, R. and Moen, E. (2005). *Changing Capitalisms?: Internationalism, Institutional Change, and Systems of Economic Organization*. New York: Oxford University Press.

Morganti, F. (1990). *Le telecommunicazioni*. Rome: SIPI/Confindustria Centro Studi.

Morrison, S. and Winston, C. (2000). 'The Remaining Role for Government Policy in the Deregulated Airline Industry', in S. Peltzman and C. Winston (eds.), *Deregulation of Network Industries*. Washington, DC: AEI and Brookings Institute, pp. 1–40.

Muniesa, F. (2003). *Des Marchés comme algorithms: sociologue de la cotation électronique à la Bourse de Paris. Thèse de Doctorat*. Paris: Ecole Nationale Supérieure des Mines de Paris.

Murillo, V. (2002). 'Political Bias in Policy Convergence: Privatization choices in Latin America', *World Politics* 54: 462–93.

Nardozzi, G. and Vaciago, G. (1994). 'Introduzione e principali resultati', in G. Nardozzi and G. Vaciago (eds.), *La Riforma della Consob nella prospettiva del mercato mobilaire europeo*. Bologna: Il Mulino.

Natalicchi, G. (2001). *Wiring Europe*. Lanham, MD: Rowman and Littlechild.

Negrine, R. (1985). 'Cable TV in Great Britain', in R. Negrine (ed.), *Cable Television and the Future of Broadcasting*. London and Sydney: Croom Helm, pp. 103–33.

Neiertz, N. (1998). 'Air France: An Elephant in an Evening Suit', in H.-L. Dienel and P. Lyth (eds.), *Flying the Flag. European Commercial Air Transport since 1945*. Basingstoke: Macmillan, pp. 18–49.

Newbery, D. and Green, R. (1996). 'Regulation, Public Ownership and Privatisation of the English Electricity Industry', in R. Gilbert and E. Kahn (eds.), *International Comparisons of Electricity Regulation*. Cambridge: Cambridge University Press, pp. 25–81.

Newman, K. (1986). *The Selling of BT*. London: Holt Rinehart and Winston.

Noam, E. (1992). *Telecommunications in Europe*. New York: Oxford University Press.

NYSE *Factbook Historical Statistics*, http://www.nysedata.com/factbook.

O'Brien, R. (1992). *Global Financial Integration: The End of Geography*. New York: Council on Foreign Relations Press.

OECD (Organization for Economic Cooperation and Development) (1983). *Telecommunications, Pressures, and Policies for Change*. Paris: OECD.

――― (1988*a*). *The Telecommunications Industry*. Paris: OECD.

――― (1988*b*). *Satellites and Fibre Optics*. Paris: OECD.

Oftel (annual). *Annual Report*. London: HMSO.

Ohmae, K. (1990). *The Borderless World: Power and Strategy in the Interlinked Economy*. London: Collins.

Oster, S. (1995). 'The Failure of Postal Reform', in P. W. MacAvoy (ed.), *Deregulation and Privatization in the United States*. Edinburgh: Edinburgh University Press, pp. 109–20.

Padgett, S. A. (1992). 'The Single European Energy Market: The Politics of Realization', *Journal of Common Market Studies*, XXX(1): 53–75.

—— (2003). 'Between Synthesis and Emulation: EU Policy Transfer in the Power Sector', *Journal of European Public Policy*, 10/2: 227–45.

Page, E. C. (2004). *Future Governance and the Literature on Policy Transfer and Lesson Drawing*. Hull: ESRC Future Governance Programme, www.futuregovernance. ac.uk/Papers

Palast, G., Oppenheim, J., and MacGregor, T. (2003). *Democracy and Regulation*. London: Pluto Press.

Paoli, L. de (2004). 'Blackout, sviluppo delle reti e liberalizzazione del settore elettrico', *Mercato, Concorrenza, Regole*, 6/1: 103–26.

Parkinson, C. (1992). *Right at the centre: an autobiography*. London: Weidenfeld and Nicolson.

Parsons, D. W. (1996). *Public policy: an introduction to the theory and practice of policy analysis*. Aldershot: Edward Elgar.

Passera, C. (2000). 'Cara Italia ti riscrivo', *Il liberismo sociale*, Sept./Oct. (http://www. liberalfondazione.it/In_fl.htm).

Perez, R. (1996). 'Autorità Indipendenti e Tutela dei Diritti', *Revista trimestrale di diritto pubblico*, 1: 115–47.

—— (2002). *Telecomunicazioni e concorrenza*. Milan: Giuffrè.

Pérouse, M. (1980). [Commission chargée de moderniser les methods de quotation, d'échange et de conservation des valeurs mobilières-chaired by Maurice Pérouse] *La Modernisation des methods de quotation, d'échange et de conservation des valeurs mobilières*. Paris: La Documentation Française.

Perrazzelli, A. and Fratini, A. (2002). 'The Liberalisation of the Italian Postal Market and the Case of "Special Services"', in D. Geradin (ed.), *The Liberalization of Postal Services in the European Union*. The Hague: Kluwer, pp. 279–96.

Perri, P. (1994). *Sauver Air France*. Paris: l'Harmatten.

Peters, B. G. (1999). *Institutional Theory in Political Science: The 'New Institutionalism'*. London: Pinter.

—— Pierre, J., and King, D. S. (2005). 'The Politics of Path Dependency: Political Conflict in Historical Institutionalism', *The Journal of Politics*, 67/4: 1275–1300.

Pfeiffer, D. (1990). *Déontologie Boursière*. Paris: Journal Officiel.

Phillips, S. and Zecher, R. (1981). *The SEC and the Public Interest*. Cambridge, MA: MIT Press.

Pickrell, D. (1991). 'The Regulation and Deregulation of US Airlines' in K. Button (ed.), *Airline Deregulation. International Experiences*. Exeter: David Fulton, pp. 5–47.

Piga, F. (1986). 'Nuovi profili dell'ordinamento del mercato mobiliare e la posizione della Consob', *Banca, Borsa e Titoli di Credito* XLIX : 281–97

Pigeat, H. and Virol, L. (1980). *Du Téléphone à la Télématique*. Paris: Commissariat du Plan.

Pitt, D. (1980). *The Telecommunications Function in the Post Office: A Case Study in Bureaucratic Adaption*. Hampshire: Saxon House.

Plender, J. (1980). 'The Rise and Rise of the Institutional Investor', *The Banker*, September: 41–48.

—— (1986). 'London's Big Bang in International Context', *International Affairs*, 63/1: 39–48.

Pohl, H. (ed.) (1992). *Deutsche Börsengeschichte*. Frankfurt am Main: Fritz Knapp Verlag.

Pollack, M. (2003). *The Engines of European Integration: Delegation, Agency, and Agenda Setting in the EU*. Oxford: Oxford University Press.

Poniatowski, L. and Revol, H. (2003). 'Prudence est mère de sûreté', *Revue Politique et Parlementaire*, 1026: 72–75.

Pontarollo, E. (1983). 'La politche di acquisto nel settore delle telecomunicazioni in Italia', *L'Industria*, 4/2: 273–300.

Pontorollo, E. (1984). 'Monopolio o liberalizzazione nelle telecomunicazioni: incentivi ed ostacoli ad un cambiomento', *L'Industria*, 5/2: 193–213.

Poppe, M. and Cauret, L. (1997). 'The French Electricity Regime', in A. Midttun (ed.), *European Electricity Systems in Transition*. Oxford: Elsevier, pp. 199–230.

Poser, N. (1988). 'Big Bang and the Financial Services Act Seen Through American Eyes', *Brooklyn Journal of International Law*, 14: 317–37.

Prévot, H. (1989). *Rapport de synthèse*. Paris: PTE Ministry.

Pringle, R. (1966). 'Why American Banks Go Overseas', *The Banker*, November: 770–85.

Pritasche, K. and Klauer, S. (2005). 'Germany', in P. Cameron (ed.), *Legal Aspects of EU Energy Regulation: Implementing the New Directives on Electricity and Gas across Europe*. Oxford: Oxford University Press, pp. 145–71.

PTT Ministry (1988). *Texte de travail pour un avant projet de loi*. Paris: PTT Ministry.

Putnam, R. D. (1988). 'Diplomacy and Domestic Politics: The Logic of Two-Level Games', *International Organization*, 42/3: 427–60.

Quilès, P. (1989), 'Dix questions à M. Paul Quilès', *Revue Française d'Administration Publique*, 52: 7–16.

Radaelli, C. M. (2000). 'Policy Transfer in the European Union', *Governance*, 13/1: 25–43.

_____ (2003). 'The Europeanisation of Public Policy', in K. Featherstone and C. M. Radaelli (eds.), *The Politics of Europeanisation*. Oxford: Oxford University Press, pp. 27–56.

_____ (2004). 'The Puzzle of Regulatory Competition', *Journal of Public Policy*, 24/1: 1–23.

_____ and Schmidt, V. A. (eds.) (2004). 'Policy Change and Discourse in Europe', Special Issue, *West European Politics*, 27/2.

Ranci, P. (2003). 'Regulating Energy in Italy', in C. Henry and A. Jeunemaître (eds.), *Regulation of Network Utilities*. Oxford: Oxford University Press.

Regierungskommission Fernmeldewesen (1987). [Witte Report]. *Neuordnung der Telekommunikation. Bericht der Regierungskommission Fernmeldewesen*. Heidelberg: v. Decker.

Reid, M. (1988). All *Change in the City: The Revolution in Britain's Financial Sector*. Basingstoke: Macmillan.

Revell, J. (1973). *The British Financial System*. London: Macmillan.

Rhodes, M. and Apeldoorn, B. van. (1998). 'Capital Unbound? The Transformation of European Corporate Governance', *Journal of European Public Policy*, 5/3: 406–27.

Richeri, G. (1985). 'The Difficulties Involved in the Control and Organization of Telecommunications in Italy', *Media, Culture, and Society*, 7: 49–70.

Richter, L. (2004). 'Une nouvelle conception du service public de l'électricité et du gaz', *Actualité Juridique Droit Administratif*, 38: 2094–99.

Ritter, Eva-Maria (2004). *Deutsche Telekommunikationspolitik 1989–2003: Aufbruch zu mehr Wettbewerb. Ein Beispiel für wirtschaftliche Strukturreformen*. Düsseldorf: Droste Verlag.

Rizzo, D. (1975). 'La Banque dans les operations de Bourse en France', *Annali della facultà di Economia e Commercio* 13/1: 505–90.

Robbes, F. (2000). 'L'ouverture du marché de l'électricité et l'adaptation du service public', *Cahiers juridiques de l'Electricité et du Gaz*, June: 211–34.

Robert, M.-C. and Labboz, B. (1991). *La Commission des opérations de bourse*. Paris: Presses Universitaires de France.

Robertson, J. H. (1947). *The Story of the Telephone*. London: Isaac Pitman.

Robinson, H. (1948). *The British Post Office: A History*. Princeton, NJ: Princeton, University Press.

Rodrigues, S. (2002). 'The French Postal Sector', in D. Geradin (ed.), *The Liberalization of Postal Services in the European Union*. The Hague: Kluwer, pp. 233–54.

Rogowski, R. (1989). *Commerce and coalitions: how trade affects domestic political alignments*. Princeton: Princeton University Press.

Rose, R. (1993). *Lesson-Drawing in Public Policy: A Guide to Learning Across Time and Space*. Chatham, NJ: Chatham House.

Roulet, M. (1989), 'France Télécom, l'opérateur national des télécommunications', *Revue Française d'Administration Publique*, 52: 85–94.

―― (1994). *Rapport sur l'avenir du groupe France Télécom*. Paris: Ministère de l'Industrie, des Télécommunications et du Commerce Extérieur.

Rueschemeyer, D. and Skocpol, T. (1996). *States, Social Knowledge, and the Origins of Modern Social Policies*. Princeton, NJ: Princeton University Press.

Sachverständigenkommission (1966). *Gutachten der Sachverständigenkommission für die Deutsche Bundespost vom 6.11.1965 in Bundestag 5*. Bonn: Wahlperiode, Drucksache V/203.

Saissi, O. (1997). 'La privatisation d'Air France. Les enjeux d'une nécessité', *Direction et Gestion Des Entreprises*, 166: 49–54.

Sandholtz, W. (1992). *High-Tech Europe*. Berkeley, Los Angeles and Oxford: University of California Press.

―― (1993) 'Institutions and Collective Action. The New Telecommunications in Western Europe', *World Politics* 45: 242–70.

―― (1998). 'The Emergence of a Supranational Telecommunications Regime', in W. Sandholtz and A. Stone Sweet (eds.), *European Integration and Supranational Governance*. New York: Oxford University Press, pp. 134–63.

―― and Stone Sweet, A. (eds.) (1998). *European Integration and Supranational Governance*. Oxford: Oxford University Press.

Sardesai, M. (1997). 'Collusion within Nasdaq: Motives, Practices, and Consequences', *Michigan Journal of Economics*, 13/1: 35–56.

Savage, J. G. (1989). *The Politics of International Telecommunications Regulation*. Boulder and London: Westview.

Scharpf, F. and Schmidt, V. A. (2000). *Welfare and Work in the Open Economy*. Oxford: Oxford University Press.

Schmidt, S. (1991). 'Taking the Long Road to Liberalization. Telecommunications Reform in the Federal Republic of Germany', *Telecommunications Policy*, 15/3: 209–22.

―― (1996). 'Sterile Debate and Dubious Generalisation: European Intergation Theory Tested by Telecommunications and Electricity', *Journal of Public Policy*, 16/3: 233–71.

―― (1998). 'Commission Activism: Subsuming Telecommunications and Electricity under European Competition Law', *Journal of European Public Policy*, 5/1: 169–84.

Schmidt, V. A. (1996). *From State to Market? The Transformation of French Business and Government*. Cambridge: Cambridge University Press.

―― (2002*a*). 'Europeanization and the Mechanics of Economic Policy Adjustment', *Journal of European Public Policy*, 9/6: 894–912.

―― (2002*b*). *The Futures of European Capitalism*. Oxford: Oxford University Press.

Schmidt, V. A. (2004). 'Policy Change and Discourse in Europe', *West European Politics*, 27/2: 183–210.

—— (2006). *Democracy in Europe: The EU and National Polities*. Oxford: Oxford University Press.

—— and Radaelli, C. M. (2004). 'Policy Change and Discourse in Europe: Conceptual and Methodological Issues'. *West European Politics* 27/2: 183–210.

Schneider, V. (2001a). *Die Transformation der Telekommunikation. Vom Staatsmonopol zum globalen Markt (1800–2000)*. Frankfurt: Campus.

—— (2001b). 'Institutional Reform in Telecommunications: The European Union in Transatlantic Policy Diffusion', in M. Green Cowles, J. Caporaso, and T. Risse (eds.), *Transforming Europe: Europeanization and Domestic Change*. Ithaca, NY: Cornell University Press, pp. 60–78.

—— and Werle, R. (1990). 'International Regime or Corporate Actor? The European Community in Telecommunications Policy', in K. Dyson and P. Humphreys (eds.), *The Political Economy of Telecommunications*. London and New York: Routledge, pp. 77–106.

—— —— (1991). 'Policy Networks in the German Telecommunications Domain', in B. Marin and R. Mayntz (eds.), *Policy Networks: Empirical Evidence and Theoretical Considerations*. Frankfurt: Campus Verlag, pp. 97–136.

—— Dang-Nguyen, G., and Werle, R. (1994). 'Corporate Actor Network in European Policy-Making: Harmonizing Telecommunications Policy', *Journal of Common Market Studies*, 32/4: 473–98.

Schwark, E. (1994). *Börsengesetz - Kommentar zum Börsengesetz und zu den börsenrechtlichen Nebenbestimmungen*. Munich: Beck Juristischer Verlag.

Schwarz-Schilling, C. (2002). 'Market Results of Postal Reform in Germany', in M. A. Crew and P. R. Kleindorfer (eds.), *Postal and Delivery Services*. Boston, MA: Kluwer, pp. 355–74.

Scott, C. (1995). 'Changing Patterns of European Community Utilities Law: An Institutional Hypothesis', in J. Shaw and G. More (eds.), *New Legal Dynamics of European Integration*. Oxford: Oxford University Press, pp. 193–215.

—— (2001). 'Analysing Regulatory Space: Fragmented Resources and Institutional Design', *Public Law*, Summer: 329–53.

—— and Audéoud, O. (eds.) (1996). *The Future of EC Telecommunications Law*. Cologne: Bundesanzeiger.

Seristo, H. (1993). *Airline Strategies*. Helsinki: Helsinki School of Economics and Business Administration.

Shepherd, W. G. (1968). 'Alternatives for Public Expenditure', in R. E. Caves (ed.), *Britain's Economic Prospects*. Washington, DC and London: Brookings Institute and Allen and Unwin, pp. 381–447.

Sherman, R. (1991). 'Competition in Postal Service', in M. A. Crew and R. R. Kleindorfer (eds.), *Competition and Innovation in Postal Services*. Boston, MA: Kluwer, pp. 191–214.

Shonfield, A., *Modern Capitalism*. Oxford: Oxford University Press, 1969.

SIB [Securities and Investment Board] (1995). *Regulation of the United Kingdom. Equity Markets: Report*. London: SIB.

Simmons, B. (2001). 'The International Politics of Harmonization: The Case of Capital Market Regulation', *International Organization*, 55/3: 589–620.

—— and Elkins, Z. (2004). 'The Globalization of Liberalization: Policy Diffusion in the International Political Economy', *American Political Science Review*, 98/1: 171–89.

Sinha, D. (2001). *Deregulation and Liberalisation of the Airline Industry*. Aldershot: Ashgate.

Slaughter, A.-M. (2004). *A New World Order*. Princeton, NJ: Princeton University Press.

Smith, M. (2001*a*). 'Europe and the German Model: Growing Tension or Symbiosis?', *German Politics*, 10/3: 119–40.

——— (2001*b*). 'In Pursuit of Selective Liberalization: Single Market Competition and Its Limits', *Journal of European Public Policy*, 8/4: 519–40.

Smith, R. W. (1993). 'Review: International Economy and State Strategies: Recent Work in Comparative Political Economy'. *Comparative Politics* 25: 351–72

Sobel, A. (1994). *Domestic Choices, International Markets*. Ann Arbor, MI: University of Michigan Press.

——— (1999). *State Institutions, Private Incentives, Global Capital*. Ann Arbor, MI: University of Michigan Press.

Sotgia, S. (1966). 'Riforma della borsa valori', *Rivista delle Società* XI : 735–55.

Spalek, B. (2001). 'Policing the UK Financial System: The Creation of the "New" Financial Services Authority and its Approach to Regulation', *International Journal of the Sociology of Law*, 29: 75–87.

Staniland, M. (2003*a*). *Government Birds: Air Transport and the State in Western Europe*. Boulder, CO: Rowman and Littlefield.

——— (2003*b*). 'Competition versus Competitiveness in the European Single Aviation Market', in M. L. Campanella and S. C. W. Eijffinger (eds.), *EU Economic Governance and Globalization*. Cheltenham: Edward Elgar, pp. 55–78.

Stehmann, O. (1995). *Network Competition for European Telecommunications*. Oxford: Oxford University Press.

Steil, B. (1996). *The European Equities Markets. The state of the union and an agenda for the millennium*. London: Royal In statute for International Affairs.

Steinmetz, H. (1960). 'Die Deutsche Bundespost—Wirtschaftliches Unternehmen und öffentliche Verwaltung', *Archiv für das Post- und Fernmeldewesen*, 12/2: 57–62.

Stevens, H. (2004). *Transport Policy in the European Union*. Basingstoke: Palgrave Macmillan.

Stone, D. (2004). 'Transfer Agents and Global Networks in the "Transnationalization" of Policy', *Journal of European Public Policy*, 11/3: 545–66.

Stone Sweet, A. (2004). *The Judicial Construction of Europe*. Oxford and New York: Oxford University Press.

——— and O'Reilly, D. (1998). 'The Liberalization and European Reregulation of Air Transport', in W. Sandholtz and A. Stone Sweet (eds.), *European Integration and Supranational Governance*. Oxford: Oxford University Press, pp. 164–87.

Story, J. (1997). 'Globalisation, the European Union and German Financial Reform: The Political Economy of Finanzplatz Deutschland', in G. R. D. Underhill (ed.), *The New World Order in International Finance*. Basingstoke: Macmillan, pp. 245–73.

Strange, S. (1986). *Casino Capitalism*. Oxford: Blackwell.

——— (1988). *States and markets*. London: Pinter.

——— (1996). *The Retreat of the State: The Diffusion of Power in the World Economy*. Cambridge: Cambridge University Press.

——— (1997). 'The Future of Global Capitalism; or Will Divergence Persist Forever?', in C. Crouch and W. Streeck (eds.), *The Political Economy of Modern Capitalism. Mapping Convergence and Diversity*. London: Sage, pp. 182–91.

Streeck, W. and Thelen, K. (eds.) (2005*a*). *Beyond Continuity: Institutional Change in Advanced Political Economies*. Oxford and New York: Oxford University Press.

——— ——— (2005*b*). 'Introduction', in W. Streeck and K. Thelen (eds.), *Beyond Continuity. Institutional Change in Advanced Political Economies*. Oxford: Oxford University Press, pp. 1–39.

Surrey, J. (ed.) (1996). *The British Electricity Experiment*. London: Earthscan.

Swank, D. (2002). *Global Capital, Political Institutions, and Policy Change in Developed Welfare States*. Cambridge and New York: Cambridge University Press.

Syrota, J. (2003). La réglementation de l'électricité en France et dans l'Union européenne', *Revue Politique et Parlementaire*, 1026: 18–22.

Tallberg, J. (2002). 'Delegation to Supranational Institutions: Why, How, and with What Consequences?'. *West European Politics*, 25/1: 23–46.

Tedoldi, C. (1977). *Il Telefono Nemico*. Milan: Mazzotta.

Terzo, T. (2000). Finanza Publicca e Privata. La Disciplina dell'Economia in S. Cassese (ed.), *Trattato di Diritto Amministrativo*. Milan: Guiffrè.

Thatcher, Margaret (1993). *The Downing Street Years*. London: HarperCollins.

Thatcher, M. (1995). 'Regulatory Reform and Internationalization in Telecommunications', in J. E. S. Hayward (ed.), *Industrial Enterprise and European Integration*. Oxford: Oxford University Press.

—— (1999). *The Politics of Telecommunications*. Oxford: Oxford University Press.

—— (2001). 'The Commission and national governments as partners: EC regulatory expansion in telecommunications 1979–2000', *Journal of European Public Policy* 8/4: 558–84.

—— (2002). 'Delegation to Independent Regulatory Agencies: Pressures, Functions and Contextual Mediation', *West European Politics*, 25/1: 125–47.

—— (2004a). 'Varieties of Capitalism in an Internationalized World: Domestic Institutional Change in European Telecommunications', *Comparative Political Studies*, 37/7: 1–30.

—— (2004b), 'Winners and losers in Europeanization: Reforming the national regulation of telecommunications', *West European Politics* 27/2: 102–27.

—— (2005). 'Sale of the century: 3G mobile licences in Europe' in J. Black, M. Lodge and M. Thatcher(eds.), *Regulatory Innovation*. Aldershot: Edward Elgar, pp. 92–113.

—— (2007). 'Reforming National Regulatory Institutions: the EU and cross-national variety in European network industries', in B. Hancke, M Rhodes and M Thatcher (eds), *Beyond Varieties of Capitalism*. Oxford: OUP 2007, pp.147–72.

Thelen, K. (1999). 'Historical Institutionalism in Comparative Politics', *The Annual Review of Political Science 1999*. Palo Alto, CA: Annual Reviews.

Thimm, A. L. (1992). *America's stake in European Telecommunication Policies*. London: Quorom Books.

Thomas, S. (1996). 'The Privatization of the Electricity Supply Industry', in J. Surrey (ed.) (1996). *The British Electricity Experiment*. London: Earthscan.

—— (1997). 'The British Market Reform', in A. Midttun (ed.), *European Electricity Systems in Transition*. Oxford: Elsevier, pp. 44–88.

Thomasset-Pierre, S. (2004). 'Autorité des marchés financiers', in J.-J. Daigre and H. de Vanplane (eds.) *La loi Sur la sécurité financière*. Revue Banque: Paris.

Tomasi, M. (2002). *La concurrence sur les marchés financiers*. Paris: L.G.D.J.

Torchia, L. (1992). *Il Controllo Pubblico della Finanza Privata*. Milan: CEDAM.

Touret, B. (1974). 'Le financement privé des télécommunications', *Actualité Juridique-Droit Administratif*, June: 284–97.

Travis, R. (2001). *Air Liberalisation in the European Community 1987–1992*. Uppsala, Sweden: Acta Universitatis Upsaliensis.

Treasury Committee of the House of Commons (1996). *Seventh Report, The Future of the London Stock Exchange*, vol. 1. London: HMSO.

Tricot Commission (Ministère de l'Economie) (1985). [*Rappprt Tricot*], *Le Coût de l'intermédiation financière*. Paris: Ministère de l'Economie.

Tsebelis, G. (1995). 'Decision Making in Politicial Systems: Veto Players in Presidentialism, Parliamentarism, Multicameralism, and Multipartyism', *British Journal of Political Science*, 25: 289–326.

——— (2002). *Veto Players*. Princeton, NJ: Princeton University Press.

Turmes, C. (2003). 'L'Europe sous tension: menaces et opportunités de la deuxième directive européenne', *Revue Politiqiue et Parlementaire*, 1026: 76–79.

Turot, P. (1973). 'Les Mutations Boursières', *Analyse Prévision* XV/1 : 1–28.

Ungerer, H. and Costello, N. (1988). *Telecommunications in Europe*. Brussels: Commission of the European Communities.

Ure, J. (2003). 'Deconstructing 3G and Reconstructing Telecoms', *Telecommunications Policy*, 27: 187–206.

Valsecchi, F. (2004). *Poste Italiane, Una sfida fra tradizione e innovazione*. Milan: Sperling and Kupfer.

Van Ness, B., Van Ness, R. A., and Warr, R. S. (2003). *A Comparison of NYSE and Regional Trading (1993–2002)* (unpublished manuscript).

Vella, F. (1998). 'L'autoregolamentazione nella disciplina dei mercati mobiliari', in G. Ferrarini and P. Marchetti (eds.), *la Riforma dei mercati finanziari*. Rome: Edibank.

Verdier, D. (2002). *Moving Money*. Cambridge: Cambridge University Press.

Viandier, A. (1989). 'Sécurité et transparence du marché financier', *La Semaine Juridique*, 49: 46–61.

Vibert, F. (2001). *Europe Simple, Europe Strong: The Future of European Governance*. Cambridge: Polity Press.

Vickers, J. and Yarrow, G. (1988). *Privatization: An Economic Analysis*. Cambridge, MA: MIT Press.

Vincenti, C. de and Vigneri, A. (eds.) (2006). *Le virtù della Concorrenza, Regolazione e mercato nei servizi di pubblica utilità*. Bologna: Il Mulino.

Vogel, D. (1995). *Trading Up: Consumer and Environmental Regulation in a Global Economy*. Cambridge, MA: Harvard University Press.

Vogel, S. (1996). *Freer Markets, More Rules*. Ithaca, NY: Cornell University Press.

Walker, J. L. (1969). 'The Diffusion of Innovations among the American States', in R. H. Walker (ed.), *The American Political Science Review*, 63/3: 880–99.

Walmsley, J. (1980). 'Moving towards Competitive Equality', *The Banker*, February: 97–101.

——— (1985). 'New York's "Big Bang"—10 Years After', *The Banker*, March: 35–39.

Walter, I. (1996). 'Global competition and market access in the securities industry', in C. E. Barfield (ed.), *International Financial Markets: Harmonization versus competition*. Washington: AEI Press.

Waltz, K. N. (1954). *Man, the State and War: A Theoretical Analysis*. New York: Columbia University Press.

Weir, M. (1992). *Politics and Jobs. The Boundaries of Employment Policy in the United States*. Princeton, NJ: Princeton University Press.

Weiss, L. (1998). *The Myth of the Powerless State: Governing the Economy in a Global Era*. Cambridge: Polity Press.

Werle, R. (1990). *Telekommunikation in der Bundesrepublik. Expansion, Differenzierung, Transformation*. Frankfurt: Campus.

——— (1999). 'Liberalisation of Telecommunications in Germany', in K. A. Eliassen and M. Sjøvaag (eds.), *European Telecommunications Liberalisation*. London: Routledge, pp. 110–27.

Whalley, J. (2004). 'Flagship Firms, Consolidation and Changing Market Structures within the Mobile Communications Market', *Telecommunications Policy*, 28: 161–75.

Wildavsky, A (1987). *Speaking Truth to Power. The Art and Craft of Policy Analysis*. New Brunswick: Transaction Publishers

Williams, G. (2002). *Airline Competition: Deregulation's Mixed Legacy*. Aldershot: Ashgate.

Wood, S. (2001). 'Business, Government, and the Patterns of Labor Market Policy in Britain and the Federal Republic of Germany', in P. A. Hall and D. Soskice (eds.), *Varieties of capitalism. The Institutional Foundations of Comparative Advantage*. Oxford: Oxford University Press, pp. 237–74.

Wright, V. (ed.) (1994). *Privatization in Western Europe: Pressures, Problems, and Paradoxes*. London: Pinter.

Wymeersch, E. (1977). *Control of Securities Markets in the European Economic Community*. Collection Studies Competition-Approximation of Legislation Series no. 31.

―――― (1998). 'The Implementation of the ISD and CAD in National Legal Systems', in G. Ferrarini (ed.), *European Securities Markets*. London: Kluwer Law, pp. 1–44.

Zahariadis, N. (1992). To Sell or Not to Sell? Telecommunications Policy in Britain and France. *Journal of Public Policy*, 12/4): 355–76.

Zysman, J. (1996). 'The Myth of a "Global" Economy: Enduring National Foundations and Emerging Regional Realities', *New Political Economy*, 1/2: 157–84.

Index